CW01024078

CELEBRATING
50 YEARS
Texas A&M University Press
publishing since 1974

LOVE AT THE
FIVE AND DIME

SERIES IN TEXAS MUSIC
Sponsored by the Center for Texas Music History
Texas State University
Jason Mellard, General Editor

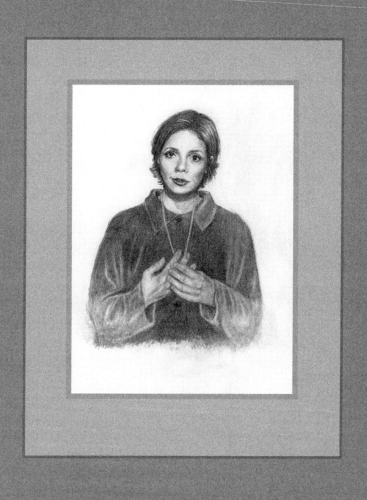

Love
at the
Five
and
Dime

The Songwriting
Legacy of
Nanci Griffith

BRIAN T. ATKINSON

TEXAS A&M UNIVERSITY PRESS
College Station

♾ This paper meets the requirements of
ANSI/NISO Z39.48–1992 (Permanence of Paper).
Binding materials have been chosen for durability.

Library of Congress Cataloging-in-Publication Data

Names: Atkinson, Brian T., author.
Title: Love at the five and dime: the songwriting legacy of Nanci Griffith
    / Brian T. Atkinson.
Other titles: Texas music series.
Description: First edition. | College Station: Texas A&M University Press,
    [2024] | Series: Texas music series | Includes index.
Identifiers: LCCN 2024022255 (print) | LCCN 2024022256 (ebook) | ISBN
    9781648432385 (cloth) | ISBN 9781648432392 (ebook)
Subjects: LCSH: Griffith, Nanci. | Singers--Texas--Biography. | Folk
    singers--Texas--Biography. | Lyricists--United States--Biography. |
    Country musicians--Texas--Biography. | BISAC: MUSIC / Individual
    Composer & Musician | MUSIC / Genres & Styles / Folk & Traditional |
    LCGFT: Biographies.
Classification: LCC ML420.G859 A8 2024 (print) | LCC ML420.G859 (ebook) |
    DDC 782.421642092 [B]--dc23/eng/20240515
LC record available at https://lccn.loc.gov/2024022255
LC ebook record available at https://lccn.loc.gov/2024022256

Front cover. Photo by Jim McGuire. Courtesy The Grand Ole Opry

Frontispiece drawing by Amanda Melchert

For Nanci

. . .

Invisible

(a previously unpublished poem by Nanci Griffith)

Through the slashing, cutting Dylan Thomas rain
    of Wales that has finally arrived
I've walked the streets of Cardiff
    Walked from book shop to docks
        In the anchor of my own heritage

An ex-patriot for a second time around from America
    once an American known and recognized
        in my hooded gray linen raincoat
            famous on the streets of Dublin
Once dubbed the Garbo of folk music by John Stewart
    once called the Queen of Folkabilly by ROLLING STONE
        and then the Garbo of Dublin by their press
            for the hood of that gray linen raincoat

I wear that raincoat now, the Garbo of nothing
    My country dissolving in its shelter
And the state of my birth, still a geographical beauty
    While myself an exile from its ugly politics

Born of a family who were dirt poor farmers of soil
    Who did laundry for oil money . . . foreign of their kind
        Who made bootlegged single malt amidst a dry arid
flatland
and complained not of their own cracked and dust blown
lives
They had no voice
    Yet their men fought a war and then another
        and their women folk waited without breath
            and in simple hope . . . blending the single malt
                washing the clothes of capitalism

I understand nothing as a middle aged, childless
woman
    Yet, I understand in study
        I read and I hope

I follow the words of Molly Ivins, Bobby Nelson, and
    Gloria Steinem
        . . . and then I hope
            Will I ever be a good girl?
                Ever be homeward bound?
                    or just invisible?

My steps crunch gravel beneath the feet of a woman
            who wonders of three thousand gone in two hours time
        and then the millions of women gone in spirit to darkness
            gone in physical mutilation from their cultures . . .
        I no longer wish to understand
    Because the consequences of understanding may revolve
            around believing it the right of ignorance

One woman walking, thinking, or asking . . .
        "Do we belong here at all . . . any race . . . though we're all
human?"
And then I return to my own grief of Garbo
        Not near as stunning, but well said, spoken, and sung
Knowing the Welsh of my blood will sing out loud in harmony
        my own music, my own lyrics of a woman returned to
                a homeland of any given night

From the cliffs of St. David's Cardiff Bay
    The heart of Episcopal trenches and birth
I am a Catholic, again a Garbo,
    I am more comfortable alone.

I refuse to believe or understand a humanity
    Intolerant of a woman alone, without a veil, without a child
        of her own,
    Who still wishes and prays for those who are forced to walk
without a crunch of gravel beneath their feet
    of their own free will, alone
        without a voice any of us can hear along their path
    A path so different of my own
Walked in a hooded gray raincoat against the grain

Nanci Griffith, Cardiff, Wales, October 1, 2001

CONTENTS

Galleries of images follow pages 51, 113, 195, and 255.

FOREWORD

A Conversation with the Indigo Girls, Kathy Mattea, and Lyle Lovett

EMILY SALIERS (INDIGO GIRLS): I'll never forget how I discovered Nanci Griffith. Amy [Ray] and I were playing in a local club, and a guy came up after a show and said, "Do you know this person's music?" "No." "I think you'll really like it." He handed me a cassette of Nanci's album *Once in a Very Blue Moon*, which I took home and listened to obsessively.[1]

AMY RAY (INDIGO GIRLS): I was drawn to the images in her songs. She was such a small, soft-spoken person, but her songs were full of vigor. They were edgy and had strong images. Also, Nanci delivered something that could be so sad and with such heartache but was so sweet. That weird clash always drew me to her.[2]

LYLE LOVETT: Nanci's songs seemed like they were about something real with genuine writing that made you want to listen again and again. You aspire to that quality as a songwriter. Her songs worked on the surface, but they also gave you a deeper understanding and revealed something over time in an even deeper way. What a wonderful thing.[3]

EMILY SALIERS: I liked Nanci's storytelling and voice and that she was folky but not sappy. She was very direct and playful. I found her really compelling. Then I started listening to other albums and would put "The Wing and the Wheel," "More Than a Whisper," and "Love at the Five and Dime" on repeat.

KATHY MATTEA: I could not get arrested on the radio before I recorded "Love at the Five and Dime." Nothing. I got one song to number twenty-five, another to number forty, and then one that didn't chart at all. I was someone everybody was rooting for but couldn't get traction. The record label came to me and said, "We believe in you, but we've got to find what's gonna connect. We want you to do singles until we can get something going on the radio. We'll finish a record when that happens." Steve Popovich, who had discovered Meat Loaf and started Cleveland International Records, came in. He was a quirky guy who loved Nanci.

We cut four sides for a single, and Steve said, "Here's your single: 'Love at the Five and Dime.'" Seems so obvious now, but I was like, "Oh, I'm not sure. Really? Quirky song." I looked at the producer Allen Reynolds. "This guy is brand new," I said about Steve. "Do I fight him?" "No," Allen said. "You give him his way, and you make your suggestion if it doesn't go your way." "Love at the Five and Dime" floated up the charts like a balloon was on it. I got nominated for a Grammy. Nanci got nominated for a Grammy for her album *The Last of the True Believers*, which had her cut of "Love at the Five and Dime."

"Hey, we like you," everyone said then. "Come on in."[4]

AMY RAY: Oh, I should have said this up front. We were signed to Epic Records because a guy heard us opening a show for Nanci at Center Stage in Atlanta around 1988. They were in a bidding war for R.E.M. when this guy came by the club where we were playing. He went back to Los Angeles and told his boss, "You have to hear these girls." So, we opened a show with Nanci and got signed to a record deal. Nanci was a quiet storm in the true sense of the word.

LYLE LOVETT: You stepped into Nanci's world as much as she stepped into yours when you went to see her perform. You heard about what personal and social issues were important to her in songs like "Trouble in the Fields." Nanci's songs were a world of their own. She was very socially conscious, very herself, and she didn't play to the audience. Nanci said things in her songs and performed them the way she felt compelled to do. She said those things regardless of how the audience would receive her. That was a very valuable lesson for me as a performer and songwriter when I was starting out.

EMILY SALIERS: Nanci was very, very passionate and had a big personality about human rights and women. We would hang out after shows and talk about politics and social issues. Nanci was really fun to hang out with. She always made me laugh and want to pay attention to her.

AMY RAY: She was superhumble when you first met her, but then you [recognize] her crazy, risqué, fun sense of humor when you're around her more. Nanci was not reverent and also very nonjudgmental.

EMILY SALIERS: Nanci exploded out of this tiny person, but she was full of ideas and thoughts. She was very fierce and alive. I remember one time when we were having a drink and she pounded the bar and said, "I'm a goddamn pacifist."

AMY RAY: Nanci's complexity drew me to her as a writer and as a human. I didn't know enough about her through her songs to know about that clash personally, but then I met her. The whole thing made me constantly curious about her. Where is all that powerful storytelling coming from? I felt like there was a world inside her that came out in songs like ["Love at the Five and Dime"].

KATHY MATTEA: Nanci and I got to sing "Love at the Five and Dime" at the Summer Lights Festival here in Nashville one year [before] ten thousand people. We were on a big stage at the steps of the courthouse. That night has always been seared into my brain. I think it was because we were in Nashville and "Love at the Five and Dime" had started my career. She had a big fan base. That was the first time I got to sing it with her. The perfect night. That song is a great gift. I got to be with Nanci in our hometown crowd, and all the songwriters in town knew her and her career.

LYLE LOVETT: Robert Earl Keen and I would talk about songwriters like Townes Van Zandt, Guy Clark, Nanci Griffith, and Eric Taylor. Their songs gave Robert and me permission to think that way. Guy's "L.A. Freeway" made me realize it's okay to mention somebody's name in a song. Willis Alan Ramsey defining a character like [he did in "The Ballad of] Spider John" made me realize you can tell real stories. Nanci's songs represented that quality and style in the very best way.

KATHY MATTEA: I do not get tired of singing "Love at the Five and Dime." The sweetest moment in my show is when people sing along to the chorus. Everybody remembers the chorus. I enjoy the lilting rhythm of the song. I had been singing the song to Nanci from wherever I was in recent years since her health got bad. "Love at the Five and Dime" is a touchstone with my audience all these years later. I would send it to her, but I never got a chance to tell her. I was just like, "You can't be out there doing your own songs, but I can carry the torch."

AMY RAY: Nanci went through [so much] with the industry. She was a survivor who came up as a woman writing her own songs being a troubadour who sang those songs. Nanci was a trailblazer in many ways and showed that you can do what you do and stick to your guns, be a nice person, and come out okay. Doing all that and standing up for yourself at the same time is a tricky thing to learn. Nanci was fearless living in Nashville, singing country songs, and speaking out for people for real before many others did.

LYLE LOVETT: Nanci championed me when I started playing Anderson Fair in Houston in 1978. Those gigs allowed me to play other places. How did I get where I am today? Maybe I could have gotten into Anderson Fair another way if I was looking forward from then. Maybe I could have started playing credible original music venues if Nanci didn't introduce me to the folks at Anderson Fair, but it didn't happen that way. Everything started happening for me because Nanci Griffith introduced me to them.

AMY RAY: Nanci was friends with us. I can definitely say that there were many musicians and singer-songwriters who felt a little trepidation about associating with us in the midnineties because we were so gay. We never got the energy that us being gay was ever a thing with her. We were friends with other writers, but we could just feel that they were hesitant to be associated with us. We just always dealt with that, but there was never anything like that with Nanci. She had the most open energy.

Nanci was a gift for us.

We were still trying to make our way and [dealing with] self-hatred about being gay. We had a hard time standing up for ourselves sometimes as humans, so it's an amazing balance to know someone like Nanci, who has so much self-confidence and is so well spoken, sweet, and kind about her perspective. Having a person like Nanci believing in you is pretty amazing. She was an ally, and we knew it. There were always kind words when we would cross paths. She was very good at acknowledging what was going on in our musical life. We did the same because we were such fans.

Nanci would have always listened to our latest record and had heard this or that song.

KATHY MATTEA: I've been hosting the National Public Radio show *Mountain Stage* recently, and we had on a trio called Nobody's Girl from Texas—[the Austin-based singer-songwriters] BettySoo, Rebecca Loebe, and Grace Pettis —just after Nanci passed. They asked me if I would sing "Love at the Five and Dime" as a tribute. "Thank you," they said after. "Nanci Griffith blazed the trail for us as Texas singer-songwriters. We might not be doing this if she didn't start it." That showed me how far Nanci's ripple goes and how many musicians she touched. Countless songwriters tell stories of her championing them and giving them a leg up.

Nanci Griffith had a different sense than anybody else.

EMILY SALIERS: I was absolutely crushed when Nanci passed away. A light went away. She's right up there with the most important songwriters in my life. Her passing was a huge personal loss even though I hadn't seen her in years. She was such a big figure in our eyes. Nanci was a good woman with a great heart.

AMY RAY: Nanci was such a fixture, an inspiration, and a compass who was always around in the first twenty years of our career. We who got to know Nanci even in a little way knew she was so humble. She didn't toot her own horn. We're so thankful you're writing this book about Nanci because it will help people understand what she was and still is. They need to know.

People can learn from Nanci Griffith.

PREFACE

We spent nine months tossing ideas back and forth for my next book. Many names almost sealed the deal, but none really stuck. Then Nanci Griffith passed away. I remembered Jenni had mentioned her several times as a potential book over the years, so I spent the next two days reading appreciations, celebrations, and occasional condemnations. People from all walks uploaded post after post after post on social media. They all made one thing very clear: Nanci Griffith's impact on the world—whether as a friend, mentor, songwriting inspiration, or just a thoughtful human being—was far greater than I had ever imagined.

Hers clearly was a legacy worth celebrating.

I spent the next two months with Nanci's music on repeat twenty-four seven before we sealed the deal with a book contract. Honestly, I had never spent much time with her songs before then. Imagine the world that opened up during those two months—and the ten that followed until today as I write this. Nanci Griffith's music has been playing in this house almost nonstop for a full year. I initially was taken aback by an obituary headline in our local daily declaring her Austin's greatest songwriter, but I now understand. No question: no better songwriter has been raised in Austin, Texas.

So many more people than ever before helped this book take shape. Thank you first and foremost to Jenni Finlay for pushing me toward Nanci in the first place. This book likely would never have happened without her patience, persistence, proofreading, and endless research assistance. As always, very special thanks to the Series in Texas Music at Texas State, Thom Lemmons and everyone at Texas A&M University Press, as well as series editor Jason Mellard for making this idea a reality. Thank you to Gary Hartman for bringing me on board years ago. Great gratitude to my parents, Ted and Ruthanne Atkinson, who have supported (nearly) every wild and crazy idea I've had during the past half century. I especially would like to thank Muddy, Lefty, and Lil for filling the strange pandemic days this book was written in with constant companionship.

Additionally, huge thanks to Dalis Allen, Dave Alvin, Winifred Booth, Tony Brown, Mary Keating Bruton, Peter Cooper, John T. Davis, Adam Duritz,

Janet and Jimmie Dale Gilmore, Julie Gold, John Gorka, Tish Hinojosa, Melanie Smith-Howard, Thomm Jutz, Maura Kennedy and Pete Kennedy, Ken Levitan, Joy Lewallen, Lyle Lovett, Kathy Mattea, Terry Myers, Bobby Nelson, Steve Price, Amy Ray and Emily Saliers, Tamara Saviano, Darden Smith, Todd Snider, Charley Stefl, Burt Stein, John Terzano, Kathi Whitley, Mike Williams, Jamie Lin Wilson, and Brian Wood for going extra miles and opening several important doors. Extra special thanks to Robbin Bach for all the conversations and contacts, as well as legendary Nashville photographer Jim McGuire for the cover photo and especially for all the priceless and previously undeveloped and unpublished photos from his Cambodia and Vietnam trip with Nanci, Dave Alvin, and Chris Noth. Of course, biggest thanks to all the singers, songwriters, players, and music industry pros who offered time to talk.

A few I wished to interview remained unavailable despite several requests, but nearly everyone more than jumped at the chance. In fact, as the list immediately above suggests, an amazing number voluntarily pitched in one way or the other to push this book onward and upward. Dozens upon dozens interviewed thanked me for recognizing Nanci with a book. The gratitude everyone showed was nothing less than overwhelming. Nanci obviously was—and is—well loved. Now, that last sentence is very important in understanding Nanci's place in the songwriting community. Countless people shifted from past to present tense midsentence while they talked about Nanci during these interviews.

She clearly remains a living, breathing, ever-present entity and inspiration.

Many thanks to everyone who has supported our Squeaky String Productions, Eight 30 Records, Barefoot Recording, Catfish Concerts, and Burgundy Red Films over the years. Importantly, thank you to Billie Joe Armstrong, Chet Baker, Kathleen Edwards, and the Grateful Dead for filling in the necessary spaces between the constant Nanci Griffith soundtrack guiding this book toward the finish line.

Love at the Five and Dime: The Songwriting Legacy of Nanci Griffith does not thoroughly dissect Griffith's musical catalog. Also, the book—although as chronologically accurate as possible—is not a straight biography. Instead, *Love at the Five and Dime* provides insights into Nanci Griffith's career and her songwriting legacy by those who knew her best, worked with her the most, and have been most significantly influenced by her. Additionally, you'll notice that some sections have significantly more material than others. For example, more were eager to talk about Nanci's most popular album, *Other Voices, Other*

Rooms, than, say, *Blue Roses from the Moons*. So goes a book based on memories like this one. Quick note about the end notes: each interview is cited only the first time used. The following entries can be assumed to be from the same interview unless noted differently. Otherwise, the notes would trample the text in a book as conversational as this.

Finally, I told everyone who would listen that Townes Van Zandt one day would be ranked among the modern era's greatest songwriters when my first book, *I'll Be Here in the Morning: The Songwriting Legacy of Townes Van Zandt*, came out more than a decade ago. Look now. Townes is a legitimate legend worldwide. Many songwriters simply exist in a time when recognition isn't ready. I hope Nanci Griffith's legacy—as a songwriter, a humanitarian, and a genuine wild child—eventually will find as broad an audience as all the other Texas singer-songwriters people call heroes today. Listen through the essential lists near this book's close for evidence. You'll hear. Those songs deserve recognition across the globe.

The best change something inside a person.

Brian T. Atkinson
August 13, 2022

PRELUDE

Nanci Griffith

I wanted to be a songwriter like Harlan Howard and Jimmy Webb [since] child-hood. Being a good songwriter means paying attention and sticking your hand out the window to catch the song on the way to someone else's house. My songs are [mostly] fiction even though they may sound very personal. [Songwriting] is a great way for me to be able to live a fantasy life as a writer because I get to be someone else and go someplace else for three and a half minutes just like the listener. I feel like I'm a journalist in some ways. I think [many] women are made to feel that they have not done the one thing they were put on the earth to do if they didn't do the "normal" thing [on] the most traveled path. Unfortu-nate. Your own voice is the voice that carries you through life the best.[1]

Introduction

Nanci Griffith stands center stage smiling sweetly. The festival cheers spread pride all across her face. Griffith's cherubic complexion, slight stature, and girlish gaze belie her thirty-three years by a decade. She looks like a care-free spirit, young, wild, and free, completely charming and eternally engaging. Then she shows soul. Griffith introduces a song she's recently written in her sleep, an achievement reachable only by someone whose thoughts corner their every move. She introduces the song and soars her voice skyward over the melody line, singing savagely, softly, supernaturally. Griffith might be everything youthful, but she's equally weary, wise, and worldly. She sees layers beyond deepest depths.

Nanci Griffith sang six seasons into every sunset.

After all, the fiery Austin-raised singer-songwriter and fierce human rights activist, a fragile spirit effectively sainted throughout Ireland and the United Kingdom for her earthy empathy but largely below radars elsewhere, frequently framed lifetimes in a breath. "One of the boys in Eddie's band took a shine to Rita's hand / So Eddie ran off with the bass man's wife," Griffith sings in her hallmark "Love at the Five and Dime." "Oh, but he was back by June, singing a different tune / And sporting Miss Rita back by his side."[1] "You feel like you've traveled this couple's whole life with them from youth to old age in 'Love at the Five and Dime,'" says country star Kathy Mattea, who notched her first top ten hit and Grammy nomination with the song in 1986. "Nanci articulated an epic love. Such economy of language.

"'Love at the Five and Dime' is a timeless piece of music."[2]

Griffith doubled down with dozens more.

Nanci Caroline Griffith, who was born in Seguin, Texas, on July 6, 1953, but was raised in Austin, and who died in Nashville, Tennessee, on August 13, 2021, effortlessly backed each sharp story song ("Gulf Coast Highway," "Trouble in the Fields") and vibrant vignette ("Late Night Grande Hotel," "Drive-In Movies and Dashboard Lights") with combustible compassion ("It's a Hard

Life (Wherever You Go)," "The Wing and the Wheel") and strength in vulner-ability ("Ford Econoline," "So Long Ago"). She fully embodied the characters she sang. "Nanci didn't sing at a distance from herself," says Counting Crows lead singer Adam Duritz, who cowrote Griffith's high-water mark "Going Back to Georgia." "She takes you there with her.

"Her music has real depth, heart, and soul. Nanci wrote truly moving music."[3]

Common lyrical themes easily emerged. Griffith captured moments fleet-ing, relationships evolving, and everymen struggling for purchase on brighter days. She fought tirelessly for broken hearts and false starts. "I'm a writer first," she said. "Giving those little stories that mean something to people is all that matters to me. I don't think [my music] will ever have a mass audience, but I've done my job as a writer if it does."[4] "Nanci stood out by being a strong female presence [in Austin in the eighties]," says longtime *Austin American-States-man* music writer John T. Davis. "She wasn't tentative. Nanci was a tough cookie. Her deceptively fragile demeanor contrasted the control she had over her [storytelling] craft."[5]

Mystical melodies winged her words. Her most elegant—"I Wish It Would Rain," "On Grafton Street," "Anyone Can Be Somebody's Fool," "Brave Com-panion of the Road," and "Listen to the Radio"—simply steal breath away, equal measures familiar and fanciful, fearless and ferocious. "I'm most drawn to her songs by those incredible melodies," celebrated songwriter Dar Wil-liams says. "I don't know how many times I've stayed awake listening to the melody on 'Listen to the Radio.' I lead a songwriting retreat and always say about melodies, 'If you're not sure how to proceed in writing a song, make it pretty for yourself.' Nanci made sure the melodies were as interesting and pretty as the lyrics."[6]

Griffith's consecutive classics—*Once in a Very Blue Moon* (1984) and *The Last of the True Believers* (1986) on Philo Records as well as her major label debut *Lone Star State of Mind* (1987) on MCA Records—ascended her star. "I started studying Nanci Griffith when she had a hit with 'Love at the Five and Dime' [on *The Last of the True Believers*]," says MCA Records executive Tony Brown, who spearheaded country music's legendary Great Credibility Scare in the eighties. "Nanci was a poet who raised the bar for me. I put her on a ped-estal. MCA raised Nanci's profile, but her success was not at the level of a Toby Keith or Garth Brooks."[7] Her destiny demanded as much. After all, true poets rarely beguile masses.

Griffith became a songwriter's songwriter instead. "Nanci Griffith was a short story writer like Faulkner," Nashville-based singer-songwriter Amy Space says. "I recently did 'It's a Hard Life (Wherever You Go)' at a tribute here in Nashville and was like, 'Holy crap. There's a whole world in there.' Her songs like ['It's a Hard Life'] and 'Love at the Five and Dime' are novels in three minutes."[8] "Nanci's songwriting was pristine," echoes Nashville Songwriters Hall of Famer Beth Nielsen Chapman, whom Griffith saluted in her song "1937 Pre-War Kimball." "Her songs were original and blew you wide open into a movie. They're so visual. You could watch the movie of 'Love at the Five and Dime' in your head."[9]

Griffith's songs provided currency for country stars in the late eighties and nineties. Suzy Bogguss (the top ten single "Outbound Plane"), Emmylou Harris, and Willie Nelson ("Gulf Coast Highway"), and a young Kasey Chambers and her family's Dead Ringer Band ("I Wish It Would Rain") are among those who followed Mattea in recording her songs. "Trouble in the Fields" joins the latter two as her most covered. "Lots of people are cutting [my] songs," Griffith said at the time. "I'm really happy because I would rather someone else have the hits. I'm happy just being a cult artist, loving my audience, growing and changing with them, and not being pigeonholed."[10]

Griffith's most commercial efforts—her final MCA albums *Little Love Affairs* (1988), *Storms* (1989), and *Late Night Grande Hotel* (1991)—cemented her small but spirited fan base, who celebrated when Griffith earned an opening slot for Americana icon John Prine at New York City's legendary Carnegie Hall in 1988. Additionally, Griffith performed on several national television shows including *The Rosie O'Donnell Show*, the *Today* show, eight times on *Austin City Limits*, and most frequently *Late Show with David Letterman* starting around that time. Her crowning achievement followed: Griffith sold out a coveted headlining slot at Carnegie Hall touring behind her benchmark album *Other Voices, Other Rooms* five years after her opening set debut.

The visionary project delivered singular takes on modern masters near (friends Vince Bell, Townes Van Zandt, and Kate Wolf) and far (legendary songwriters Bob Dylan and Woody Guthrie). *Other Voices, Other Rooms* connected the Greenwich Village sixties folk boom with younger folksingers today. In short, Griffith kept alive the fading genre by resuscitation. She followed five years later with the less successful *Other Voices, Too (A Trip Back to Bountiful)*, but both brought her back home. "The most treasured gift my father ever gave me is a book by Alan Lomax [called] *Folk Songs of North America*," Griffith said. "It is an incredible collection of musical history that I have referred to like a bible throughout my life. My two volumes of *Other Voices* are a mere tip of the iceberg."[11]

"Nanci was so aware of others' greatness," said late Country Music Hall of

Fame director Peter Cooper. "She was a window for me into so many [song-writers]. She just loved songs so much. She always had her ears open for people who wrote great songs."[12] *"Other Voices, Other Rooms* was my introduction to Nanci's music," Griffith's later-years producer Thomm Jutz says. "Those songs really influenced me by introducing me to songwriters I didn't know. Nanci's choice in material represented the very best in contemporary folk music as far as what I had heard at that point. I thought it was interesting that she found the commonality between songs that people in England and Ireland had written and those written by Americans. Plus, Nanci's voice was so individualistic and unique."[13]

Griffith became a community leader among songwriters through her unparalleled generosity both personally and professionally. Her impact resonated broadly. "Nanci put me on the map as a songwriter," says New York City–based songwriter Julie Gold, whose "From a Distance" Griffith recorded before iconic torch singer Bette Midler brought the song worldwide fame. "Kathy Mattea, Judy Collins, and the Byrds suddenly recorded 'From a Distance' [after Nanci did]. Then came Bette Midler and her international hit with the song." Importantly, Griffith always acknowledged writers before performing their songs in concert. "Nanci gave so many of us credibility when she put us on the map," Gold continues. "She always credited me [onstage]. I found her generosity a really beautiful trait.

"I won the lottery [with Nanci]. She made my dream came true."[14]

Griffith peaked in the *Other Voices, Other Rooms* wake. She occasionally bottled lightning later on (1994's *Flyer*, 1999's gorgeous *The Dust Bowl Symphony* backed by the London Symphony Orchestra), but her songwriting muse visited fewer and farther between. She slowly faded into relative extinction as her drinking increased over the following quarter century. Griffith felt forgotten as fame faded. "Nanci wanted praise and felt underappreciated," Austin-based singer-songwriter Darden Smith says. "What the fuck was she taking about? She was the queen. The songwriter world is littered with people who have figured out ways to self-destruct, which is the chink in the armor they can't get past. Human nature.

"You get famous and complications are given fertilizer."[15]

Griffith certainly received recognition. She scored several awards and honors throughout her career—four Grammy nominations with one win, an induction into the Austin Music Hall of Fame in 1995, the Americana Music Association's Lifetime Achievement Trailblazer Award in 2008, and BBC Radio 2's Lifetime Achievement Award in 2012. Additionally, she was posthumously inducted into the Texas Heritage Songwriters' Hall of Fame in 2022. Griffith anticipated the award as well as former manager Ken Levitan's all-star tribute album *More Than a Whisper: Celebrating the Music of Nanci Griffith*—featuring acolytes Steve Earle, Mary Gauthier, Lyle Lovett and Kathy Mattea, Todd Snider, and Aaron Lee Tasjan, among others—before she passed away. "Nanci lit up when I told her she was going to be inducted," her manager Burt Stein says. "She said, 'That is so important to me. I'll go if you go.'"[16]

Griffith simply undershot her worth. She was—and is—beloved among friends and followers. "You know someone has had a profound impact on you when the mention of their name makes your heart and feelings swell until they wrap all the way around that name," legendary sacred and secular pop star Amy Grant says. "Her voice's vulnerability makes her music dear to me."[17] "I know the effects she had on my life, and I can only imagine how it was for others," Adam Duritz echoes. "Real artists like Nanci impact so much beyond just record sales. They teach us how to write songs, be artists, and treat other artists. Being decent to artists improves the work you get out of them. Nanci has changed the world in a way."

Verse: There's a Light beyond These Woods

THE AUSTIN YEARS

NANCI GRIFFITH signs with singer-songwriter Mike Williams's Austin-based B.F. Deal Records in her early twenties. Her first recorded songs—the original compositions "Texas Boy," "If I Were a Child," and "Double Standard Blues"—appear on the B.F. Deal Sampler, Vol. 1 in 1977. Griffith's debut full-length album, *There's a Light beyond These Woods*, releases the following year. The collection includes the early high points "Alabama Soft Spoken Blues" and "West Texas Sun," but the title track best showcases her songwriting potential. "There's a Light beyond These Woods" highlights relationships with Griffith's best friend Margaret Mary Graham ("Mary Margaret" in the song) and her late high school boyfriend John.

Griffith most frequently performs at the Hole in the Wall at the University of Texas as *There's a Light beyond These Woods* hits shelves. She's already a seasoned performer. "I did my first professional gig at fourteen at a Thanksgiving party at the Red Lion Cabaret," Griffith says. "It was a wonderful night [even though] no one came. I was terrible, but I made eleven dollars."[1] Griffith further sharpens her craft as a performer at Bobby Nelson and Martin Wigginton's Austin clubs, the Alamo Lounge and Emmajoe's, throughout the late seventies and early eighties. "I went to the Hole in the Wall to see Nanci Griffith play around 1978," Nelson says. "I was so impressed because she could quiet their crowd."[2]

STEPHEN DOSTER: Nanci always seemed pissed off because the audience was too loud. She was not a shrinking violet. She would say, "Y'all mind shutting the hell up for a while while I do a few songs?" Anyone hanging around the Hole in the Wall in Austin was aware that she was the most apt to tell you to shut the hell up. Her persona onstage was a pretty soft person and almost like a southern belle, but she was a tough person who held her own. Nanci and I both had residency nights at the Hole in the Wall. Mine was Tuesday. Hers was Sunday. Those were her first gigs. Nanci had original songs and a real Texas thing about her.[3]

Austin-based songwriter and producer Stephen Doster has produced more than sixty albums. He appeared on Austin City Limits *with Nanci Griffith in 1985.*

DOUG CUGINI: [Nanci] was the first person to bring in a PA when she played [at the Hole in the Wall], and she actually brought a following with her. She had twenty or thirty people who would come to see her, and that was a big crowd at the Hole in the Wall in those days. She commanded the room. She insisted on the people paying attention to her, and the power of her presence onstage got it. [Hers are] the only nights I remember the crowd being quiet during the music.[4]

Doug Cugini was the original owner of the Hole in the Wall when it opened in Austin in 1974. The venue remains active today.

CHARLEY STEFL: Nanci wanted people to listen. She was very serious about her [craft] and didn't want to be background music even when she was just starting to play out around Austin. Nanci rocked the Hole in the Wall just with her voice [and guitar]. She wouldn't have to demand attention. She could capture it with her voice and guitar playing. So, yeah, she would give unruly customers this look and usually didn't have to say anything beyond the look. She had the audience's attention even from the first time I saw her play. Everybody was focused on her singing, and this was really early on. They hadn't even put out the *B.F. Deal Sampler* at that point.[5]

Nashville-based artist Charley Stefl has cowritten songs recorded by major artists including Lee Ann Womack ("The Fool") and George Jones ("The Visit").

MIKE WILLIAMS: I met an unknown lady with a thrilling voice named Emmylou Harris, and we partnered up for a couple years starting in 1965. Emmylou was the standard in my mind. Then I heard Nanci Griffith and thought, She's another one. Nanci was singing at the Hole in the Wall in Austin at the time. Her songwriting was crafty enough, but her voice really lifted the songs. I wasn't sure what her ambitions were, but she didn't have a record deal. I had started B.F. Deal Records for my first album in 1975 with more money than sense.

We had produced albums for Allen Damron [*The Old Campaigner*] and Ladd Roberts [*Lady Up the Stairs*, both in 1976], and I was casting about for ideas. How about a sampler with three songs for each artist? Nanci was one of the four artists we recorded in January 1977. We released the *B.F. Deal Sampler, Vol. 1* that year with her songs "Texas Boy," "If I Were a Child," and "Double Standard Blues." "Texas Boy" was a gem. I could feel the buzz for Nanci, but there were no sales to speak of with the sampler. I asked if she would want to do an album in spring 1978. She said yes. We went into the studio that summer for four or five days. Nanci was ready to do *There's a Light beyond These Woods*. Her people were rehearsed.

We recorded the album two-track and sat around cutting and splicing tape with a real good engineer named Bill Blacksley, who had worked for Motown. We might record fifteen takes of a song and listen back on cassette, then go back in and take a knife to the tape. Nanci's album sounds like the songs are one single take, but they're very edited. Her performance was good from take to take. Bill was able to keep the levels right. I'm real happy with that album, which is probably my best work. Nanci wasn't famous yet, but she had all that talent. I'm glad we did that record. Nanci was a neophyte in the studio but not new as far as singing her songs.[6]

Singer-songwriter Mike Williams founded B.F. Deal Records. The label released Nanci Griffith's debut album, There's a Light beyond These Woods, *in 1978.*

LYLE LOVETT: I opened two shows for Nanci Griffith at the Basement coffee house when I was a student at Texas A&M University and she [came over from Austin] in 1978. The Basement was in the student union and had a scheduled open mike, but we had enough budget to bring in regional professional performers like Nanci two or three times a year. I was a journalism student and had interviewed her for the daily paper *The Battalion*. Nanci came across as confident, and I remember viewing her as a well-established performer because she commanded the room. Nanci was a great, thoughtful, and deliberate performer who knew how to impact an audience. I was thrilled when she listened to my set the first night.

Nanci closed the first Basement show with the Mike Williams song "Wichita Falls Waltz." I was standing in the back in a packed house and have a distinct memory of Nanci walking offstage in her white jeans halfway through the end of the song. She sang the remainder off mike, which was very effective and had a big impact on the crowd. She was gone with the last word of the song. Very well done. Her storytelling and voice really drew me to the songs. Nanci asked me the second night if she could sing with me and got up to sing harmony on my song "Walk through the Bottomlands." She just had *There's a*

Light beyond These Woods out at that time, but her voice made you want to dig in and listen.[7]

Lyle Lovett has released nearly a dozen albums since entering consciousness with his self-titled debut in 1986. His album Step inside This House *(1998) salutes songwriting influences such as Vince Bell, Guy Clark, and Townes Van Zandt.*

MICKIE MERKENS: Nanci Griffith truly loved songs and songwriting. She lived for the songs and was gonna make sure her audience was gonna hear a song she loved. She wanted to share songs with everybody. She also had a real love for detail, knowing who wrote the song, when it was written, and who performed on the [record]. Details were very important to her. For example, I recorded "Are You Tired of Me My Darling" for the *Texas Summer Nights Volume 2*. Nanci made sure that I knew that she went through the copyright office and looked up all that information.[8]

Mickie Merkens wrote "Yarrington Town," which Nanci Griffith recorded on Other Voices, Too *(A Trip Back to Bountiful). She is married to guitarist Brian Wood.*

NANCI GRIFFITH: "Are You Tired of Me My Darling" was my dad's barbershop quartet song. I researched it and found out the song was written in 1877.[9]

MICKIE MERKENS: She called and said, "I want you to know that I've researched that song. The song isn't a traditional. It was written by G. P. Cook and Ralph Roland in 1877. Did you know that?" Nanci was very excited about sharing those details. She saw her place in that lineage early on as a songwriter whose songs would be passed down. She knew she would mark her place in time in the legacy of folk music if she kept writing and introducing people to other songs. Nanci had to really love and relate to a song when she recorded it. She was like a person going out and excavating for the perfect jewel and showing them to everyone. Nanci went on to record "Are You Tired of Me My Darling" on her *Other Voices, Other Rooms* album in 1993.

RUELENE STRAWSER: Nanci [was] musical [from when] she was about two years old. She used to perform the little kids' songs for my grandmother standing on an aluminum tub they turned upside down on the patio. Nanci would do her thing and Grandmother would applaud. Nanci loved to write. She wrote poetry. She wrote her first song, called "A New Generation," when she was twelve.[10]

Ruelene Strawser was Nanci Griffith's mother.

10 • THERE'S A LIGHT BEYOND THESE WOODS

NANCI GRIFFITH: I started [singing] when I was six growing up in Austin. My dad was a tenor in a barbershop quartet who taught me how to sing harmony. Then I learned how to play guitar and piano. I had those abilities to go out and be the backup vocalist and rhythm guitar player and started playing on my own when I was about fourteen. My parents were beatniks who were very unusual, very odd, and had a lot of very odd friends. One friend owned a folk club cabaret in Austin. One day there was a cancellation. I was fourteen and was called in to come and play [my first show].[11]

PETE KENNEDY: Nanci always said she grew up in a beatnik house. She was a schoolteacher for a while, but she couldn't do anything besides what she did. I'm always inspired to be around people like that. [Following your muse] takes courage. People will always tell you that you need something to fall back on or fit more into the mainstream. They say you shouldn't be so weird. There are all the variations on them saying, "You're doing the wrong thing." You have to develop the hard outer shell and inner resolve that Nanci definitely had.[12]

Singer-songwriter Pete Kennedy performed with Nanci Griffith from the nineties through the end of her career. He previously played guitar for Kate Wolf.

NANCI GRIFFITH: Everyone else in my family played piano, but I couldn't wrap my brain around playing piano. So, I started watching a public television program on Saturday mornings [with] Miss Laura teaching guitar lessons. She used Phil Ochs songs as examples. Watching those guitar lessons every Saturday morning basically was how I learned to play guitar. That and watching Buddy Holly and the Crickets on [the] *Ed Sullivan [Show]*. Buddy Holly's hand was a blur because it moved so fast. I grew up listening to [Nashville's legendary 650 AM radio station] WSM every Saturday night and waiting for Miss Loretta [Lynn] to come on the Grand Ole Opry. There was a station in Juarez that would cut in and out of WSM's signal. I always hoped that it wouldn't cut into Loretta.[13]

VALERIE SCHUSTER: Nanci and I lived across the street from one another. Her next-door neighbors were [local Austin counterculture legend "Crazy" Carl] Hickerson and his family. Nanci and I were involved in numerous plays like *Stop the World I Want to Get Off* at the Austin Civic Theater when we were ten years old. *Gypsy* was our first musical. Nanci and I bought the *Gypsy* album and loved all the songs. We would put on music, start singing and dancing, and become different, joyous people. We worked out one song and dance and performed it for the director, who had us perform for the audience on closing night. We got a standing ovation.

Nanci wasn't very outgoing. She was awkward and kept to herself. I remem-

THE AUSTIN YEARS • 11

ber her coming over after we moved to [the north Austin suburb] Westwood in junior high, sitting in our living room, playing guitar, and singing. She had an amazing voice even then. We sat there mesmerized in disbelief over this awkward girl who wasn't superpretty singing with this amazing voice. Maybe the way she presented herself onstage later on was for theatrics. I don't recall her speaking quite that way when we were younger. She could have developed that onstage.[14]

Valerie Schuster grew up in the same Austin neighborhood as Nanci Griffith. She owns Upper Crust Bakery in North Austin today.

NANCI GRIFFITH: I started out wanting to play French horn, [but] I was so bad. I came home from school one day, went to my room to practice, and it was gone. There was so much great music going on in the house so their ears couldn't take it. They took the French horn back. I was also a child actor and did a lot of acting in musicals like *Stop the World I Want to Get Off*, *Gypsy*, and *Li'l Abner*. I was very comfortable with the stage by the time I started performing music.[15]

VALERIE SCHUSTER: Nanci and I kept in touch after my family moved when I was in seventh grade. Nanci became somewhat estranged from her family later. She was nerdy and unpopular and didn't get along with her older sister and brother. They were extroverts, and she was an introvert. Nanci taught me how to play guitar at one point. Then she wrote the song "There's a Light beyond These Woods" for Margaret Graham. Nanci and Margaret were really close. We all hung out, smoked dope, and did drugs together. Margaret's parents took us to San Antonio to see Blind Faith when we were fifteen. We checked into our hotel, got in the elevator, and Steve Winwood, Eric Clapton, and the guys in the band got in the elevator. We rode in the elevator with Ginger Baker after the show. Crazy.

MARGARET MARY GRAHAM: I was a loose cannon, and Nanci was more sensible and subdued. We loved to play, sing, and party and would spend time at the Vulcan Gas Company, the Paramount Theatre, Red Lion, Woolworth's, and Piccadilly Cafeteria. We did what most people our age did at those places and were wild by our parents' standards. Her parents didn't like me and mine didn't like her when we were teenagers. We loved all the music of our youth. I was a rock and roller at heart, but the music I played and liked to sing was more like Dylan. We both thought we would be musical performers. I knew she would.[16]

Margaret Mary Graham was Nanci Griffith's childhood best friend. Griffith immortalized her in the title track to her debut, "There's a Light beyond These Woods."

RILEY HICKERSON: Nanci grew up next door to Valerie Schuster across my street. Nanci was so sweet, generous, and kind. She would come to all our Holy Cross High School reunions. Then I would go to her concerts at Bass Hall here in Austin years later and couldn't believe how she would fill that place up and play guitar without making a single mistake. She would let us go backstage.[17]

Riley Hickerson grew up in Nanci Griffith's Austin neighborhood. He taught the Berlitz method for nearly three decades.

DARDEN SMITH: Nanci Griffith [taught me] two things. The first was when I was opening for her in Austin. I was in the parking lot early when Nanci showed up and watched her unload the sound system from her car. This small woman was carrying these big-ass speakers, a mixing head, and microphones. I was like, "Why are you bringing your own sound system?" "They don't have a sound system," she said. "I have to bring my own." I was like, "I'm selling my sound system." I did the next day. I didn't want to spend my life lugging one around. They have to take care of the sound and respect you in a different way. I still own as little gear as possible.[18]

Darden Smith has released more than a dozen albums from his debut, Native Soil *(1986), through* Everything *(2017). He cofounded the nonprofit Songwriting With: Soldiers, which employs songwriting as a healing resource for veterans.*

BOBBY NELSON: We had Nanci do a couple twilight concerts at the Split Rail, but then it burned down and within a year my partner Martin [Wigginton] and I opened the Alamo Lounge, which stayed open until 1981. Nanci went on to play there regularly. We became friends. Nanci was writing beautiful songs at the time. Martin and I were really into the songwriters [who were playing our clubs] like Nanci, Townes Van Zandt, Jimmie Dale Gilmore, and Butch Hancock.[19]

Bobby Nelson played a major role in Austin's folk music scene during the seventies and eighties as owner of the Split Rail Inn, the Alamo Lounge, and Emmajoe's.

MICKIE MERKENS: Denice Franke and I used to play music together in San Marcos. Franke was constantly telling me about Nanci Griffith and would take the bus to Austin to see her play. I didn't go to Austin much, but Franke was very persistent [that] we go see Nanci perform at the Alamo Lounge. The Alamo was very tiny and bizarre. Nanci sang onstage in the corner. Very intimate. Nanci made me think of the legendary folksingers I had grown up admiring from the first time I saw her perform. She was very sincere and very professional with an innocence, but she was a very skilled performer. Her songs blew me away. The early stuff was beautiful. I'm into the narrative story songs, and Nanci loved telling tales and love stories.

DENICE FRANKE: I had known about Nanci Griffith since a friend turned me on to her record *There's a Light beyond These Woods* in 1978. Nanci was everything and more than her record. I was in a folk quartet called the Beacon City Band who started putting songs from *There's a Light beyond These Woods* into our set list. We lived in San Marcos but were trying to break into Austin and wanted to play this shotgun bar run by Bobby Nelson and Martin Wigginton called the Alamo Lounge on 5th Street. I didn't have a driver's license, so I had been taking the Greyhound from San Marcos up to Austin to go see Nanci's shows at the Alamo. The bus station was on Congress Avenue in Austin so I just had to trot a few blocks down to see her.

We got a call from Martin one night saying Jimmie Gilmore canceled last minute on a Thursday night [and we could fill in]. We sound-checked that night with a Nanci song before I saw she was there at the end of the room. Bobby Nelson apparently told her that we were doing one of her songs. Nanci had come in to see Jimmie perform, so we were a surprise. Nanci came up before we even got started and introduced herself. I was like, "Yeah, I know who you are." She asked me to sing her song "Alabama Soft Spoken Blues," which is the song we did during sound check. She sat right up front, so that made me more nervous.

Then she came over and thanked us at the end of the set. [Nanci saw that] I hadn't figured out the chord progression in "Alabama Soft Spoken Blues" and had just made something up. "Do you mind if I show you the chord progression?" she said. "Sure." She showed me the change, and I did it that way from there on out. I always would have to leave early when I went to see her shows because the last bus left at eleven, but she would ask me to sing with her after that night when she saw me in the audience at the Alamo and later at Emmajoe's and the Cactus Cafe.[20]

Denice Franke is a Houston-based singer-songwriter featured in the documentary For the Sake of the Song: The Story of Anderson Fair.

BOBBY NELSON: The Alamo Lounge and Emmajoe's were almost entirely songwriter shows. Nanci and I spent time together over the next decade and a half after Emmajoe's. We both liked to read southern literature and James Harrison, who wrote the short story that became the movie *Legends of the Fall*. We were both on a Charles Bukowski reading streak. We also read newspapers and magazines and were immersed in the political news both nationally and globally. Nanci read so much and knew about so many issues.

What we did not have in common was a love of Lyndon B. Johnson. She defended him staunchly. I appreciated the civil rights work he did, but he really messed up the Vietnam War. We had big arguments about that. We would get really drunk during our arguments, but they were always friendly. Emmajoe's closed at midnight, but we often would go down the street a block to [legendary Austin blues club] Antone's to catch the last set. Nanci sometimes would stay at my house after Emmajoe's. She loved to be around people drinking and singing songs.

NANCI GRIFFITH: I [felt] Lyndon B. Johnson was very naive on an international policy level, but he was a brilliant man when it came to domestic issues. We had Lyndon Johnson cramming Medicare down the throat of Congress in order to have what we have because everybody was very against Medicare. They were calling it socialization. Thanks to Lyndon Johnson we have the Voting Rights Act. We have Medicare. We have all kinds of relief programs, but nobody ever mentions him, which is sad. He was such a great senator and president other than the Vietnam War.[21]

BOBBY NELSON: Eric Taylor would play Emmajoe's as well. Nanci was very up-front about giving him credit for teaching her guitar and songwriting. His life had calmed down by the time we got to know each other, and he was a really nice guy. He had his own problems, but he eventually became a counselor later. He influenced a lot of songwriters in the Austin, Dallas, and Houston areas. Eric was an influence on Lyle Lovett. Lyle and Robert Earl Keen both played at Emmajoe's. Townes played at the Alamo and Emmajoe's regularly. I have a postcard from Lyle to Martin and me saying, "Do you have any opening acts?"

Nanci was good friends with all those guys like Eric, Lyle, and Jimmie Dale Gilmore, but she didn't hang out with them when she was still in Austin like they hung out with each other. She was one of the first to say, "Okay. I've got to travel the country if I'm serious about music and songwriting." She traveled a lot and saw that as really important to do. There was always something that set Nanci apart from the rest. She was very literary and serious about her songwriting, but I could sit around the room with the Flatlanders at three in the morning and feel an easiness I would feel that I wouldn't when Nanci was around.

JIMMIE DALE GILMORE: I played the grand opening of the Armadillo World Headquarters when I was living in Austin in the early seventies and had been involved in the music scene that later developed into the cosmic cowboy thing. I was in the more underground, psychedelic movement with a band called the Hub City Movers back then. We were hardcore hippies who were the last house band at the Vulcan Gas Company on Congress Avenue. I was a hippie doing country music more than folk even though I was deeply influenced. Then I left town.

I went to Lubbock first and the Flatlanders happened. Then I went to Denver and lived there most of the seventies. Jerry Jeff Walker and Michael Martin Murphey and the cosmic cowboys mainly happened in the seventies and had exploded by the time I came back. Willie Nelson had moved here. [Marcia Ball's band] Freda and the Firedogs were doing band-oriented straight-out country music. Nanci, Butch, and I were still more associated with the acoustic music–oriented songwriter [venues] than to dancing or big crowds. We were playing listening music.

Folksingers were a pretty tight-knit group in Austin in the late seventies and early eighties when I met Nanci at the Alamo. We became very close friends. Nanci was opening shows for Butch and me, but she was really popular and had her own big following. She was one of the few who actually originally came from the Austin area. The rest of us—Lyle Lovett, Robert Earl Keen, Butch, and I—were transplants from all over [Texas], but we did shows together pretty often. Townes started hanging out at Emmajoe's and would stay until late night. Townes, Nanci, and I did a number of shows together.

Everybody looked up to Townes, but they also knew that on any given night you might wish you were somewhere else instead [of with him]. Townes was pretty noted for that. I had some strange nights with him, but Nanci and I were huge fans. I used to get into arguments with Townes. "I'm gonna be like Hank Williams," he would say. "Nobody's gonna know anything about me until I'm dead, and then I'll be well known." I used to argue with him about that becoming a self-fulfilling prophecy. He thought it was fated. Well, it came true.[22]

Legendary singer-songwriter Jimmie Dale Gilmore is a founding member of the Flatlanders with fellow Lubbock, Texas, natives Joe Ely and Butch Hancock. His solo album Spinning around the Sun *was nominated for a Grammy award with Bob Dylan, Shawn Colvin, and others the year Nanci Griffith's* Other Voices, Other Rooms *won.*

DARDEN SMITH: Townes Van Zandt, Calvin Russell, and Pat Mears all circled around Big Larry, who liked me for some reason. Big Larry was a posthippie biker guy who was a drug dealer and a preacher. He was huge but had a tiny little biker chick wife. I met Big Larry at a place called Beer Park at the intersection of 26th Street and Manor Road. He was my entrée into the inner world around Townes. I was a suburban kid and was a little petrified by these guys. I knew drugs and alcohol were my weak spots and could seriously mess my life up. I was having a hamburger with Larry one time, and he goes, "Darden, those guys . . ." He was pointing at Townes and Calvin. "I love them, but they're dangerous for people like you. Be really cautious. Don't let them get too close."

JIMMIE DALE GILMORE: Townes was totally brilliant and totally self-destructive. I loved the guy a whole lot, but it was hard to be around him during some periods. I think Nanci probably was a good influence on him, but not enough to alter his whole trajectory. I think Townes would tend to be on better behavior around Nanci unless he was just totally whacked out, which also could happen. Townes and I both were trying to get sober together at the same time. There were lots of ups and downs, but I ended up being a little more successful than he was.

JANET GILMORE: I enjoyed Nanci's company when we met at Emmajoe's in 1981. We were [living in] a rare and magical moment in a rich music scene where Nanci, Lucinda Williams, Jimmie Dale Gilmore, Butch Hancock, Lyle Lovett, Robert Earl Keen, Townes Van Zandt, and Uncle Walt's Band were offering their music in an intimate and reverent setting. Nanci's voice was transcendent. Her songs were about ordinary life and troubles. She sang to us about us. Her song "Marilyn Monroe/Neon and Waltzes" was my favorite. "Farewell you old tinsel city / With your waltz in the mornin' and your neon at night," she sang in the song. "I've bathed in your loneliness, drank of your wine / I lived on DiMaggio time."

Nanci was a champion of the underdog, a talented and strong woman in what was pretty much a man's world. She held space magnificently—regally even—with her performances and would weave a spell with her audience, who were pin-drop quiet and transfixed. Nanci was gentle and wild, strong and fragile. We bartenders and waitresses would shoot some pool with a few regulars and some of the other regular musicians like Jimmie, Butch, Townes, or Blaze Foley, who would drop by for a free beer to wind down the night and sometimes even wind up again and keep going till it was daylight—or we would walk down the street to the Hole in the Wall and catch the last few songs and then be welcomed into the after-hours party.

Nanci and I weren't close, but we all played our parts in creating the magic of that time. Nanci was a private person even then, and I felt like I knew her best through her voice and her songs. Emmajoe's closed in 1983 after bringing indescribably great music most every night for two years. Nanci left for Nashville a couple years later with record contracts, bigger audiences, and a well-earned successful career awaiting her there. Our paths crossed over the years and I was always glad to see her and felt the connection to that time no matter how many years had passed. I think she felt it too. Emmajoe's and the early eighties music scene was Austin's Camelot, a romantic, sweet, crazy, wild time. Nanci might have been our queen.[23]

Janet Gilmore worked as a bartender at Bobby Nelson's club Emmajoe's during the early eighties. She lives with her husband, Jimmie Dale Gilmore, in Austin.

JIMMIE DALE GILMORE: We were all each other's fans and would all go to each other's gigs when we weren't playing. Nanci and I spent the most time together when would go out to eat after gigs and then sometimes over to someone's house late at night. We would eat at Katz's Deli because it was good food and stayed open late. We also ate at Hill's Cafe. The Night Hawk was still around then. Katz's and the Alamo were both on 6th Street. Farther east was Antone's on 6th. The Alamo and Antone's were the only two places on 6th Street that had music back then. Antone's had the band music.

We knew something really special was going on. This was before the city council decided to embrace Austin as the "Live Music Capital of the World." The thing is, it really was. There were blues clubs, country cover bands, and cross-fertilization between different groups. Nanci and I were around each other a lot at Emmajoe's, which was pretty wonderful. Nanci was the one woman in the group that had the most staying power. Lucinda Williams came into our group a little later. Lucinda and her boyfriend Clyde actually lived with Janet and I for a while.

MIKE WILLIAMS: I didn't know what to do with *There's a Light beyond These Woods*. Neither did Nanci. I guess she was doing well by local standards because people were liking her music. I forget how she got connected with her next record company [Featherbed Records], but she came to me about a year and a half after we released *There's a Light beyond These Woods*. "Mike," she said, "I've gotten some interest from a record company, and I could negotiate much better with them if I had the rights to *There's a Light beyond These Woods*."

I'm such a brilliant businessman. I gave her the rights.

STEPHEN DOSTER: The first thing I recall recording with Nanci was called *The B.F. Deal Sampler, Vol. 1* before they put out *There's a Light beyond These Woods*. I started playing what she called acoustic lead guitars for her on occasion before that, but I played much more when we got to *There's a Light beyond These Woods*. She called me her music director because I knew the chord changes. She played with [different] tunings and moving her capo around. Her most literary piece, "There's a Light beyond These Woods," was my favorite song back then and still is today. Nanci was well into that before naming [*Other Voices, Other Rooms*] after Truman Capote.

MARGARET MARY GRAHAM: "There's a Light beyond These Woods" always haunts me. I stayed lost for so many years of my life [because it] wasn't what I imagined it to be. I didn't do the things I wanted to do, but I have real riches in life. I am wealthy and need nothing. So that song is a reminder to me of how tangled up things can look at times. The song meant different things during different times. Every word reflects a true event or time with Nanci. I think we spent some time being jealous of each other. She thought I had something she could never have because I was always in a relationship I took seriously, [and] I wanted to be a musician.

We did *There's a Light beyond These Woods* and then went our separate ways. We didn't hang out much during [our twenties and thirties]. I was too busy getting involved in an abusive relationship, and she was moving up in her career. Nanci did make me get up onstage and sing with her once at the album party. I was petrified. I was not very involved in the songwriting process when we were young. I just wrote some lyrics, and Nanci did some initial revision for "Saint Teresa [of Avila," later released on 1997's *Blue Roses from the Moons*]. Then a friend died and Nanci did some more revisions based on my involvement with [the Roman Catholic religious order] the Carmelites. Nanci's sister Mikki also added a line.

Nanci would play her guitar and sing the song over the phone for me during the revision process. Then it took off, and she sent me demo tapes as revisions. The song ended up totally different than it had begun. The other song I wrote with her was "Alabama Soft Spoken Blues" in 1976. We were sitting on the bed in a house I was renting in Austin at the time. Nanci was sort of homeless and staying with me and helping with rent. This was when she was still playing the clubs in Austin. The song was written about Gary, but I won't give his last name. He was a cutie and a real heartbreaker from Alabama. There never was another friend like Nanci. I had other best friends, but never another Nanci.

STEPHEN DOSTER: The sessions for *There's a Light beyond These Woods* were very organic. We sat around in a circle and played songs live without much overdubbing. Recording live was really good, and I still think so all these years later. Playing live is everything, which is what is missing in music today. You can't get that by overdubbing. The acoustic mike bleeding through the electric mike and the other way around makes a sound. What comes through the speaker moves me so much more. I don't remember stopping and punching in overdubs at all during the *There's a Light* sessions. You're gonna have some guitar string squeaks if you move your hand around, but that's my favorite part. *There's a Light beyond These Woods* had a very strong folk music vibe. Nanci was best at being a folksinger.

BRIAN WOOD: I played with Nanci for six years starting in 1981. She introduced herself and invited me to sit in with her at the Alamo Lounge where she played every week. I went to hear her the next week just to listen. Magic. The next week I went back with my guitar and played. More magic. We usually played as a duo but also with other incredible players and singers. I played on her first *Austin City Limits* show, her first time at the Kennedy Center in Washington, DC, and her first time at Carnegie Hall. Nanci was very generous with a great sense of humor and clearly was a major singer-songwriter, but more than that she was a great friend always.

Nanci was all about the music. We had the same ears musically, liked the same music, and heard the same arrangements in songs. We were kindred spirits, which helped the music sound wonderful. I liked the content of her songwriting, her musicality, and performance. You know it when you hear it as a sideman. "Yeah, I can do this. I can add to the songs and enjoy and revel in them." We were mostly playing the songs on her second album, *Poet in My Window*, when I started with her. We had been playing them for about three months when we went in to do that album. Man, what a wonderful [experience]. I played guitar and pedal steel on the album and was coproducer with Eric Taylor.[24]

Instrumentalist Brian Wood played guitar with Nanci Griffith early on. The longtime Austin resident coproduced her second record, Poet in My Window.

•   •   •

Nanci Griffith releases *Poet in My Window* in 1982. Griffith's sophomore album features several highlights like "You Can't Go Home Again," "October Reasons," "Workin' in Corners," "Wheels," and the title track. She includes Jimmie Dale Gilmore's "Tonight I Think I'm Gonna Go Downtown" as the penultimate song before the closing title track. "Nanci recorded 'Tonight I Think I'm Gonna Go Downtown' right in the period when she was beginning to make the transition to Nashville," Gilmore says. "We were close friends, but we had different social circles. We wouldn't see each other for a long time if we didn't have gigs together. I wasn't really keeping up with her all the time, but we remained close. We had a connection, a real friendship, and a mutual admiration."

Griffith and the musicians—Brian Wood (guitar), Wells Young (keyboards, bass), Eric Taylor (bass), Evelyn Taylor (harmony vocals)—join drummer John Hill at his hill country studio for the sessions. "We recorded *Poet in My Window* out at Loma Ranch Studio about twelve miles outside Fredericksburg [Texas]," Wood says. "Magic. Everything came together and worked. Boy, I learned so much. The music was great. Recording that album wasn't my first time in a studio, but it was close. The engineer John Hill taught me a lot as we went along. I learned about the technical aspects of recording and what producing means. I think Nanci wanted me in there for my ears when it comes down to it."

BRIAN WOOD: Nanci, Eric, and John knew that I'm mostly guided by my ears. I was listening for the obvious stuff [as coproducer] like making sure no one was out of tune or playing clams, but I was mostly listening to the overall ensemble sound. Does everything work together here? Anything sticking out like a sore thumb? Are people contributing at the right times during the song to make things work? You know, I got offstage one time at Kerrville and Townes Van Zandt was at the bottom of the stage. Townes looked at me and said, "I like your spaces." He was saying I knew what not to play, which is another measuring stick when producing. Spaces are very important. You don't have to fill up every single note. Townes was right.

I wanted to make sure that every note that happened belonged on *Poet in My Window*. I made sure the ones that didn't weren't there. Sometimes you have to dump [parts] of a masterful performance if it doesn't fit the ensemble sound. Eric Taylor played absolutely lyrical and masterful bass lines on that record. I love the studio because that's where you get it right. You can correct mistakes and craft the songs. Songs are raw playing live. There are so many outside forces. We mostly played those *Poet in My Window* sessions live in the studio, but obviously there were some overdubs. Nanci had her dad's barbershop quartet come in to do a song.

We were constantly playing live around then either at the Cactus Cafe in Austin or Anderson Fair in Houston. We would make occasional forays up to Dallas to play Poor David's Pub. Pretty busy time. We had played the Alamo Lounge and Emmajoe's in Austin regularly before that. I think we played every week for a long time. Griff [Luneburg] had it down with how [to run] the Cactus. He's a hero in my opinion. The Cactus would be full when we played there. They have a full bar in the back, but you could hear a pin drop when the music started. The acoustics in there with the hard stone walls is wonderful.

JOHN HILL: -The weather was so cold during the *Poet in My Window* sessions. Nine degrees outside. We usually wear many hats here: engineering, camp counselor, producing, barbecue specialist—but there wasn't any barbecuing going on when Nanci was here to record [*Poet in My Window*] because we had a snowstorm. Eric slipped and slammed down on the patio. Crazy. We had a few slippages from the studio to the house. We just roared the fireplace, sat on the couch, and tried to get back and forth into the studio to do the best we could. Good days here are magic because everyone is just sitting and playing on the patio and getting ready to go back into the studio.

There are various ways Nanci might have come out [to Fredericksburg] to record here. [My wife] Laurie and I were highly visible in Austin back then. I was drumming for five different bands, and we had a sound company. Willis Alan Ramsey was among our clients. Nanci might have sat in on some of those sound gigs and watched us. She also might have seen me sit in with bands like Bill and Bonnie Hearne's or Michael [Martin] Murphey's. Also, we did the Eric Taylor album *Shameless Love* around then when they were still married. We met through the Kerrville Folk Festival crowd. She might have known about us through that.

We recorded Nanci's album in five days or less. Nanci, Brian, Laurie, and I produced her album collaboratively. We didn't plan on anything. We would decide when things were going backward and would quit and come back another time when that was the case. Nanci's song "October Reasons" was gonna be her album title song, but she couldn't get it. We finally figured out that she was meant to be essentially by herself to record. All the guys got kicked out of the studio. Laurie and Nanci successfully got the song down. Nanci needed to get into the mindset she wanted. She wanted to cut down to bare bones and emote the song the way she heard it in her head. She did with Laurie.

Songs like "Working in Corners" were magic. We knew. Very few songs had to be microscoped to the point of exhaustion. They were just there because Nanci [was prepared] going into the studio. Brian was instrumental in putting that together, too. He was very specific about what he wanted. Of course, he knew what to do, having been with Nanci for quite some time. Everything basically came together as planned. Brian is quite the expressionist on the melodic side, which is exactly what you need for folk music. Lead guitar should be non-obtrusive, very melodic, and exquisite. Brian was that and did most arrangements.

I didn't really arrange during my production process. I just ask the right questions and go in the right suggested directions. You have to do that to figure out what to express and how to reproduce it. As a drummer producing, I just play the way I feel the song. I've really memorized the vocal stabs and guitar expressions and where I need to be and not to be. I don't usually get much direction as a drummer in that situation. I usually have drums down in my head already going in. Playing with Eric was wonderful. Eric was a master technician. Working with Eric and Nanci together wasn't a problem at all. Eric was more technical about saying what he wanted to his players than Nanci was.

We would know instantly if something didn't work. Eric and Nanci were always [open to suggestions]. The conversation between all parties was really easy. Sometimes someone would ease the mood and ask, "Why don't we put bagpipes on it there?" They were good about not being overly serious and getting back to being an artist. The main thing is we had fun. I try to create that atmosphere even if people come in stiff. "Here you are at the ranch. No big deal. We have a barn with some really good gear. Have fun." That usually works. The room is what you make of it with your crowd, your humor, and your sense of artistry.

We started with mastering labs on the East Coast for the record. The actual lacquers came back sounding like there were radar pings. "What the hell is this?" We called various mastering labs on the East Coast and found out that something had attacked the actual storage warehouse at Lacquer Masters, which were bugs akin to the ones who eat oil slicks. They would start in the center and eat their way out to the side of the record. So, you lay grooves on the record, and it just goes "ping, ping, ping." The whole way through. "Oh, shit." We finally found Wakefield Mastering in Arizona. The bugs hadn't gotten there yet. We got a good pressing. Nanci had been going crazy. "What is this?"[25]

John Hill owns Loma Ranch Studio in Fredericksburg, Texas, where Nanci Griffith recorded her second album, Poet in My Window.

Verse: Once in a Very Blue Moon

The Houston (and Back) Years

NANCI GRIFFITH lives the next several years in Houston. Legendary listening room Anderson Fair, a springboard for future icons Townes Van Zandt, Guy Clark, Vince Bell, Eric Taylor (Griffith's new husband), Lyle Lovett, and Robert Earl Keen becomes home base. "Anderson Fair is a magical place all about the music," Griffith says. "Eric Taylor introduced me to [club owners] Tim Leatherwood and the late Roger Ruffcorn, and I opened up for Eric the first time I played at Anderson Fair. So many generations of artists have come through and played at Anderson Fair."[1]

Clark describes the venue's bohemian Montrose neighborhood as "feel hippie."[2] Songwriters encourage each other. They clothe and feed less fortunate. Buy guitar strings for friends short on cash this week. Songwriting remains top focus throughout the era as the hallowed club with the red-brick floor serves as epicenter. "Anderson Fair has historically brought those generations together," Griffith says. "We've met each other there. I think everybody just migrated here, which had a lot to do with Guy Clark and Townes Van Zandt and all of us being such big fans. [Our Anderson Fair days] were a time as songwriters when you got up and you woke up every morning to write. You couldn't wait to write."[3]

JOY LEWALLEN: Nanci started playing Anderson Fair in 1975. She was a fabulous performer who had been playing in Austin and San Marcos. Nanci had been a kindergarten teacher and was very sweet, innocent, and stunningly beautiful naturally. Her hair was curly and cut in a bob. She had the clearest and sweetest voice and was a great writer. Nanci could create characters you wanted to meet. Many were based on her really interesting family who were farmers. Nanci had a real affinity for people who worked the earth, which came from her grandparents. We became friends because she was the new girl in town, and I was at the Fair every day. I was three years older and like a big sister to her.

We knew she was going somewhere from the very beginning.[4]

Joy Lewallen has worked at Anderson Fair since 1974.

DALIS ALLEN: Nanci and her dad owned a house in the Heights in Houston where she lived in the garage apartment. We hung out at this neighborhood bar called the Rising Star. Nanci would usually be writing at a table. People were always trying to get me to get her to hang out at the bar, but she didn't interact much. She only came up to the bar once. She was in her process, and you don't interrupt someone writing. We hung out at Anderson Fair, which opened the same as the Kerrville Folk Festival in 1972. What a really cool time to be in Houston. Nanci was so focused on writing.[5]

Dalis Allen served as producer of the Kerrville Folk Festival for eighteen years.

LYLE LOVETT: Nanci was always generous of spirit. She would extend her hand to up-and-coming performers like me. "My boyfriend Eric is playing at Anderson Fair," Nanci said a week after the gigs at the Basement. "Come down and do a guest set?" "Are you sure?" I asked. Of course, I was aware of Eric. "He's okay with it?" A guest set at Anderson Fair was a very exclusive gig. Having someone speak up for you was one of the only ways to get in the door in those days. Nanci jumped onstage the next week at Anderson Fair and sang "Walk through the Bottomlands" with me. She and Eric were instrumental for me being introduced to that audience.

I had been going to [shows at] Anderson Fair for a couple years by then and knew the importance of playing there for original music. I was aware of Don Sanders, Vince Bell, Bill Staines, Odetta, and Ramblin' Jack Elliott. Anderson Fair was like Club Passim [in Cambridge, Massachusetts], but in Texas. Even Austin had nothing like it in those days. Eric, Vince Bell, and the "Mayor of Montrose" Don Sanders were [top draws at Anderson Fair].

There was a cliquish division [among Houston songwriters]. Shake Russell, then Shake and Dana Cooper, John Vandiver, and Michael Marcoulier all were Houston staples, but they played Corky's a few blocks away in the Montrose. Nanci, Eric, Vince, and Bill Cade played Anderson Fair. The venues had some crossover, but Corky's was more of a nightclub bar where people talked. You would go there to meet people. Anderson Fair was a serious listening room. You just didn't speak when you were in Anderson Fair's listening room. I saw the owners politely go up to the uninitiated and offer them their money back a couple times. The bar where you would buy beer and wine even was quiet. Anderson Fair was folk music church.

STEVE EARLE: I first saw Nanci play at Anderson Fair. I had known about her as long as I had been writing songs because she played the same places I was playing when I was seventeen. I was banned from Anderson Fair because Townes Van Zandt was banned, and I was considered in his crowd. Townes wasn't living in Houston back then. He actually didn't live anywhere for eight years, but he would come through Houston. Everyone including my mentor Eric Taylor waited around for Townes to come back. Eric was a Townes disciple and was supernice to me, but he was competitive because he wanted to be Townes as bad as I did. Maybe worse.[6]

Legendary songwriter Steve Earle and fellow Texan Lyle Lovett boosted country music's Great Credibility Scare with their debut albums arriving on MCA Records in 1986. Nanci Griffith joined them with her major debut on the label in 1987.

WAYNE MILLER: Nanci was constantly writing and playing Anderson Fair. Townes also played there and would go to his car in between sets to nap. Nobody ever wanted to be the one to wake him up for the next set, so Tim Leatherwood and Nanci always would push me into going out to get him. Townes would be a little grumpy.[7]

Austin-based director and producer Wayne Miller has worked with Lyle Lovett on several music videos.

STEVE EARLE: Eric actually assimilated the Townes look early on. He wore a short-rimmed cowboy hat and wide-rimmed wire glasses like Townes did on the cover of [Van Zandt's 1969 album] *Our Mother the Mountain*. He even wrote a song about Townes very early on. Eric got me in to play [the Houston venue] Sand Mountain [Coffee House]. He had seen me play one night by accident when I opened for him because [Old Quarter Acoustic Cafe owner] Dale Soffar [double] booked us both to play. Eric was a really, really good entertainer. Eric also had me play a guest set with him at the University of Houston coffee house, which got me a gig opening for him there next time. I opened for him the only time I played Anderson Fair.

LYLE LOVETT: Eric Taylor had such complete guitar arrangements. They supported his songs. Plus, the narrative quality in his songs was a draw. Eric was a twenty-year-old kid from Georgia who would open for Townes and Guy. He was my friend who taught me guitar, tunings, and different songs. I could listen to Guy Clark's records, but I didn't know Guy then. Being able to go to Eric's apartment was powerful when I met him [as a young songwriter]. I always thought Eric and Nanci had the ultimate respect for each other's ability. They encouraged each other and their art without exception. "Hey," Eric would say, "check out this song Nanci just wrote." He was very enthusiastic about her writing and performing and likewise she was with him. Nanci revered Eric.

DEE MOELLER: I was around Eric Taylor one time when our friends played a show at Anderson Fair. We went to his house that afternoon. He was real quiet and seemed like an introvert but was really kind and nice. Eric's house back in the seventies looked really hippie-homey and like it was built in the thirties or forties. Lyle Lovett and I used to do a bunch of shows together throughout Texas. Lyle was so charming, witty, and smart. He and Eric showed up one night at our house when I was playing the Longbranch [because] the Office Club had closed. They came up and visited at the house, and then we went to the club. We had a big time. Eric had a dry wit and was very pleasant. Meanwhile, Nanci was gathering experiences from herself and people around her for her songs. Her song about Mary Margaret ["There's a Light beyond These Woods"] is very sweet.[8]

Nanci Griffith recorded Dee Moeller's songs "Tequila after Midnight" and "Party Girl" later in her career. Moeller married legendary guitarist Wayne Moss (Barefoot Jerry, Area Code 615). They own Cinderella Sound in Madison, Tennessee, where influential singer-songwriter Mickey Newbury recorded his most lasting albums.

LYLE LOVETT: Nanci and Eric both seemed like stars who were just waiting to be discovered for a major label record deal in those days. Nanci performed [like a star] and her audience regarded her that way. [We weren't just] watching someone starting out. This was "Nanci Griffith" from the very first time I saw her. She had the ambition and confidence to match. Nanci was always aware of her value, but she was generous. I'm not the only one she extended a [helping] hand to. She did the same for Denice Franke and Doug Hudson. Nanci was either your biggest champion or you were on the other side, which I experienced as well.

VINCE BELL: Nanci Griffith was well suited to be in the songwriter crowd at Anderson Fair [in Houston] and naturally became part of our group writing original songs. Writing and playing music typically are alienating environments. You're not too close with your fellow songwriters when you're together because you're working, and then you're like passing trains when you're apart. You're trying to make your dream visible, and so is everybody else in the room. We all were racehorses trying to break that damn tape. So, it's hard to be close to people in that environment, but close we were—Townes, Guy, Eric, Lyle, and Nanci. One hundred percent. We had a bond being around those song-writers.

We had a riot together back then. We were required to pull a tune out of the ozone every day as good as anything we had ever heard at Anderson Fair, and every damn day there was a new tune. We also had a new play or a new ballet around town. We were all very competitive, but nobody was crazy or too much. We all kept our art going. I thought Nanci's songs were very good, plus I enjoyed her including my song "The Woman of the Phoenix" on her Gram-my-winning album *Other Voices, Other Rooms* years later. She changed genders in the song and made it work. She also recorded my song "Sun and Moon and Stars."[9]

Vince Bell's promising songwriting career was derailed by severe brain trauma caused by a life-threatening car accident after a recording for what should have been his debut album in 1982. The triumphant Phoenix *marked his return in 1994.*

LYLE LOVETT: I love Vince Bell's song "Sun and Moon and Stars" [which Griffith recorded on 1991's *Late Night Grande Hotel* and Lovett recorded on *Natural Forces* in 2009]. What a wonderful thing to say to your friends. The song really spoke to me where I was in life back then. Life is transitional at twenty-one. You're leaving behind familiar things in a leap of faith. "Sun and Moon and Stars" really speaks to the vastness of the choices lying ahead, and "I've come to miss a few." The song is not just about people. The song is about your whole life that you're forsaking for the next step. You're leaving behind the familiar for what's next. Whatever that might be.

Also, Vince was—and is—so compelling. I opened for him back then, too. Nanci recorded his "Sun and Moon and Stars" before me, but I was hearing it back in those days too. Vince's voice had more power than it did after his accident. Vince was more of an outgoing performer than he is now, but his quiet quality draws you in [today]. His voice met you as soon as you walked in back in those days. He had a very rapid-fire delivery that oozed confidence in a big way. He was a bold performer.

NANCI GRIFFITH: Vince Bell was the most amazing, electric songwriter and performer I had seen in my life. I mean, he did a tour opening up for ZZ Top.[10]

JOY LEWALLEN: Vince Bell was right: the music at Anderson Fair was all original. We were encouraging the musicians to [work on] their craft instead of copying someone. I had started at the Old Quarter before Anderson Fair. You can hear my voice in the background of Townes Van Zandt's album *Live at the Old Quarter*. I was tending bar and asking if he wanted something, and

Dale Soffar was asking me to turn off the popcorn machine. Townes and I were really good friends. I taught his son JT in second grade and dated his guitar player Mickey White. Someone the other day asked me why I got involved with music, and I said, "Well, I like the musicians." I liked the music as a result.

Anderson Fair was the laid-back neighborhood bar in the heart of the Montrose area, which was all artists, hippies, and poor students. Everybody who worked there was a volunteer and stepped up to the task. The songwriters were really young, starting out in their early twenties. I lived in a duplex for fifty dollars a month. Finding a place you could afford in Montrose was easy. Anderson Fair started out where you could get a cheap spaghetti, garlic bread, and pie lunch. A co-op and clothing store with recycled jeans were around the corner. The building had been a washateria next to Texas Art Supply so artists started coming over for lunch.

Anderson Fair was like the old salons where people would gather and have intellectual conversations. We had some pretty high-profile people like Mayor [Fred] Hofheinz and other Democratic politicians who would stop by. People would play for tips, but no money changed hands. I think Vince said in the Anderson Fair movie *For the Sake of the Song*, "Sometimes you would play your heart out and walk away with fifty cents." Everybody was poor. The Family Hand [which became Liberty Hall in 1971] was another neighborhood place. Eric Taylor was living with Nanci and got his first job there.

Eric and I were good friends. I heard this noise downstairs one night, so I went into my roommate's room and said, "I think someone has broken into the house." We grabbed something to hit people with and went downstairs. Eric and Blaze Foley were in our kitchen making breakfast. They knew we had jobs and always had food. Blaze and Eric were notorious for breaking into people's houses. There was something about Anderson Fair. You genuinely got to know the people. Eric used to come over to my house to play songs before he ever debuted them onstage. I guess he had to pass my litmus test. We were like a family because we spent so much time together.

Nanci had a part-time job when she lived with me for a while after she and Eric got a divorce. She drove a Pinto. We always joked about that thing going down in flames if she kept driving it. Nanci had a naturally hysterical dry, evil sense of humor. She would pack everything in that Pinto and drive herself around to play gigs. I was the person who stood on the side of the stage, held her brush, and fluffed up her hair before she went on. We had been in that environment where we were all equal. I was a student. They were struggling musicians. We were in the same boat financially.

Nanci was easy to hang out with and trusted me. She didn't trust anybody

[else]. We ended up being friends for life because she knew I would never do or say anything that would belie that trust. I understand why people say they never knew her beyond a certain point because she was very guarded with them. I don't know where that [trait] came from. She adored her stepfather and had a good relationship with her mom. Her dad was fabulous. He sang in a barbershop quartet and had a printing business in the Montrose neighborhood. He printed the handbills for the ballet. Her dad would come to the Fair and sing duets. Her being guarded had more to do with disappointing relationships. She and Eric got divorced, but they had a lifelong bond.

DENICE FRANKE: Nanci and Eric were apples and oranges. There was lots of passion between them, which is why their marriage didn't work. There was clashing. You can't have two people like that and have it be compatible. The wheels keep banging and clashing into each other. You need someone who isn't invested in the drive when you have a strong spirit. People saw lots of sparks and jabs in the midst, but I saw a deep love between them.

They both had a deep passion to write and have people acknowledge their work. I didn't know them together because they were already divorced when I met them, but they drove each other crazy. You feel constantly under attack when you're in that situation. You almost need a prayer to make those personalities work in a relationship. They either had too much yin or yang, but they were deeply connected because of what they were to each other.

LUCINDA WILLIAMS: Eric Taylor tried to kill himself when he and Nanci split up. [Eric] drank a bunch of whiskey, took some pills, turned the gas on in the stove, and passed out next to the stove. Eric forgot to close the windows and doors in the kitchen. He didn't die.[11]

Grammy award–winning singer Lucinda Williams established herself as a sharp and singular songwriter with the consecutive classics Lucinda Williams *(1988),* Sweet Old World *(1992), and the career-making collection* Car Wheels on a Gravel Road *(1998).*

WAYNE MILLER: Nanci and I became boyfriend and girlfriend when I was living in Austin, and she was in Houston. Nanci and Eric stayed friends, but I'm not sure that Eric ever was totally over her. Interesting guy. Sometimes we would be at Anderson Fair, and Eric would create some uncomfortable situations. There was always some degree of tension between them, but Eric and Nanci had a certain level of tension with everybody. You didn't want to get on her wrong side. They were just two difficult personalities. Nanci certainly [put up emotional walls] professionally, and how she dealt with people could make me uncomfortable. I certainly would have interacted differently than she did. [Her behavior] caused difficulty between us.

• • •

Meanwhile, Nanci Griffith instantly clicks with the legendary New Folk song-writing competition at the Kerrville Folk Festival in 1978. "New Folk [in 1978] who got our attention were Jon Ims from Colorado, Nanci Griffith from Austin, and Steve Earle from [Schertz]," festival founder Rod Kennedy says in his coffee-table memoir *Music from the Heart: The Fifty-Year Chronicle of His Life in Music (with a Few Sidetrips!)*. "There were so many high points during the weekend—Butch Hancock sitting in with Joe Ely . . . Guy Clark sitting in with Buck White, New Folk finalist Nanci Griffith sitting in with Eric Taylor."[12]

Folkies love Nanci Griffith.

Nanci Griffith loves folkies.

Her strongest musical bond officially takes shape.

CAROLYN HESTER: I helped start the Kerrville Festival in the early seventies. Young people by the hundreds were writing to [Kerrville founder] Rod Kennedy and saying that they wanted to come play the festival.[13]

Iconic Greenwich Village folksinger Carolyn Hester joined Nanci Griffith to sing "Boots of Spanish Leather" at Bob Dylan's Thirtieth Anniversary Concert at Madison Square Garden in New York City in 1991.

STEVE EARLE: Eric and Nanci rescued me from the Kerrville Folk Festival one time when I was playing the New Folk competition. I had no place to go while the rain was pouring. They were pulling out of the site after Eric's set, saw me literally ready to roll up under a van for the night, and gave me a ride. They let me sleep on their hotel room floor. Kerrville was weird. Townes kept getting into trouble there, but I went every year before I left [Texas for Nashville] in 1974. I had gone to Kerrville one time before I knew Townes, too. The next time I went back to Kerrville was playing bass with Guy Clark.

LYLE LOVETT: Nanci already was established as a main stage performer at Kerrville when I played the New Folk competition in 1980. She and Eric were both booked to play, but Eric had a gig in Denton and wouldn't be able to get to Kerrville until Saturday. Nanci asked if she could ride with me. I remember that as a particularly nice trip. We had a little Anderson Fair enclave with James Gilmer, Bob Felder, Eric, and Nanci, who were all camping there. Kerrville was—and is—a great way to be around your favorite performers in a social setting.

TOM RUSSELL: A bunch of us were swapping songs and passing the guitar late night around a campfire when I noticed this young gal waiting in the distance with her guitar. She was shy and working on her chops. I invited her to sing one. She came to the campfire and sang her song "If I Were a Child." Nanci Griffith's gentle voice blew us all away. Patricia Hardin and I [had each been established by winning] the New Folk Award at the Kerrville Folk Festival in the early seventies, and we invited her to open a few shows for us at a hamburger joint in Houston. Nanci had this wonderful, soft-spoken, literate way with the song that was Texan yet universal.[14]

Folksinger and David Letterman favorite Tom Russell has had his songs recorded by Johnny Cash, the Sir Douglas Quintet, Dave Alvin, and Nanci Griffith. He and Nanci Griffith sang Dave Alvin's classic "Bus Station" on Russell's album Modern Art *(2003).*

LYLE LOVETT: Kerrville was not that far removed from Woodstock and that cultural ethic where it was more about sincerity than ambition when I got my first gig in 1980. Ambition was more about getting your song out in front of people at Kerrville than how much money you were gonna make. Kerrville was "Hey, check out this song." Also, performers actually camped at Kerrville in those days. We zip in and out of festivals today and leave the camping to the audience, which is one reason Kerrville is fifty years old this year.

ROBERT EARL KEEN: I met Nanci Griffith and Eric Taylor when I played Kerrville in the New Folk songwriter competition. I had been an honorable mention but got to play as a finalist the next time when Nanci was a judge. I played "Rollin' By" and "The Armadillo Jackal." I won. I had never won anything in my life up until that time. I was really excited and went over to thank the judges. Nanci says, "You almost lost because of that damn Armadillo song." Some people didn't realize that song was serious, but it made me feel like I had figured out something. I started to go see Nanci play, and we talked to each other. She would get up onstage with me sometimes and sing "Swervin' in My Lane." She was a real pro.[15]

Robert Earl Keen has released a dozen albums over the past four decades including the consecutive peaks Gringo Honeymoon *(1994),* Picnic *(1997), and* Walking Distance *(1998). His live album* No. 2 Live Dinner *(1996) remains a fan favorite.*

CAROLYN HESTER: I was one of the first judges when Rod Kennedy decided to have a songwriting contest. We heard from Nanci when she was a New Folk judge in 1983. She came up and said, "I met you when I was ten years old in Austin. You were playing at the Aqua Festival. I handed your record to you to sign." "Oh," I said. "You had an ice cream cone in your hand."

NANCI GRIFFITH: I had been eating cotton candy and had it all over. "Do not touch Carolyn Hester," my dad had warned me. "You'll get cotton candy all over her." I was so nervous about meeting my childhood idol, my hero, my vocal mentor. I was crying by the time I got to the front of the line. I was afraid that she would shake my hand, and I would make my dad mad because I got cotton candy on Carolyn Hester.[16]

CAROLYN HESTER: We became buddies. I asked Nanci if she wanted to sing a song during my set at Kerrville one year. "Oh," she said, "that would be wonderful." Then I was going on a trip to the Northeast a few months later, and this local Austinite lady came up with an idea: "What if you took Nanci with you? It could be a whole package with an opening act." This gal managed to get herself on the tour with us too. "I should know these places we're booking," she said. "Then I can book other Texans there." Apparently, Nanci had done a few things outside Texas by then, but she had never been past the Mason-Dixon line.

JOHN GORKA: Nanci came through Godfrey Daniels Coffee House in Bethlehem, Pennsylvania, where I went to school with Carolyn Hester on one of her first Northeast tours in summer 1982. Nanci had sent me her *Poet in My Window* album. I was struck by the songs and remember asking Rosalie Sorrels about her. "She's a really great songwriter," I said. Rosalie said, "She's a superior person, too." I always remembered that: "a superior person." The next time I saw Nanci was a year later at an open mike at the Speakeasy in New York City. She was visiting with her dad. Then I opened for her at Godfrey Daniels the next year. She liked my songs. I remember we sat up quite late that night. Nanci encouraged me to enter the New Folk song contest at Kerrville in 1984. I won. Nanci had me open for her at Anderson Fair that fall.[17]

Rolling Stone *magazine called John Gorka "the leading singer-songwriter of the New Folk movement" after he won Kerrville's contest. Gorka sang Townes Van Zandt's "Snow Don't Fall" with Nanci Griffith on his 2006 album,* Writing in the Margins.

TOM PAXTON: Carolyn had taken Nanci under her wing, and they were touring coffeehouses in the East to introduce Nanci around. My wife and I went to see Carolyn and Nanci play at [Gerde's] Folk City in New York, but we were late and didn't hear Nanci's opening set. I hadn't heard her sing a note when Carolyn invited me up to sing my song "Can't Help but Wonder Where I'm Bound." I was standing about two feet from Nanci when we got to the chorus and that voice came out. Nanci just about blew me off the stage. I could not believe that such a big voice could come from such a small woman. I became an instant fan.[18]

Tom Paxton has been a folksinger for more than half a century. His songs have been recorded by Pete Seeger, Bob Dylan, the Weavers, Judy Collins, Doc Watson, Joan Baez, and several others. He was awarded a Lifetime Achievement Grammy in 2009.

CAROLYN HESTER: Nanci was only twenty-eight when she went on the road with me. She was so lovely looking. The music business loves youth, but her talent overruled that concern anyway. I was very happy all that success came to her later. Her talent and ability to accomplish things was so striking. You would fail Nanci if you didn't get her idea or keep up with her. She was astonishing. I got the sense that it was meant to be with her and me. She wrote [an unreleased] song about me called "Angel in the Wasteland." I thanked her by writing a song called "Nanci's Song" [on Hester's 1996 album, *From These Hills*].

We did shows [somewhere] in Arkansas, at the Birchmere in Virginia, Gerde's Folk City in New York City, and Club 47, which is now Club Passim, in Cambridge, Massachusetts. I hadn't been on the road for the [previous] ten years while I was raising my two daughters. I had only been playing Kerrville during that decade, so this tour was a great coming out for Nanci and I both. We had people sign up for a mailing list, which propelled us back out on the road. Nanci's songwriting was so great. I thought she was a genius. Her dad's business created a bandanna in all kinds of colors that said "NG" and then "Nanci Griffith" in smaller letters under that.

The "NG" became a symbol for her. Nanci gave us a lot of credit for starting her singing, but I think her father being a barbershop quartet singer and showing her she had to overrehearse, make travel plans, and have places to stay was the real example for her. She got the discipline from him. She had no hesitancy booking all the people, all the gigs, all the recording. She was a phenomenal professional.

JOHN GORKA: I played a song called "Burning through the Wind" that I've never recorded when I won the Kerrville New Folk competition, which was a huge deal. I didn't sleep the night before at the hotel in Kerrville. I had cramps. I had never been in that kind of competition. Playing was a huge relief. I did a song called "That's How Legends Are Made" to open the set in 1984. The song is about my musical hero Stan Rogers. Stan's last show was at the Kerrville festival. He died on the way back in a plane fire. I got to meet Jerry Jeff Walker that year. There were magical campfires. Nanci, Denice Franke, Lyle, Robert Earl Keen, and I played at one. What Nanci gave to other songwriters was really a remarkable thing. She loved folk music.

STEVE GILLETTE: Rod Kennedy invited me to be a part of the songwriting school and perform at the Kerrville Folk Festival in 1984. I could hear music coming from the main stage as I arrived at the Quiet Valley Ranch for the first time and made my way out front to hear Nanci's performance. I was enchanted. *Sing Out!* magazine editor Mark Moss introduced me to Nanci later, and she was very cordial and sweet. I was staying in Austin a couple weeks later and gave her a call to invite her to lunch. We had a very nice time. I enjoyed talking and left her a cassette tape of my songs.[19]

Steve Gillette's songs have been recorded by Garth Brooks ("Unto You This Night") and Carolyn Hester ("2:10 Train"). John Denver, Josh Ritter, Linda Ronstadt, and Nanci Griffith are among the hundreds who have cut his song "Darcy Farrow."

TISH HINOJOSA: I went to Kerrville a couple times before I entered the songwriting contest and knew about Nanci. I thought she was totally cool. I was singing cover songs on the Riverwalk in San Antonio at the time. I saw Nanci and thought, I can do it if Nanci can. I liked the way she told stories to introduce the songs. I was a sponge during that time trying to convince myself I could be a songwriter, and here was a gal like me writing songs. She's up there onstage at this folk festival. I was in awe. I met her a couple times around then. I liked her down-to-earth stories.

Nanci inspired me to write my best-known song called "The West Side of Town." The song is about growing up in San Antonio and my parents' struggle to give us a good life. Nanci's songs were stories, and that wasn't something I had paid attention to before. I was listening to pop music. Yeah, I loved Joan Baez and folk songs, but Nanci captured my attention about writing story songs with her songs like "Love at the Five and Dime." I remember sitting in the audience at the Kerrville festival and watching a Texan. I liked that she was from our neighborhood.

I was in awe of Joan Baez, but she was off in the distance. Nanci was someone close who was my age doing that. That really captured and empowered me because Nanci was just a couple years older than me. I didn't consider myself a songwriter so going to Kerrville was like watching the creative process in person. There was a hippie-outlaw-country Texas vibe that I was drawn to. Rod Kennedy came to hear me play at San Antonio College. I couldn't believe it. That was like God coming to my set. He said, "You have a really good voice. Do you write?" "Well," I said, "I've tinkered with it, but I'm not really a songwriter." "I would like you to play the festival," he said, "but you have to be a songwriter."

I loved Nanci's command of the stage and audience. I watched her very closely. She had confidence and a mastery of her craft in her early twenties.

Nanci came across onstage as very simple and direct, but I think she was very complicated. I tried to be friendly with her when we became peers on record labels. She was friendly enough but was never like, "Hey, let's go hang out." I think she was very reserved and had few friends. She didn't seem open to letting other people in. I always felt sorry for her because I saw a sadness in her. I would catch a glimpse of her backstage and see that sadness.[20]

Tish Hinojosa has released nearly twenty albums as well as a few best-of collections. Her album Culture Swing *won the National Independent Record Distributors' Indie Folk Album of the Year award in 1992.*

JAMES MCMURTRY: I started buying Nanci's records after I saw her play at Kerrville. I liked her songs, the ones she picked [to cover], and her singing and phrasing. Nanci was more about the song than anything. Her songs were really well crafted and literate. Kerrville was like school to me. Fledgling songwriters were hanging around Kerrville and learning their craft. I won the songwriting competition in 1987 and was around there in 1988, but then I got a record deal. The last time I played before I went back this year was being Fred Koller's sideman in 1988.[21]

James McMurtry's literate storytelling has fueled peak albums such as Childish Things *(2005) and* Just Us Kids *(2008). His latest,* The Horses and the Hounds *(2021), marked his debut for Nashville-based New West Records.*

FRED KOLLER: James McMurtry was always in the background. James was playing with Peter Rowan the first time I saw him. Kerrville was rained out that year. There was high-tide deep water. I didn't know who he was. He was just some kid from Texas writing great stuff. I think his father, Larry, had bought him a muffler shop out in the middle of nowhere. James was just banging around back then, picking up books for his father. We got to talking at one point, and I figured out his father was Larry McMurtry [most famous as the writer behind the series *Lonesome Dove*]. I always tried to encourage his writing, then he got the deal [for his 1989 debut record, *Too Long in the Wasteland*] with John Mellencamp.

James was one of the best writers.[22]

Fred Koller has written several hit songs (Jeff Healey Band's "Angel Eyes" with John Hiatt, and Kathy Mattea's "She Came from Fort Worth" and "Goin' Gone," the latter also recorded by Nanci Griffith). He owns and operates Rhino Booksellers in Nashville.

PETER ROWAN: Nanci brought a sense of literacy to the folksinging style. She read lots of Larry McMurtry. Larry's son James is so caustic and funny about Texas. So refreshing. The first time I played with James was so weird. There was a woman connected with the Kerrville festival who said there was a great young guitarist named James McMurtry who would love to play with me. James played the whole set until we got rained out and were [sent to] the Holiday Inn. I never asked him to sing a song because I didn't know he sang. He was very young, fresh faced, and so game.[23]

Music legend Peter Rowan has played everything from bluegrass (Bill Monroe) to rock and roll (Seatrain) and the folk between (Steve Earle's Train a Comin' band). His songs "Midnight Moonlight" and "Panama Red" are bluegrass standards.

JOHN GORKA: I was at Kerrville with Mark Moss from *Sing Out!* magazine, which was how I was able to go. I wouldn't have been able to afford the plane ticket if it was just up to me. Nanci put Mark and me up at her place in Austin and took us to see Townes Van Zandt that night. Townes had been drinking, and Nanci cried to see him that way.

DARDEN SMITH: I would sit around at Kerrville and watch and listen to Nanci listening to Townes and talk with Butch Hancock. They were talking in [songwriter] shorthand. Having Nanci [vouch] for me was like being accepted into the songwriter's club. The songwriter's club is a private one like in jazz. You're in once you're in. Then you have to work really hard and really piss people off to get kicked out. You can even do average work and stay. You get access to this cache as well as secret knowledge, which is the coolest thing. You get to sit around while the older kids talk.

I probably met Nanci at the Kerrville festival when I was nineteen, and she was a judge in the songwriting contest. I had been going to clubs like the Alamo Lounge in Austin and then was opening shows for her around 1982. I was the young punk kid then. I knew how to write some songs, but I didn't know about real songwriting or the music business. I wouldn't say I hung out with Nanci, but I did spend time with her while touring with her.

The second thing I learned from Nanci was when I opened shows for her in California. Nanci was very generous with young acts, which was partly ego. She wanted to be known as the benevolent one. Anyway, we were playing at a great club in Sebastopol, California, the night Kate Wolf died. Kate's guitarist Nina Gerber had been playing with Nanci, and I remember looking up after the show and Nanci and Nina were a wreck. We drove into San Francisco the next day. Nanci said when we were driving in, "Where are you staying?" "I think I'm staying with this friend of mine," I said, "but I haven't heard from him." "You don't have a place to stay tonight?" "Well, no, I don't." "How about I get you a hotel room." "Okay, I guess that's a good idea."

I had never had someone book a room for me before. I had never had someone go, "I have your back. I'm gonna show you how this is done on the road. You have to plan out a place to sleep." We were staying on the Wharf in San Francisco when there was a knock at my door the next day at nine in the morning. I open the door, and Nanci goes, "You need to take the key out of the door when you come in at night." I felt like such a dumbass. She taught me to look out for people on the road. Nanci was dealing with her own thing from Kate Wolf dying, but she was still kind enough to help me out. Big Lesson.

Then she sang on my first two records, which was a huge boost for my confidence. There's no guidebook to [being a songwriter]. Making a living as a songwriter is not like the legal profession where you're an intern out of law school, then you become a junior partner and then a partner. The music business isn't just a meritocracy. The music business is luck. Some have to bang on doors forever. Sometimes they never open for certain people even though they're just as good as others. Doors magically open for others. Who knows why?

DALIS ALLEN: Nanci hugged me one time at Kerrville. People said, "Oh. Nanci Griffith hugged you." They would freak out. Nanci had a beautiful, generous spirit and used to hang out in the campground. She had been on B.F. Deal Records with Mike Williams and would hang out with the artists in that camp. I'm not sure that Nanci was overly social in most circumstances, but she was very supportive. She and [Kerrville festival founder] Rod Kennedy were close for a while. Nanci would play the festival and donate her fee back to us. She loved the festival.

TOM RUSSELL: We all knew Nanci had begun a profound journey at Kerrville when she sang "If I Were a Child" on the main stage years later.

• • •

Nanci Griffith's initial ascent begins with her third album. Griffith leaves Houston for a few more years in Austin and sets up shop in Nashville for the *Once in a Very Blue Moon* sessions during that time. Griffith enlists elite Music City studio musicians as well as her best Texas pals for backing on her Philo Records debut. The session players—Philip Donnelly (lead guitar), Pat Alger (guitar), Stephen Doster (guitar), Béla Fleck (banjo), Roy Huskey Jr. (bass), Mark O'Connor (fiddle), Kenny Malone (drums), Lyle Lovett (background vocals), and Denice Franke (background vocals)—guide her journey spectacularly.

Griffith discovers the title track at Nashville's most iconic listening room. "I was playing the Bluebird Cafe in winter 1983, and Jim Rooney came by to see me," songwriter Pat Alger says. "He brought with him what looked like a little girl. I played my song 'Once in a Very Blue Moon' for the first time, came offstage, and Jim introduced me to Nanci. She said she really liked that song. Jim hired me to be a guitar player on that record. Nanci became part of our scene, and I became part of hers." Meanwhile, Griffith's success draws ire from Texas press. After all, you can never be a hero in your hometown, as the saying goes.

• • •

LYLE LOVETT: My relationship with Nanci was inconsistent over the years. I was on the other side of the fence when she and Eric broke up. Nanci didn't have anything to do with me for a couple years because I was Eric's friend. Then she started inviting me to stay at her place in Austin all of a sudden when I would come in town to play. "Come stay with me," she would say. "Meet my new boyfriend Wayne." I resisted those invitations, thinking I didn't want to step in the middle of something. I felt weird because Eric was my friend.

Finally, we were doing a show together with me opening for her at the old Waterloo Ice House. Nanci asked me to come stay with Wayne and her, then we would do the gig. I did. Nanci was out doing stuff all that weekend so it was just Wayne and me at the house. We immediately got along very well. We watched football games. I remember Nanci was out doing something and the Jonathan Sayles film *The Brother from Another Planet* was playing in theaters. Wayne and I went to see that together.

WAYNE MILLER: Nanci and I lived together for about three years when she moved back to Austin. Nanci and Joy stayed very, very close when we lived together. Nanci was nervous about coming back to Austin and how she would be accepted. She had a bunch of new material that became the record I financed, *Once in a Very Blue Moon*. Nanci really had turned her writing up a notch at that point. She was very focused on being accepted beyond Texas and had a following in the Northeast.

Nanci would play me songs she was writing, but I wasn't involved in the creative process. She probably was working on the songs for the *Once in a Very Blue Moon* album when we were together. I was interested in Nanci doing well personally and professionally and made a conscious effort with things like album cover photography. I didn't have lots of money, but I wanted to do the album right because the material was very strong.

There was a conscious effort to take Nanci to the next level as far as her deal and distribution. I remember the record cost under twenty thousand dollars. I started negotiating with Rounder Records to license and put out the album [on Philo]. I remember visiting their offices in Boston. We went back and forth with negotiations. I wanted them to pay for some marketing and promotion things that they didn't want to pay for. We finally came to an agreement. The deal was done.

JIM ROONEY: Nanci asked me in summer 1983, "Could you help me make a record in Nashville?" Nanci was partners with Wayne Miller at the time, and they gathered some money together and made a plan. She would come to Nashville every two or three months, and we started working on [ideas] toward the record. Then she came back to Nashville and recorded in June 1984. [It helped that] Pat, Mark, and Roy knew her songs going into the studio. Nanci brought Stephen Doster with her as well as Lyle Lovett and Denice Franke to sing. I added a mixture including Philip Donnelly. I liked that Nanci would give you an answer if you asked a question. For example, she was quite clear that she wanted [legendary steel guitarist] Lloyd Green to play with her because her aunt liked [his playing on] the Don Williams records.

I met Lloyd through Jack Clement. He agreed to do the session [even though] it didn't pay union scale. I also got the wonderful drummer Kenny Malone. I had come up through the bluegrass world and knew that Mark O'Connor and Béla Fleck had moved to town and thought Nanci's music could [use] some banjo and fiddle. Jack's studio was an attic in a big house, which was perfect for acoustic music. You could get a few musicians sitting around a room without too much baffling. I think we wound up with eight or ten people playing at once and recorded thirteen songs in two days. We were all impressed that Nanci was very well prepared.[24]

Jim Rooney's storied career includes managing the legendary Club 47 venue in Cambridge, Massachusetts, coordinating talent at the Newport Folk Festival during Bob Dylan's electric era, and producing records for Nanci Griffith, John Prine, and Iris DeMent.

LLOYD GREEN: Jim Rooney called me to play on *Once in a Very Blue Moon*. He said this Texas girl was a real intellectual and scholar. She had this guy with her to sing background vocals on the sessions who was dressed in a tight-fitting black thing. He had funny-looking black hair that was sticking straight up and wouldn't make eye contact with anyone. He walked around with his hands behind his back and didn't say anything, but he sounded really good when he sang with her. I thought, This guy has cognitive problems. Well, the guy was Lyle Lovett. I never misjudged someone so severely. He's actually one of the smartest guys in Nashville.[25]

Legendary steel guitarist Lloyd Green has performed on several thousand record-

ings including records by Tammy Wynette, Bob Dylan, and Paul McCartney. Green's work on the Byrds' iconic 1968 album, Sweetheart of the Rodeo, alone cemented his legacy.

LYLE LOVETT: Nanci was the first person to cut one of my songs when she recorded "If I Were the Woman You Wanted" for *Once in a Very Blue Moon*. I was thrilled. The song came from a personal experience of mine and speaks to the emotion of being in a relationship and standing your ground to say, "This is who I am. That's important to me. I have to be myself." The song is just about standing up for yourself. I met Jim Rooney during the sessions for *Once in a Very Blue Moon* in June 1984, which was the first time I had gone to Nashville.

Working with Nanci on those sessions gave me a chance to set up meetings around Nashville. I was there for a week and would start my days at the studio. Then I would go off to my meetings and come back to the studio after. Great veteran players like Lloyd Green on steel, Kenny Malone on drums, Pat Alger, Roy Huskey, and Mark O'Connor were always really encouraging. I would come back from a meeting and they would go, "Well, how did it go?" Very supportive. I felt a little like the upperclassmen were letting me find out how it would work on my own. Even Cowboy Jack would be downstairs in his office.

I was thrilled being there and meeting people I had read about. "My god, that's Cowboy Jack Clement right there." Of course, Jim Rooney couldn't have been more gracious, inclusive, and very nice to be around. They all treated me like I belonged, which is generally how I felt as I went around Nashville meeting ASCAP reps and publishers and producers. My introduction to Nashville was very much the Anderson Fair ethic and Texas sense of community.

STEPHEN DOSTER: Lyle back then was the way he is today. I don't know anyone who is more of a gentleman than him. He came from such a loving family. I think that's what made him what he is today.

DENICE FRANKE: Lyle and I ended up staying at Rooney's tiny little apartment, which was no different than when you're on the road sleeping on couches. Very relaxed. These were new friends, but they felt like hanging out with old friends. Rooney is a natural producer. He was big in the Boston and Cambridge folk circle and was so easygoing. Rooney could speak technically, but his approach was very organic. He knew what he wanted to come out of the song when he was producing.

JIM ROONEY: All vocals on *Once in a Very Blue Moon* were recorded live. We did very little fixing. Most overdubs we did were vocals from Denice and Lyle. Nanci was very good with harmonies and was very clear about her singing and that she wanted pizzicato stuff on cello. Her ideas made it very easy for me [as producer]. I just hung on by the seat of my pants. We didn't have much money and had to get things done. I had been working for Jack Clement for five years by then and had recorded all the demos for Johnny Cash's publishing company House of Cash. They would routinely record five or six songs in a session. You get used to working fast.

DENICE FRANKE: What a wonderful experience recording at Cowboy Jack Clement's studio and meeting Jim Rooney. This was a much broader world opening to me than the one I was in. The only experience I had had in the studio before Cowboy's was recording to track live. You can only really do that in a really tight band. I was around these musicians who did charts and spoke this other language for the first time. I'm more intuitive, but they were speaking this one-three-five language that I didn't understand. These guys really didn't rehearse together. They heard the main vocal and guitar track and built from there. These are famous people or at least people who run around in circles with famous people, but they were just ordinary people in the studio. They just plugged in, nailed it, and were done.

I wasn't accustomed to working that quickly. Being in that studio with studio musicians was a growing experience for me. I was a real purist in those days. I wasn't used to big productions, but for some reason I wasn't intimidated by the process. The only thing I was intimidated by was the language of music. "I'm gonna hit the three and go to the one." Working with Jim Rooney and the musicians was very easy. They met you on your level and made you feel relaxed so you don't get all worked up about messing up. You just go in and do what you do.

PAT ALGER: Those session players were all interested in what the others were doing, and there was no pressure to do anything besides good music. So Nanci fit right in. She stood up there with a guitar and played and sang live, which was interesting. Most Nashville session guys were used to laying down the track and having the singer come in and putting a vocal on it. Nanci stood up there, sang, and played live. She did the songs very quickly and was a great singer. She was used to standing up and playing and singing. Her voice was really strong.[26]

Nashville Songwriters Hall of Fame member Pat Alger has written four number one hits for Garth Brooks, including "Unanswered Prayers" and "Thunder Rolls," as well as "Once in a Very Blue Moon" and "Lone Star State of Mind" for Nanci Griffith.

JIM ROONEY: We would have songs down within an hour with Nanci. My job was to keep things rolling without getting in the way. My philosophy about producing is to let people do what they do if they know what they're doing. Steer a little from time to time, but don't get in the way if they don't need it.

I did work with Nanci picking the songs, but she also had a clear vision there. The only song I introduced her to indirectly was Pat's song "Once in a Very Blue Moon." Nobody had recorded his songs in Nashville then, so I was happy to get him a cut.

PAT ALGER: [My "Once in a Very Blue Moon" cowriter Eugene Levine] and I were not really close friends, so I don't know what he was channeling when we wrote "Once in a Very Blue Moon." He had the idea for the title. I know I had just gotten a letter from this woman I had lost my mind over before moving to Nashville. Moving to Nashville and getting remarried was my antidote to that. So, I had just gotten this letter from her that was very nice and pleasant, so I was pissed off. That's the last thing I wanted to feel [about her] as I was just now getting over it. I know that came out in the song. Gene mentioned the title and I thought, I know what that means.

I did a piano and vocal demo for "Once in a Very Blue Moon" that was completely different than what Nanci did, so she couldn't have heard that. I must have made a work tape for her. I originally pitched the song to Dolly Parton, who ended up cutting it much like the demo that I produced [on her 1985 album, *Real Love*]. Chris Smither does a really powerful performance of "Once in a Very Blue Moon" [on his 1984 album, *It Ain't Easy*]. Crystal Gayle cut it too [on 1990's *Ain't Gonna Worry*]. The song has a very simple lyric, but I guess it touched a nerve. We did the demo in the same studio that we did Nanci's record in so that's another great coincidence. I might have shown Nanci the chords because it has one little tricky part to the bridge. Nanci didn't do bridges.

I was trying to write a hit song, not make a mythological career. I had a two-year-old son and was trying to [get by]. I actually love that bridge. I showed Nanci how it hits the major seventh and then the major, but otherwise she had the song down. She delivered that song with conviction. People think Nanci wrote that song. I always say if they think you wrote a song that means you really nailed [the performance]. I considered that to be a great compliment.

JIM ROONEY: Nanci's own songs had a very good variety. "Mary and Omie" is a really good story song involving race. "Friend Out in the Madness" and "I'm Not Driving These Wheels" are totally personal. "Time Alone" is a beautiful, quiet favorite even though not many people paid attention to that one. "Daddy Said" is a really good one with an easy message and sing-along. "Spin on a Red Brick Floor" is about Anderson Fair. What a range. They weren't all love songs about her broken heart.

We started recording on Monday, and Nanci had a mastered album to take home by Sunday. We called ourselves the "Once in a Very Blue Moon Sink or Swim Team" because I lived in the Americana apartments, which had a pool on the roof. We started going upstairs to the pool near the end of the week. We were celebrating because we felt like we had done something. The album had a freshness. Nobody had a guitar sound like Philip Donnelly, and Nanci's material was all good. No filler songs. Really great album. Béla, Mark, and Pat Alger were just starting, but people like Lloyd Green and Kenny Malone had incredible and lengthy experience.

WAYNE MILLER: The *Once in a Very Blue Moon* sessions were great, with Jim Rooney producing those phenomenal players. I remember Nanci and John Prine having the same sense of humor when we went over to Prine's house a couple times when we were doing *Once in a Very Blue Moon*. They became fast friends. John and Nanci obviously had a lot of respect for each other. Nanci loosened up around John. Sometimes John Hartford came around during the sessions. Marty Stuart came over at some point too. There was usually a joint going around.

STEPHEN DOSTER: I was about two feet from the drummer Kenny Malone during the *Once in a Very Blue Moon* sessions. We were doing our first run-through, and he goes, "You're a real metaphysical player, aren't you?" "Well," I said, "I hope so." We were in Jack Clement's Cowboy Arms Hotel and Recording Spa. The blue recording room was upstairs. "Let's go downstairs, man," Kenny said. "Let's talk about time." We sat in the kitchen and he said, "Time is everything. Every movement is part of time, when you walk down the street, the way the waves roll in at the beach, the way the moon comes and goes. You just have to lock into it." That's a beautiful thing.

Talking with Kenny was like when scientific codes fly through the air in the movie *A Beautiful Mind*. "Energy is not speed," Kenny said. "Energy is time." Lovely man. I remember really locking in with him during those sessions. "Find out what hand someone keeps time with, and don't listen to anything else," he said. Probably the best advice I've ever gotten. I still tell everyone I work with, "Don't just listen to the singer. Watch their right hand." I'm grateful to Nanci for the experience.

DENICE FRANKE: Rooney was great at bringing all these genres together. He took Nanci's folk elements and covered them with country instruments like Dobro and fiddle so it didn't feel like a Nashville record. Refreshing. He made you feel at ease working in the studio and knew what you were about when you stepped up to the microphone. He wanted to pull out what makes each musician unique into the mix. He wasn't about the massive production sound without any character [like mainstream Nashville]. He wouldn't talk over you.

Rooney met you where you were and brought out the best and more. That's invigorating and doesn't have to apply to music. He senses potential and raises you even higher than your expectations. "Wow, I didn't know I had that in me." You can free-fall more as a vocalist like that. Nanci gave her input [as coproducer]. Rooney was always checking in with her to make sure she liked it, and she was pretty accepting of what he was doing. They had a very symbiotic relationship.

PAT ALGER: I've done a lot of sessions, but the ones for *Once in a Very Blue Moon* were pretty special. Jim Rooney was the perfect guy to produce. He created an anything-goes atmosphere where the song was the star. I had never heard anyone quite like Nanci. "Wow, she's really shy," I remember saying early on. "Do you think she really wants to make it in the music business?" "Oh yeah." She wasn't shy. She knew what she wanted.

WAYNE MILLER: I remember flying to Boston and driving her back one time when she was playing Club Passim. She broke her foot stepping onstage but still played the whole show.

JOHN GORKA: Passim was really crowded the first time I opened for Nanci in May 1985. That was the Friday night when she stepped wrong on the way to the stage and broke a bone in her foot and did two sets with a broken foot. You never would have known it. She went to the emergency room after the shows. Nanci was such a pro. She didn't do things like others did in the folk world. She really paid attention to her presentation and the whole song and had the ability to become larger than life onstage. She was a great performer. Also, she was doing everything herself. She was putting together promo kits to send out that time Mark Moss and I stayed with her during Kerrville. She was booking herself. She eventually got an agent and things started happening for her in New York and Boston, where she had a big audience.

Nanci was complicated but very generous. I lived in a place that was nicknamed the Blues Palace where Nanci stayed a couple times on her way to the Northeast. I gave her my room and slept on the couch downstairs. The first time she drove up by herself. There was a bar across the back seat of the car, and she had all of her outfits taking up the whole seat. She brought a cooler with her. That was the first time I had Shiner Bock beer. I got a call from her after she had stayed, and she said, "There are fleas in my suitcase." We didn't have pets, so how we got fleas was a mystery. They must have come from one of the other Blues Palace resident's furniture in the living room. She didn't stay there after that.

JOY LEWALLEN: Nanci worked hard. Nobody ever gave her anything. She had a fragility even though her songs were really strong. That caused her to be really protective of herself. She came across onstage like she was very vulnerable, but deep inside there wasn't a vulnerable bone in that woman's body. She got a terrible review one time from the *Austin American-Statesman* and felt so betrayed because that was her home. She told me, "I'll never play in Austin again." She wasn't saying that because of the review, but she was saying, "I'll never put myself out there again."

WAYNE MILLER: Nanci was a tortured and troubled soul and never was able to deal with whatever those demons were. They stuck with her until she passed. She had resentment I didn't understand. She would be very sensitive to the music critics in town at the time who weren't very nice. Michael Corcoran in particular was pretty relentless in taking shots at her, which always upset her quite a bit.

MICHAEL CORCORAN: I did a three-page story on Nanci Griffith and Lyle Lovett for *Spin* magazine in 1985. The story was ninety percent positive, but I had been put off when I saw Nanci at the Austin Opera House backed by a band in matching suits. I thought that was hacky for her, and I wrote so. Well, it turned out she had some major cats in her band—including Danny Flowers, who wrote "Tulsa Time"—so she dashed an angry letter to editor Bob Guccione Jr. at *Spin*. She was totally justified, but I thought it went too far. Yes, I made a mistake. I was a jerk, but I did get her a full page in the hip magazine whose readers probably never heard about her before.

The letter seemed bent on making sure I never wrote for *Spin* again. Then she did an interview in the *Houston Chronicle* with Marty Racine where she trashed me by name in the first paragraph. A couple catty comments [in *Spin*]—I also said that she was the type to be married in a white Victorian dress—in an otherwise favorable piece really set her off. My style was more like a roast comedian with press credentials back in the eighties, and I needed targets for my barbs. I usually went after those who went after me. Those and my best friends like Alejandro Escovedo, who I knew could take a joke.

This led to a feud with Nanci that I regretted over time.[27]

Longtime Austin American-Statesman *and* Dallas Morning News *music writer Michael Corcoran authored* All Over the Map: True Heroes of Texas Music *(University of North Texas Press, 2017) and* Ghost Notes: Pioneering Spirits of Texas Music *(Texas Christian University Press, 2020).*

BUDDY MONDLOCK: Nanci was really sweet and a beautiful human being. We didn't talk long when Guy Clark introduced us at the Kerrville festival, but she was superpolite. I think Guy must have shared some of my music with her around then. Nanci was no shrinking violet as both [a person and songwriter]. She would tackle any subject, which is harder for women in our society, but she was a sensitive soul. She wouldn't let those bad reviews roll off her back.[28]

Nashville-based songwriter Buddy Mondlock's songs have been recorded by Guy Clark, Nanci Griffith, and Janis Ian. Griffith's cover of his song "Comin' Down in the Rain" on Other Voices, Other Rooms *has become a favorite among fans.*

WAYNE MILLER: There was a cloud trying to take her down a notch during her rise as an international artist in the eighties, but John T. Davis was another prominent writer around Austin and wrote wonderful things about her. They became friends.

JOHN T. DAVIS: Nanci and I both loved to read. Her best songs had such a short-story quality. Also, Nanci had a very dry sense of humor, which I found really appealing. We cultivated a friendship. I felt very close to her, and I think that was reciprocated. We developed a friendship that transcended the professional relationship, and I'm not sorry about that. Nanci and I had lots of commonalities in our sensibilities and sense of humor, which drew us together. She liked to read Katherine Anne Porter and Flannery O'Connor and her book *Wise Blood*. We were both drawn to writers like them who had a strong sense of place and voice.

Nanci's songs were so beautifully self-contained, even more than Guy Clark's or Rodney Crowell's. They were complete little universes. I admired that quality. Nanci had a really great melodic sense and knew exactly what she wanted out of her music. She was always working really hard at her craft, but the songs seemed to come really effortlessly. She had a real command of the medium, plus she was a great performer. She could command a stage.[29]

Former Austin American-Statesman *music writer John T. Davis has authored several works of nonfiction (*The Flatlanders: Now It's Now Again, *2004) and fiction (*Ransom Island, *2014). He lives in South Austin.*

BRIAN WOOD: The last time I played with Nanci was at the Berklee Performing Arts Center in Boston. I don't remember one single off note during the entire night. I couldn't believe it. I called my wife at my hotel afterward. "This is probably my last gig with her," I said, "but we went out with a bang." We could not have played better. The whole thing was like, "Boy, this is the way to go out." Everything came together. You know my favorite question: "Where is the music in all this?" That's where the music was that night. Wonderful. Then Nanci was on the trajectory to Nashville.

WAYNE MILLER: I talked to Terry Lickona, who was producing and directing the *Austin City Limits* television program. Terry agreed to have Nanci on the show, and we got many players from the album to come in and play on her first *Austin City Limits*, which was after the release for *Once in a Very Blue Moon*.

TERRY LICKONA: Lyle [Lovett] and Nanci Griffith represented an antidote to the more rowdy outlaw and cosmic country of the seventies. Especially Nanci. She really stood out for her songwriting, voice, and her whole style.[30]

Terry Lickona has been executive producer for Austin City Limits *since 1979.*

WAYNE MILLER: Nanci was nervous and excited as a hometown girl to play *Austin City Limits*, but she would never show it. The nervousness went away as soon as she started playing. The taping went well. She had a special dress made.

STEPHEN DOSTER: Nanci and I both were nervous and tense taping [*Austin City Limits*], but like most things, after the first song we were like, "Hey, we're here to play." We had a lovely time. Someone mentioned that someone was out of tune from tuning before putting a capo on. You have to put the capo on first. Things like that happened, but I was really happy about our set after. I asked the guy running the board for a copy of the audio, and I played it later. "Man," I said, "this sounds fantastic." You never know when your nerves are high going into the performance. Denice Franke was singing harmonies with Lyle. I was playing acoustic lead guitar. Nanci probably was happier that night than any other time that I had been around.

They started the television show with our third song because you could only be on for thirty minutes, and we were sharing the set with the Gatlin Brothers, of all people. People probably thought we taped on the same night, but we didn't. Nanci later released a video on Country Music Television of the second song we played that night. I've heard everything from that show except the first song. I told Nanci after *Austin City Limits*, "I came to help you get this thing rolling, but I have to get back to my own songs." She looked like she was heading to Nashville. I had some offers to move up to Nashville to produce some records, but that isn't where I wanted to be or to inevitably raise my family. Nanci and I argued, but there was no animosity.

WAYNE MILLER: Our breakup was as amicable as breakups can be. Nanci decided she wanted to live in Nashville, but I was not going to move there. The relationship fizzled quickly. I still own the masters for *Once in a Very Blue Moon* and was paid for a while but then was not paid for a very long time.

LYLE LOVETT: Wayne is still one of my best and closest friends in the world. He has directed half the music videos I've done. He and Nanci split up [between *Once in a Very Blue Moon* and *The Last of the True Believers*]. Regrettably, that put distance in my relationship with Nanci once again.

WAYNE MILLER: Nanci had her dark moments but could be a very open and loving person. Terms like "tortured soul" and "demons" are vague, but there were times she would go there. She would go into a funk and almost be paranoid about people accepting her as an artist. I'm guessing there are lots of people who feel that she deserved more acknowledgment and recognition, which she got when we did *Once in a Very Blue Moon* and [even more so later] with the *Other Voices* album.

JOHN T. DAVIS: She had come to have such a conflicted relationship with Austin that she hardly ever came back. I lost touch with her after she went to Nashville and obviously regret that now. Nanci was getting an honorarium the last time I remember seeing her perform here in Austin. Something rubbed her the wrong way. She broke down in tears and rushed out into the parking lot. I went after her, but she didn't want to be touched or consoled.

That was the last straw.

STEPHEN DOSTER: Well, she might have been a little perturbed with me. She was on a tour bus coming in from Nashville the next time I saw her. "Look at my bus," she said. "You could have been traveling around in this." I think she might have been going, "Hey, why did you leave [then]?" "Hey, this had been fun. We did a great record. We did *Austin City Limits*. I had to move on." Someone flying down to visit from Nashville was seated next to Nanci years later. "What are you doing in Austin?" Nanci said. "I'm coming down to see this guy Stephen Doster." Then Nanci said the nicest things to her about working with me and me helping her out.

JIMMIE DALE GILMORE: Nanci was more commercially ambitious than the rest of us. There really wasn't an infrastructure in Austin to become a real recording artist. Now, I love Nashville. I've made several records in Nashville, but I have always preferred to live in Austin. I never had that distaste for Nashville that a lot of the folkie people had—or pretended to have—but Austin has always just had a different atmosphere. The stereotypical description was that Austin was more focused on the art and love of music and Nashville more focused on the business.

KEN LEVITAN: I represented Guy Clark and Townes Van Zandt legally but shifted to management when I realized I didn't like practicing law. I had fallen in love with Nanci Griffith's music when I saw her play in a small club in Nashville. We would go to a place called the Kettle of Fish in New York City. She really knew the whole early New York folk scene, and the Kettle of Fish is a famous place where Dylan sang. She and I started working together around the end of 1985, and I worked the very tail end of *Once in a Very Blue Moon* and then helped out with *The Last of the True Believers*. Nanci was getting some nice critical acclaim by then because *Once in a Very Blue Moon* had gotten some great reviews. I thought she could work internationally, which worked out very well.[31]

Ken Levitan's high-profile Vector Management has represented several bold names including Emmylou Harris, Trisha Yearwood, Lyle Lovett, Meat Loaf, and the B-52s.

BOBBY NELSON: Some musicians here in Austin were very critical of her when she went to Nashville. Nanci took that very hard. She felt that she reached down to musicians when she could and had them be her opening act or put them in her band. She did everything she could to be inclusive, but there was [friction]. People thought Nanci was a prima donna. She wasn't old Austin, which was relaxed and could take things as they came. She was thick skinned, but not entirely. Nanci was a businesswoman.

JOHN GORKA: I opened again for her at Club Passim in January 1986. Tony Brown signed her to MCA Records around then.

ANDREW DANSBY: Going to Nashville does not undermine anyone's credibility to me, but she could hold a grudge. Guy Clark and Townes Van Zandt didn't stick around in Texas either. Her booking agent and manager were in Nashville. She just decided to take a swing out there.[32]

Former Rolling Stone *magazine writer Andrew Dansby has covered music and visual arts for the* Houston Chronicle *for nearly twenty years.*

JOY LEWALLEN: I think moving to Nashville helped her become her own person. Eric was well established in Houston and had a huge following here. She was in his shadow. I think the competition between them might have broken them up. They were able to stay close friends until Eric died because there was no competition when she moved away. Eric's career didn't end up going the same way. He ended up being very popular with a big following in Europe. Nanci had management and record companies [behind her] when she went to Nashville. Her star took off.

• • •

Nanci Griffith performs at Carnegie Hall in New York City during folksinger Tom Rush's revolving-cast tour. "We played places like the Kennedy Center and Carnegie Hall on shows presented as Club 47 reunions," guitarist Brian Wood says. "Tom Rush put them together. He mixed the new and old crowds for those shows. Carnegie Hall was first. I couldn't believe we were playing there. I had a day job as an IBM geek. I would go in and tell my boss, 'I have to take seven days off to do this other thing.' 'Really? Where are you going?' 'Ah, we're playing Carnegie Hall.' The boss's jaw hits the floor. 'No way.'"

PETE KENNEDY: I saw Nanci a couple times at the Birchmere starting in 1985. I had met her before at the after-party for the Tom Rush Club 47 show, but it wasn't an ongoing friendship. Everyone would just play a couple songs on that Tom Rush tour. Emmylou, Shawn Colvin, Peter Rowan, Jerry Douglas, and Mark O'Connor all played. Tom wanted to create a coffeehouse vibe at these venues. He had dedicated fans sitting at tables with checkered tablecloths onstage in every town. I was one of those people sitting onstage. Emmylou would come out and it would be like you were at Club 47 back in the sixties except you were on the stage at a giant concert hall.

BRIAN WOOD: Emmylou Harris, Maria Muldaur, John Sebastian plus Nanci, Robert Earl Keen, and Bill Morrissey were playing at the Kennedy Center. Tom Rush wanted a mix of new and old. I arrived at baggage check at the same time as Emmylou Harris. She was an idol. I grabbed my suitcase. I already had my guitar in a gig bag. I would just hang my gig bag up in the airplane with the suit bags back then in 1986. She acted like she had never seen one. She said, "How did you do that?" She was on the bill as a duo with Barry Tashian. We talked about that for a while, and she got her guitar. She joked that these were the days of being your own road manager.

She asked where I was staying. "I'm staying at the Mayflower Hotel." "That's where I'm staying," she said. "Why don't you ride with us?" We all got a cab and went to the hotel. We went to the gig later. I heard her in the dressing room with the door cracked warming up. "Oh, man," I heard her say. "I sound like crap." I thought, Man, that sounds like angels to me. Amazing. So, we did the gig and then played Carnegie Hall. I remember better the Kennedy Center show. We played with John Sebastian, Maria Muldaur, and Emmylou Harris. Bill Morrissey might have played the Carnegie Hall show. Nanci's sister Mikki was at the gig.

CAREFREE LIFE—David Jessie, playing the comic character that serves as the hero of "Stop the World—I Want To Get
Off," leans back and lets the girls carry the load in this scene
from the Austin Civic Theater's production of the offbeat musical hit. The young ladies bearing the carefree clown are Valerie Schuster, Nancy Griffith, Debbie Doyle, Kim Jones, May-
nette More, Dianne Doyle and Cassandra Haddox. The An-
thony Newley satire, which has been on the Playhouse stage
since early March, is proving ACT's most popular attraction
this season. It's presented each Friday and Saturday night
with an 8:30 p.m. curtain.

Austin American-Statesman article on the Austin Civic Theater's production of *Stop the World—I Want to Get Off.* Front row, L–R: Valerie Schuster, unknown, Nanci Griffith. Courtesy Valerie Schuster

Austin American-Statesman article on the Austin Civic Theater's production of *Stop the World—I Want to Get Off.* Front row, far L–R: Valerie Schuster, Nanci Griffith. Courtesy Valerie Schuster

Nanci Griffith, Kerrville Folk Festival, Kerrville, Texas, late seventies. Photographer unknown. Courtesy Bobby Nelson

SUN	MON	TUES	WED	THURS	FRI	SAT
					1. GEORGE BASHAM	BILL NEELY
3. GORDEE HEADLEE	4. ELLIOTT LEONARD	5. DANNY EVERITT	6. JEANNIE KITCHENS	7. LEIF & MANDY KAHAL	8. DOUG BLASER	9 DAVID RODRIGUEZ
10. ECLIPSE OF AUSTIN	11. PRISSY MAYS	12. 4-7 p.m. TWILITE CONCERT BUTCH HANCOCK 9 p.m. ABNER BURNETT	13. PAT MEARS	14. JIMMIE GILMORE	15. JOE GRACEY & BOBBY EARL SMITH	16 NANCI GRIFFITH
17. JIM DIXON	18. ELLIOTT LEONARD	19. HARVEY THOMAS YOUNG JIMMIE GILMORE	20. GEORGE BASHAM	21. MANDY & LEIF KAHAL	22. DOUG BLASER	23 BILL NEELY
24. DAVID RODRIGUEZ	25. SPENSER & SUE PERSKIN	26. ABNER BURNETT	27. PAT MEARS	28. JIMMIE GILMORE	29. JOE GRACEY & BOBBY EARL SMITH	30 NANCI GRIFFITH
31. DON LEWIS					6th & Guadalupe 472-0033	

Alamo Drafthouse calendar, late seventies. Nanci Griffith was scheduled to play two Saturday nights that month. Photo by Brian T. Atkinson. Courtesy Bobby Nelson

Front cover art for songwriter and label owner Mike Williams's *The Radio Show*, which was B.F. Deal Records' first release in 1976. Courtesy Brian T. Atkinson archives

Back cover art for songwriter and B.F. Deal Records owner Mike Williams's *The Radio Show*. Courtesy Brian T. Atkinson archives

THE PARTICIPANTS

MIKE WILLIAMS: lead vocals, acoustic 12-string guitar.
DENNIS COATS: acoustic guitar, banjo, harmonies.
STEVE HILL: bass, acoustic guitar, enthusiasm.
KELLI WILLIAMS: supper, occasional mysterious harmonies.
THE AUDIENCE: energy.
JIM WHEELER: instant mixing, mechanical wizardry.
DENVER SOUND STUDIO: that living-room feeling.
KIMN RADIO: sponsoring the "Denver in Concert" radio series.
CAROLYN WILLIAMS, artwork, photography.

All selections written by Mike Williams, except "Weaving" by Dan McCrimmon. Side One #1, 2 and Side Two #1, 2, 3, 4, 5. © Michael R. Williams. Side One #3, 4, 5 © Cross-Keys Pub Co.. Side Two #6 © Ampco Music, Inc.. All selections ASCAP.

LIFE'S FINEST ADVENTURES seem to happen when I am trying to do something else. Actually, we were trying to record a commercial for a feminine hygiene product, but the company turned it down because of a few missed licks. Dennis (who is really George Gobel in a very thin disguise) pointed out that what we had was probably a record album. That's all right — last time I tried to cut a record album it came out sounding like a commercial for a feminine hygiene product. This business is so weird, I just take 'em as they come.

SIDE ONE

1. DADDY'S GONE TO TEXAS   3:47   (3:15)
2. SMOKE OUT THE MEMORY   2:51   (2:04)
3. MORNING IN SUNSHINE CANYON   4:08   (4:08)
4. DECISION   2:36   (2:33)
5. THE BILL BLACK SONG   3:02   (2:10)

SIDE TWO

1. 4/4 WALTZ   2:26   (2:16)
2. RAGTIME KICKOFF WHOOPEE   2:27   (2:27)
3. MISSISSIPPI   3:03   (3:03)
4. DUMB-ASS, TEXAS   3:06   (1:54)
5. THE DONUT MAN   3:47   (2:57)
6. WEAVING IS THE PROPERTY   4:44   (4:16)
   OF FEW THESE DAYS

B.F. DEAL

A B.F. DEAL PRODUCTION
© 1976 B.F. DEAL, INC.
4325 E. 18th AVE
DENVER, COLO. 80220

54

Front cover art for *B.F. Deal Sampler, Vol. 1,* which included three tracks each from songwriters John Garza, Will Walker, Frank Zigal, and Nanci Griffith. Griffith's first recordings "Double Standard Blues," "If I Were a Child," and "Texas Boy" were on the record. Photo by Brian T. Atkinson. Courtesy Bobby Nelson

Back cover art for *B.F. Deal Sampler, Vol. 1.* Nanci Griffith is described as "either a butterfly or a Bird of Paradise . . . or maybe a sparrow just in out of the rain." Photo by Brian T. Atkinson. Courtesy Bobby Nelson

Promotional material for Nanci Griffith's debut album, *There's a Light beyond These Woods*, B.F. Deal Records, 1978. Photo by Brian T. Atkinson. Courtesy Bobby Nelson

Promotional photograph for Nanci Griffith's debut album, *There's a Light beyond These Woods*, B.F. Deal Records, 1978. Photo by Brian T. Atkinson. Courtesy John T. Davis archives

There's a Light beyond These Woods, original cassette pressing, 1978. Courtesy Brian T. Atkinson archives

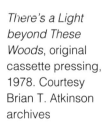

fOCUS

Nanci Griffith is coming to town

By Lyle Lovett

Nanci Griffith makes her Texas A&M debut tomorrow and Saturday at the Basement Coffeehouse.

Nanci who? Never heard of her.

It's easy to get lost in the shuffle of popular music these days. To get the ear of the public, a musician almost has to be a bonafide superstar, or at least a good imitation of one.

Many listeners prefer being told what is good by disc jockeys and record promoters rather than deciding for themselves. If you are one of those people, you won't enjoy Griffith. She is neither a superstar nor an imitation.

She is a 26-year-old folksinger-songwriter who has been playing her guitar and singing professionally since she was 14, performing full-time for the past two years.

On stage, she sings with a strong clear voice and tells stories in a way that can turn a bar full of rowdies into an attentive, quiet audience. But off stage, it's another matter.

"I don't talk that much, and when I do talk it's usually not anything very intelligent," she said, laughing. "It's a pretty big contrast and I guess a lot of people write it off, thinking I don't want to talk to them. But it's not that. I'm just a very shy person — always afraid I'll say the wrong thing.

"I guess I could get a pretty bad reputation from audiences for

not being the type that will go out and laugh it up with everybody. But I'm too shy, I can't get to know them and then get back on stage and do what I do. There really is a contrast in what I am on stage and what I am as a person."

Though she does speak more freely on stage, Griffith's quiet, sensitive demeanor is reflected in songs like "Alabama Soft-Spoken Blues," which she co-wrote with Maggie Graham:

Southern man, you sure are pretty,
Got a smile to still the city,
And Lord, you know, you got those sleepy eyes.
Alabama sweet-talking baby,
Calmed the heart of a lonely lady,
You kept me flying high,
And the living easy.
And it's Dallas in the rain,
And I was dreaming.

Griffith is from Austin. She left her home town about a year ago for Houston.

"I enjoy Houston a lot," she said. "More than Austin, I enjoy other musicians here. In Austin there was a very heavy air of competition because there were so few jobs for so many musicians. Everyone hated one another.

"In Houston, everybody can get along and work with each other because, God knows, the club owners talk to one another.

Musicians in Houston realize that they need to talk to one another and have a bond between them. There's not as much competition at all."

Griffith performed in this year's Kerrville Folk Festival as a participant in the New Folk songwriting contest, and will be performing next year as a headline act. She also has an album that was released this year on a small Austin-based record label, B. F. Deal Records. She wrote seven of the nine songs on the album.

"I really don't have any plans," she said, "because if you don't have any plans, you don't have anything to get knocked down. I enjoy what I'm doing — just being a free spirit in the music business

right now. Because once you get on a larger scale you're really tied down to agencies and things of that sort. Right now it's the happiest time. You're just playing music for yourself and making a good living."

Griffith said she enjoys playing college coffeehouses because the crowds come primarily to listen and not just for alcohol.

"In a club, the musician is just an afterthought," she said. "Liquor is the first thing. It's a real challenge because I don't ever want to be an afterthought. I'm not there to play to myself. I have to change their mind and make them believe that I am the reason they're there, not the bottle of beer in front of them."

Griffith has been to Bryan-College Station twice before to perform at Ginns, a live music-oriented bar in Bryan. This time she said she hopes to see her Aunt Lani and Uncle Charles, who live in Bryan.

"Uncle Charles teaches at A&M," she grinned, "but I don't know what his last name is. I asked my grandmother a couple of weeks ago and she told me but I forgot. So give been meaning to find out before I go back so they can come hear me."

Maybe they will if they see this story.

"Yeah, I hope so," she said with a laugh.

Lyle Lovett, "Nanci Griffith Is Coming to Town," *The Battalion*, College Station, Texas, late seventies. Photo by Brian T. Atkinson. Courtesy Bobby Nelson

NANCI GRIFFITH

COLLEGE REFERENCES

```
AMARILLO COLLEGE........................AMARILLO, TX
ANGELO STATE UNIVERSITY..............SAN ANGELO, TX
UNIVERSITY OF ARKANSAS...........FAYETTEVILLE, ARK
UNIVERSITY OF CENTRAL ARKANSAS.........CONWAY, ARK
UNIVERSITY OF HOUSTON/CLEARLAKE......CLEARLAKE, TX
LAMAR UNIVERSITY.......................BEAUMONT, TX
UNIVERSITY OF SOUTHEASTERN LOUISIANA.LAFAYETTE, LA
SAM HOUSTON STATE UNIVERSITY.......HUNTSVILLE, TX
SAN ANTONIO COLLEGE................SAN ANTONIO, TX
STEPHEN F. AUSTIN STATE............NACADOCHES, TX
SOUTHWEST TEXAS STATE...............SAN MARCOS, TX
TEXAS CHRISTIAN UNIVERSITY..........FORT WORTH, TX
TEXAS LUTHERAN COLLEGE..................SEGUIN, TX
TEXAS TECH UNIVERSITY..................LUBBOCK, TX
TEXAS A&M UNIVERSITY..........COLLEGE STATION, TX
WEST TEXAS STATE.......................CANYON, TX
```

RADIO SHOWS

```
KUT FM.................................AUSTIN, TX
KPFT FM/THE CRYSTAL EGG SHOW...........HOUSTON, TX
KBOR/THE CONNIE GREEN SHOW........BROWNSVILLE, TX
NATIONAL BROADCASTING SYSTEMS.....................
                         /KERRVILE FOLK FESTIVAL
```

TELEVISION APPEARANCES

```
KTBC/CHANNEL 7/THE NOON SHOW............AUSTIN, TX
KTRK/CHANNEL 13/SPOTLIGHT..............HOUSTON, TX
KPRC/CHANNEL 2/THE LITTLE 'OLE SHOW....HOUSTON, TX
```

RECORDINGS

B F DEAL SAMPLER ALBUM VOL. 1
THERE'S A LIGHT BEYOND THESE WOODS

SPECIAL REFERENCE

THE KERRVILLE FOLK FESTIVAL

Nanci Griffith performance résumé, late seventies. Photo by Brian T. Atkinson.
Courtesy Bobby Nelson

CLUB REFERENCES

Hole in the Wall .... Austin, Texas
The Backroom .... Austin, Texas
Valentines .... Austin, Texas
Liberty Lunch .... Austin, Texas
Symphony Square .... Austin, Texas
Uncle Stanley's .... Austin, Texas
Split Rail .... Austin, Texas
La Bodega .... Houston, Texas
Houlihan's #2 .... Houston, Texas
Anderson Fair .... Houston, Texas
Fat Dawgs .... Lubbock, Texas
The Pirate Ship .... Port Isabel, Texas

RECORDINGS

B F Deal Sampler Album Volume I

RADIO SHOWS

Connie Green Show, KBOR .... Brownsville, Texas

TELEVISION APPEARANCES

KTBC Noon Show .... Austin, Texas

TAPES AND RECORDS AVAILABLE UPON REQUEST

Contact: SUGAR BEAR BOOKING:

Nanci Griffith club references, late seventies. Photo by Brian T. Atkinson. Courtesy Bobby Nelson

60

Kerrville Daily Times article, Wednesday, March 13, 1979. Photo by Brian T. Atkinson. Courtesy Bobby Nelson

NANCI GRIFFITH is one of six performers appearing at the Kerrville Municipal Auditorium at 2 and 8 p.m. on Saturday, March 17, in a Preview of the Kerrville Folk Festival. The pair of concerts honor the 170 members of the Kerrville Festivals Sponsors Assn. and include performances by Don Sanders, Louis Real of Kerrville, Lindsay Halsley, Peter Rowan, and the exciting progressive bluegrass band Southern Select. Festival producer Rod Kennedy will emcee and the Texas States Arts and Crafts Fair will have a lobby exhibit.

8-F—LUBBOCK AVALANCHE-JOURNAL—Sunday Morning, February 5,

SMALL PACKAGE — Good things are supposed to come in small packages, and singer Nanci Griffith is further proof of that fact. The young Austin singer played a University Center courtyard concert Wednesday for Texas Tech students, and earned applause with every number. Not bad for a free concert. As Allen Damron told an A-J reporter earlier in the week, "This lady is little, really little, but she's got a voice that will just knock you out." (Staff Photo by Holly Kuper)

Lubbock Avalanche Journal article, Sunday, February 5, 1978. Photo by Brian T. Atkinson. Courtesy Bobby Nelson

L–R: Brian Wood, Nanci Griffith, Central Texas, late seventies. Photographer unknown. Courtesy Bobby Nelson

Nanci Griffith, Kerrville Folk Festival, 1980, from Rod Kennedy, *Music from the Heart: The Fifty-Year Chronicle of His Life in Music (with a Few Sidetrips!)*. Photo by Brian Kanof. Courtesy Dalis Allen

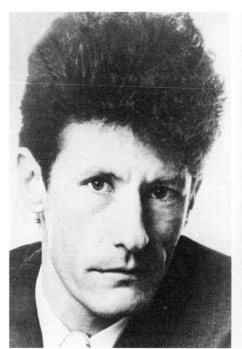

L–R: Lyle Lovett, Nanci Griffith, promotional photo. Photo of photo by Brian T. Atkinson. Courtesy John T. Davis archives

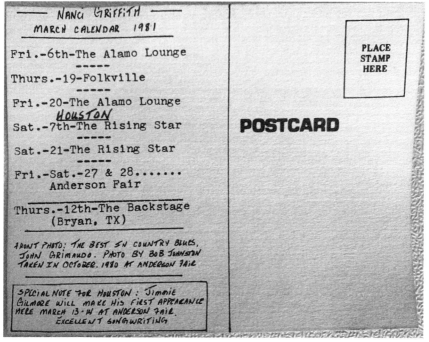

Nanci Griffith's tour calendar, March 1981. "Special note for Houston," the note reads. "Jimmie [Dale] Gilmore will make his first appearance here March 13–14 at Anderson Fair. Excellent songwriting." Photo by Brian T. Atkinson. Courtesy Bobby Nelson

Outtake from *Poet in My Window* photo shoot, 1978. Photo by Brian T. Atkinson.
Courtesy Bobby Nelson

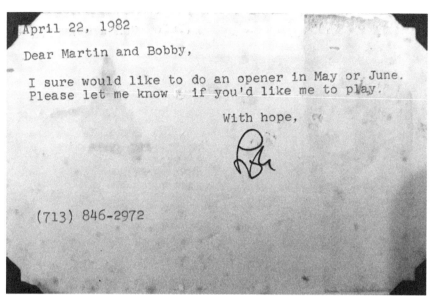

Note from Lyle Lovett to Martin Wigginton and Bobby Nelson, April 22, 1982. The note reads, "Dear Martin and Bobby, I sure would like to do an opener in May or June. Please let me know if you would like me to play. With hope, Lyle." Photo by Brian T. Atkinson. Courtesy Bobby Nelson

Philo Records promotional photograph, 1986. Courtesy Bobby Nelson

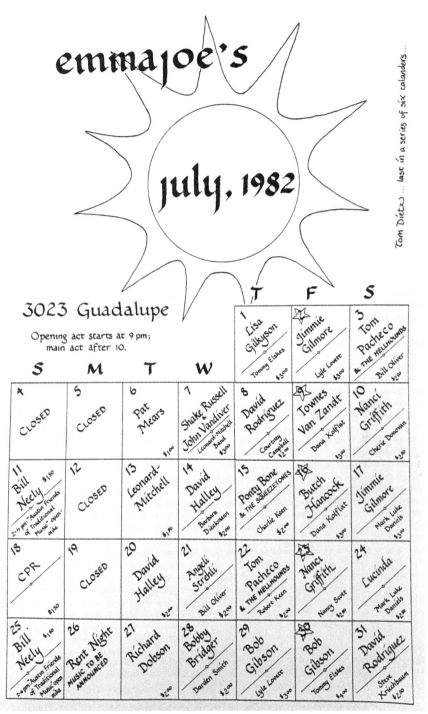

emmajoe's

july, 1982

(Tom Dietz) ... last in a series of six calanders...

3023 Guadalupe

Opening act starts at 9 pm;
main act after 10.

S	M	T	W	T	F	S
				1 Lisa Gilkyson — Tommy Elskes $3.00	2 ☆ Jimmie Gilmore — Lyle Lovett $3.00	3 Tom Pacheco & THE HELLHOUNDS — Bill Oliver $2.00
4 CLOSED	5 CLOSED	6 Pat Mears	7 Shake Russell & John Vandiver — Leonard-Mitchell Band $3.00	8 David Rodriguez — Courtney Campbell $2.00	9 ☆ Townes Van Zandt — Dana Kolflat $5.00	10 Nanci Griffith — Cherie Donovan $2.00
11 Bill Neely $1.50 — 2½ pm Austin Friends of Traditional Music open mike	12 CLOSED	13 Leonard-Mitchell	14 David Halley — Barbara Dieckmann $2.00	15 Ponty Bone & THE SQUEEZETONES — Charlie Keen $2.00	16 ☆ Butch Hancock — Dana Kolflat $5.00	17 Jimmie Gilmore — Mark Luke Daniels $3.00
18 CPR $1.50	19 CLOSED	20 David Halley $2.00	21 Angeli Strehli — Bill Oliver $2.00	22 Tom Pacheco & THE HELLHOUNDS — Robert Keen $2.00	23 ☆ Nanci Griffith — Nancy Scott $2.00	24 Lucinda — Mark Luke Daniels $2.00
25. Bill Neely $1.50 — 2½ pm Austin Friends of Traditional Music open mike	26 Rent Night MUSIC TO BE ANNOUNCED	27 Richard Dobson $2.00	28 Bobby Bridger — Darden Smith $2.00	29 Bob Gibson — Lyle Lovett $3.00	30 ☆ Bob Gibson — Tommy Elskes $4.00	31 David Rodriguez — Steve Krichbaum $2.50

Emmajoe's calendar, July 1982. The spectacular lineup includes Lisa [Eliza] Gilkyson on July 1, Jimmie [Dale] Gilmore on July 2, David Rodriguez on March 8 and 31, Townes Van Zandt on March 9, Nanci Griffith on July 10 and 24, Lucinda Williams on July 24, and Richard Dobson on March 27.

Nanci Griffith, Kerrville Folk Festival, 1986, from Rod Kennedy, *Music from the Heart: The Fifty-Year Chronicle of His Life in Music (with a Few Sidetrips!)*. Photo by Brian Kanof. Courtesy Dalis Allen

Chorus: Gulf Coast Highway

Nashville (The Early Years)

NANCI GRIFFITH MAKES NASHVILLE HOME in the mideighties. The move pays high dividends. "I was a little surprised that someone who was so quintessentially Texan like Nanci—and she knew when she should start twanging it up and be more Texan—would end up moving to Nashville," Pat Alger says. "Women usually come to Nashville and try to fit into the Nashville scene. Nanci did not. She wasn't trying to fit in at all, but she realized [Nashville] was an opportunity. Jim Rooney wanted her to be the best Nanci Griffith she could be. He [wanted to] make her songs the stars."

Griffith delivers straightaway with *The Last of the True Believers* in 1986. The same studio aces from *Once in a Very Blue Moon*—Pat Alger, Roy Huskey Jr., Béla Fleck, Lyle Lovett, Kenny Malone, Mark O'Connor, and Philip Donnelly—transcend on her final Philo album. In fact, most consider *The Last of the True Believers* Griffith's most successful collection with original songs. "We had pulled everything together so well the last time, so we figured we would try that again," Jim Rooney says. "Everyone was happy to come back and do a new album with Nanci."

The Last of the True Believers features Griffith's signature "Love at the Five and Dime" as well as the timeless "The Wing and the Wheel," "One of These Days," and the Bobby Nelson cowrite "More Than a Whisper." "Griff let us stay late and drink one night after Nanci's show at the Cactus," Nelson says. "We got into an argument about what we could expect from the loves in our lives. She called the next day and said, 'I went back to the hotel last night and wrote a song called 'More Than a Whisper.' 'I'm putting your name down as a cowriter because you inspired it.' That was Nanci." Griffith again covers Pat Alger with the Alger, Fred Koller, and Bill Dale cowrite "Goin' Gone" and records Tom Russell's "St. Olav's Gate."

The collection earns her first Grammy nomination. However, future Oh Boy Records executives Al Bunetta and Dan Einstein's *Tribute to Steve Good-*

man ultimately edges out *The Last of the True Believers* in the Best Contemporary Folk Recording category at the twenty-ninth annual ceremony in February 1987. Another near miss: Kathy Mattea scores a nomination for Best Country Vocal Performance for her "Love at the Five and Dime" cover but comes up short against Reba McEntire's "Whoever's in New England." Either way, Griffith's attention to detail—down to constructing *The Last of the True Believers*' iconic album cover as a nod toward both "Love at the Five and Dime" and "Lookin' for the Time (Workin' Girl)"—turns heads throughout the industry.

LYLE LOVETT: Nanci was very complete in her thinking. Setting up the cover shot for *The Last of the True Believers* outside the Woolworth's in Houston was all her idea conceptually. The female characters in the photo for *The Last of the True Believers* are all intended to be different versions of her.

PAISLEY ROBERTSON: Nanci said, "What are you doing for Thanksgiving?" I'm standing on a street corner in front of the Woolworth's in Houston next thing I know. We were standing there in the cold with some real prostitutes. Security guards were guarding us while they shot photos for the cover of *The Last of the True Believers*.[1]

Former Texas Chili Parlor bar waitress and Uncle Walt's Band manager Paisley Robertson appears on the cover of Nanci Griffith's The Last of the True Believers.

JOHN T. DAVIS: We were all friends who Nanci asked to get together [to shoot] the album cover for *The Last of the True Believers*. Nanci rounded us up when she had a gig at Anderson Fair. We went downtown to set up shop outside that Woolworth's. I was talking to Paisley Robinson, who had her back to the camera. Nanci had us set up to look like the guy and working girl in her song "Lookin' for the Time (Workin' Girl)." The song [goes], "If you [ain't got] money, [I ain't got] time for you." I'm asking Paisley what time it is and getting the cold shoulder in that cover photo. Real working girls hung out on that corner. They stood there in the dark giving us dirty looks when we showed up with our camera and lights.

JIM ROONEY: Nanci had moved to Nashville by *The Last of the True Believers*. Nashville was an easy place to get around back then. Her first apartment was by the Vanderbilt University Medical Center. You could live in a nice one for not much money. Then she got one in a vintage building out on West End near Woodlawn Avenue. The apartment had really nice hardwood floors and plaster walls and really worked for her. Then time came to record *The Last of the True Believers*.

The first song we tried was "Lookin' for the Time (Workin' Girl)," but it wasn't coming together. Then the power went out after we had only been working for maybe two hours. We would have been working on at least the second song by then on the last album, but we didn't have anything. [I always say] you need to be ready to come out with nothing when you go into a session—and especially when you think you have everything figured out like we did [on *Once in a Very Blue Moon*]. "There isn't anything we can do," I told everyone. "[Let's] go to an early lunch. Let's try something else when we get back." We did "Goin' Gone" when we came back. Then we were rolling and never looked back. The lesson: don't count your chickens before they hatch. I already had learned to never beat a dead horse in the studio.

KATHY MATTEA: I lived a block from Jack's Tracks on Music Row and found the door was closed one day. "Somebody's using the studio today?" I asked. "Who's in there?" "Jim Rooney's making a record on Nanci Griffith." I was like, "Nanci Griffith is here?" "I have this friend in Texas," my friend Richard Dobson had been saying, "and you would love her. She would love you. You've gotta meet." Unfortunately, I had been unavailable every time Nanci [was around]. I waited for a lull in their sound and knocked on the door. We went, "It's me. It's you." They were cutting "Love at the Five and Dime" and listening to a playback. "Love at the Five and Dime" struck me. I went, "Great song. Who do you think should do that?"

[Noted producer] Allen Reynolds and I were listening to music later, and he said, "There's an unusual song called 'Love at the Five and Dime' I want to send you. I think it's special." "I remember hearing this," I said. "I would love to do it." I've lived with that song for so long now that I can't remember what it felt for it to be new. "Love at the Five and Dime" for me is like trying to remember what your favorite blue jeans felt like after you've been wearing them for more than thirty years. You know them so well broken in.[2]

Country star Kathy Mattea reached number one four times with songs including "Goin' Gone" *and Susanna Clark's* "Come from the Heart." *She hosts the popular* Mountain Stage *on West Virginia's public radio today.*

NANCI GRIFFITH: Kathy Mattea had her first number one hit with my song "Love at the Five and Dime." I was out on the road with the Everly Brothers that summer when she was climbing up the charts. *Last of the True Believers* was getting a lot of attention. Phil Everly kept saying, "['Love at the Five and Dime'] is gonna go to number one for you." "It's just a little folk song with a little bit of everything in there like adultery and alcohol," I said. "I mean, how could that go to number one?" He said, "Oh, it's gonna do it." He was right.[3]

KATHY MATTEA: The main memory I have [from the "Love at the Five and Dime" recording session] is that Nanci and Rooney were so comfortable with each other. They were a unit with the same vision and mutual trust. His production is such a big part of her sound. Rooney had a real understanding of what was really special about her. He comes from the Allen Reynolds tradition [as a producer], which is that you just create a vibe where everybody feels like they're specifically there to contribute their piece. Every musician is very respected. No one senses that we're not gonna get something special. Rooney is always listening for the feel. He has the instinct to just look up and say, "Hey, pal, I think you need mandolin instead of acoustic guitar there." Then the whole thing comes together.

TOM RUSSELL: Nanci recorded my song "St. Olav's Gate" on *The Last of the True Believers.* She was so generous and loved stories about my Norwegian experiences with the Tom Russell Band and how we would work the honky-tonks there two months a year back in the eighties. I wrote "St. Olav's Gate" about a street with that name in the center of Oslo where there was a dormitory for musicians from around the world. Wild times. The Scotsman was one of the original bars, and it's still there. Doug Sahm also recorded the song later.

KATHY MATTEA: I dug into the *Last of the True Believers* album and became a huge fan. I'm really drawn to storytelling songs, and Nanci was a brilliant storyteller, but what made Nanci so special wasn't just the storytelling. There was something about the way she approached songwriting that was like nobody else. Her songwriting was literary simplicity. She wrote beautiful melodies with variety. I'm always struck by the way she writes rhythm into her lyrics.

Also, her percussive Texas accent bled into her performance. I always think about that with the beginning of the [third] verse of "Love at the Five and Dime." She says, "Now, one of the boys in Eddie's band took a shine to Rita's hands." That's all pickup before you even get to the verse's downbeat. You look at it and think, That doesn't work, but it's quirky, interesting, and works. Nanci had a way of doing things outside the box. We spent long hours talking about music, and I saw why [Townes Van Zandt and Guy Clark] really respected her.

Nanci really was the first woman to break into that boy's club. Townes and Guy were hard-living, hard-partying, hard-drinking guys, and they had high standards for songwriting. They looked at her as an equal. We talked about that over the years. My connection to her is as a contemporary and a fan, but I have this window into this one song that I've sung for thirty-five years and changed my life. I have been struck by how many layers there are to that very simple song. I was doing an interview with a guy who teaches writing and writes novels, and he asked about that song. "You know, Kathy," he said, "that song is a movie of someone's entire life in three minutes."

"Love at the Five and Dime" is never stiff or forced. I was onstage once after singing this song hundreds of times. The second verse comes out of my mouth, and I was like, "Oh my gosh. Who writes, 'Sportin' Miss Rita back by his side' or 'one of the boys in Eddie's band took a shine to Rita's hand / So Eddie ran off with the bass man's wife / Oh, but he was back by June'?" Nanci was so conversational. That's the mark of a great writer. I don't think she liked that song very much, but I sure did and came to love it more and more.

BUDDY MONDLOCK: Nanci's voice was so clear, effortless, and exact on *The Last of the True Believers*. She sang with such feeling that sounded sweet one minute and growling the next about being a prostitute and not having time for you. She was especially playing exactly the music I was attracted to on the records Jim Rooney produced. Rooney's sound perfectly captured what she was doing. Also, Nanci's writing wasn't all belly-button gazing. So many modern singer-songwriters talk about their feelings endlessly. I love someone who can step in like a short-story writer who fleshes out a character and then tells the story like Nanci, Guy Clark, and Eric Taylor.

PETER COOPER: I would go straight to the Jim Rooney–produced projects if someone asked me why Nanci was so good: *Once in a Very Blue Moon*, *The Last of the True Believers*, and later the first *Other Voices, Other Rooms*. There was an incredible array of players on *Once in a Very Blue Moon* and *Last of the True Believers*, and the musicians clearly are coming up with arrangements in the studio that are spectacularly musical. You had Lloyd Green, who is the greatest steel guitar player ever. Lloyd had total freedom to be Lloyd Green on the records Rooney produced. Some players carried over into the Tony Brown–produced MCA records. Tony was like, "Why doesn't this sound like *The Last of the True Believers*?" "Well, you have synthesizers and drum triggers [on *Lone Star State of Mind*]."[4]

Longtime writer Peter Cooper was a senior director, producer, and writer for the Country Music Hall of Fame in Nashville.

LLOYD GREEN: Nanci's sessions always were a calm and intellectual environment. You recorded for three hours and took a break. I do remember playing the role of who she was talking about in the song "Love at the Five and Dime" because [Eddie] was a steel guitar player in the lyrics. Nanci was just easy to work with. She seemed to appreciate my approach and music. I would ask her about her interest in books. We could talk. I loved her as an artist and a person.

PETER COOPER: Then you had Kenny Malone on drums, who was a remarkably intuitive percussionist. You had this conjunction of younger and older musicians who worked together beautifully.

LLOYD GREEN: Kenny Malone and I had different approaches to find the end result. We were two opposing solutions with the same logical ending. You always take the simplest approach with the least problems. Kenny and I were always looking for fewer notes to get there. So many steel guitar parts are too cluttered with notes. I look at music as a conversation. Look at what the instrument is saying. Is he stuttering? Does he have coherent sentences? Is it articulate or just a bunch of dumbass notes to fill the space? Kenny was always looking around and hitting everything to get him into the emotion of the songs. He would hit something and "Let's record this."

Creativity transcends IQ. You can't measure it, but I have a lot of recall from childhood memories that are all in color that I tap into to find the emotion in the songs. I can still feel the emotions from all those wonderful times playing Tom Sawyer as a kid in Mobile, Alabama, or going to the swimming hole or stealing watermelons out of someone's patch. Those memories become locked in as a solidified picture. Those memories are the best vehicle to transfer emotion into a song. Another avenue is using a former romance I had with a girl in the song. You need to use that emotion for the song. The music is always the ultimate purpose in life.

PETER COOPER: Rooney and Nanci didn't tell anybody what to play. They just called the best players in the world. How old they were or what their résumés were didn't matter. Go to the song "The Last of the True Believers." Listen to the way the arrangements support Nanci. Absolutely undeniable. She was bringing in people who weren't truly professional musicians by then like Lyle Lovett and was mixing her remarkable songs with songs by amazing writers. Jim Rooney and Nanci offered such an open musical conversation on the record.

The Last of the True Believers was a high point.

LLOYD GREEN: Jim Rooney was the prototypical scholar-producer. Rooney hired musicians who listened to the lyrics, melodies, and ambience. The best producers hire musicians they trust and let us create the music behind the singer and the song. Bingo. Great philosophy. Why hire the best musicians in the world and then come out and tell us how to play? I had worked with Jim Rooney before when we recorded John Prine's song "Let's Talk Dirty in Hawaiian." Rooney was always a calm, quiet guy, not demonstrative about anything. He had ideas, but he left the music up to us. I'm sure Nanci had specific ideas, too. I would have done whatever Rooney told me to do, but I can't remember him ever doing that.

Nanci's lyrics were smarter than most. Her songs were like Kris Kristofferson's in conveying vivid stories. She was an intellectual songwriter whose songs didn't have clichés. Her songs were vignettes, complete short stories. They were several levels above the ones like [the Tammy Wynette songs] "D-I-V-O-R-C-E," "Stand by Your Man," and the drinking songs, which were just trying to get people's attention.

PETER COOPER: Nanci's guitar playing sometimes gets overlooked. She came from a guitar tradition that went from Lightnin' Hopkins to Eric Taylor to her [generation], which included Lyle Lovett. Nanci was a masterful guitarist. Having that lyrical command at the same time as the instrumental command was very rare. Her style involved the deep blues from Houston and also the folk music of Carolyn Hester. She played with these thumb picks that were bradded to a finger pick. She often used alternate tunings. Hers was a fascinating way to play, and I know Eric had a lot to do with that, as he did with Lyle Lovett. Nanci was something else. I don't just mean she was wonderful. I mean she was something else.

MAC MCANALLY: Nanci played with these thumb picks that Guy Clark made for her. He would cut the end off a thumb pick and rivet your favorite guitar pick onto that frame. The thumb pick's purpose is to play a bass line that's a little stronger than what you're playing with the rest of your fingers because you want it to stand out, but there wasn't a thumb pick that did both the job of strumming and the job of a thumb pick. Guy's thought process was to take your favorite pick that stands alone as a thumb pick, but then have your favorite flat pick if you need to break into a strum. He made it easy to go back and forth, which was the magic. Guy was ahead of his time.

Nashville Songwriters Hall of Fame member Mac McAnally has released more than a dozen albums between his self-titled debut in 1977 and his latest, Once in a Lifetime *(2020). The ten-time Country Music Association's Musician of the Year toured with Jimmy Buffett's Coral Reefer Band.*

• • •

Nanci Griffith discovers a trusted instrument around this time: her Taylor guitar. "[Nanci] bought a Taylor in a music store in New York in 1986," company founder Bob Taylor says. "She later ordered a custom Taylor 512ce with a Florentine cutaway and sunburst top, which became a performance staple for many years." Taylor—today a leading manufacturer in the same league as heavyweights Gibson and Martin—designs its first signature guitar for Griffith years later. "Nanci Griffith was the reason Nashville took off for us in a big way and put our company on the map," says Terry Myers, who helped design Griffith's signature Taylor guitar. "We were still struggling to be heard and become known as Taylor guitars in the eighties."[5]

TERRY MYERS: Nanci would be called an influencer in modern times.

She became a big ace card for us. She would buy guitars for her friends a couple years later. Then she started doing studio sessions in Nashville, and her Taylor 512ce became like a lightning bolt for us. She started influencing everyone from engineers to producers. They all fell in love with the guitar's dynamics. Nanci picked that model because it was stable and behaved from climate to climate as she traveled. All these up-and-coming artists wanted to borrow Nanci's guitar.

We had all these Nashville people who would become big names all of a sudden calling us and wanting a Taylor. "Wow," we went, "this is everything we could have hoped for." Nanci started the ball rolling. Suzy Bogguss, Kathy Mattea, Clint Black were playing that smaller-bodied Taylor guitar and putting us on the map. Vince Gill bought six guitars for his friends one time. Nanci was a hell of a catalyst, so we thought, Why don't we make you a guitar? Let's make a guitar that defines you.

Terry Myers has worked at Taylor Guitars in El Cajon, California, for more than thirty years. The company designed Nanci Griffith's signature 512ce in the eighties.

NANCI GRIFFITH: I got two phone calls when I first came to Nashville. The first was from [iconic guitarist] Chet Atkins, who welcomed me and told me he had my earlier records. The second was from [the "dean of Nashville songwriters"] Harlan Howard asking if we could get together because he had my albums and admired my writing. [Harlan] said it had been a long time since Nashville had an honest female songwriter who wasn't afraid to write songs about controversial subjects. I felt very welcome. [Singer-songwriters and session players alike] would be vying to borrow my guitar whenever we would be in the studio.

I bought a regular 512 in New York, a beautiful guitar. I was endorsing [another brand] at the time, but I was unhappy with them. I just could not get them to stay consistent worldwide through different environmental changes. I eventually called Taylor and said I would really like to get another 512, but I would really like a sunburst finish. That little cutaway sunburst has been in every video and every photo shoot I have done since then. Suzy Bogguss and Kathy Mattea saw my Taylors when I started playing and liked them. They started playing Taylors. I have so many friends who have converted to them including Harlan Howard.[6]

MELANIE SMITH-HOWARD: Billy Joe Shaver wanted to get back to his wife, Brenda, in Texas and asked Harlan for four hundred dollars. Harlan gave it to him, and Billy Joe gave him an old Martin guitar [in exchange]. I told Harlan that I wanted to play the guitar, and he said, "You can play that Martin. It's too small for my hands." Well, Harlan gave it to Nanci one night after drinking. Nanci gave him a Nanci Griffith signature Taylor guitar in return. Harlan fell in love with [the guitar]. He marched down to the guitar store and picked up two more Taylors.

Nanci and Harlan met not long before I met him. He had heard Jim Rooney's records [on Nanci] and loved Nanci's writing. He wanted to meet her and called Rooney. They had lunch at Maude's Courtyard. Harlan got there early as he was known to do, and Nanci showed up by herself. Harlan thought for sure she would come with a manager and an entourage. Instead, she showed up wearing bobby socks and carrying a book. They became instant friends. They talked about their love of books, songwriting, and words. They both smoked and drank. They had a great time. "Hey," Harlan said to me one time. "We have to go over to my friend Nanci's house."

She was living close to Elliston Place. We went to her house, and I thought, Gosh, Harlan has such cute young friends. Nanci was one of the first people I met with Harlan. I got to know her and her music and could see why Harlan was drawn to her. Harlan was a lyricist first. He thought the melody was dictated by the words. He loved Nanci's writing style coupled with her voice and performance. He loved her storytelling. The love of words is what really got their friendship off to a good start.

I was over at Nanci's one night after Harlan was gone. "I know you thought this was gonna be your guitar," Nanci said about the Martin. "I would like to give it back to you." She was drinking. "Nanci," I said, "I'd rather you be sober when you tell me you want to give me the guitar." Never got the guitar. Never talked about it again.[7]

Melanie Smith-Howard is legendary songwriter Harlan Howard's widow. She runs Melanie Howard Music in Nashville today and is writing a book about Harlan.

SUZY BOGGUSS: I had two Martins stolen on the road. I reached out to Bob Taylor when I was just over having my M-38 stolen. He said, "I can make you one exactly like that." He did. I still play it. Bob built the neck to the specification to the other guitar. He's done two others with the same neck since then. One of my Taylors was run over by a van. They're so dependable. I'm loyal to them because they've been so good to me. "Oh my god," I said, "this gut string hurts my hand and gives me a backache because it only has fourteen frets." They said, "We can fix that. We'll put more frets on it."[8]

Suzy Bogguss's platinum-selling third album, Aces *(1991), featured hit singles including the title track and the Nanci Griffith and Tom Russell cowrite "Outbound Plane." She performed at the White House with Kathy Mattea and Alison Krauss in 1995.*

NANCI GRIFFITH: Taylors also have made a difference for me in the studio in that they're so consistent. All the guitarists I've worked with from Byrd Burton to Lee Satterfield have converted to Taylors because of that consistency and the sound. I flat pick and finger pick at the same time. Taylors are lovely to play for that. I need a guitar I can travel around the world with that will stay in tune. So many people have wanted this guitar over the years.[9]

BOB TAYLOR: Nanci taught me how to use the Mastercam and Fadal back in the day because I listened to her album *Storms* on loop several hours a night for weeks on end while I learned to draw, program, and machine guitar parts. The mention of her name or the sound of her voice always takes me back. She kept me focused on absorbing this CAD/CAM world that eventually helped me make her signature guitar. To make guitars that she played was unplanned but meant a lot to me. I'll miss her even though I never personally knew her.[10]

Bob Taylor founded Taylor Guitars after working at San Diego's "hippie guitar shop" American Dream in 1974. The company employs more than 1,200 people today.

TERRY MYERS: Nanci's became our first signature guitar. We wanted to salute Nanci for starting the windstorm with us, so we made one hundred. We had a few talks. Nanci wanted the sunburst top for an interesting reason that wasn't about aesthetics. "I use several guitars onstage with different tunings," she said. "It's really easy for me to pick up the wrong guitar." She literally wanted a sunburst so she could look back and go, "Yeah, there's the 'burst. It's tuned this way." Hers was the smallest body we made. We call it the grand concert. Her signature guitar was basically just a different version of the 512 she originally bought, but we put a sharp cutaway called the Florentine. She liked the sharp cutaway look. We used the same wood.

We figured out how to do the design and upgrades by talking with Nanci. We lasered her signature into the truss rod cover. Her 512 just had a plastic rosette, which is the trim around the sound hole, so we put an abalone rosette to upgrade her signature model. We wanted to give it a little more flair and pop. We put gold tuners on the signature, which is another upgrade. We also did tortoiseshell binding around the edge of the body. The signature guitars came with a signed label, a signed copy of her [*Flyer*] album, and certificate of authenticity. We really wanted to make the guitar for Nanci because of what she had done for us. Nanci's Taylor was her baby. She used the guitar all the way through.

PAT ALGER: Nanci obviously had more experience with [*The Last of the True Believers*], so she had more authority. I remember that album being fun. Players in Nashville usually labor over doing solos until they're 3-D perfect.

Sessions can be tedious because someone wants to get it perfect, but my favorite records aren't. The little slipup the bass player did makes the chorus work. Nanci's sessions were like that. Loose but tight. The songs on that record really stuck with me.

Nanci could be one of the boys very easily, which was very important. The fact that she could play guitar made her part of the band, which had a lot to do with how the record came out sounding. We played to her guitar. Of course, we had Philip Donnelly's unique sound on the record. Nobody sounded like Philip. Nobody played drums like Kenny Malone. Playing with Lloyd Green was a thrill. I got to meet Lyle Lovett when he was just a guy named Lyle. I wasn't assuming we were working on a gold record or that I would find a mystery check in the mail I could use to buy my wife a new Porsche. I had realistic expectations.

I had some interesting songs covered at that point, but I hadn't crossed over into any mainstream territory. Nanci said that MCA was interested. A lot of the guys were hired back for *Lone Star State of Mind*, so it was different but not wildly different. We were in a $225-an-hour studio instead of Cowboy's place, which is whatever the freight can handle. More businesslike. We were on the clock. Nanci and I were still friendly after that, but we lost touch. I did play gigs with her, though. I was usually in the band when she did television shows and videos. I even came down to Anderson Fair in Houston to play with her once.

We were a real congenial bunch. You could take *The Last of the True Believers* and *Once in a Very Blue Moon* and make a good set list. You could mix it up in all kinds of ways and it would still be a good, fast-moving show. No throwaway songs. Great songs. Then Nanci really took off. She was on the road all the time. So was I as the opening act for the Everly Brothers when they got back together. Nanci ended up joining that gig later on. We just weren't around. Life changed—for the better in a lot of ways—but I missed the pace of being in town and then not being in town. You make new friends when you get famous. She was doing European tours, and we weren't hanging out.

• • •

Griffith joins powerhouse MCA Records for her major label debut *Lone Star State of Mind* in 1987. Her singular take on Julie Gold's "From a Distance" alone makes her a star across the pond—especially in Ireland. Additionally, Griffith joins fellow Texans Rodney Crowell, Steve Earle, and Lyle Lovett in refocusing Music City's mainstream on singer-songwriters who chart their own songs. Earle tells anyone who will listen that modern country music is now entering into MCA executive Tony Brown's Great Credibility Scare era.

"Nanci was extremely important to the Great Credibility Scare, which came about when country music was at a low sales point," Peter Cooper says. "A company making no money can either double down on the little they have or take some chances. Tony Brown was willing to take chances." *Lone Star State of Mind* also contains the staples "Trouble in the Fields," "Ford Econoline," a rerecorded and alternatively titled "There's a Light beyond These Woods (Mary Margaret)," and the title track.

Griffith enlists many familiar players including Pat Alger, Philip Donnelly, Béla Fleck, Emory Gordy Jr., and Lloyd Green, but one notable exception doesn't make the cut for *Lone Star State of Mind*: MCA Records label mate Lyle Lovett. "We were cordial, but Nanci and I never were close again after [she and Eric Taylor divorced]," Lovett says. "I saw her occasionally because we shared business, but we didn't run into each other at the record company after Tony signed us to MCA. We never toured or did gigs together that probably would have happened if we were closer personally, but I never lost my appreciation for what she did for me early on."

Lone Star State of Mind affords Griffith a cover photo session with legendary Nashville photographer Jim "Señor" McGuire. "The first cover I shot for Nanci was the portrait for *Lone Star State of Mind*," McGuire says. "Nanci always had her own good ideas when she came in for photo sessions. She really thought about how she wanted to present herself and would bring her own props. I probably shot about six hundred fifty album covers during my career in Nashville, and the major labels almost always came with an art director, manager, or publicist who had ideas for what the cover should be. They always let Nanci do her thing. Guy Clark was one of the few others who was the same. Very refreshing."[11]

TONY BROWN: Guy Clark gave me the demos cassette that turned into Lyle Lovett's first album. Lyle was singing with Nanci Griffith on the demo. "Go see Nanci," Guy said. "I think you'll like her too." I went to a guitar pull where she was playing, and her charisma blew my mind. Then I went to see her with a full band at a showcase at the Cannery Ballroom here in Nashville. She was like Rodney Crowell and Vince Gill, who can sing with just their guitar. [Other MCA artists like] George Strait and Reba can't. I looked to the right and saw a guy in a real nice suit and Lucchese boots. "That's the guy Guy Clark told me about."

So, I discovered Lyle and Nanci at the same time.[12]

Tony Brown helped birth the Great Credibility Scare in country music by signing literate singer-songwriters and future hitmakers Steve Earle, Nanci Griffith, and Lyle Lovett to MCA Records in the mideighties.

JIM ROONEY: We felt [*The Last of the True Believers*] was really good in every way. Nanci was ambitious and clearly wanted to move up beyond being on Rounder Records. Well, I knew Tony Brown was under Jimmy Bowen at MCA Records, and Tony was interested in these new writers and singers. Tony was paying attention to artists who were not necessarily commercial country. I knew I would not be allowed to produce her if MCA made Nanci an offer because they're a closed shop, but there was potential for Nanci to get bigger with a major label. I ran into Jim Foglesong, who signed George Strait and Reba McEntire. Foglesong was a capable, nice, quiet person who was not a boaster. I ran into him at a party and said, "I want to take a meeting with you. I have an artist." "Sure," he said. "Can we set up a time?"

I played him "Once in a Very Blue Moon" and "Love at the Five and Dime" when we met. Foglesong was very straightforward with me. "These are fine," he said. "There's nothing wrong with them, but I don't think the current state of radio will take them. That's what I have to work with." I accepted that. Foglesong was at Capitol Records and was the only person who I thought would understand Nanci. So, Nanci did move on to MCA, and I wasn't allowed to go with her. [Letting go] was difficult, but you have to get over it.

We eventually got to work together again.

KEN LEVITAN: Tony Brown and I were friendly so I got him to fly up to Club Passim to see Nanci. He produced *Lone Star State of Mind* and *Little Love Affairs*.

RODNEY CROWELL: Tony Brown had a creative side for his MCA label for a while, which is how Lyle Lovett, Steve Earle, and Nanci came up. I was close friends with Tony. He made me aware of Nanci by signing her for her first MCA recordings. Tony became so successful producing mainstream country after he had been playing with Elvis Presley, Emmylou's band, and then my alt-country band the Cherry Bombs. He loved that music and eventually landed himself in a situation where he became a powerhouse with mainstream. He was inclined to sign artists like Steve and Nanci and myself later on when he landed that job.[13]

Eighties country radio star Rodney Crowell launched his creative renaissance with the seamless singer-songwriter albums The Houston Kid *(2001) and* Fate's Right Hand *(2003). His memoir,* Chinaberry Sidewalks, *tells his coming-of-age story.*

TONY BROWN: I joined MCA Records in 1984. My first Wynonna and George Strait records both sold six million copies. I had so many records that sold, but what defined my career to the critics was working with the Austin crowd: Steve Earle, Nanci Griffith, Lyle Lovett, and Kelly Willis.

RODNEY CROWELL: The Great Credibility Scare during that time would eventually become the property of indie labels. The corporate labels had to report to their shareholders and go for the fast buck. The Nanci Griffiths of the world are a long-term investment. Her music was a variation on a theme. She played alt, pop, country singer-songwriter, but it wasn't until I started touring that I started to realize that she had some real serious roots in folk music. My blinders came off when I discovered she really was a folkie [at heart]. I understood and loved that about her. She was seriously dedicated to the folk music mindset in the late fifties and early sixties.

Nanci was serious about songwriting. Third-person storytelling is a noble pursuit and the highest form of art when it's done right. I'm sure Joni Mitchell would question that, but you better know some truth about yourself if you do confessional storytelling. You better know some truth about what's out there to do the third-person narrative and make it resonate with people who understand that and recognize who can go there as an artist. Nanci also could be two fisted, which was a delightful thing to learn when we were touring. That girl was a tough boot.

Nanci brought a good, enlightening conversation. She was no dilettante. We who were influenced by Mickey Newbury, Guy Clark, and Townes Van Zandt are [going for] truth telling and achieving something akin to poetry with our songs. You want your songs to resonate with truths and not something vain like, "Hey, look at me. Ain't I great?" The job at hand is to make the narrative great, not the deliverer of the narrative. Nanci understood the Guy Clark school of "stand up straight and write your songs." He would bust you when your ego is like, "Look at me." Guy was about, "Look at the song." Nanci already possessed that knowledge when she came onto the scene and just slipped right on in.

TONY BROWN: I started noticing that there were different vibes at the sessions. Baseball players and golfers would be hanging around Vince Gill's sessions. People who worked in the cattle business would drive by during the George Strait sessions. Phil Everly and a whole different group would show up at Nanci's sessions. I felt a little more in sync with her people than I did with the mainstream ones. There was [something about] Nanci. I realized then that success in the record business isn't always measured in sales but in impact instead. Nanci made an impact. She had a serious career and would get invited to the king and queen's castle in England when George Strait wouldn't.

LYLE LOVETT: There was an overriding ethic in art in those days in the same way that performers wouldn't dare do a jingle for a commercial product because it would damage artistic credibility. That's how artists worked then. I remember being offered twenty-five thousand dollars to do a Burger King jingle when my first record came out in 1986, which was huge money. I had met David Wylde, who did a nice piece on us for *Rolling Stone* magazine, so I called him and said, "What do you think?" "Well," he said, "do you want to be known as the Burger King guy?" "Okay, good enough."

TONY BROWN: I was at MCA for twenty-five years. I started as the vice president of A&R and ended up as president. People were always saying, "You ran MCA." No, I didn't run MCA. Bowen was the CEO and a producer. He hired me to become a producer. Bruce Hinton was the president, the money guy. My title changed when I became president, but I was still an A&R guy. You start learning that you have the people who pay the bills. We had a serious roster with Wynonna, Trisha Yearwood, Vince Gill, George Strait, and Reba. Then you have the artists like Mark Chesnutt or Chely Wright who are called established but don't make or lose money. They give your label activity on the charts.

We also had artists like Joe Ely, Nanci, and Steve Earle. Steve's record *Guitar Town* took ten years to go gold. I don't think Nanci ever had a gold record at MCA. Lyle's first two went gold. We already had the artsy artists like Nanci, Mary Chapin Carpenter, and k.d. lang selling records when Lyle came out. We could never get traction with radio on Nanci, but the press loved her. I remember when Julie Gold sent Nanci a demo of "From a Distance." "Hey," Nanci said, "my friend Julie just sent this to me. She wants me to cut it. I think this song is amazing."

•   "From a Distance" (Julie Gold)   •

NANCI GRIFFITH: My friend Christine Lavin introduced me to this wonderful singer-songwriter in New York named Julie Gold one day. [Then] I got a package in the mail from Julie and a note [that said], "Can you listen to this song 'From a Distance'? I really think it's special, but it's been rejected by everybody." She couldn't even find a publisher. I said, "There's absolutely nothing wrong with this song. In fact, I'm in the studio recording right now. I'll call Tony Brown and have him listen to this song because I really want to record it." The rest is history.

KEN LEVITAN: I remember Julie Gold had sent "From a Distance" on a tape to my office. I gave it to Nanci, and she loved the song immediately. I did a deal with Julie for Nanci to [own] part of the publishing on the song.

JULIE GOLD: I was here in New York as a songwriter trying, trying, trying and pitching, pitching, pitching and performing whenever I was given the chance. I wrote "From a Distance" on the piano I grew up on right before my thirtieth birthday in December 1985. I pitched the song to anyone and everyone like I did with all my songs. Most songs went, "Rejection, rejection, rejection," but then my singer-songwriter friend Christine Lavin asked me to bring ten copies of "From a Distance" to a gig she had at the Speakeasy on MacDougal Street that night.

Christine sent "From a Distance" to Nanci Griffith. Nanci loved the song, which was the moment like when the match from *Mission: Impossible* got lit. "From a Distance" became unstoppable. Nanci started playing "From a Distance" all around the world and gave me songwriter credit whenever she played it. "Here's a song," she would say, "by my friend Julie Gold." She set fires of interest all over the world. Nanci would call me from Ireland. "Julie, I just sang your song in Belfast," she would say. "Catholics and Protestants cried and embraced in the aisles. You don't know what you've done here." Our friendship was sealed. She became the messenger for that song. Many other artists recorded that song because of her. All I ever wanted as a songwriter was to have a song be widely known, loved, and remembered.

My mother fled Russia with her family for freedom in 1930 and taught my brother and me about compassion, freedom, love, and America. For this song written by the granddaughter of an orthodox rabbi who fled oppression in Moscow to be sung as a unifying message in a club in Belfast was a magnificent dream. You know, the music business is a really cruel, terrible business. There are many cruel, terrible people. That Nanci included me in all the happiness [is amazing]. I'm dumbfounded. Nanci tried so hard to make "From a Distance" a hit. She did the original "From a Distance," a live version, a symphonic version, then a multilingual version with Raul Malo and Donna Summer [on the 1996 Olympics album *One Voice*].

Nanci recording "From a Distance" would have been the pride of my life and the greatest feather in my cap imaginable if that's all that happened, but it would not have freed me financially. Bette Midler recording it was a whole different story. The song was a radio hit back when there was no downloading, Spotify, Rhapsody, none of these things that rob songwriter income. A hit song still could be a life-changing event then. "From a Distance" was my game changer.[14]

New York City–based songwriter Julie Gold's "From a Distance" won the Song of the Year Grammy for Bette Midler in 1991. Nanci Griffith first recorded the song on her album Lone Star State of Mind *in 1987. She performed it around the globe for years.*

MAC MCANALLY: I will always remember singing on "From a Distance." That song killed me from the first time I heard it. Nanci knew the song was fabulous and the real deal. I remember putting the vocals on and literally playing it over and over and over in the studio. We ran out into the parking lot and grabbed anyone we could and said, "You gotta listen to this." I've been playing on records a long time, and I've been blessed ten or fifteen times where a song took over half the day like that. We spent the other half talking about how blessed we are to do this.

The title "From a Distance" is awesome because it's a two-edged sword. There's a little sting in "god is watching us from a distance." She's not just saying, "God is great, god is good. Say the prayer. Thank him for our food." She was saying there's some distance between us and the good and bad happening in the world. You didn't hear that in songs. What's so wonderful is that the song says, "There are all kinds of blessings that you've miscounted or didn't notice if you back up from your own troubles." There was a commercial aspect in Nanci's version and Bette Midler's obviously as well. The song was great for them both.

BOBBY NELSON: Nanci could be really snippy at people, like she was about Bette Midler for getting the hit with "From a Distance." Nanci doing that song was such a big hit in Ireland, so Bette doing it pissed Nanci off—and she could really be pissed off. I forget what the occasion was the next time she came to Austin, but she had a road manager with her at all times. She went to a radio show to do an interview with him along. Well, you didn't bring your managers to the radio shows here in Austin. We were much more laid back. People would think, Who does she think she is? Nanci was such a big hit over in England and Ireland like she never was here.

KEN LEVITAN: [Nanci's popularity in] Ireland came about because [she performed "From a Distance"] on a television show called *The Sessions* done by David Heffernan.

JOHN T. DAVIS: Nanci talked about moving to Ireland and becoming a librarian. I could never tell if she was joking. She would get disenchanted with the music business and say, "Screw it. I'm moving to Dublin to work in a library." The Irish love their poets and writers and the literary tradition, which existed long before James Joyce. The Irish responded to Nanci very powerfully because of that literary tradition.

KEN LEVITAN: The Heffernans fell in love with Nanci, and she exploded in Ireland. Then [her popularity] continued over to England around 1987. Julie had never had a cut before, and Nanci did a publisher's job, which is partly to exploit a song. I thought it would be a good move for her. Nanci was very ambitious early in her career and wrote a lot. We toured her all around the world with fantastic bands. Those guys mostly stayed with her through the years.

• • •

PAT ALGER: I had the idea for "Lone Star State of Mind" when I was living in New York because Billy Joel had this big hit with "New York State of Mind." I was like, "Nobody calls it the New York State." It's the Empire State. I casually mentioned one day that I would call a song "Lone Star State of Mind," not "Texas State of Mind," if I would write it. I thought that sounded pretty good, but I had never been to Texas when I wrote the song. I called my friend Richard Dobson, who was in Houston, and said, "You've been to Corpus Christi, right?" He said, "Yeah." "That's on the coast, isn't it?" I wasn't sure. I somehow captured the flavor of the area writing the song with Fred Koller. We got lucky.

[Having Nanci's title track cuts on] *Once in a Very Blue Moon* and *Lone Star State of Mind* helped my confidence, which is really important. "Goin' Gone," which I wrote about the same woman as "Once in a Very Blue Moon," is as close to a campfire song as I can imagine writing. Fred Koller came up with the idea for the lighthouse. I pictured this lighthouse in Cape Neddick, Maine. The woman who wrote me the letter was from York, Maine, which is right down the road. I wrote about the lighthouse she claimed was hers. I took a photograph of the Cape Neddick lighthouse myself. Nanci did a great version of "Goin' Gone."

FRED KOLLER: Pat Alger and I did a simple demo for our song "Goin' Gone." I was taking "Goin' Gone" around to publishers, who were saying it was a folk song, which was the last thing they were looking for at the time. Pat said, "I know a folksinger from Texas who just recorded one of my songs." Pat had been messing around with the chorus with a man named Bill Dale by the time he brought the song to me. The nautical imagery was from my mind. We wrote it in an afternoon and then did "Lone Star State of Mind" a week later.

LUCY KAPLANSKY: [MCA Records] flew me to Nashville and paid me the most money I had ever made [to sing on *Lone Star State of Mind*] when I was twenty-six. Nanci, Tony Brown, Mac McAnally, and I were in the studio for two days with the engineer [Steve Tillisch]. This was the first time I had ever sung with Nanci, which was so incredibly exciting and thrilling. I was being paid major label money and singing on an album by someone famous. Nanci hired me because she had come by the studio and heard me sing when I was on John Gorka's first record [1987's *I Know*] in Nashville. The way she sang and wrote for her singing was so perfect, and those songs were simpatico with my singing. Nanci said, "You do Nanci Griffith better than I do Nanci Griffith."

Tony said he liked my singing on the *Lone Star State of Mind* sessions and would recommend me to Reba McEntire. Reba was looking for new people, but I never heard from her. I don't remember Tony and Nanci telling me much as far as how to sing on *Lone Star State of Mind*. I just did my thing, and they just liked it. The process wasn't painstaking because Nanci and Jim Rooney most definitely liked people to be themselves. That was the whole Rooney thing. We just played. I showed up after the instruments were played and [sang harmonies]. I don't mind being produced, but I also like when people trust my instincts like they did.[15]

Lucy Kaplansky sang harmonies on Shawn Colvin's Grammy-winning album Steady On *and Nanci Griffith's* Lone Star State of Mind *and* Little Love Affairs.

• "Trouble in the Fields" (Nanci Griffith) •

MAURA KENNEDY: Of course, Nanci loved Woody Guthrie because she was connected with the Dust Bowl era with her family coming from Wales and settling in West Texas. I think "Trouble in the Fields" is like a minimovie. You hear it and see the song in your mind in sepia tone. She nailed that song. I love the part in that song where she sings, "You be the mule / I'll be the plow." The melody is the same three times, but there's a different chord under each one so the quality of that melody in relation to the chord changes. I think that's genius.

Her melodies arc with the emotion in the song.[16]

Maura Kennedy toured with Nanci Griffith behind her Grammy-winning album Other Voices, Other Rooms *and played a key role in Griffith's later years in music.*

NANCI GRIFFITH: Most of my mother's family came from way out in West Texas in a little town called Lockney, which is somewhere close to Lubbock but not too close to Lubbock. Nobody likes to be too close to Lubbock. I have five great-uncles who were all farmers during the Great Depression. Four sold off their family farms and bought liquor stores and dry-cleaning businesses after the Depression. [They were] getting ready for the oil boom. My great-uncle Tootie never sold his farm. He pushed a plow for almost eighty years. ["Trouble in the Fields"] is a tune I wrote for him and my great-aunt Nettie May.

My great-aunt Nettie May said surviving the Great Depression on a farm was not easy. She understands why the young farmers nowadays are having such a hard time because she went through it herself. The dust blew through so hard during the Great Depression that she was afraid to go to sleep at night because she was afraid the dust would blow so hard one night that she would wake up one morning and find herself living in Oklahoma. She, by god, didn't want to live in Oklahoma.[17]

LAURIE MACALLISTER: The "Trouble in the Fields" melody is brilliant. Nanci isn't giving you a three- or four-note range. She's way up there right at the start. "Baby, I know we've got trouble in the fields." Then she comes down. "When the bankers swarm like locusts turning away our yields." She was a master. The human ear wants that variety. Her songs are extremely catchy. I probably have heard "Trouble in the Fields" a hundred times. The chorus is something different and more challenging than you would expect. Think about starting out the songs with those lyrics. Incredible. "Baby, I know we've got trouble in the fields / When the bankers swarm like locusts turning away our yields."

So delicious for a person who loves words.[18]

Red Molly's Laurie MacAllister has released solo albums outside her group, including These Old Clothes *(1999),* Things I Choose to Do *(2002), and* The Lies the Poets Tell *(2018). She frequently covers Nanci Griffith's "Gulf Coast Highway."*

• • •

TONY BROWN: I started looking at the record business as a whole different deal after working with artists like Nanci Griffith and Garth Brooks. You've got to cut stuff that makes the company money with mainstream music, but you can do both. I'm proud of records I did with Reba, but you can also make records that really cool, hip people and critics are gonna love. You can keep them on the label as long as you don't lose money. You know, I signed Joe Ely and made a record called *Love and Danger*, but [MCA executive] Bruce Hinton told me I had to drop Joe because we were in the red.

I dropped him. Then the entire building came to my office and said, "You have to undrop him." I called business affairs and said, "Can you undrop an act?" It took a while for Steve Earle to catch on. Nanci had more fans than Steve back then. They finally caught on around [Earle's second album] *Exit 0* [in 1987]. We started having lots of attention from the press when Nanci put out *Lone Star State of Mind*. The first session for that record was a big deal. That was like the Peter principle where you rise to the level of your incompetence. Bowen was great. "Hey, T," he said. "You don't get in the way when an artist knows what they want. You just have to produce with an artist who's green and doesn't know what they want."

I knew right off the bat that Nanci knew exactly what she wanted to do. She hired this player Philip Donnelly from the UK who was a big part of that record. I learned a lot from Nanci because of that. One player made that record sound different from anybody else. Nobody in town knew who he was.

He wasn't for everybody, but "Ford Econoline" and "Trouble in the Fields" were interesting songs. Nanci definitely made social statements. Most songs weren't like the country norm. Faith Hill wouldn't cut those songs. Nanci was a teaching moment for me.

Her first week when a record would come out was big because the press would build it up. Her hardcore fans would go out and buy it, but it would disappear off the radar if there wasn't a hit. I told somebody that the only way you can enjoy being in the music business is if you're idealistic, but the only way you can stay in it is to be realistic. Otherwise, you won't have a job. Nobody quite knew Nanci. I didn't. I was just around her for the sessions. She wasn't one to call you and say, "Hey, let's go have a beer or dinner tonight." I felt like I would be disturbing her if I called her after the session. You knew she was a very intelligent person.

Intelligence is very intimidating in this world. Look at pictures of her. She's like Alison Krauss. Alison's not a babe, but she's so beautiful on her album covers. Nanci's drop-dead gorgeous on her album cover for *Lone Star State of Mind*. The way she carried herself and dressed made her seem unapproachable, but she was sweet as could be if you did approach her. Reba would run at you if you walked into the room, "Hi. I'm Reba McEntire." Nanci was not that person. She would say hello when I walked in the room. Then we would spend six weeks making a record.

Our conversations usually weren't about business. We usually talked about politics. She was a different animal. I think me signing Nanci, Steve, and Lyle might not have worked back in those days, but I think it opened the door for Americana to become a genre. It was a big deal when they made Americana a Grammy genre you could vote for. People would argue about people like Nanci. "Come on, man. She gets more press than someone who has sold ten thousand copies." John Prine was a part of that world Nanci ran in. Nanci, Steve, John Prine, and Lyle were a big beginning of what became Americana, which now seems to be the minor league of country.

Nanci's songs were so good. There was no doubt that she wrote great songs. I just didn't realize how hard a deal it would be to make [her famous]. I thought Steve Earle was the next Waylon Jennings, but the press said he was the next Mellencamp or Springsteen. Now I realize that Steve was jumping on top of all that small-town shit they were doing. I don't think Nanci really copied anybody's narrative. She had her own going on. She really stands out in my career. I consider her one of the greatest artists that I worked with. She was all about the songs. People who have never heard about her never talk about her voice when I play Nanci for them.

They talk about the songs.

JIM ROONEY: Tony did a good job shifting [Nashville's focus]. I like and respect him. Tony played piano on all those House of Cash demos I was doing back at Jack's, so I had known him that way. He was very complimentary to me. "Boy," he said, "I think those records you did with Nanci are really good." He took lots of the same players with her to MCA and didn't try to change her sound. I just don't think MCA's marketing had much clue what to do with her.

JULIE GOLD: Nanci's management called me and asked if I would go with her when she started to promote "From a Distance." They just wanted me to accompany her on the song. Nanci was a guitar player, so she needed piano accompaniment. I was thirty-two years old by then and had dreamed of playing these hallowed halls and touring, but I had never experienced it. I was still a secretary at HBO so I took a week off and went in a recreational vehicle for five shows with Nanci and her band.

The opening band was the New Grass Revival with Béla Fleck. Incredible journey. I liken my times with Nanci to being in the circus. I got to be completely privy to that life. We started at the Bottom Line in New York City and then drove through the night to play the Lisner Auditorium in the Washington, DC, area. I remember it like it was yesterday. We drove right back up the New Jersey Turnpike and played Connecticut. Then we played in Boston and Northampton, Massachusetts. We said goodbye after, and Nanci flew back. We took the bus back.

Nanci never went up [vocally] on a lyric or a chord. She never had to start a song over. She was professional, the band was slick, and she gave the audience what they wanted. I would sit out in the audience all those nights and study her. I knew what song was right before "From a Distance," so I would come backstage then and would see her from that angle. She would give me exquisite introductions. Then I would usually walk out to find a seven-foot black Baldwin or Steinway piano. I could easily cry telling this from missing her and knowing it will never happen again.

• • •

Griffith doubles down on momentum from *Lone Star State of Mind* with *Little Love Affairs* in 1988. The second and last studio album Tony Brown coproduces with Griffith yields another country hit when Suzy Bogguss covers Griffith's cowrite with Tom Russell ("Outbound Plane") and offers her own finest ("Gulf Coast Highway"). The album reaches number twenty-seven on the country charts. "The song Nanci and I wrote called 'Outbound Plane' was a major gold record for Suzy Bogguss," Russell says. "We wrote the song when I was visiting Nanci at her apartment in Nashville."

Little Love Affairs—featuring other highlights such as "Anyone Can Be Somebody's Fool," "Love Wore a Halo (Back before the War)," "So Long Ago," and "I Wish It Would Rain"—earns rave reviews. "Our second album was *Little Love Affairs*," Brown says. "Those were days when *Rolling Stone* magazine was more like *Rolling Stone* than it is today. They would have the latest releases in the back ranked from one to five stars. *Little Love Affairs* was the number one five-star album in *Rolling Stone* when it came out. That was money to me. Big deal."

TONY BROWN: I learned not to make Nanci more mainstream. *Little Love Affairs* had a really good and commercial single called "I Knew Love." A few stations played it, and Bowen had me bring in one of the big program directors. "Bring him to the session after you've mixed it," he said. "Then play him the album. Play it in the control room and make him feel like no one else gets this opportunity but him." The guy sat there listening and said, "Man, this is really good. I have to admit something. I have never listened to a Nanci Griffith album until now. Thanks for inviting me."

JAMES HOOKER: Tony Brown didn't get in our hair when he was producing *Little Love Affairs*. He was a stand-off, hands-on guy who wasn't in there for every knob twiddle. Many producers are there from the first note to the last and don't leave the board. Tony stepped back, left us alone, and let us do what we wanted to do.

James Hooker served as Nanci Griffith's keyboard player and band leader for twenty years. He and Griffith cowrote several songs including "Gulf Coast Highway." Hooker previously played with the Amazing Rhythm Aces and Steve Winwood.

SUZY BOGGUSS: Nanci was a great mentor. Her song "Outbound Plane" from *Little Love Affairs* felt incredibly great. I was compelled to sing "Outbound Plane" on [Bogguss's best-selling 1991 album] *Aces* and cut the song at Emerald Studios in Nashville. Jimmy Bowen was the label head and was trying to be progressive, but he was trying to make me into a Reba clone. I had always been a guitar player and singer-songwriter, and we weren't gelling. I had a big fight with him. "That's not who I am. You keep talking down to me about being a folk artist, but you had Cheryl Wheeler and Nanci Griffith. Why can you not understand that this is who I am?"

It finally dawned on him, and I ended up on both Cheryl's song "Aces" and Nanci's "Outbound Plane." It was awesome once we clicked. I later brought

Cheryl and Nanci on to do [The Nashville Network's show] *American Music Shop*. The reason I wanted to do it was Nanci's generosity. She started all that by being Harlan Howard's protégé. Her vibe was being a generous, gracious artist who wanted to share the stage and the music. She came from folk music where it wasn't about making money or becoming a big star. Her thing was how many people we could reach with a good message. Nanci would put both happy and sad in songs like "Outbound Plane." It sounds so upbeat, like "Okay, let's get on," but . . . "We're breaking up, by the way. You go your way, and I'll go mine."

TOM RUSSELL: Nanci came into the kitchen one morning with a rough set of lyrics and said, "See what you can do with this." I scratched around for a while and added ideas here and there—especially on the chorus for "Outbound Plane." She gave my ideas the stamp of approval. We signed the deal right there ten minutes after finishing the song. She went for an idea that had a good chorus hook, then put her own personality and life experiences into the verses. Nanci had a poetic base, a delicate sense for the word, metaphor, and rhyme. She had what Joni Mitchell has in that sense—that ability to describe landscape and emotion in a way that doesn't sound too academic. Words float. Choruses ring. Nanci was a Texan.

SUZY BOGGUSS: I'm getting ready to play "Outbound Plane" at a Merle Haggard tribute at the Opry in a week because he loved that song. I found this out when I was doing a fair with him before *Aces* came out. Merle came up to me when I was singing "Outbound Plane" during sound check and goes, "Where did you get that song?" "Merle," I said, "please don't take it. The song's not out yet." He loved that song so much. He went on and on about it. I said, "It's a Nanci Griffith song." "Oh," he said, "I totally understand. She's really something."

I initially found "Outbound Plane" when I bought *Little Love Affairs*. I would clean the house to that song because I had just gotten married and everything was new and I wanted to keep the house really nice. "Outbound Plane" would get me moving really fast. I would spin through the house and get stuff done. Then I was getting ready to record my third record for Capitol and I thought, I'm just gonna call Nanci and ask if it's okay to cover this. She said, "Hell yes. You can cut all my songs if you want to." I really believed in that song and that album. I loved her stories and the intelligence in her poetry. I've always admired her metaphors and descriptions. They're classic and not flowery. You get the picture of what she's talking about in "Gulf Coast Highway," "I Wish It Would Rain," and "Outbound Plane." She didn't make things hard to understand. Her lyrics were perfect [for the] common man.

MELANIE SMITH-HOWARD: Nanci included Harlan's song "Never Mind" on *Little Love Affairs*. In fact, she included several songs Harlan wrote or they cowrote on her albums over the years. "Nanci really didn't have to do that," he would say. "She's a great writer herself." Music Row is a brotherhood and sisterhood. Harlan wanted to make sure that songwriting was a proud profession. Most people think the artists wrote their songs. Music Row was such a microcosm of just a couple streets. There are five watering holes where everyone would congregate. There were shared friendships and interests. You knew that Harlan Howard loved Nanci Griffith if you were on Music Row. Nanci made everyone shine like diamonds, which made us want the same for her. She made masterpieces. Harlan would study Nanci. He liked finding out what she did and how she did it and when and why she did.

LLOYD GREEN: Nanci's [cover of "Never Mind"] was used on the soundtrack to John Grisham's movie *The Firm*. There wasn't any designated player on [*Little Love Affairs*]. I happened to be designated session leader on the song, so I got paid double. I probably made fifty thousand dollars by accidentally being leader on that session.

• "Gulf Coast Highway" (Nanci Griffith, Danny Flowers, James Hooker) •

Bruce Springsteen performs "Gulf Coast Highway" during sound check for his show on June 25, 1988, at London's Wembley Stadium. Springsteen doesn't play the song in concert during that tour supporting his *Tunnel of Love* album, but he records the song with his wife, Patti Scialfa, for her solo album the next year. Their recorded version still has not been released. "This next song is a tune that Bruce Springsteen and Patti Scialfa just recorded," a proud Nanci Griffith says, introducing "Gulf Coast Highway" at her show on May 26, 1989, in Dallas. "It's a song that they're doing as a duet."[19]

Griffith cowrites "Gulf Coast Highway" with bandleader James Hooker and guitarist Danny Flowers as a Mac McAnally duet on *Little Love Affairs*. "I was noodling around one day and wrote the instrumental that would become 'Gulf Coast Highway,'" Hooker remembers. "I had inherited a boatload of keyboards for free when I left Steve Winwood which were leftovers from tours. I hooked them all up and wrote some instrumental songs. I played a couple of these one night on the tour bus with Nanci, who was sitting up in the front lounge. She wanted to hear a couple but then jumped up when I started playing this one and ran out of the lounge."

JAMES HOOKER: Well, I thought, this must really suck, but she had gone back to her room to grab a pencil and notepad. She started jotting down [ideas]. We set up a writing date a week or two later. She and Danny Flowers came over to the house. "Gulf Coast Highway" was a classic Nashville "word for a third." Danny came up with the line "She walked through springtime," which is how he got writing credit. Nanci wrote [all] the [other] lyrics, and I wrote the music. The chorus just worked out right as a minor six to the one [chord]. I don't know why. You get these little chills when the muse hits you because you don't know where it came from. You think, I didn't write that. Somebody else gave me this idea. I don't see them in the room, but they did. That's your muse. It's freaky.

The muse has freaked me out more than once.

MAC MCANALLY: Lucy Kaplansky and I were the regular background singers for Nanci for a while. I remember Lucy and I had sung on all the songs we had to do the day we [recorded] "Gulf Coast Highway." Danny Flowers had written the song with Nanci and James Hooker, but he was on the road with Don Williams. Nanci and Tony Brown were in the studio and said, "Do you want to take a whack at this one?" Well, Danny had done something unusual on the demo for "Gulf Coast Highway." He sang the harmony as the melody in the duet in the second verse. I loved that demo, so I did the same thing Danny did in their work tape. I'm a natural baritone, which meant I had to sing higher than god had intended.

Something felt special from the first time I sang it. Singing high put my voice in a more emotional place. People teared up. The two-part harmony in the last line just came out. "Oh, my goodness," everybody said. "That's special." People usually tolerate my singing because I'm a decent songwriter and guitar player, so I felt almost my full driver's license height that night because people were bragging on me as a singer. I still feel that it was a special thing when I hear the record now. "Gulf Coast Highway" was a particularly wonderful song written by some particularly fine people which caught me on a particularly good day.

AMY GRANT: The [original] version of "Gulf Coast Highway" with Mac McAnally rips your heart out every time. I worked with Mac a few years ago. A conversation with Mac is like you stepped into a radio show with a southern Garrison Keillor. Every piece of conversation seems like effortless storytelling with him. I love invested and conscious conversation like Mac's. I would say his pendulum swings much wider than Nanci's, but they have a similar lyrical approach in that it's all in the details. Their songs don't just have two people in a room. You see all the furniture in the room and the view out the window.[20]

Sacred and secular music star Amy Grant has sold more than thirty million records and won six Grammy awards, with more than a dozen other nominations.

NANCI GRIFFITH: ["Gulf Coast Highway"] is the first song James Hooker and I ever wrote together. It just goes to show that you can put your mind anywhere you want your mind to be. We wrote the song riding along a Pennsylvania highway thinking about James's wife, Connie, back in Alabama and the baby they had on the way, and thinking about springtime in South Texas.[21]

LLOYD GREEN: Listen to "Gulf Coast Highway." I love that song. Nanci described the bluebonnets so vividly. I remember playing Dobro during the "Gulf Coast Highway" session. "Hey," I said to Nanci, "how about I approach it this way? That's such an emotional song. Let's have the Dobro come in and disappear." "You know," she said, "you're not a steel player. You're an artist."

• • •

PETER COOPER: I was a high schooler living in the Washington, DC, area when Nanci was playing the Birchmere often. I remember reading a review of her *Little Love Affairs* album in the *Washington Post*. The review quoted her lyrics, "I remember waving back at you from a silted windowpane" [from "So Long Ago"]. I thought, That is a different level of poetic country music. She was coming to the Birchmere shortly thereafter. The Birchmere show tickets were general admission, and my habit during those days was to go early [to shows]. The doors opened two hours before the show, so I got there four hours before the show so I could be at the front of the line. I remember you could hear sound check even from outside.

She was playing "Listen to the Radio" with her band. I thought, This is something else. Nanci's voice had such power. Then I saw she had such charisma when I did get in there to see the show. I knew I was in the presence of something very special. Of course, she was beautiful. I had a crush on her instantly. I remember her eyes searching the room to make sure everyone there knew she was paying attention and not going through the motions. She would set those eyes on you, which was magnetic when you're a high school student who had showed up four hours early. Nanci was playing guitar at such a high level.

Eric Taylor [must have taught] her some. Eric was one of the greatest songwriters. I don't mean Texas songwriters. I mean one of the greatest songwriters who wrote in the English language. He was a tremendous influence on so many [songwriters]. Eric was irascible and difficult, but a truer friend you'll never find. There's no way Nanci or Lyle exists without Eric. A constant irritation to me—it hurts my heart—is when people write about the Texas folk songwriting tradition and mention Townes and Guy but don't mention Eric. You would never meet a stronger personality. He was so giving of his musical knowledge [to her and others]. There's no way to overstate his influence, although it's so often understated.

Listen to Eric's song "Dollar Matinee," which Nanci recorded on her first album. The song is so rich in imagery. Then there's Eric's song "Deadwood," which Nanci retitled "Deadwood, South Dakota," to Eric's eternal aggravation. You got the story of American racism in the way that's never been told. Nanci deserves a lot of credit for releasing that song on a major label, MCA Records, on the live at Anderson Fair album *One Fair Summer Evening*. Nanci could be incredibly gracious.

• • •

Nanci Griffith brings heart back home for her first live record. *One Fair Summer Evening*—featuring a dozen songs recorded at Anderson Fair including "Once in a Very Blue Moon," "From a Distance," Eric Taylor's "Deadwood, South Dakota," and "Spin on a Red Brick Floor"—captures a soaring set recorded in late summer 1988. "I had sung with Nanci for about ten or twelve years before she moved to Nashville," Denice Franke says. "Then Nanci was doing the *One Fair Summer Evening* record at Anderson Fair when I got back from Asia and she asked if my singing partner Doug Hudson and I would sing on the album."

Griffith returns a hero overseas.

"[Griffith] can slip into Bert's Bar-B-Q near the University of Texas for a brisket fix," John T. Davis wrote in the *Austin American-Statesman*, "[but] she has metamorphosed into a major star in Great Britain, Ireland, and Europe. A tour used to mean a weekend away from home to play in Dallas or College Station. Now, it is a commitment that can devour a year." *One Fair Summer Evening* showcases a mix-and-match band—James Hooker on keyboards, Denny Bixby on bass, and Franke, Hudson, and Eric Taylor on harmony vocals—and serves as the fulcrum between her four studio albums on MCA Records. She employs new producers for the following two collections.

TONY BROWN: The last album I did on Nanci was *One Fair Summer Evening*. They moved Nanci to the Los Angeles division because Nashville wasn't getting her attention. The publicity person Susan Levy was getting all the attention from *Rolling Stone* and *Village Voice*. I brought Susan to Nashville to work for me for fifteen years just because of Nanci. Nanci played a big part in my career. She didn't buy my house like George and Reba did, but she gave me credibility. People thought I had big balls. Someone said when I signed her, "Who's gonna play that?" "Somebody will."

JOHN LOMAX III: I really started beating the drums about Nanci when *One Fair Summer Evening* came out. What a remarkable live record.

Longtime journalist, artist manager, and music distributor John Lomax III has worked closely with Townes Van Zandt, Steve Earle, and Kasey Chambers. He is the son of John Lomax Jr. and grandson of John Lomax Sr., both renowned folklorists.

JAMES HOOKER: I remember that the dressing room was right off the stage at Anderson Fair [the night we recorded *One Fair Summer Evening*]. Pat McInerney called me in January 1987. I was living in Nashville and had just left Steve Winwood after we did the *Back in the High Life* tour. Pat said Nanci was putting together a band. Pat and I had toured with Don Williams. I liked Nanci's music before I even knew her. I was driving down the interstate years before when I heard "There's a Light beyond These Woods" on AM radio. I fell in love with the song even though they didn't say who wrote the song before or after it played. She was a damn good songwriter who wrote these simple little stories. Her vignettes drew you in for three minutes and you went, "Wow. I'm glad I heard this."[22]

AMY GRANT: I toured a great deal during the years [around *One Fair Summer Evening*'s release] and discovered Nanci Griffith through the nanny we hired when my son Matt was born. People typically hire touring coaches so you can sleep on the bus at night and wake up in the next town, but we actually traveled during the day for the first ten years touring. We would finish the gig, go to the hotel, sleep, then travel the next day. Our nanny Phyllis would bring Nanci Griffith cassettes so we would travel down the road listening to her. Nanci's music is driving music to me. She was our go-to music for two years with songs like "Love at the Five and Dime" and "Ford Econoline."

Her songs are so palpable and remind me of the October reds driving through New England and sitting around in the company of people I loved surrounded by her musical storytelling. Her voice is so familiar to me because we listened to [*One Fair Summer Evening*] so much. Nanci was such a story-teller. Music like hers that provides companionship during times in your life always stays precious to you. I got her records through the years, but there's [something about] that captive audience of being in a bus for at least three or five hours. We travel at night now, and I miss those days when we were stuck in a comfortable chair with the ever-changing landscape of the open road and how much dedicated time we had listening to music.

Nanci painted great pictures of love, the Dust Bowl, and the common man struggling. Everything was a picture. Maybe I was so drawn to Nanci's work because [her songwriting] was so different than what I did. I still play her songs because she has a definitive sound and style, and her songwriting is so vivid and full of details. She will always be a conversational reference when I'm talking about writing songs. You know, my daughter is a songwriter. It had not occurred to me until now to say, "Check out this artist," but I'm gonna text her right now. She's twenty years old and just getting started, but she also puts lots of good furniture in the room when she's writing. I'm gonna text her right now: "Check out Nanci Griffith."

DENICE FRANKE: Singing on *One Fair Summer Evening* was like being home. Anderson Fair is one of the home base venues for songwriters, like the Cactus Cafe was in Austin. Then we went out on tour with Nanci to sing background vocals on the tour with her. Incredible. We were playing before audiences where you could hear a pin drop. We had a great year for performing and people coming into our lives. We got to pal around with John Prine. We met Mary Black in Dublin. Her voice really spoke to me in her band De Dannan, which sang all in Gaelic. I became friends with the great guitar player Philip Donnelly.

There weren't women writers out there writing about topics people generally didn't want to talk about. Eric Taylor and Nanci Griffith both had the courage to write about those characters and talk about those subjects. They might get flak from the press, but they're speaking their truths and how they saw them. Writing the truth is one of the greatest qualities in a writer. Eric and Nanci had the courage to write those songs and stand behind them. The press [treated her badly]. Nanci didn't stand down if she believed in something, and they called her a difficult bitch. It wasn't in her nature to be silent if something really bothered her.

It isn't comfortable when you're reading an article and see [a writer] put down someone you care about. Nanci didn't tolerate that. John T. Davis understood her, but the other Austin writers did not. I got the feeling they didn't understand her or how much she had to fight and work and pick herself up when people were hard on her when she was trying to do her art. I commend her courage for speaking out when criticized. My tendency is to shut up. Nanci made a point when she was trying to enlighten me. I was young and didn't know anything about the business. I understood what she was saying [in an email to Bobby Nelson criticizing Texas]. "I love the Cactus and Griff, but there's nothing in Texas for me."

GRIFF LUNEBURG: [Nanci] would tell other artists about this little club in Austin [when she was touring]. I started getting calls. She was such a great ambassador for Austin and the Cactus. She really put the Cactus on the map because she was the queen of Austin folk music at the time.[23]

Griff Luneburg booked the iconic Cactus Cafe (Townes Van Zandt's "home club") at the University of Texas at Austin for more than a quarter century starting in 1983.

BOBBY NELSON: There are about three places in Texas where people can come hear the song without chicken-fried steak going by or brothers in a corner throwing a bunch of drinks back. The band is basically a jukebox in Texas. Then you go to California or New England and experience people who welcome you. They invite you in and appreciate you. Then it's a slap in the face when you come back to Texas, except those three venues where people listen. People are so hungry to hear your music in places like California and New England—even more so in Europe—and they appreciate you. They were so eager to hear anything you played and said and wanted to hear more. "Somebody pinch me. Is this real?"

ROBERT EARL KEEN: I opened for Nanci for eighteen days in Ireland in spring 1988. We went all over the country to some backwoods country places and dance halls and some beautiful theaters. We played this beautiful theater in Galway. I only played for twenty minutes during those shows, and as far as I know people hated me, but Nanci was always cool and never told me what I needed to play. The drummer from U2 [Larry Mullen Jr.] came to a show one time. Everyone was excited, but I didn't know who U2 was. Nanci mostly loved to talk about all that Bob Dylan lore and Joan Baez stuff. She truly was like one of those Greenwich Village people.

JULIE GOLD: Nanci's manager called me again when she was playing Carnegie Hall with John Prine on June 16, 1988. She wanted me to accompany her on "From a Distance" like I had on that weeklong tour. My whole family rented a van and my brother drove everybody up to watch me at Carnegie Hall. Carnegie Hall is the biggest imaginable, with food, hotels, and transportation. Everything. Nanci gave me that gift. I played a song I had just written called "Heaven" at sound check that night while Nanci was milling around onstage. "What's that?" "That's a brand-new song called 'Heaven.'" She said, "I'm gonna record that for my next record." She did.

LUCY KAPLANSKY: I also sang with Nanci at Carnegie Hall the night she opened for John Prine. She started singing "Listen to the Radio," which I had never heard. I panicked but had the idea by the second chorus. Who needs to rehearse? She would pick people who didn't have to. Guy Clark sat in that night at Carnegie Hall. He [was walking] offstage and Nanci asked me, "How does it feel to have just sung with the great, legendary Guy Clark?" I don't know where this came from in me, but I said in a very dry way, "Frankly, I'm devastated." The place totally broke up. I remember being backstage with John Prine and Nanci that night. She was always kind to me backstage.

Not rehearsing before playing Carnegie Hall takes real moxie.

• • •

Rock royalty Glyn Johns—engineer for the Beatles, the Rolling Stones, Led Zeppelin, and dozens more—steers the ship for Nanci Griffith's *Storms* (1989). The superlative album offers one classic after another: "I Don't Wanna Talk about Love," "Drive-In Movies and Dashboard Lights," You Made This Love a Teardrop," "Brave Companion of the Road," "It's a Hard Life (Wherever You Go)," "If Wishes Were Changes," and "Listen to the Radio." All-stars such as British guitarist Albert Lee, Rock and Roll Hall of Famer Phil Everly, and Waterboys drummer Fran Breen lead the charge. Griffith's stock soars overseas and especially in Ireland.

Storms marks her penultimate MCA Records album before the swan song *Late Night Grande Hotel*. The recording sessions are adventurous. "I had known Glyn Johns since we did the ARMS concerts and tour in 1983," James Hooker says. "I was still with Winwood then. Eric Clapton, Jimmy Page, Jeff Beck and others were on the tour. We're doing the *Storms* album next thing I know, and there's Glyn, who was great to work with. He would do things in the control room that you would never expect. We would walk in after a take and go, 'I didn't play that.' He would do weird tape-loop effects."

JIM "SEÑOR" MCGUIRE: Nanci brought the outfit and umbrella for the *Storms* photo shoot because they were special to her. We shot that through a screen door with water on it for the rainy feel.

PAT MCINERNEY: I think *Storms* is a brilliant album. Nanci wanted to get more back to feet-on-the-ground acoustic music.[24]

Longtime Blue Moon Orchestra drummer Pat McInerney has worked with John Prine and Mac Wiseman, Doc Watson, Tom Paxton, and Tom Rush.

KATHY MATTEA: "Listen to the Radio" [on *Storms*] was really joyful, which is something Nanci was really good at doing. I love the rhythmic stuff in that song and the way her phrasing stretched me as a singer. The chorus is rhythmic. Her writing was cinematic like it was in "Trouble in the Fields" and "Gulf Coast Highway." My god. What melodies. What lyrics. What pictures.

JAMES HOOKER: I won't mention any names, but there was some truth to [the *Storms* track] "Drive-In Movies and Dashboard Lights." Nanci knew someone who she didn't get along with then and still didn't until the day she died. My understanding is that she was singing about that person in this song. I always got tickled by that line, "Heavy on thigh and light on integrity."

I remember the beginning of "It's a Hard Life (Wherever You Go)." Fran Breen had played this simple, odd tom-tom intro. Glyn put an old-school tape delay on the song unbeknownst to us. Totally changed the intro. We loved it. Fran's eyebrows went up two feet. [The droning sound] at the beginning of "Hard Life" was the lowest possible D note I could find on the Korg synthesizer. A cello doubled it. Glyn did some alchemy on that song.

BOBBY NELSON: The Irish adored Nanci because of "It's a Hard Life," which was like a secondary national anthem. Also, Nanci was speaking about the Irish in her songs even though she didn't write "From a Distance." They could embrace that song because there has been so much turmoil in that country. Experiencing that tour was wild. Nanci over there was like a Mother Teresa savior, an iconic person who in her songs spoke so intimately to that nationality of people and their culture and history. She was speaking their life in songs. She adored them as much as they adored her because she felt so welcomed there. She could do no wrong in Ireland. Nanci had an almost spiritual connection to them in her writing. She was speaking about families, injustice, and ordinary things that Americans seem pulled away from because they're so busy and connected to technology.

FRAN BREEN: Nanci was a great songwriter whose songs touched a nerve for anybody who came across her. The idea on the Irish television show *The Sessions* was to bring in some American artists and sprinkle them with Irish ones. I got a call to one of the shows with a girl called Nanci Griffith [because] Philip Donnelly was the musical director. I didn't know her from Adam, but she came in with fiddler Mark O'Connor and Dobro master Jerry Douglas. We did rehearsal the day before. The show was hugely successful at the time. It was like, "Who's this girl?" She had a great knack for telling stories.

I remember doing gigs and hearing people go, "Shh. Shh." They were trying to catch every word she was saying. *The Sessions* was a big launching pad for Nanci in Europe. She was known in America but not that well. [She had] Philip Donnelly on guitar, a bass player named Denny Bixby, and James Hooker from the Amazing Rhythm Aces. Great vibe in the room during *The Sessions* for the first time "From a Distance" was aired. The manager said, "Nanci really likes you. She would like you in the band." "Great," I said, "there's my phone number."

I kept looking at the phone, but it never rang. Her manager called a year later and said, "Hey, look. We're going to make [*Storms*] in Los Angeles, and Glyn Johns will produce. We want you to come over and play." I had just been talking to Mike Scott [because] the Waterboys were setting up a tour. I went home and went, "Oh god. What am I going to do?" I always wanted to record in America. Mike was very gracious and let me go so I went to Los Angeles and met the great Glyn Johns and did *Storms*. That was the start of gigging with Nanci.

I was terrified [during the recording process even though] Glyn was such a nice, easygoing guy. I was just chuffed to be there in America recording. Nanci was very humble and would hold on to the root of what she had written and composed, but she would leave the songs open to the musicians. Nanci really was flying high, and we went all over America [on tour]. We were packing them out in Ireland. I had never seen such crowds and couldn't believe it. We did three weeks in Ireland and four in England. Someone texted me yesterday asking me about a particular track on *Storms*, and I listened and went, "Wow." Sometimes you walk away and don't listen for years to something you've done.[25]

Irish drummer Fran Breen has toured with the Waterboys, the Everly Brothers, Lucinda Williams, Gilbert O'Sullivan, and several others.

LUCY KAPLANSKY: I sang with Nanci a couple times. Once was on [the television series] *New Country*. "Don't let those women do your hair," she said. "You'll look like Loretta Lynn." So I didn't let them. I also sang with Nanci when she was performing solo at the Bottom Line in New York. I remember hanging out backstage. She was wearing a dress that I had just bought from The Limited, and we were laughing that we had the same dress. I don't ever remember rehearsing with Nanci. I just went up and sang with her at the Bottom Line.

JAMES MCMURTRY: I played the TNN show *American Music Shop* with Guy Clark and Nanci in 1989. Great house band with top Nashville guys like Jerry Douglas and Mark O'Connor. I played a couple songs, Nanci did a couple, then Guy did. Then we did a couple songs together like "Love at the Five and Dime" and Guy's "Homegrown Tomatoes." We must have run through the songs before they shot it for television. I flew in for that gig. Our first tour together was before the *American Music Shop* show. We started with the BoDeans, then opened for Arlo Guthrie on the East Coast, then we switched and started with Nanci on that Fillmore gig.

I did my first band tour with Nanci [to support] my first record, *Too Long in the Wasteland* [in 1990]. We went all the way across the country from San Francisco to Washington, DC. Nanci had a tour bus, but we had a van, which was hard. Buses can do long after-show drives. Vans have a problem with that. I had a tour manager back then who did most of the driving. Then I did another tour with her in 1995. I had my own band and was doing most of the driving.

The first gig was at the old Fillmore in San Francisco. I had tour support from Columbia Records and had David Bromberg on guitar.

PETER COOPER: James McMurtry was another person Nanci effectively introduced me to. I was nineteen and living in San Francisco. I was working at the Wharf gift shop. Nanci came to the Fillmore West with an incredible band that included David Halley, Doug Hudson, and Denice Franke. I did my same trick, getting there very early so I could have a seat at the front table. Her opening act had had an album out for about a week. The opener was James McMurtry, and the album was *Too Long in the Wasteland*. His band included David Grissom. Explosive. Some headliners don't want an opener who will be incredible, but Nanci seemed so gracious and thankful to have James there. His performance was masterful.

Nanci stopped in the middle of her show that night. She told everybody who David Halley was and said his song "Rain Just Falls" was one of the best songs she's ever heard. She asked him to sing it. Halley got up there and just stunned people. That night was Texas songwriting at its best. Many other headliners would have considered having [McMurtry open and Halley sing during their set] a distraction from their show, but she was like, "This is my guitar player. He's an incredible songwriter. You need to hear this." Also, James's band was loud.

JAMES MCMURTRY: We came out, did the first song, and about ten women stood up in the front rows and said, "Turn the drum down. Do you think you're in a stadium?" We clowned our way out of it. Nanci's fans were really folky, and we didn't know what we were up against. There was another time in Wisconsin where a promoter said after the show, "You know, for a folk-oriented act you're too fucking loud." Nobody told us we were a folk-oriented act, but that first show at the Fillmore was the only one where they yelled at us. Nanci had a cool band and was nice to us on the tour, but she had darkness. She would snap at her dog, and I saw something really dark in her face when she was yelling.

• • •

Nanci Griffith skyrockets her stardom overseas with *Late Night Grande Hotel*. Clear evidence: her Irish tour itinerary now includes events like off-night dinners in Dublin with Bono and the guys from U2. "There was a big push from the label to do European press on that tour because the Irish particularly loved her," says Vector Management's Kathi Whitley. "We had a great time." Another artist popular in the Pale connects the dots. "Ireland has an oral tradition, and storytelling has always been important in Texas," Steve Earle says. "I learned as much about what I do now from guys my dad hunted deer with as I did from singers and songwriters. Nanci charmed Irish audiences [with her stories]."

Late Night Grande Hotel predictably comes packed with them. Standouts like "It's Just Another Morning Here," "Down 'N' Outer," and "The Power Lines" as well as the superlative covers "Heaven" (Julie Gold), "The Sun, Moon, and Stars" (Vince Bell), and "San Diego Serenade" (Tom Waits) fuel the wildly popular collection produced by Mike + the Mechanics drummer Peter Van Hooke and Zombies keyboardist Rod Argent. Griffith makes national television appearances on the *Today* show, *Late Show with David Letterman*, and *Austin City Limits* as she promotes her final album with MCA Records.

PAT MCINERNEY: The first album I played on was *Late Night Grande Hotel*. We recorded that at the Farmyard studio with Rod Argent producing in [Dublin]. We had the core band with James Hooker and Danny Flowers. Nanci didn't want to be trapped in the folk world, so she was attracted to having a piano and [Hammond] B-3 [organ] player like James. We also used synthesizers for more variety in the sound.

Nanci wanted an extra textural sound that expanded beyond acoustic guitar and bass, and James certainly brought that. Peter Van Hooke and Rod Argent were very involved as producers. We went to a residential studio that was very close to my hometown in the Hertfordshire region. Peter Van Hooke had been a member of Mike + the Mechanics and Van Morrison's band. Of course, Argent was [a main composer for] the Zombies, so the pedigree was there.

JAMES HOOKER: I remember the Farmyard and the freezing cold. The studio was nice and had good atmosphere. We had good catering with lots of good barbecues and home-cooked food. Those producers were encouraging but pretty hands-off too. They [occasionally] tried to say "do this or that" but failed. The record came out Nanci's way. I remember recording the song "Late Night Grande Hotel." What a great autobiographical song. I never got tired of playing that one in the studio and onstage.

PAT MCINERNEY: The producers knew what they wanted, but Nanci was resistant to pressure about what she should sound like. She had a vision. She didn't mind taking direction, but you couldn't cross a line. "You should sound like this." "Well, no, I shouldn't. I know exactly how I should sound." We recorded the song "Late Night Grande Hotel" at Rod's place called the Red House. Fran Breen was the main drummer. I mainly was playing percussion. I remember the session for "Down 'N' Outer," which was a weird one we did at the Red House. We didn't quite understand that song, but she was very keen on doing it. Nanci knew Vince Bell and his song "Sun and Moon and Stars" for a long time. She was keen on doing that song and wanted to preserve Vince's sound.

I liked being behind the drum set. I road managed her quite a bit over the years, but I was just floundering around doing the job. Being her road manager wasn't my favorite position. We got along fine at the end of the day, but Nanci could be quite demanding and testy. I thought, Why are you doing this? I had been running around and going up to London. They eventually found someone who actually knew how to do the job. I was good enough being her pal. We were playing theaters when I was road managing, but then Ken Levitan told me, "I think you're a little out of your depth here." "Oh boy," I said. "Tell me about it."

KATHI WHITLEY: Ken Levitan came in one day randomly in 1991. "Do you have a passport?" he asked me. "Somebody needs to go with Nanci on this European press tour." I was the day-to-day person for her from that point forward. We went to Dublin and London on that press tour. Richard Wooten was the press agent who set us up in the Langham Hilton hotel in London. People would come in to interview her about her new *Late Night Grande Hotel* album. Nanci was such an accomplished singer and guitarist. I loved her storytelling. She really could put you in somebody else's life with these really intimate details.

Going overseas with Nanci was my first trip outside the United States. I was supposed to be helping her, but Nanci was very kind and generous helping me get through. So many people wanted to see her. We went over to Dublin after a couple days in London, and Bono and his crew adopted her. They made sure we had good dinners and nice drinks. We stayed at Blooms Hotel, so it was quite the thing. Nanci loved [the attention] over there. You know, everything feels easier when you're around people who get what you do.

She felt a real kinship with the European audience. Her family has Welsh ties, so she felt close to her ancestors over there. Also, she had just gotten her apartment in Dublin before we went. We had such a blast decorating things, getting sheets, and setting her up on that trip. Nanci was a couple years older than me, and I felt like my big sister was taking me around because she knew [her way around] in Dublin. I just followed her lead. Nanci knew everyone. She did her work and was professional. She was upbeat and excited to have people on her side. I only found out later that she had bigwigs at the record label behind her.

We went to two big concerts back to back while we were in Dublin: Bob Dylan and Van Morrison at the Olympia Theatre. Then there were dinners with the U2 guys. Bono's brother had a restaurant in Dublin and invited us over. The person who escorted us in said, "Okay, we're gonna go through the curtain to the back of the private room. We have chairs for you at the end of the table. Just move quickly when you pass the booth on your right. Bob Dylan's there talking with some people." We sat next to Bono and the Edge, and Chrissie Hynde and Kris Kristofferson. I was starstruck, but Nanci took it all in stride. She fit right in.[26]

Artist manager Kathi Whitley has worked at Nashville's Vector Management for three and a half decades.

JAMES HOOKER: The Blooms Hotel was like the Gramercy Park Hotel [in New York City]. What a place. The Blooms wasn't a dump, but it wasn't a top-shelf hotel. I don't think the bar had locks on the doors. Everybody hung out there. Wonderful place. A little tattered around the edges. I remember Bono coming by. Nanci wasn't intimidated by anyone on earth. She would walk right up to the president and say, "How are you doing?"

KATHI WHITLEY: Everybody shoots to be a level above where they are. The thing about artists and artist managers is that the job is never done. The bar is being raised every day. What does someone do five minutes after they have a number one record? They turn around and go, "What do we do next?" Your popularity is gonna ebb and flow. Sometimes you get stuck when you feel low. Nanci was a wonderful but really fragile person. People weren't paying much attention to singer-songwriters after the nineties. They were doing other things musically.

TOM KIMMEL: Nanci was finishing up *Late Night Grande Hotel* when I met her. I went over to Ireland with her when she was playing five sold-out nights in a beautiful old theater in Dublin. She wanted to reproduce *Late Night Grande Hotel* to some degree on that tour, so she had a much bigger band. Anyway, she was very excited to introduce me to Ireland on that trip because I had never been. There was so much joy for her over there even after things started getting crazy [between us]. There were still times of joy, fun, and surprise, but that began to ebb. The crazy started getting the upper hand after a while.

I've asked myself [why she was so popular in Ireland] many times. They were crazy about her. This brings up a larger question: Why was she so charismatic as a performer? She could be unapproachable backstage and walk onstage with her winsome, delightful demeanor in spades. The personality she brought to the stage matched who she was to some degree. She loved the way they adored her and responded in a big way. It was something to behold. These people were ecstatic to have any contact with her.[27]

Singer-songwriter Tom Kimmel's songs have been recorded by Johnny Cash and Waylon Jennings ("Heroes"), Joe Cocker ("A to Z"), and Linda Ronstadt ("The Blue Train"). He was engaged to Nanci Griffith and toured with her in the nineties.

JAMES HOOKER: We had a caterer come with us on that tour and a couple others in England and Ireland. Same chef every night in a mobile van-slash-kitchen. Wonderful food. Nanci was charging big bucks and playing big arenas. Nanci only made a small mark in America, but we would sell out seven nights at the [Royal] Albert Hall in London. We would sell out two or three weeks at the National Concert Hall in Dublin. Those are no small feats. She caught fire over there because her music touched them where they lived.

She was a fucking superstar in England and Ireland.

TOM KIMMEL: I remember leaving to go to the tour bus. Security was [everywhere]. I thought, Maybe that was what it was like to be in the Beatles with a crazy throng of people and security going, "Let her through. Let her through." She had toured hard over there early on to support "From a Distance." Nanci told me later that she had played every little place that had a stage. They really worked Ireland. Nanci had developed the relationships for so long that she was the queen of Ireland by the time I came along. Quite amazing. I remember at one gig in Ireland where some girl brought her blind sister backstage. She wanted her sister to be blessed by Nanci. Holy shit. There's the blind girl and Nanci.

Nanci was blessing her like the Pope.

I said to her one time, "I have watched you play night after night and don't understand how audiences just adore you. They're in from hello." This is a quote I will never forget. "Sweetheart," she said, "all you've got to do is love them." That was monster big for me. That idea still comes up for me when I perform—especially if I'm struggling. "Okay, this is a relationship with the audience. I'm not playing at them. I'm playing with the audience and for the audience. Breathe. Be with them." She was comfortable with the audience, but she struggled with personal relationships.

Nanci had many moods. For example, she was pacing back and forth smoking backstage at one show I remember. Smoking, pacing, muttering to herself. Everyone in the band knew to give her lots of room when she got like that. Stand back. Everyone was standing back when she threw down her cigarette, stomped it out with her foot, and said, "All right, dammit. Let's do this thing." She walked out onstage and the crowd was like, "Oh, Nanci." Holy shit. What did I just see? Flame off. Flame on.

She would tell me about when she was younger and built her audience by touring in Texas and the [Northeast]. She was booking herself and had to be aware of how far ahead she had to have shows booked and get the press out. She would lay out her press kits. She knew that she might be booked the next couple months, but she knew she would run out of money if she didn't keep booking past that. She talked about how hard she worked and how she had earned everything she had.

PETER ROWAN: She [did]. Nanci Griffith had started touring back then all on her own up and down the East Coast as the sole outrider of folk music, which we would call Americana these days. Nanci was on her own driving from Austin, Texas, stopping to play every little place up to Boston and back again. The market was sleepy at the time. There were only sixty-seat rooms to play, but they were gigs she was able to do on her own. Nanci was devoted. I learned the first time I was in Nashville that Nanci's commitment to the Texas tradition of Townes Van Zandt and Guy Clark was huge. Jim Rooney had brought her up.

Jim really believed in Nanci when she showed up in the mideighties, but I think it was stressful for Nanci to be the torchbearer for this whole thing. She spent so much energy just getting to where she could reach the starting line. She did that all on her own on those drives from Austin to Maine by keeping the singer-songwriter thing alive. Her songs are very detailed and have a shape. Sometimes in bluegrass it's like, "Another chorus." Nanci was nothing but a charming, wonderful companion during those moments playing together even though we came from different places. We would play the Townes Van Zandt song "No Lonesome Tune" together at Telluride. She knew her predecessors.

TOM KIMMEL: She also would talk about artists she didn't respect who she felt hadn't earned their place. She was really angry when Bruce Springsteen won the Best Folk record Grammy. "He puts out one damn folk record and wins the Grammy?" She could cuss like a sailor, but she had a point.

Nanci had strong opinions.

PETER ROWAN: Jim Rooney, Bill Keith, and I were touring Ireland when the country had discovered bluegrass. You would go to sessions wanting to hear Irish music, but they would want to play bluegrass. Then I went back a couple years later. Nanci Griffith was on the speaker system in every bank I went into to change money back to dollars. Every one. Perfect. Nanci was really, really big in Ireland. She was the voice of the time for the Irish.

STEVE EARLE: I'll never forget producing Bap Kennedy's record [*Domestic Blues*] in the nineties. Nanci was a very big deal in Ireland by then. Bap talked about getting Nanci on the record, and I said, "I can probably get her in to sing." She came in and sang on "Shankill and the Falls," but Bap couldn't talk to her. He started blathering when she left, but he just couldn't talk to her when she was there, which was ridiculous. She had that effect on people.

You felt like she was letting you in on something by telling stories on herself [in songs and in concert]. That's the job. People don't give a fuck about what happened to you, but they do give a fuck about what happened to you that happened to them. They have to be able to relate to your personal life. Also, she knew she was cute and wasn't afraid to use it. There's a fine line in using that and still being taken seriously, but her songs were so good and she was so fucking funny.

• • •

Nanci Griffith hosts a songwriters' special on *Austin City Limits* with guests Mary Chapin Carpenter, Indigo Girls Amy Ray and Emily Saliers, and Julie Gold in late 1991. The show airs as season 17's first episode on January 17, 1992. Griffith opens with "It's a Hard Life (Wherever You Go)" and closes by leading everyone singing the Rolling Stones' "No Expectations." She performs "Late Night Grande Hotel" with Gold on piano and "Listen to the Radio" with the Indigo Girls and Chapin on harmonies between. "I remember sitting in the makeup chair next to Nanci when we played *Austin City Limits* [on the *Late Night Grande Hotel* tour] with the Indigo Girls and Mary Chapin Carpenter," Gold says. "Nanci looked like a porcelain doll.

"She's getting her makeup put on, and I'm being fan blasted the best they can. Nanci went over to this washbasin right after the two makeup artists left and wiped everything off her face. She still looked so beautiful even without the makeup. The Indigo Girls came in five minutes before the show all messy and wearing ripped jeans. 'Hurry, guys,' someone said. 'You go on in five minutes.' 'Oh,' they said, 'we're ready.'"

EMILY SALIERS: We couldn't believe we were getting to play [with Nanci] on that *Austin City Limits*. I became a superfan of Chapin's early on as well. Nanci was nice and Chapin is so great to harmonize with. Those women loved harmony and collaborating. We came out of the same folk tradition. I found that evening a combination of being starstruck and finding our people. Nanci had such a sensitivity to songwriters.

AMY RAY: I thought it was so unusual to for her to [ask us to] learn the Rolling Stones song ["No Expectations" to close] that *Austin City Limits*. Interesting choice.[28]

Amy Ray and Emily Saliers are the Grammy-winning folk duo Indigo Girls. The LGBTQ pioneers have released more than a dozen albums between their debut, Strange Fire *(1987), and their latest,* Long Look *(2020).*

PETE KENNEDY: I joined Nanci's band at such a unique moment in my life. I had known Mary Chapin Carpenter from when she was leading the open mike at a little club in Washington, DC, and didn't have a record deal. Then she got a deal with Columbia Records [for her 1987 debut, *Hometown Girl*] and went on the road. Her producer John Jennings did the first year or two on the road but wanted to get back into the studio. They asked me to take his place in the band. So I got on Mary Chapin's bus in spring 1991. We went all over the US. The last gig was taping an episode of *Austin City Limits*. The band had shut down while she was about to make another album, so it was just Mary and me playing *Austin City Limits*.

Nanci was hosting a round robin with Mary Chapin and me, Julie Gold, and the Indigo Girls. We all set up in a circle in the old *ACL* studio on campus. I knew Nanci's drummer Pat McInerney. He beckoned me over during sound check and said, "There might be an opening for lead guitar in Nanci's band." So I did something crazy for a live broadcast. I [went onstage and] played with Nanci after I played with Chapin even though I was hearing most songs for the first time. Nanci had [been touring behind] *Late Night Grande Hotel* so they played those songs plus the Rolling Stones song "No Expectations" at the end.

Nanci handed me her Nanci Griffith model sunburst Taylor when my guitar started acting up. "Here," Nanci said, "play this." I thought, Man, giving a stranger your signature guitar is really generous. Pat McInerney came over after the show and said, "Nanci's manager would like to have a word." I thought, Oh, man. I'm in trouble now. I went backstage and found Ken Levitan. "Nanci wants to know if you can join the band right away," he said. "We're leaving for England in ten days. You have to learn all her songs by then." That gig was my last for Mary Chapin. I said yes immediately. Weird happenstance that my very last gig with Mary was my first with Nanci. What a significant break.

MAURA KENNEDY: I met Pete when he was coming through town on his first full tour with Nanci, and I had wanted to see her in person on *Austin City Limits*. I had never seen her live, but her music was everywhere around town in Austin. Everybody like Kelly Willis, Bruce Robison, and Don Walser knew Nanci. Pete had started touring with Nanci on the *Late Night Grande Hotel* album. Nanci was beginning her tour while Chapin's was ending so it dovetailed very nicely for Pete. I had never been on the road at that point. I had just played around Austin and the Hill Country and had never backed up anybody.

PETE KENNEDY: Ken Levitan's assistant Kathi Whitley sent me every Nanci album besides the BF Deal one. I immersed myself in them and learned enough to play on all her songs. Then I went down to rehearse in Nashville for a couple days. I was used to Mary Chapin's [approach]. She was a brand-new artist and Columbia was really trying to get her on the charts so we were playing all her songs just like on the record. Nanci didn't care about that. Nanci wanted you to play recognizable bits like the riff at the opening to "Listen to the Radio," but she wanted everyone to play however they played. I liked that better than Nashville's way of reproducing the records. Nanci had the Texas attitude, like "we're just playing some music together."

Playing with Nanci was not like playing a tribute to Woody Guthrie, who deliberately used two or three simple chords. He didn't want the chords and melodies to be complicated. Nanci took both wherever they wanted to go. We were playing to an audience who had grown up with Peter, Paul, and Mary, and they were looking for that smart songwriting. They were the same people who would have gone to see Bob Dylan or a Neil Young solo show. Nanci's audience was great and exuded so much love for her. There was a great vibe onstage.

JULIE GOLD: Nanci continued validating me by recording five more songs I wrote ["Heaven," "Southbound Train," "Good Night, New York," "Mountain of Sorrow," and "Love Is Love Is Love"]. Nanci Griffith gave me credibility as a songwriter. You've heard the expression, "If a tree falls in the forest and nobody hears it, does it make a sound?" I would have been the tree falling in the forest if not for Nanci. No one would have heard me. Period. The name of the game for most songwriters and artists is rejection, rejection, rejection. Rejection wears on you. Nanci gave me confidence to be rejected again because she gave me a little more resilience.

TOM KIMMEL: Nanci would have lightning strikes, little creative eruptions, and there would be a song. She would have these songs that would burst out whole. I never observed her rewriting. I thought she was a creative genius. I was in awe of her creative spark. All writers have some experiences writing like that, but there's something really charming that she didn't take every song and hammer out every line so that it made perfect linear sense. Her song "I Wish It Would Rain" from *Little Love Affairs* has a line that really blew me away: "When the diamonds fall / They burn like tears." So poetic. "They *burn* like tears." I love poetry in music. She had that.

Nanci and I were in a relationship most of the time we were around each other, but I never really knew what she was thinking. She was an enigma, mercurial, a very private person. Hello to goodbye for us was about fifteen months, and I felt like I didn't know her, which was crazy. We were engaged for a while and met each other's families. We had a real relationship, and I did the whole tour opening for *Late Night Grande Hotel*. We had a powerful relationship personally and professionally. The relationship changed my life in many ways.

We were having a rough time on the road one night when I got on the bus. I had gotten to be pretty tight with the guys in the band. "Wow," I said, "she's just an enigma to me. I don't know what to do." Fran Breen said, "Nanci is a complex, fascinating woman." I've used that line when people have asked me over the years. I loved Nanci and cared about her. I don't just mean that in a romantic way. I still care about her as an artist. There was a time when we were close. I relate to guys who have said they felt the need to protect her even though she didn't ask. Being protective was a powerful feeling early on.

There were times when I thought she was just plain nuts. I've studied therapy and don't mean that in a flippant way, but I thought there was no explaining her in any rational, reasonable way. We're all neurotic to a certain extent, but it was hard to tell where she was on the gradation of mild neurosis to ungrounded wild imagination that shades into psychosis. She was a brilliant artist who had a big heart. I witnessed great acts of generosity on the road with people and donating merch sales to local food banks, but then there was this wild, withdrawn person who had a switch that could be flipped. She could be incredibly angry. She could go from incredibly happy to sad and withdrawn. She would be deeply hurt in ways that I didn't understand. I still couldn't anticipate her moods even after we were together a while.

Saying [she became a chore to deal with] is a good way of putting it. I grieved over her when we broke up. I knew it wasn't sustainable, but I missed something about her spark. I was fascinated by her. I had a guy who was a big fan of hers ask me one time, "Come on, man. Just tell me one thing. Tell me one thing about her." I said, "She's a very private person." I always say that I wouldn't trade that time with her for anything, but I also wouldn't relive it for anything. I didn't feel like she acted in her own best interest when we were together.

PETER ROWAN: It's a roll of the dice. You're so exhilarated from the thrill of the road and the reaction from the audience that you forget about your spiritual rejuvenation. You've paid other dues. Your spirit never goes away, but your body has to support the consciousness of living. Dangerous waters to be out there too long. I've felt that myself, and maybe I'm just sympathizing that Nanci might have felt that way too. She rode the high wire. I also knew Janis Joplin pretty well when my band Seatrain used the same manager [Albert Grossman] as her. Janis had to get so up for her shows because she couldn't deliver a mellow show.

Janis always delivered at the top of her lungs. She shredded her voice and fell apart emotionally onstage even though she kept it together with this incredibly focused vocal delivery. I would see her after a show where she was like a rag doll. You could see her paying the price. She would be in tatters. Nanci was expending the same energy, just in a more classical and controlled way. Every arrangement was very clean, clear, straight ahead. Having a good, tight musical shape can contain that energy. I'm only comparing Janis and Nanci because they were two ladies I knew on the road. The road is a rough place.

TOM KIMMEL: I remember we were on the road when I got a call from her manager, Ken Levitan. "Tom," he said, "I need your help. Maybe you can talk to Nanci." You immediately know it'll be trouble. "Nanci's been invited to open the summer tour for Crosby, Stills, and Nash," he said. "This would be a huge opportunity. She would play for a gajillion fans and make lots of new ones, but she doesn't want to do the tour. She won't talk to me, but maybe she'll talk to you." I should have said, "No way, man. I'm out here on the road opening these shows and am trying to get along."

She was absolutely furious with me when I brought it up. "I'm not opening for anyone again," she said. "I only headline. I can't believe you have the gall to say this. It's none of your business." She used much worse language than that. "This is not starting over as an opener," I said. "This is a monster opportunity. Their fans would love you and this could be a huge boost to your career." I can't remember how long she stayed angry at me for bringing it up, but I know I wished I never had.

We were backstage somewhere another time when Levitan's management people came back and said, "We have all the radio people lined up for you to speak to." "No," she said, "I'm not talking to them tonight." "Nanci, they're here as our guests, and they're huge fans." "I'm not dealing," she said. "You can handle it." She just left. There are times I wished I would have said something, but it wasn't worth it as time went by. Those are practical examples, but she didn't take care of herself physically either. Addiction is very common in writers, poets, and artists. I used to look at Nanci and her idols in the Texas world who were addicts and alcoholics and think, Do you have to be in the club? You have to do this to feel legit? I never bought it.

Nanci very badly wanted to have a child with me. I loved the idea because there was an aspect that was exciting, but then there would be that perspective of my inner voice saying, "Tom, this could be a disaster of a bigger magnitude than you could ever imagine." The first big fight we ever had was because I wouldn't set a wedding date. We talked about getting married and she was like, "Well, let's do it. Let's do it now. We already met our families." "Let's not go too fast." I think it was huge for her to want a baby, but I realized at a certain point that it wasn't gonna happen—and not just the baby. You just realize it's not gonna work, but you don't break up right then. You try to make it work. You keep saying "maybe," but you know in your heart.

I loved Nanci's winsome side. We had fun when we started dating. She was really quirky. I used to feel like I was dating the librarian. You think she's superconservative, perfect, polite, and tight, but she could let her hair down.

She could have fun and had a sensual side. I loved the time when I was getting to know her and we were exploring together. She loved showing me places to eat. We rode bikes. I loved Nanci. I was crazy about her. No question.

I couldn't believe she even knew who I was when we met and got acquainted. She knew my songs and was a fan. I was flabbergasted. What an honor for her to care about my music. She wanted people to hear my songs, she talked me up, and she introduced me to people. Nanci was unfailingly respectful as a writer and artist. She really wanted to see my songs get more out there. It meant a lot for her to put me out there and say, "You need to hear this guy." I've heard stories from others like Frank Christian, John Gorka, Cliff Eberhardt who say she did the same for them.

CLIFF EBERHARDT: I was really close with Nanci's fiancé, Tom Kimmel. Nanci was such a force in all our lives. You didn't have a casual friendship with her, but you never knew what you were gonna get. We were at Julie Gold's one time, and she drank a whole bottle of Courvoisier. Can you imagine? Then she turned to me and said, "Hey, Cliff, will you be a sweetie and bring me another of these?" She drank a whole other bottle. Think about Townes. Eric Taylor would drink a half gallon of vodka when he was here. These people were drinkers, which led to health problems. Nanci was getting out of control. Nanci got to where she was singing at Carnegie Hall with Emmylou Harris singing background vocals for her. All the celebrities were at a private party at the Russian Tea Room after, but that wasn't enough for her.[29]

Former New York City taxi driver Cliff Eberhardt has had his songs recorded by folk icons Richie Havens ("The Long Road") and Buffy Sainte-Marie ("Goodnight").

PETER ROWAN: Watching Nanci grow was interesting. She was even playing a Stratocaster guitar instead of her folky acoustic guitar at one point. Nanci was flexible and gave her all. This often happens in the business. You have to pull back and regain your strength if you give yourself to it like that. Music and crowds are so addictive. They reinforce your own need for [approval]. You're doing it because you love it, but then you're doing it because the crowd loves it. Her career got so big. I remember when Nanci left Nashville and made a comment that was really a country girl's expression in the local paper. She said, "We know when we're not wanted." Whoa. What was she up against in the business?

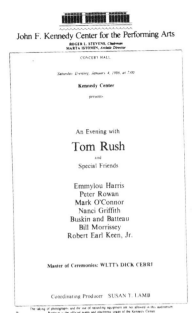

Stagebill for "An Evening with Tom Rush and Special Friends," John F. Kennedy Center for the Performing Arts, Washington, DC, January 4, 1986. The show marked Griffith's first performance at the hallowed hall. Emmylou Harris, Peter Rowan, Buskin and Batteau, Bill Morrissey, Robert Earl Keen, and others performed. Courtesy Brian Wood

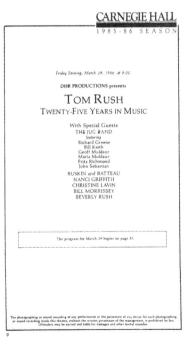

Stagebill for "Tom Rush: Twenty-Five Years in Music," Carnegie Hall, New York City, March 28, 1986. The show was Griffith's first performance at the legendary venue. Geoff and Maria Muldaur, John Sebastian, Christine Lavin, Bill Morrissey, Buskin and Batteau, and others performed. Courtesy Brian Wood

AMERICAN FEDERATION OF MUSICIANS OF THE UNITED STATES AND CANADA

The CASE Company

1016 16th Avenue South
Nashville, TN 37212
615 255-1313

JUN 12 1986

CONTRACT

Agreement #8503
Local 257

Whenever The Term "The Local Union" Is Used In This Contract, It Shall Mean The Local Union Of The Federation With Jurisdiction Over The Territory In Which The Engagement Covered By This Contract Is To Be Performed.

THIS CONTRACT for the personal services of musicians on the engagement described below is made this 14th day of May, 19 86, between the undersigned purchaser of music (herein called "Purchaser") and the undersigned musician or musicians.

1. Name and Address of Place of Engagement: The Paramont Theater 713 Congress Austin, Texas

Name of Band or Group: Nanci Griffith
Number of Musicians: one

2. Date(s), Starting and Finishing Times of Engagement: Friday, September 12, 1986 One 60 minute show at 8PM. Nanci will receive 80% special guest star billing.

3. Type of Engagement (specify whether dance, stage show, banquet, etc.): Stage show

4. Compensation Agreed Upon $1750.00 plus $250 bonus TBA. (Amount and Terms)

5. Purchaser Will Make Payments As Follows: 10% with the return of this contract, 40% by August 1, 1986, and the balance in cash during engagement.

6. No performance on the engagement shall be recorded, reproduced or transmitted from the place of performance, in any manner or by any means whatsoever, in the absence of a specific written agreement with the Federation relating to and permitting such recording, reproduction or transmission.

7. It is expressly understood by the Purchaser and the musician(s) who are parties to this contract that neither the Federation nor the Local Union are parties to this contract in any capacity except as expressly provided in 6 above and, therefore, that neither the Federation nor the Local Union shall be liable for the performance or breach of any provision hereof.

8. A representative of the Local Union, or the Federation, shall have access to the place of engagement covered by this contract for purposes of communicating with the musician(s) performing the engagement and the Purchaser.

9. The agreement of the musicians to perform is subject to proven detention by sickness, accidents, riots, strikes, epidemics, acts of God, or any other legitimate conditions beyond their control.

10. It is expressly agreed that The Case Company acts herein only as agent for artists and is not responsible for any acts of commission or omission on the part of either the artist or purchaser. In consequence hereof and for the benefit of The Case Company it is agreed that neither purchaser nor artist will name or join The Case Company as a party in any civil action or suit arising out of, in connection with, or related to, any acts of commission or omission pursuant to this agreement by either purchaser or artist.

IN WITNESS WHEREOF, the parties hereto have hereunto set their names and seals on the day and year first above written.

Susan Walker
X Susan Walker
Rt. 6 Box 41 L
Austin, Texas 78737
512 288-1695 Theater 472-5411

Nanci Griffith
X Nanci Griffith
433
1016 16th Avenue South
Nashville, Tennessee 37212
615 255-1313

Keith Case, Booking Agent

▲ Contract for Nanci Griffith's sixty-minute guest appearance opening Jerry Jeff Walker's show, September 12, 1986, Paramount Theatre, Austin, Texas. The contract, dated June 12, 1986, stipulates that Griffith would receive $2,000 for her set. Photo by Brian T. Atkinson

NANCI GRIFFITH — THE LAST OF THE TRUE BELIEVERS

The Last of the True Believers album cover. Courtesy Brian T. Atkinson archives

Cactus Cafe poster, late eighties. Photo by Brian T. Atkinson. Courtesy Bobby Nelson

116

MCA Records publicity photo, eighties. Courtesy John T. Davis archives

Nanci Griffith Live: One Fair Summer Evening cover, MCA music video, VHS tape, 1989. Griffith's first live album and concert video opens with "Once in a Very Blue Moon" and closes with "There's a Light beyond These Woods," with "Love at the Five and Dime," "Working in Corners," "From a Distance," and others between. Courtesy Brian T. Atkinson archives

Ticket stub for Nanci Griffith with James McMurtry, Bass Concert Hall, Austin, Texas, October 9, 1989. Griffith was on tour supporting her record *Storms* with McMurtry, whose John Mellencamp–produced debut album, *Too Long in the Wasteland*, was released the same year. Photo by Brian T. Atkinson. Courtesy Bobby Nelson

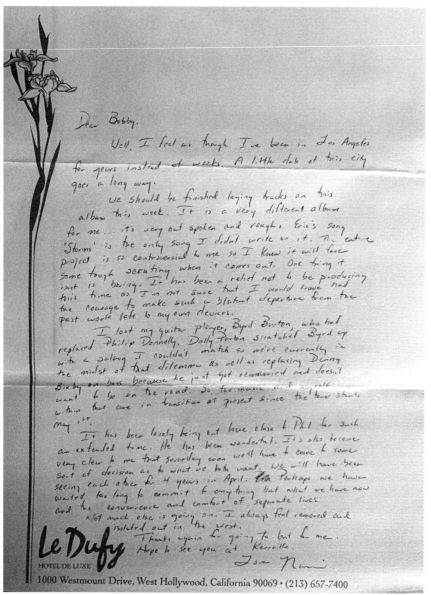

Letter from Nanci Griffith to Bobby Nelson during recording sessions for Storms, late eighties. "Well, I feel like I've been in Los Angeles for years instead of weeks," the letter opens. "A little dab of this city goes a long way." Photo by Brian T. Atkinson. Courtesy Bobby Nelson

Autographed poster for the *Austin Chronicle's* Austin Music Awards, 1989–1990. Signatures include Nanci Griffith, Townes Van Zandt, James McMurtry, Daniel Johnston, Alejandro Escovedo, and others. Courtesy Brian T. Atkinson archives

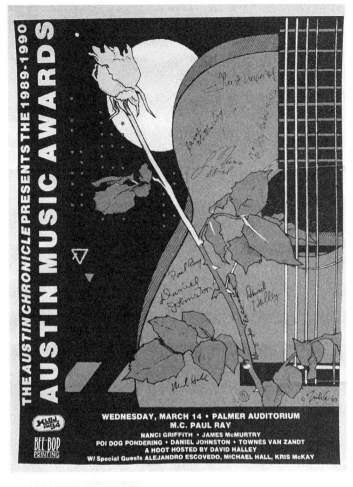

"American Music Shop," a concert series hosted by David Holt, premieres on TNN: The Nashville Network on Saturday, March 31, at 10:00 PM (Eastern). The first episode features Nanci Griffith (top) with her friends (below) James McMurtry (left) and Guy Clark.

Top photo: Nanci Griffith. Bottom photo, L–R: James McMurtry, Nanci Griffith, Guy Clark, flyer for *American Music Shop*, The Nashville Network, March 31, 1990. Courtesy Brian T. Atkinson archives

Nanci Griffith bandanna. Photo by Brian T. Atkinson. Courtesy Bobby Nelson

BMI event honoring the Julie Gold song "From a Distance," first recorded by Nanci Griffith, Friday, November 9, 1990. The handbill shows that both songwriters owned publishing for the song. "[Publishing] was a typical thing for a manager to ask for," Mac McAnally says. "Nanci did accept it, but it never would have been required. That was literally the way it was put to her. Julie knew she was out of her field and needed a favor to get something going [so she offered half]. I knew Nanci fairly well. She never would have asked for that leverage. She was so just enamored with the song because it was amazing and accepted." Photo by Brian T. Atkinson. Courtesy Bobby Nelson

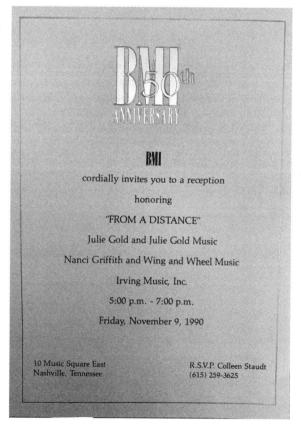

BMI 50th ANNIVERSARY

BMI

cordially invites you to a reception

honoring

"FROM A DISTANCE"

Julie Gold and Julie Gold Music

Nanci Griffith and Wing and Wheel Music

Irving Music, Inc.

5:00 p.m. - 7:00 p.m.

Friday, November 9, 1990

10 Music Square East
Nashville, Tennessee

R.S.V.P. Colleen Staudt
(615) 259-3625

All-access pass for the Late Night Grande Hotel tour, 1992. Photo by Brian T. Atkinson. Courtesy Bobby Nelson

Program for *Austin City Limits*' "Songwriters Special Featuring Nanci Griffith, Indigo Girls, Mary Chapin Carpenter, Julie Gold," recorded in late 1991, first aired January 17, 1992. Guitarist Pete Kennedy had been touring with Mary Chapin Carpenter but joined Griffith's band that night. Photo by Brian T. Atkinson. Courtesy Bobby Nelson

Ticket stub for Nanci Griffith and Jerry Jeff Walker's appearance on *The Texas Connection* television program, March 9, 1992. Photo by Brian T. Atkinson. Courtesy Bobby Nelson

Nanci Griffith's *Other Voices, Other Rooms* vocal and guitar demo tape, 1992. Courtesy Maura and Pete Kennedy

Elektra Records' *Other Voices, Other Rooms* tour advertisement, 1993. Photo by Brian T. Atkinson. Courtesy Bobby Nelson

All-access pass for *Other Voices, Other Rooms* tour, 1993. Photo by Brian T. Atkinson. Courtesy Bobby Nelson

Set list for Nanci Griffith, *Other Voices, Other Rooms* tour, Paramount Theatre, Austin, Texas, April 27, 1993. Photo by Brian T. Atkinson. Courtesy John T. Davis archives

SPEECH: SPOT ON NAN
CURTAIN DOWN,
BAND LOW GLOW

X-TRA SPOT

AUSTIN
PARAMOUNT
4/27

SPOT ON PIANO 1. TROUBLE IN THE FIELDS (G) GREEN CURT., NANCY + BAND

BACK UP SINGER 2. LISTEN TO THE RADIO (A) BRI· BLUE CURT. GOLD, NANCY SPOT

— 3. SO LONG AGO (C) MAROON CURT., BLUE BAND,

GUITARIST 4. THREE FLIGHTS UP (A) GOLD CURT., GOLD BAND, NANCY SPOT

* 5. I WISH IT WOULD RAIN (A) with Iris GREEN CURT., BLUE BAND,

BACK UP SINGER * 6. ACROSS THE GREAT DIVIDE (A) with Emmy MAROON CURT., SILHOUETTE BA

PIANO EMMY * 7. GULF COAST HIGHWAY (D) Emmy and James duet -Nanci Guitar BLUE CU

TWO BACKUP 8. ARE YOU TIRED OF ME (C) Emmy & Iris BLUE CURT., FOOTLIGHTS, PIANO

* >9. IRIS SONG With Band

BACKUP SINGER 10. ONE OF THESE DAYS (B) MAROON CURT., GOLD BAND,

BACK UP SINGER 11. SPEED OF THE SOUND OF LONELINESS (C) GOLD CURT., BAND SILHO

SPOT PIANO —12. TECUMSEH VALLEY (F) BLUE CURT., FOOTLIGHT GLOW, PIN SPOT

* >13. TOWNES VAN ZANDT SONG - Nanci harmony

14. OUTBOUND PLANE (E) GREEN/GOLD, BAND GOLD,

* 15. DO RE MI (A) with Guy Clark

16. FORD ECONOLINE (D) MAROON/GOLD CURT., GOLD BAND,

* 17. NIGHT RIDER'S LAMENT (G) with Don Edwards

* 18. BOOTS OF SPANISH LEATHER (A) with Carolyn MAROON CURT., BLUE BAND

BACK UP SINGERS 19. CAN'T HELP BUT WONDER (A) Carolyn, Lee, John Gorka, Tom Paxton

* >20. TOM PAXTON SONG Nanci & Carolyn Harmony BLUE CURT., GOLD BAND

21. DON'T FORGET ABOUT ME (B) GREEN CURTAIN, GOLD BAND + FOOTLIGHT,

* >22. JOHN GORKA SONG Nanci Harmony

* 23. WIMOWEH (B♭) full stage call all guests/ intro Rooney, Griff, etc GREEN CURT., FOOTLIGH

* 24. HARD LIFE(C) all guests remain + kids (Nanci's niece & nephew) GOLD BLUE CURTAIN, GOLD + FOOTLIGHTS,

THIS HEART (E) with Carolyn and Iris
THE WING AND THE WHEEL (B)

WHAT BAND BLUE?

4/27/93

"Across the Great Divide" sheet music from *The Kate Wolf Songbook*, Another Sundown Publishing Company, San Francisco, California, first printing, May 1988. Courtesy Brian T. Atkinson archives

All-access pass for the *Flyer* tour, 1994–1995. Photo by Brian T. Atkinson. Courtesy Bobby Nelson

Band itinerary for Retro Tour 1995, supporting the *Flyer* album, 1995. Courtesy Brian T. Atkinson archives

Show-day band itinerary for performance at Rose Garden Amphitheatre, Portland, Oregon, Retro Tour 1995, supporting the *Flyer* album, 1995. Closing entry notes that the band travels to Seattle after the show and arrives late "(after bar closes)." Courtesy Brian T. Atkinson archives

Set list for Nanci Griffith on *Flyer* tour stop at the Paramount Theatre, Austin, Texas, March 3, 1995. Photo by Brian T. Atkinson. Courtesy John T. Davis archives

3/4/95
Paramount Theatre
Austin, TX

1. FLYER (G)
2. FROM A DISTANCE (F#)
3. SAY IT ISN'T SO (E)
4. ALWAYS WILL (G)
5. ACROSS THE GREAT DIVIDE (A)
6. TROUBLE IN THE FIELDS (G)
7. IF THESE OLD WALLS (A)
8. DON'T FORGET ABOUT ME (B)
9. TIME OF INCONVENIENCE (E)
10. SPEED OF THE SOUND (C)
11. LISTEN TO THE RADIO (A)
12. HOW COULD YOU (Lee) (D)
13. THESE DAYS... (A)
14. GULF COAST HIGHWAY (D)
15 OUTBOUND PLANE (E)
16. GOIN' BACK TO GEORGIA (F)
17. ANYTHING YOU NEED (G)
18. FIELDS OF SUMMER (E)
19. THINGS WE SAID TODAY (B minor)
20. THIS HEART (E)

Encore: #1 HARD LIFE (C) (with SARA)
#2 GOODNIGHT..DREAM (G) .."open G" tune

GOING BACK TO GEORGIA

OH THE CITY SNOW MAKES YOUR BROWN EYES SHINE
WE'VE GOTTA LOOK REAL HARD TO FIND A REASON TO CRY
NEW YORK, NEW YORK IS A FRIEND OF THE TRAVELLING KIND

AND I'M COMING AROUND FROM YEARS OF HARD TIMES
HE'S CHASED ME DOWN THROUGH THE TOWNS AND THE MILES
ONCE STILLED BY LOVE HE WAS BOUND TO ROLL ON BY

-CHORUS: AND IF YOU FEEL MY LOVE WON'T LEAVE YOU
AND IF YOUR SORROW HAS BEEN YOUR SHARE
IF YOU ARE TRAVELLING BACK TO GEORGIA
WON'T YOU TAKE ME WITH YOU THERE

WELL I'M LONG GONE DARLIN', LONESOME BLUE
I BEEN THINKING OF LEAVIN', I BEEN THINKIN' OF YOU
BUT THAT BIG CITY SINGIN', MAN, I LIKE THE WAY THAT IT SHINES

I WAS HALF A MILE FROM CANADA WAITIN' ON A TRAIN
WANDERIN' AND WISHIN' I COULD DISAPPEAR AGAIN
I BEEN KILLED BY LOVE STILL IT TAKES ME TO THE END OF THE LINE

-CHORUS:

I'VE BEEN TROUBLED BY A LOVE UNTRUE
HE'S A FOOL WHO'LL DROWN IN HIS FOUNTAIN OF YOUTH
I CAN SEE THAT NOW AS I'M WALKIN' AND TALKIN' WITH YOU

I BEEN BLINDED BY THE SUN, WASHED IN THE RAIN
SCATTERED IN AMERICA, I'M SCATTERIN' AGAIN
BUT IF YOU'RE GOIN' SOUTH DARLIN I GUESS I'M TRAVELLIN' WITH YOU

-CHORUS:
-CHORUS:

-TAG: TAKE ME WITH YOU...

(WORDS & MUSIC BY NANCI GRIFFITH, ADAM DURITZ & BRIAN CLAFLIN/PONDER HEART
MUSIC/IRVING MUSIC/EMI BLACKWOOD MUSIC, INC./JONES FALLS MUSIC/BMI
GRIFFMILL/ ALMO/ASCAP)

Nanci Griffith's typewritten lyrics to "Going Back to Georgia," *Flyer* album, written by Nanci Griffith, Adam Duritz, and Brian Claflin. Photo by Brian T. Atkinson. Courtesy John T. Davis archives

Lady

and the

Scamp

Front cover of program for "Lady and the Scamp," featuring Nanci Griffith, Jerry Jeff Walker, and Steven Fromholz, Paramount Theatre, Austin, Texas, September 8, 1995. Photo by Brian T. Atkinson. Courtesy Bobby Nelson

Back cover of program for "Lady and the Scamp," featuring Nanci Griffith, Jerry Jeff Walker, and Steven Fromholz, Paramount Theatre, Austin, Texas, September 8, 1995. Photo by Brian T. Atkinson. Courtesy Bobby Nelson

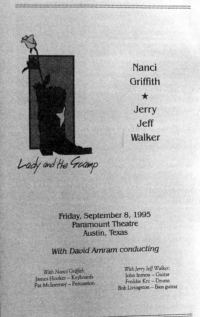

Lady and the Scamp

Nanci
Griffith
★
Jerry
Jeff
Walker

Friday, September 8, 1995
Paramount Theatre
Austin, Texas

With David Amram conducting

With Nanci Griffith:
James Hooker – Keyboards
Pat McInerney – Percussion

With Jerry Jeff Walker:
John Inmon – Guitar
Freddie Krc – Drums
Bob Livingston – Bass guitar

Nanci Griffith publicity photo, Elektra Records, nineties. Courtesy John T. Davis archives

Nanci
Griffith

Nanci Griffith

Nanci Griffith publicity photo, Elektra Records, nineties. Courtesy John T. Davis archives

Nanci Griffith

Nanci Griffith

Nanci Griffith publicity photo, Elektra Records, nineties. Courtesy John T. Davis archives

Nanci Griffith

Nanci Griffith
publicity photo,
Elektra Records,
nineties.
Courtesy
John T. Davis
archives

First signature inside Nanci Griffith's Other
Voices: *A Personal History of Folk Music*,
Three Rivers Press, 1998. Courtesy Brian
T. Atkinson archives

Cover photo,
*Nanci Griffith's
Other Voices: A
Personal History
of Folk Music*,
Three Rivers
Press, 1998.
Courtesy Brian T.
Atkinson archives

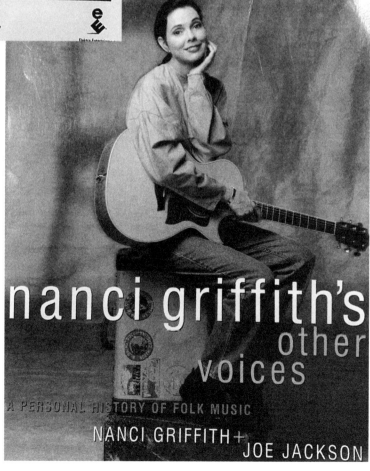

nanci griffith's
other
voices

A PERSONAL HISTORY OF FOLK MUSIC

NANCI GRIFFITH + JOE JACKSON

Second signature inside Nanci Griffith's Other *Voices: A Personal History of Folk Music*, Three Rivers Press, 1998. Courtesy Brian T. Atkinson archives

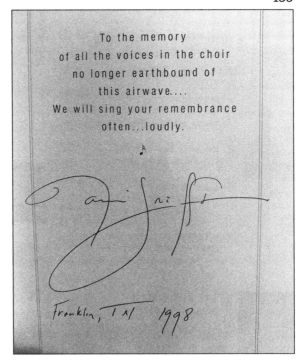

To the memory
of all the voices in the choir
no longer earthbound of
this airwave....
We will sing your remembrance
often...loudly.

Franklin, TN 1998

Negative review of *Other Voices, Too* (A Trip Back to Bountiful) in the *Austin American-Statesman*, July 21, 1998. Photo by Brian T. Atkinson. Courtesy Bobby Nelson

Tuesday, July 21, 1998

Entertainment

Griffith goes overboard with 'Other Voices, Too'

'Other Voices, Too (A Trip Back to Bountiful)'
Nanci Griffith
Elektra
★★½

By ROB PATTERSON
Special to the American-Statesman

Nanci Griffith's 1993 tribute to her musical roots, "Other Voices, Other Rooms," was a musical high point for the native Austinite. A loving and lush (if occasionally overly lush) paean to the music that has influenced and inspired her, it was a revelatory window on her muse, and a signpost for those music fans who might not know the rich folk heritage that informs Griffith's own songs and style.

"Other Voices, Too" reprises that concept, once again gathering a host of singers and players to celebrate the vitality of the contemporary folk song. But with 19 tracks, and some 60 musicians involved, all too often it feels like "Other Voices, Too Much." Although one of Griffith's gifts is the ability to fuse roots music simplicity with a pop richness, her "Trip Back to Bountiful" is frequently a cluttered and crowded affair that, for all its inclusive spirit, ends up burying the basic point of the project underneath the vocal and musical contributions. For all Griffith's ability to zero in on the heart of a song, her takes here on some genuine classics seem to be more concerned with the trappings she can cram on tape than with the soul of the songs.

The problems start cropping up on the first track, Richard Thompson's "Wall of Death," which is delivered like some carny barker's upbeat pitch, missing the implicit menace and drama of the piece (and mysteriously lacking Thompson's guitar-playing genius, though he does appear on other tunes here). On "You Were on My Mind," a folk hit for Peter, Paul and Mary in the 1960s, Griffith undermines herself with overly mannered vocals, while on "Walk Right Back," the Sonny Curtis song made famous by the Everly Brothers, she sounds

misses on this collection sadly stacks up far too much in the negative column rather than the positive. Yes, one can have way too much of a good thing, and with "Other Voices, Too," Griffith squanders the achievement of "Other Voices, Other Rooms" with sheer overkill.

'Phantom Power'
The Tragically Hip
Sire
★★½

After years of howling about Canadian politics, serial killers, nautical disasters and missing hockey players, King's, Ontario's beloved hard-rock troupe the Tragically Hip takes a new album, "Phantom Power."

Still empowered by the seeming ly deranged, hyper vocals of singer Gordon Downie, the Hip pick up on the softer, mellower tones its previous album, "Trouble at the Hen-

'Glow in the Dark Soul'
Spectacle
Supreme/Island
★★★½

'Days for Days'
The Loud Family
Alias
★★★

There is no reason to assume

baroque delicacy of the Left Banke. Plainly operating at both a geographical and generational remove from such inspirations, Blake Miller has crafted a time-warped landscape of the aural imagination, a place where innocence and irony walk hand in hand and where the sort of cheesy technology that once sounded futuristic is now hopelessly retro.

In the end, it all comes down to the songs, and Miller's got 'em, from the summertime bounce of "So Unkind" and "She Knows" to the reflectively ornate, horn-tinged "Artificial Pain" to the pop obsessive's "You Made Me Hate the Beach Boys." The album's kickoff track and first single, "Stargazing," could easily be a Weezer-size novelty smash, with its rage-rock, fuzz-toned flashbacks and improbably virginal seduction ("Close your eyes, don't be scared, it's my first time too"), but Spectacle's promise extends further and deeper than that.

(The band's first national tour brings it to the Electric Lounge on Friday with the Brian Jonestown Massacre.)

During his glory days in the '80s with Game Theory, Scott Miller seemed to embody the sort of promise that the younger Blake Miller does now, but the elder Miller remains a little too smart for his own good, like the adult equivalent of a child prodigy who embraces complexity and resists doing anything the easy way. Though the Loud Family covers much of the same sonic terrain as Spectacle, Scott Miller as a coda to crack

'El Niño'
Def Squad
Def Jam
★★★½

delicacy and lilting melody of "Way Too Helpful" reinforce Miller's reputation as prince of the perpetual sigh. Where Spectacle could well become a flavor-of-the-month radio sensation, the Loud Family is a way of life.

(The Loud Family returns to the Electric Lounge on Monday.)
— Don McLeese

The Green-Eyed Bandit, the Funk Doctor Spock and the Enigma are back.

On their latest album release as a crew, the rhyme veterans known as Def Squad have returned with little else on their minds but lyrical superiority through raw, gritty and grimy rhymes. And rest assured that the album, like its namesake weather pattern, is hot and making noise.

With a team like Erick Sermon, Redman and Keith Murray handling the rhymes and most of the production, it's no wonder it limited the guest appearances to just a handful. Biz Markie shows up on "Rhymin' Wit' Biz" and Too Short blesses the track "Ride Wit' Us" in his special way. The video of the first single, "Full Cooperation," represents the album, with the theme being vintage Eddie Murphy movies. Few videos are as funny to watch as seeing Erick play three people in the dinner scene from "The Nutty Professor," or hearing Redman say, "Hey, I got

Listening station

To hear cuts from albums reviewed today, dial 416-5700 and enter categories below:

❶ 'Other Voices, Too (A Trip Back to Bountiful)' – Nanci Griffith NANC (6262)

❷ 'Phantom Power' – The Tragically Hip, HIRT (4478)

❸ 'Glow in the Dark Soul' – Soul Spectacle SOUL (7685)

❹ 'El Niño' – Def Squad DEFS (3337)

❺ 'Days for Days' – The Loud Family LOUD (5683)

character from "Trading Places." Def Squad gives us something different on the piece "Y'all N****'s Ain't Ready," which flows over a Bone Thugs-N-Harmony-type beat but still manages to sound as original as ever. Among the few drawbacks to "El Niño" are the numerous skits and interludes. Even as funny as Redman interlude are, they start to get annoying after awhile. If you are a rap scholar, though, this album is required study material.
— Tondric Willis

■ CD neighborhood: In addition to Nanci Griffith's album, other releases hitting stores today include techno-wizards **Spring Heeled Jack's** "Songs From Suburbia," Screaming Trees singer **Mark Lanegan's** "Scraps at Midnight," South by Southwest regulars **Tina & the B Sides** "It's All Just the Same," Silkworm's "Bluechor," Color Me Badd's "Awakening," Candlebox's "Happy Pills" and the new '70s

tel: (615) 255-9000 fax: (615) 255-9001
home tel: (615) 386-9638 home fax: (615) 385-4361

Date: 17 July 1998   [1 PAGE TRANSMISSION]

Fax: **GUY CLARK**   (615)356-0967
         RODNEY CROWELL   (615)665-2570
         Walter Gibson / **JERRY JEFF**   (512)477-0095
         ERIC TAYLOR   (409)732-6810
         Dan Gillis / **STEVE EARLE**   (615)327-9455
         Mike Crowley / **IDG**   (512)847-7226

From: Nineyear Wooldridge

Re: "Desperadoes...."-Letterman TV - GROUND TRANSPORT:

You all have your flight information, below are the confirmation numbers
for airport transportation arrival AND departures.. All cars Music Express;
(800) 421-9494 EXCEPT "Letterman", which is BLS; (800)992-0570:

MONDAY, JULY 20:
CROWELL: La Guardia AA#1088   arr: 9:47a   car: #323477
GRIFFITH, CLARK, BROWN, PEARSON, WOOLDRIDGE: {CROWELL
          La Guardia AA#1192   arr: 3:47p   van: #323480
WALKER: La Guardia AA# 716   arr: 2:57p   car: #323485
          ...Nanci, Guy, Rodney, Jerry Jeff, Bruce & 9year all leave Rihga
          6:30pm (#323552):   Atlantic WFUV interview @ 7:00PM
DAWSON: JFK   TW# 044   arr: 4:40p   car: #323406
          ...Dawson directly to: Atlantic Studios
                                    619 W. 54th ('tween 11th & 12th Ave)
TAYLOR: Newark   CO# 564   arr: 5:10p   car: #323487
          ...Taylor directly to: Atlantic Studios
                                    619 W. 54th ('tween 11th & 12th A

TUESDAY, JULY 21:
GILLIS/EARLE: #323489 cancelled... arrive by train 10am / taxi to Rihga
GILMORE: OMEGA INSTITUTE   time: 1:00pm   BLS car:#HJS310-01
          ...to "Letterman" rehearsal: 4:00- 5:00p
                          taping: 5:30- 6:30p ...return Rhinebeck
WEDNESDAY, JULY 22:
GRIFFITH, CROWELL, BROWN, WALKER, STEINPEARSON, WOOLDRIDGE:
          Rihga to La Guardia: time: 8:45a   van: #323483
TAYLOR: Rihga to Newark: time: 9:45a   car: #323488
GILLIS/EARLE: #323490 cancelled... taxi now to Penn Station
CLARK: Rihga to JFK-Intl: time: 4:00p   car: #323492

Itinerary for Nanci Griffith's appearance on *Late Night with David Letterman*, July 21, 1998. Griffith assembled Texas songwriting royalty including Guy Clark, Jerry Jeff Walker, Steve Earle, Eric Taylor, Rodney Crowell, and Jimmie Dale Gilmore, who all sang Guy Clark's "Desperados Waiting for a Train" with her on *Other Voices, Too (A Trip Back to Bountiful)* for the television show taping. Griffith was a longtime Letterman favorite. In fact, the ninety-minute YouTube clip "Nanci Griffith Collection on Letterman, 1988–2005" shows her many appearances. Photo by Brian T. Atkinson. Courtesy John T. Davis archives.

Verse: Across the Great Divide

Other Voices, Other Rooms

NANCI GRIFFITH SIMPLY OVERSHOOTS the MCA Records marketing team. "It's no one's fault that [MCA Records] couldn't find a place for me," Griffith says about the late eighties and early nineties. "My records belonged on Triple A alternative radio. Well, there were no alternative radio stations then. They had no outlet. They had college radio—and college radio was great to me—but that's all they could do. I didn't fit on country radio or pop."[1] She accepts living in margins. However, Griffith fundamentally needs recognition—and MCA Records fails.

"MCA forgot to nominate me for a Contemporary Folk [Grammy award] three years in a row," Griffith says. "Your record label is the initial place where you're submitted [for Grammy consideration]. You do not get nominated if they don't. I was so disappointed. I thought, This is terrible. My record label doesn't even remember me enough to nominate me. Then I was ejected from the Contemporary Folk category by the Grammy committee for *Late Night Grande Hotel*. They said I was no longer a folk artist. Folk music was a four-letter word in the music industry for many years, [but] I think folk music is a true American tradition just as country music is."[2]

Griffith searches for a more symbiotic shelter in the early nineties.

Enter Elektra Records.

"Elektra was an unbelievably supportive label for *Other Voices*," Ken Levitan says. "MCA loved Nanci, but the radio promotions department [in the US] didn't get her like the UK did." "MCA didn't understand *Other Voices* at all, but Elektra understood her concept," Pete Kennedy says. "MCA thought she was gonna ruin her career if she did an album of folk songs. They would have said, 'How are we gonna sell this to a country audience? We can't sell it to the mainstream audience we were trying to get with *Late Night Grande Hotel*.'

Of course, they had it exactly backward. Nanci was right. Elektra gave her a free hand." "[The executives at] Elektra were elated when they found out what their first product [from me] was going to be," Griffith says. "They're one of the premier folk labels."

Griffith conceptualizes the mostly modern folk covers collection *Other Voices, Other Rooms*—named after Truman Capote's debut novel in 1948—while on tour. "Kate Wolf's 'Across the Great Divide' [inspired] the whole *Other Voices* project," Pete Kennedy says. "We were sitting in the hotel bar when we were in New York playing the Bottom Line, and Nanci started talking about 'Across the Great Divide.' She knew I had played with Kate. Nanci looked at me very resolutely and said, '"Across the Great Divide" will be the first song on an album of songs by other writers that I'm recording.' Of course, I already knew the song."

Griffith immediately assembles an unimpeachable list—"Woman of the Phoenix" (Vince Bell), "Tecumseh Valley" (Townes Van Zandt), "Boots of Spanish Leather" (Bob Dylan), "Speed of the Sound of Loneliness" (John Prine), "From Clare to Here" (Ralph McTell), "Can't Help but Wonder Where I'm Bound" (Tom Paxton), and relative newcomer Buddy Mondlock's "Comin' Down in the Rain"—that rolls the stone. Everyone knows shooting dice on folk music in the nineties risks ledding the zeppelin, but Griffith's gamble strikes gold. "Nanci's version of 'Boots of Spanish Leather' with Dylan playing harmonica is fucking transcendent," says *Texas Monthly* magazine writer Michael Hall. "So good. Same with the Prine song. Here Nanci was twenty years later going back to [honor] the people who had influenced her like Kate Wolf. [*Other Voices, Other Rooms*] had a focus and a vision."

Naturally, Griffith reenlists folk expert Jim Rooney as producer. After all, Rooney lived and played through the sixties folk music revival in New York City's Greenwich Village and Cambridge's Club 47 that *Other Voices* draws from. "Nanci had gone outside to other producers for albums like *Storms*, but then she did the right thing by calling Jim Rooney for *Other Voices, Other Rooms* for the folk thing," Pat McInerney says. "Jim had done *The Last of the True Believers* and *Once in a Very Blue Moon*. Nanci told him the concept for *Other Voices*, and he was very into it because he was a veteran of the folk scene and knew all these people. I think she wanted to get away from the slicker sound of the past few records."

Griffith wholeheartedly believes the singer-songwriter boom from the seventies carried through since as an undercurrent. "The music industry has treated folk music so badly the past twenty years, but it has been a major influence on so many artists," she says. "I told Jim Rooney, 'Hey, I would really like to do this tribute album to the songwriters who have influenced me and get this music heard.' Jerry Jeff Walker's 'Morning Song for Sally' is every bit as special as 'Mr. Bojangles.' The song had been overlooked but deserved to be passed on."[3] "I played that song for a while, but then I had forgotten it," Walker explains. "Nanci saying she was doing an album of old songs made me listen to it again. Hearing her play it gave me a fresh approach to the song and has been like finding a new song again."[4]

Griffith's best-selling album scores the Grammy award for Best Contemporary Folk Album over luminaries like Bob Dylan (*Good as I Been to You*), Janis Ian (*Breaking Silence*), Shawn Colvin (*Fat City*), and old friend Jimmie Dale Gilmore (*Spinning around the Sun*) in 1994. "I'm so pleased that the reception has been so great," Griffith said at the time. "[*Other Voices*] has sold threefold what all of my other records have sold. The album is number ten in Norway, number seventeen in the United Kingdom, and number fifty-four in the United States. We're playing a week in Dublin, a week in Belfast, three nights at the Royal Albert Hall, a week in Glasgow."[5]

"*Other Voices, Other Rooms* can be seen as a manifestation of Nanci Griffith's own attempt to cross that great divide between life and death," notable Irish journalist Joe Jackson says. "Not just in terms of folksingers who have been silenced but also in songs that have been [destined] to a similar fate [as well as] all the personal and social histories that are lost as a result of this process and which would remain lost if the market-driven and less than socially self-conscious music had its way. Moving against such forces is another motivating factor behind Nanci's involvement in the project."[6]

RODNEY CROWELL: Nanci's folk sensibility was a broad stroke coming out of the Weavers, Pete Seeger, and the black-and-white television from a time with "Hang Down Your Head, Tom Dooley." Guy Clark was very internally influenced by that music like Nanci was. I was a good deal younger so it was Bob Dylan, the Beatles, Buck Owens, and Merle Haggard who got me more than Seeger and the folkies. The folky idealism was socialist and wasn't user friendly in my current culture.

KEN LEVITAN: Nanci was a poet who read all the time. She had the idea to pay homage to her influences on *Other Voices, Other Rooms*.

STEVE EARLE: The *Other Voices* albums were acknowledging that we were literary songwriters. We're post–Bob Dylan writers who didn't learn this in college. Fortunately, I liked to read, which saved my ass. We talked a lot about books in the Townes and Guy crowd.

JOHN T. DAVIS: Nanci genuinely loved the performers and songs on *Other Voices, Other Rooms*, but she saw herself as a peer. Nanci was saying, "This is thc league I'm batting in. I don't feel any trepidation at all putting my stuff up against theirs." She wasn't trying to knock them off their pedestals, because she completely respected them, but she was saying, "I can take my place beside you." She had a great deal of confidence in what she could do musically even though she was always evolving and learning and developing her craft.

JIM ROONEY: Nanci wrote me a letter suggesting we get back together. She had left MCA and was with Elektra Records now. Well, I had my misgivings and wrote to her about them. "We can't go back and try to re-create what we've done. Let's live in the present." Nanci again had a clear vision for *Other Voices, Other Rooms*. I was impressed by her listening range. She listened to so many other writers, learned the songs, and had those songs in her. She wasn't reading lyrics off a page.

Her band was different now. I had been working with musicians I liked and got along with, but this was eight or ten years later. Well, I knew Pat McInerney from having him on some demo sessions. Of course, [fiddler] Stuart Duncan was a brilliant, wonderful player. I didn't know James Hooker, but I trusted Nanci's choice. We started with "Across the Great Divide" and the Vince Bell song ["Woman of the Phoenix"], which I would not have known about if not for Nanci. I said, "Let's do some more." We just went down that path again.

Nanci really cared and knew about music and always had ideas for how to interpret songs. It's very healthy for a writer to pay attention to others instead of just listening to their own songs. Nanci paid attention on a very deep level. John Prine and Emmylou Harris were like that. In fact, the Prine song "Speed of the Sound of Loneliness" was Nanci's pick. I thought her version was brilliant and as good as any other of that song. We recorded in Dublin. Philip Donnelly's playing had such an influence on Nanci, and recording in Dublin had the right feel.

KEN LEVITAN: The sessions were unbelievable. Legendary. Arlo Guthrie, Emmylou Harris, John Prine, Iris DeMent, Guy Clark, Odetta, Don Edwards, and her huge influence Carolyn Hester were on the record. Chet Atkins played some guitar. Greenwich Village folkie Frank Christian was her good friend and was on the record.

JIM ROONEY: I was familiar with almost all those writers when we started *Other Voices, Other Rooms*. Many were friends so the album meant a lot to me, too. Nanci wanted to record the album with me because shc knew my history. *Other Voices* was exciting and fun. Nanci led me to places where I had never been before.

KEN LEVITAN: *Other Voices* was a brilliant history of folk music. Bob Dylan even played [harmonica] on [his song "Boots of Spanish Leather"].

PETE KENNEDY: Dylan's two-note harmonica part on "Boots of Spanish Leather" was the only thing we farmed out. Nanci was adamant that we cut everything else on *Other Voices* live in the studio. Recording live also meant vocals were live. Nanci was there with her acoustic guitar and Pat McInerney counted off "one, two, three" before I played the opening riff to "Across the Great Divide." Jim Rooney's brilliance kept that on the record. He didn't want to send the record around the world to get people to overdub on it. Everyone on the record is in the room. I thought the Dylan track was charming because the song was about him as a young man. All other vocals were cut with whoever was in the studio.

Nanci's A&R guy at Elektra was completely into what she was doing and respected her decisions right down the line. That's why the record was successful. There was no battle between her and the label. They had complete teamwork. I think Nanci was so focused on the music that she didn't see it as a career move. We were fortunate to have Ken Levitan as part of the team because he was able to enlarge the whole thing in those ways. You have to be good to make a folk record a hit, but he made it happen. *Other Voices* definitely took Nanci to another level. She was playing the Bottom Line in New York the first time I played with her. We were playing the Beacon Theatre and Carnegie Hall two years later.

KEN LEVITAN: Nanci not only paid homage to her influences, she brought along so many others. She gave Lyle Lovett his [break] and put him on the cover of *The Last of the True Believers* and sang his songs. She helped people like Iris DeMent, John Gorka, and Pete Kennedy. She took Iris out as an opening act. She really sang their praises a lot because she loved songwriting. There was lots of shine on Nanci during the time I worked with her. I loved Nanci's writing and willingness to experiment with her contemporaries. She had such a love for the history of folk music. My career grew up with Nanci. She was very, very important to me.

TOM KIMMEL: Nanci and I were very close, but she was very private in a way. She had this really cool old farmhouse out on Adams Street in Franklin, which is older with lots of antebellum places. There were wood surfaces and high ceilings. Nanci would sit in there and try out songs that we were doing on *Other Voices, Other Rooms*. I got to hear those songs. Her vocal and guitar performances were the thing for me. I was talking to Jim Rooney and said, "Why spend your album budget on the studio? This is what the fans want." I thought it would be a great idea. I really enjoyed hearing those songs coming out. I have a cassette she recorded with those songs.

The tape had "Across the Great Divide," "Woman of the Phoenix," and

"Tecumseh Valley." She spoke with great reverence of all those writers. I didn't know Kate Wolf, but she was just appalled that I didn't know Townes Van Zandt's music. Nanci took it upon herself to say, "Here. Listen to this record. Listen to this record. These people are icons."

NANCI GRIFFITH: The guest artists on this album feel like this is their album too. I know Jerry Jeff probably feels like this is his album. I love the camaraderie and compassion amongst all these people who have worked together who had never met one another before. Tremendous. I didn't have any kind of premeditated intention of retreating from pop music because I've never tried to be in any genre specifically. I've been allowed to do anything I wanted to creatively. It really is just exactly what it says it is—a tribute to these songwriters who inspired me to become a songwriter. I'm very blessed to have been successful and owe a great debt to all these writers who inspired me to become Nanci Griffith.

[Other Voices] is everything from very, very wee childhood to hearing Bob Dylan do "Boots of Spanish Leather" at ten years old to hearing Gordon Lightfoot in my teenage years. You could get a good cross section of Americana back then on the radio. Unfortunately, folk music has just been swept under the rug for the past twenty years and is considered the black sheep of all the genres of music. I was tired of hearing that, which was another reason for this album. We all know that it sounds just fine on the radio. Folk music sells just fine if it's promoted and handled with the same grace that other genres are.

[Our live set] has been a mix with Other Voices songs and [my songs]. We've been pulling songs out of the back catalog that I haven't done onstage in years just because it's such an unusual tour and such a very different project. We wanted to pull the songs out of my album that haven't been done before on tour that people have written me letters about like "So Long Ago," "Gulf Coast Highway," "Ford Econoline," "Listen to the Radio," "Trouble in the Fields," "Drive-In Movies and Dashboard Lights," and "The Wing and the Wheel."

• "Across the Great Divide" (Kate Wolf) •

CAROLINE HERRING: Kate Wolf came from another planet for me. She flat out left her husband and kids, then died young of cancer. I had both her songbooks and listened to her all the time. She was in the San Francisco and Northern California folk scene and married four times. I played once at her memorial festival and met two of her four kids. Her voice was very deep, and her songs were pretty simple and self-reflective with metaphors about redtail hawks [on her cover of George Schroder's "Redtail Hawk"], love, and time. She wrote different lyrics than Nanci.[7]

Literate singer-songwriter Caroline Herring's high-water marks Lantana *(2008) and* Golden Apples of the Sun *(2009) were named NPR's best folk album of the year and the* Boston Globe's *top folk album of the year, respectively.*

NANCI GRIFFITH: We were opposites. Kate Wolf never had the capacity to get outside herself, and I never had the capacity to get into myself. *Other Voices, Other Rooms* was really helpful to take a break from Nanci Griffith and reacquaint myself with all the writers who had inspired me to become a writer—especially Kate, who wrote so personally and internally.[8]

KATE WOLF: I didn't start writing until I was twenty-eight or -nine. I meet a lot of young mothers who say, "How did you find time to write and play?" Well, I didn't. I'm glad I didn't. I think you have to wait until a point in life where you have something to say. "Here's four thousand dollars," someone in town said when I was living in Sonoma County. "Make us a record." We made [Wolf's 1976 debut album] *Back Roads* for the people in our community. I didn't know if I would ever make another record, so I made a record with songs I felt should be out there: "Legend in His Time," "Telluride," "Redtail Hawk," "It Ain't in the Wine," songs by people I knew who I felt should be recorded. The songs go from people to people, and they give each other the records.

People say my music is driving music. I love driving, traveling, and being out in the space. I write in the car sometimes. My imagery comes from that experience. My life started to stabilize around 1980. I went through a divorce and an annulment, so it was a rough time. I finally settled down in Berkeley determined to hold still and not be in any relationship. I lived in Oakland for a couple years. I didn't like being in the city, and things were up and down. I made [my fourth record] *Close to You* [in 1980 with the opening track "Across the Great Divide"]. Then I went through some profound crises and decided to move out of Oakland and live in my car. I ended up going on a vision quest down in the desert in California.

My musical influences started out with the Weavers and went into Rosemary Clooney and singers where you can hear the words like Bob Dylan and the Beatles. Folk music was always in the background. I was interested in the Kingston Trio and the Weavers. I found country music after I got into folk music and started going to libraries. I discovered Merle Haggard and Lefty Frizzell when I got into country and used to listen to Hank Williams as a kid. It's been a progression through honest songs and singers. I never thought of what I write as poetry. I just followed the models of folk and country. I write from visual imagery. [Everything] comes down to imagery.

Stories and feelings are what make country music strong. Country loses its soul when it crosses over into pop music. The country music audience is ready for the shift back [to singer-songwriters], and country would have a whole rejuvenation if it got a little more back to the folk, simplicity, stories, and good lyrics. Modern country seems to have lost its focus unless you're talking about someone like Rodney Crowell, who is a fine songwriter. I had this realization that this work I do is more important than I give it credit sometimes. I'm most whole when I'm participating in giving the music to an audience and having the audience connect with each other in the common ground of our emotions and life. We're mirrors of each other. You never have any time off as an artist.

You spend a lot of time observing things. [Being an artist] is your full life. You're not just working a job. You have to pay attention every waking and dreaming moment to live a creative life. It affects everything—your relationships and your sense of self. That's why a lot of artists struggle with addictions. You're so finely tuned that you need something to bring you back down to the ground. You're living with your eyes and senses wide open. Quiet is so important, which is why it affects your relationships. Sometimes you just need to go off by yourself in ways that aren't always constructive. It's really nourishing and wonderful once you get into the flow where you're in relationship to the world and people around you and yourself in a proper way. It's an exciting way to be alive.

People hang pictures, write songs, and listen to music because it expands their capacity to express themselves—whether you created it yourself or not. I've heard people say, "Boy, you say just what I would say if I could figure out how to say it that way." I've had that feeling about other people's work, which is why I sometimes do other people's songs. Woody Guthrie has a great quote about that: "The person told you what you already knew." Sometimes we just can't find the words but we have the same feelings. I used to learn other people's songs because I could say things I wouldn't have the courage to bring to words.[9]

Northern California folksinger Kate Wolf was a profound influence on Nanci Griffith. Her song "Across the Great Divide" inspired Other Voices, Other Rooms.

NINA GERBER: Nanci did such a huge thing recording Kate Wolf's "Across the Great Divide" on *Other Voices, Other Rooms*. So beautiful. Nanci really put Kate's music on the map. She had such reverence for Kate and treated that song with such respect. They had a connection. Kate had Nanci take over all her dates when she got sick with leukemia [Wolf passed away on December 10, 1986]. Nanci hired me to play those dates. I went on tour with her and Rosalie Sorrels in my Ford Econoline van. Nanci wrote "Ford Econoline" on that tour. Kate came to the last show at the Great American Music Hall in San Francisco and said, "That's totally my song if you just change it to a Dodge." Rosalie was a big inspiration to both Kate and Nanci.

Nanci wasn't working with a band when we were playing together in 1985. The shows were just her with me on guitar. Nanci had a great energy. She was happy and so powerful. I was thrilled to be onstage with her. I would come sit in with them later on when she was doing her band thing, too. We would hang out and talk after the show, but I was being serious about the music on that tour. We talked a lot about dogs because I brought mine with me. I've seen Nanci go off on people, but she was always good to me. I enjoyed her company and felt close to her. I also felt concerned for her. I could tell there was so much sadness in her life. I'm sure others have talked about her alcohol consumption.[10]

Nina Gerber served as Kate Wolf's guitarist from 1978 until Wolf's passing in 1986. She has performed with Dave Alvin, Peter Rowan, Lucy Kaplansky, Rosalie Sorrels, Karla Bonoff, Mollie O'Brien, and more.

KATE WOLF: [Love is] just a journey. What gets in the way of love is maybe not loving yourself first of all. You have to take time to survive unfulfilled love. You look for the gifts in what you do have from it. [Some people go through life] never feeling loved. To survive that almost always implies that you grit your teeth and say, "Well, it's never gonna happen to me, so I'm gonna do something else." Sometimes you just have to relax and not think about it, and it comes if you're wanting to be loved. I've found that if you give yourself away you get what you need. Giving your love away is the mirror we were talking about, and it creates a circle and comes back to you.

NINA GERBER: My concern was about alcohol, which was the reason Nanci would get angry and go off on people. I'm sure that anger was already inside her, but she was out of control when she drank. I could see the sadness in her even though she was really strong and powerful. She was a tortured soul who really went out of her way to champion people. She was supportive and had a really good heart. Nanci was a really wonderful, intelligent, kind person who just had a hard time.

Nanci felt underappreciated well before the end of her life. She tried so hard to be good to people and was politically active and a good person. Maybe she didn't feel that she was treated as such. I'm not sure if that's what caused her outbursts, but she was definitely getting a reputation. She was lecturing people in the audience when she was touring in the 2000s. People were talking about that. Sadly, I feel like she was getting more known for the crazy shit that she did. [Being related to her upbringing] makes sense. That stuff starts early on. She was definitely searching for approval.

Nanci supported me so much, like the time she gave me a [Fender] Strato-caster. I said one night in Nashville at a gig, "That's a sweet guitar." I was hanging out at her house I don't know how long after that, and we were drinking. I was getting ready to go and she said, "Don't leave here without everything that belongs to you." "What?" She handed me the Strat. She just did stuff like that. I hope people know Nanci's heart and talent and not the crazy shit. She had a big heart.

BRIAN WOOD: Former Texas governor Ann Richards asked Nanci to play Kate Wolf's "Across the Great Divide" at her funeral [in fall 2006]. "I don't think I can do this by myself," she said. "Would you be able to play with me?" "Of course." This gig wasn't like playing at the Cactus Cafe, Carnegie Hall, the Kennedy Center, or even *Austin City Limits*. Playing Ann Richards's funeral was very emotional. This was intensely personal. I always felt like Nanci had trust in me to get her through things. We had friendship, trust, and love. My relationship with Nanci was intense and transcended music.

• "Tecumseh Valley" (Townes Van Zandt) •

NANCI GRIFFITH: I'm grateful that my parents maintained their passion for the arts and did not abandon that love by conforming to the average American family endeavors. I would not trade my teenage memory of my father taking me to hear Townes Van Zandt for the first time in a small club in Austin for anything "normal." ["Tecumseh Valley"] forever changed my life and lent me character and strength. Thinking about [Caroline's] downfall and sorrow often saved me from making the wrong turns when I felt I had no choice.

JOHN TERZANO: Nanci was still caught up in the emotions in the song after she recorded "Tecumseh Valley." Her recording is so magnificent. She really caught what Townes was saying. I asked her about the recording session when she came back. "John," she said, "I don't want to talk about it." I could tell. She was singing that about somebody.[11]

John Terzano served as vice president of the Vietnam Veterans of America Foundation for thirty years. He's currently president of the Justice Project

NANCI GRIFFITH: I've had times even before Townes died [on New Year's Day 1997] when I would finish "Tecumseh Valley," and there would immediately have to be some other thing for me to do on the stage because I couldn't deal. The intensity of the sense of loneliness as I sang about Caroline was too much. She is someone who just tried so hard to find something in life but still couldn't get up on her feet. That hurts so bad. Townes just takes you so far into this woman that it hurts that deeply. I have to go and mess around with James Hooker and his keyboards, do anything just to have somewhere else to go, rest, and pull myself back together.

I can't go straight into another piece of music because I'm feeling Caroline's loneliness too intrinsically. The sense of her hurt does not leave me. I could have been Caroline. I guess it's my own pain I'm feeling too. Caroline became a guardian angel for me, a presence that will forever ensure that I never fall that low because I never forget that I could have been her. ["Tecumseh Valley"] kept me from being her. I always had [the] concept within myself that I cannot fail. I cannot fail because there is no place to fall. The fall is death. So, I've been given strength from Townes Van Zandt and ["Tecumseh Valley."][12]

HAROLD F. EGGERS JR.: Nanci regularly said Townes was the best song-writer who ever came from Texas. Townes really liked her "Tecumseh Valley" on *Other Voices, Other Rooms*. He sang the song with Nanci when she was touring the album at the Paramount Theatre in Austin. Townes liked that Nanci used the line about being a hooker ["She turned to whorin' out on the streets / With all the lust inside her"]. Townes was very upset when they took that line out on his first album [1968's *For the Sake of the Song*] because they didn't think [radio] would play the song.[13]

Harold F. Eggers Jr. served as Townes Van Zandt's business partner and road manager for more than twenty years. He tells his story in the book My Years with Townes Van Zandt: Music, Genius, and Rage.

JIM ROONEY: Having Arlo Guthrie on "Tecumseh Valley" was Nanci's idea. He came in after the session. That song had a deep emotional connection for Nanci. She was in tears when we finished recording. She really connected with the character Caroline. I always felt that was an extremely wonderful performance and am so glad we recorded it. Combining Arlo and Nanci on that song was terrific. Nanci had lots of good musical ideas like that. She was right there in the conversation if the subject was music.

PETE KENNEDY: Nanci was influenced by Townes's pure genius. Nanci, Guy Clark, Steve Earle, and Lyle Lovett all looked up to Townes Van Zandt. He was the guru because he came up with songs [like "Tecumseh Valley"].

ROBERT EARL KEEN: Lyle turned me on to Townes. Townes had songs [like "Tecumseh Valley"] that he called "sky songs" because they just fell out of the sky. Roger Miller said they were a gift that just happens. [You think] someone truly wrote them for you, put them in your lap, and you just play. No doubt they're a gift. You never have quite that confidence with a song when you have to chisel along word after word as you do when a song just falls out of the sky like that. You feel like those ones were meant to happen.

PETE KENNEDY: I don't know that Townes could exist comfortably in society being anything but exactly who he was. Nanci understood that. She was like that too. She only wanted to be a singer and songwriter. People had to respect that. Townes may have been a flawed person, but he had the courage to be himself, which is essential for any true artist.

HAROLD F. EGGERS JR.: We stayed at the Driskill Hotel when Nanci was doing the *Other Voices* show in Austin. Guy Clark finished sound check and was mad. "Man, that Nanci Griffith," he was ranting. "She doesn't understand my song." "Hey, Guy," I said. "Have you seen Townes?" "He's in my room," he says. "Follow me." I followed him to the room. Guy walks in the room, and I'm behind him. Townes and Susanna are sitting there with a bottle of vodka. Townes immediately jumps up. "There's nothing going on here, man. There's nothing going on." Guy is totally ignoring Townes. He's still going on. "Nanci Griffith doesn't understand. The song is supposed to be in this key. My song." Townes is saying, "Guy, nothing is going on. Nothing is going on."

Guy looks at Townes like, "What the heck are you talking about? I'm talking about Nanci singing my song." They respected Nanci. I was backstage later when they were raving about her singing their songs on *Other Voices*. They considered Nanci a peer, but Townes was very uncomfortable singing "Tecumseh Valley" with her. He was always uncomfortable singing duets. They were very rare, but when he came offstage at the Paramount, he said, "Wow. Nanci made me feel comfortable. That came off really good, H." He talked about how she did a great version of the song on her album. You know how humble Townes was.

CHARLEY STEFL: Of course, Nanci adored and loved Townes. He likewise thought she was a wonderful singer and songwriter. Their performance of his song "Tecumseh Valley" on the *Texas Connection* television show is a classic. Nanci knew Townes because her dad had taken her to see him back in the sixties. Townes would be playing at the Split Rail, which was on the left as you head out of town in Austin off Lamar Boulevard. Crazy place with bikers, cowboys, hippies, and businessmen. Nanci was playing there around 1975. Bob Dylan had mentioned something about cowriting with Townes. That would have been something.

I was with Townes one time when Dylan was playing at the Starwood Amphitheatre [in Nashville]. Townes had just gotten out of rehab. He had a nice haircut and everything [as well as] a backstage access and a poster he wanted Dylan to sign. Townes came back from backstage with his signed poster. He was just like a kid on Christmas morning. He was so happy. Guy Clark had bought Dylan's *Biograph* for Townes on vinyl. Townes played that record and put the needle back on "I'll Keep It with Mine" at least ten times. He had never heard that song—none of us had—and was in love with it. Quite a thrill.

• "Do Re Mi" (Woody Guthrie) •

JIM ROONEY: Doing "Do Re Mi" with Guy Clark singing was a perfect, spontaneous event that I enjoyed. We said, "We don't have a Woody Guthrie song." "I know 'Do Re Mi,'" Nanci said. Maybe she had heard Guy sing that. We called him up. "What are you doing? Do you know 'Do Re Mi'?" "The Woody Guthrie song?" Guy asked. "Yeah. We have Nanci Griffith over here singing it. Come over and sing with her?" "Yeah." [Lead acoustic guitarist] Pat Flynn was doing an overdub for Allen Reynolds, and I asked what he was doing. He came over, and we threw it together. Great cut.

• "This Old Town" (Janis Ian and Jon Vezner) •

JANIS IAN: Nanci called me one day and said, "I'm making a new album. I need a Janis Ian folk song." I had no idea what she meant, but she told me it would come naturally once I thought about it. She was right. I had been want- ing to write with Jon Vezner for some time and called him to cowrite with me the next day. I woke up the next day with the line "This old town should have burned down in 1929." I presented it to Jon, sure that it wouldn't work because who writes about towns that should have burned down? Jon turned it around and made it into a triumph rather than a tragedy. We finished the song that day.

I threw "This Old Town" onto a cassette and sent the song to Nanci. She was pretty happy. Nanci was amazing, a very underrated songwriter and a very lovely woman. I was truly honored that she had me on her short list of writers for what turned out to be a seminal album. We were up against one another for a Grammy that next year, and I was truly happy when she won. Her father was there, and they both were crying as she walked down the aisle to receive her award.[14]

Folk icon Janis Ian is best known for her late-sixties hit "Society's Child (Baby I've Been Thinking)" and the top ten single "At Seventeen" from her Billboard *number one album* Between the Lines. *She has won two Grammy awards.*

• "Comin' Down in the Rain" (Buddy Mondlock) •

BUDDY MONDLOCK: Nanci invited me as her guest when she was hosting an episode of the Irish television program called *Town and Country* one time when they were filming parts in Nashville. I was surprised and touched. They wanted some songwriters who weren't well known at the time. We had the place to ourselves for an afternoon taping. I played "Comin' Down in the Rain." I happened to run into Jim Rooney a couple years later, and he said, "I'm producing this folk record on Nanci doing other peoples' songs. Do you have anything?" She had ventured out with other producers by then and had tried out more rock stuff, so I was happy to hear she was getting back to acoustic music and especially that she was working with Rooney.

She ended up recording "Comin' Down in the Rain" on *Other Voices*, which was great for my self-esteem and helped [my career]. I got a call a couple years later from this Norwegian artist named Rita Eriksen who happened to go by the Bluebird and saw my poster in the window. "Oh," she said, "that's that guy who wrote 'Comin' Down in the Rain.'" She ended up recording five or six of my songs over the years. I had never even been to Norway and here someone is recording a bunch of my songs all because Nanci put "Comin' Down in the Rain" on *Other Voices*.

JOY LEWALLEN: I loved *Other Voices, Other Rooms* because she was such a fan of writers like Buddy Mondlock. I talked to Buddy when he played the Fair a couple weeks ago and said, "What did you think about that?" "It got my song out there," he said. "People heard my song and wanted to contact me as a songwriter. That was the highest compliment she could pay. She did my song on an album where she had a lot of more well-known people to choose from."

FRED KOLLER: I was in the studio when Nanci was doing Buddy Mondlock's "Comin' Down in the Rain" on *Other Voices*. Buddy was there along with quite an impressive crowd. So many people say *Other Voices* is their favorite record. Nanci had a great ear for songs. Major publishing companies would have thought "From a Distance" sounded like a summer camp song. [Julie Gold] was getting passed over, but Nanci knew what that song needed immediately. Nanci's audience and Bette Midler's weren't the same, but the song got the attention it deserved with Bette.

BUDDY MONDLOCK: Nanci's "Comin' Down in the Rain" was a little different than mine. She made very minor changes to make it make more sense to her. "Comin' Down in the Rain" came from me seeing this Clint Eastwood film about Charlie Parker called *Bird*. There's a scene where Parker is really hitting bottom in the back seat of a car at night in New York. The car pulls up to a corner as Parker tries to score heroin. The dealer pulls up to the car in a wheelchair, which was an interesting touch. The dealer looks in the car and sees it's Charlie Parker. The dealer knows Parker doesn't have any money. He shakes his head as if to say, "I'm sorry, man. I can't help you out this time." Parker doesn't say anything either. He's smoking a cigarette.

The camera moves inside the car with him and you see his silhouette in the car window with the night fitting behind him. The tip of the cigarette glows very brightly as he inhales and a little ember breaks off, catches an air current, goes outside into the city, and blinks out. I was completely floored. I thought, That ember is Charlie Parker. I woke up at four in the morning a few weeks later with the first verse to "Comin' Down in the Rain" in my head. I wrote it down and went back to sleep. I saw that the next day and said, "I'm onto something here." I finished it up over the next couple days. The song is about that little ember, not Charlie Parker. Clint Eastwood is pretty precise, so I don't think that moment was an accident.

TOM NORRIS: "Comin' Down in the Rain" was my breakup song. I listened to that song on repeat. I always thought the idea of a breakup song was a really corny thing. Who actually has a breakup song? That was the one for me. I was very, very young and still at music college, but the relationship was notable for me. The relationship ended weirdly, and I was the one who had to end it. "Comin' Down in the Rain" was the song I was left with. I didn't boot her out, but it happened that we had to go our separate ways.

I remember somebody coming into my apartment at one point and saying, "Come on, man. Pull yourself together. You can't listen to this song for the rest of your life." I find "Comin' Down in the Rain" really enigmatic and haunting, consoling and grounding. You know, sometimes you wonder if you're doing the right thing after you make a decision. I remember being very much living inside my emotions at the time. I guess that was one of the most self-absorbed moments in my life, but you do tend to remember those ones the most. Her voice on that song was [amazing]."[15]

Celebrated London Symphony Orchestra violinist Tom Norris has worked with rock acts the Who, Eric Clapton, Deep Purple, Elvis Costello, and Seal. He played with the LSO on Nanci Griffith's album Dust Bowl Symphony *in 1999.*

BUDDY MONDLOCK: Nanci tried to give me a leg up. She asked me to sing "Comin' Down in the Rain" onstage in Fort Worth one night. Then a few weeks later we were both back in Nashville, and she asked me to sing the song at the Ryman. I couldn't believe it. Playing the Ryman with Nanci was such an honor. Walking out on that stage has so much history. Backstage is a little dumpier than you would imagine, but I guess backstage always is. I don't know if I gave my best singing performance because I was nervous. Sure was a cool feeling, though. Nanci let me take the lead and sang harmonies, which was generous since she was with her whole band.

• "Speed of the Sound of Loneliness" (John Prine) •

JOHN PRINE: ["Speed of the Sound of Loneliness"] is a song about a breakup. I was thinking of somebody's heart being pulled apart by g-force like one of the astronauts of the 1950s with his face all contorted. The more the listener can contribute to the song, the better, and the more they become part of the song and fill in the blanks. You save your details for things that exist rather than tell them everything—like what color the ashtray is and how far away the doorway was. So, the listener can fill in the blanks, and you just draw the foundation when you're talking about intangible things like emotions. I still believe that's the way to tackle it.

["Speed of the Sound of Loneliness"] came out all at once from [this] broken relationship. I could not understand what went wrong, and I had to explain to myself through this song. The next day I thought, Jesus, that's beautiful. I didn't recognize it at the time. [The song] was just pouring out of me. I guess [the title] must have been a play on the words of [the 1962 British film] *The Loneliest Long-Distance Runner* [written by Alan Sillitoe and based on his short story with the same title]. Probably. I don't know where it came from when it's all said and done, but I'm thinking that's maybe where I got the idea to use "loneliness" like that. I guess I'm attracted to stuff with a long title [that is] kind of abstract.[16]

Legendary Americana singer-songwriter John Prine's timeless classics like "Angel from Montgomery," "Speed of the Sound of Loneliness," and "Sam Stone" effectively defined a genre. He nodded toward Austin by covering Blaze Foley's "Clay Pigeons" on his album Fair & Square *(2005).*

NANCI GRIFFITH: I chose ["Speed of the Sound of Loneliness"] because it says that someone clearly doesn't know what they are doing spiritually [and] emotionally in so few words. In fact, it's what John Prine says has been said about me so many times. Like, "Nanci's out on the road because she doesn't want to come home, doesn't want to face reality." "Out there running just to be on the run." Great line. I borrowed it from John for my favorite song on *Blue Roses from the Moons*, "Not My Way Home." I wrote, "You'll be out there running / I'll be here to be still." Same idea. John Prine is often compared to

Dylan. They are very, very different musically, but I think John Prine's music will be around as long as Bob Dylan's.

They're both going to be hailed as great writers of this century, but John makes it sound so easy and plays guitar and sings like everybody does. His melodies are so accessible and memorable. You never forget a John Prine song once you hear it. John is such fun to work with. I threw in those little high angels on "Speed of the Sound of Loneliness," and he's asking, "Is that going to work?" We were walking through a cemetery [while] filming the video for "Speed of the Sound of Loneliness" and realized at one point that people in cars driving by couldn't see the film crew. They just saw these life-sized angel lights. People probably said, "Ma, did you see that? Nanci Griffith and John Prine are angels. When did they die?"[17]

FIONA WHELAN PRINE: John loved [singing] with women and marveled at how the best voices in music agreed to sing with him and how good they made him sound. Nanci was maybe his first real duet partner onstage. I rode the tour bus in the early nineties with them. A golden time. Nanci and John had a real affection for each other. They both enjoyed their Major cigarettes from Ireland and had the same goofy sense of humor. He regarded her as a kindred spirit because they both saw and wrote about the experiences of everyday heartland men and women.[18]

Irish singer Fiona Whelan Prine is John Prine's widow.

JIM ROONEY: Loneliness was Nanci's life theme. Did I tell you Nanci left the rights to her novel *Two of a Kind Heart* to me [in her will]? The opening paragraph of the [essay "God's Lonely Man"] by Thomas Wolfe is about loneliness. The Carson McCullers book *The Heart Is a Lonely Hunter* was one of her favorites. I believe loneliness was Nanci's fundamental state, so John's song "Speed of the Sound of Loneliness" really spoke to her in a deep way. She did such a beautiful job on the song, but she could be really prickly. She threw a fit about the piano one time when she was opening for John at Carnegie Hall. She could be a very difficult person.

I do think that John had lots of respect for her as a writer and artist. He would have liked to be her friend, but that wasn't in the cards. That was the way with [most] people. You couldn't be her friend. Nanci just wasn't there. Whatever it was was so deep inside it destroyed her and was related to the loneliness. I don't know what caused it, but she couldn't shake it. Took her over eventually. Very sad. [Loneliness] cost her everything. Cost her her life. I'm touched that I succeeded in maintaining some sort of friendship all along the way. I also tried to get through it, but I couldn't. You have to accept that eventually.

• "From Clare to Here" (Ralph McTell) •

RALPH MCTELL: I was playing at the Cambridge Folk Festival many moons ago when Jim Rooney said, "Ralph, here are a few albums you might like." They were Nanci Griffith records. My daughter took them up to her room when I got home, and I didn't see them again. I had forgotten all about them when Nanci was coming to do a show at the Royal Albert Hall in London years later. She was going to do my song "From Clare to Here" and asked if we could have a meeting. Then she asked if I would like to join her onstage [to sing the song]. Well, yeah, I would love to join her. I told my daughter, and she freaked out. She had been a fan since she got those albums.

The band had arranged the tune with chords I didn't know, but we got through all right. I found Nanci absolutely charming, incredibly talented, and a unique person. Her version of "From Clare to Here" was absolutely lovely. Nanci told me she first heard "From Clare to Here" during a sing-around in Nashville when my friend Jim Dooley had introduced the song. I found that folk process quite charming. The guy Nanci sang with on the record [Pete Cummins] was actually a rock singer, and she was very happy with his harmonies. The song did well for her.

"From Clare to Here" goes back to my childhood when my father left our family home. The lovely, gentle fellow who lived upstairs was almost a father figure of kindliness. He took a young uncle's attitude to my brother and me as there was a big migration of Irish to England after World War II. They were rebuilding the countries after the bombings, which incidentally were our playgrounds. I'm English, but I grew up around and labored on building sites with Irish people. I love the traditional Irish music, and some of my best friends have been Irish.

The Irish dealt with prejudice. Some signs said, "Room to rent, but no Irish need apply." In fact, Pete Seeger wrote a song about that called "No Irish Need Apply." I saw how the boys would stay to themselves and not properly integrate when I got older and worked on building sites. "From Clare to Here" was really inspired by that slow breakdown of family ideals that starts off with slipping away from church and not going to mass. Anger would spill over into fighting—probably from drink—and not saving money.

The song certainly seems to have resonated. The only problem is that an Irish musician friend I gave it to got the tune slightly wrong. Now, the entire world seems to do it in a reverse chord structure in the chorus because of that. The sentiment is the same, but most play it faster than I do. You hear Paddies in the pub singing it [very upbeat], "It's a long, long way from Clare to here," but I [intended] it to be more reflective. The song is an admission that your ideals have slipped away, and you're missing home in that extremely deep way that the Irish talk about home and culture.

"From Clare to Here" probably is my second most famous song [after 1969's "Streets of London," which has been covered by more than two hundred artists]. A friend from Yorkshire recently got an Irish music book from America where "From Clare to Here" is listed as a traditional Irish tune written around 1850. They said it commemorated the Irish migration after the potato famine. I get a great buzz that the song has traveled around the world, and Nanci had much to do with that. [The song works because] short couplets are easy to remember, and people like to sing them: "When Friday comes around Terry's only into fighting / My ma would like a letter home but I'm too tired for writing."[19]

British folksinger Ralph McTell's masterwork "From Clare to Here" is eclipsed only by his most popular song, "Streets of London."

PAT MCINERNEY: Ralph McTell's "From Clare to Here" was really special. Philip Donnelly played guitar. He came up with the arrangement that he had played with Ralph.

PETE KENNEDY: Philip must have known "From Clare to Here" in his own repertoire because he laid down a solid acoustic arpeggio foundation that sounded like a grand piano. I held off playing until the chorus and then played some really simple strums so I didn't interfere with Philip's picking pattern. I also sneaked in a couple high harmonies.

RALPH MCTELL: Ireland comes from deep, passionate, beautiful music with its history of subjugation, rebellion, emigration, famine, and all the other things that have hit this island. The culture musically is extremely complex and really gets a finger on the pulse of being forced to move away from home and even move to the perceived enemy's country to survive and work. The Irish [relate to Nanci because] her songs are so honest. She had a direct way of singing and was a great poet.

I'm not surprised that some folks brought their children [backstage for Nanci to bless]. [Popular Irish singer] Christy Moore has a similar effect as Nanci on Irish people. People just want to reach out and touch singers like them. Christy has a very simpatico way about him the way Nanci had in spades. She had an understanding and wasn't afraid to show that side in poetic form. People respond. I think the record companies wanted her to break more into the overground, which is why they produced the records like they did. There have been times where I would think, Maybe we'll get more radio play when the producer said, "Why don't we try this?"

Think about how many miles Nanci traveled on the road. She worked hard. There's always that feeling about, "There's so much I want to say. I have to make it." I'm amazed. There was a deep yearning for more than what was possible to get out of her writing. She wasn't writing commercially. She was too honest. It's like, why isn't Randy Newman more famous? He's famous for *Toy Story* but not for the other songs he's written. I think he's accepted it in his own cynical and dry way. "Forget it, Mark," he said when Mark Knopfler was producing his record. "Just give me the money."

Nanci had a beautiful, creative voice you couldn't mistake for anyone else. Her melodies are so strong they almost take away from the simple honesty of the statement, but that's not intended as a criticism. I went onto my Amazon Alexa before we did this interview and listened to a whole bunch of songs, and I was totally charmed by the care with which the records [were made]. Nanci certainly was a fine, fine writer. Her voice has such a purity, and her keen observations in the songs don't need much dressing up with steel guitars.

• "Can't Help but Wonder Where I'm Bound" (Tom Paxton) •

TOM PAXTON: My biggest experience with Nanci was when she recorded "Can't Help but Wonder Where I'm Bound" on *Other Voices, Other Rooms*. She had all of us writers down to Austin for two nights at the Paramount Theatre, which was the first time I met Guy Clark and Jerry Jeff Walker. I would later become great friends with Guy. We had a wonderful time that whole weekend, but Nanci mainly kept to herself. She was shy, but Nanci was a delightful person with plenty to say when you started a conversation. She loved to laugh and have a drink. I didn't have the friendship with her that I would have enjoyed, but I did like her and respected her enormously.

The atmosphere was electric at the Paramount in Austin the night we recorded that *Other Voices* live concert. Everything was as receptive as you could ask for in your dreams. Nanci sold the songs. She sang them because she believed in them. Carolyn Hester told me later that when the album first wrapped, Nanci had not done "Can't Help but Wonder." They wrapped up recording, and she went on a vacation to Ireland. Carolyn said that Nanci had a dream on her first night in Ireland. She dreamed she was on one canyon rim, and Carolyn was on the other rim yelling to her, "Nanci, you have to record 'Can't Help but Wonder Where I'm Bound.'" Nanci called Jim Rooney when she woke up, and they recorded the song.

I wrote "Can't Help but Wonder Where I'm Bound" in 1962. I was in my early years and was very much influenced by Woody Guthrie, Pete Seeger, and their writing. I was writing a lot then and do remember writing "Rambling Boy" and "The Last Thing on My Mind." I know I was writing about everybody else in "Can't Help but Wonder," but you're always writing about yourself no matter what you write.

• "Woman of the Phoenix" (Vince Bell) •

VINCE BELL: I wrote "Woman of the Phoenix" about finding a woman who couldn't handle [being with me]. Nanci also recorded a song I wrote called "The Sun, Moon, and Stars" [on *Late Night Grande Hotel*] about my friends while I was in San Miguel de Allende, Mexico. I didn't see much [recognition from Nanci recording those songs], but I work with my head down. I see very little recognition [from the public] when Nanci or Lyle Lovett have recorded my songs [Lovett recorded Bell's "I've Had Enough"] because I've been busy writing.

PETER COOPER: *Other Voices, Other Rooms* was a masterpiece and another good example of when Jim Rooney and Nanci were in the same head space. That album also is another example of Nanci's graciousness in taking the camera that was pointed at her and shifting it around to point toward others. *Other Voices* introduced so many people to music that they didn't know about. There were famous folk songs on there, but there were also songs by writers like Vince Bell. They were songs where she brought famous people in to sing works that were not well known. *Other Voices* gave new lives to work we wouldn't even know about. You can't miss the joyfulness in the record.

Other Voices is what artists do when they're doing the right thing.

STEVE EARLE: Tony Brown had signed Lyle, Nanci, and me at the same time to MCA Records thinking singer-songwriters were gonna be the next big thing in country music. He was wrong, but Nanci stood out. She was really good and had a bigger audience than Lyle and me for a long time. Nanci invited me to do [the Woody Guthrie song] "Deportee" on the first *Other Voices* album and [Guy Clark's] "Desperados [Waiting on a Train"] on the second.

I knew Jim Rooney as soon as I moved to Nashville because my crowd had two contingents: the songwriters and the hippie bluegrass guys. One salon revolved around Guy Clark and the other around John Hartford, but they cross-pollinated quite a bit. I remember Odetta during the "Deportee" session. Nanci worshipped her. There were five or six of us around the microphone, and Rooney didn't have anything to say. Odetta starts clapping and goes, "People, people, people. There is someone in this group who's not singing. What this song says is too important not to be singing." We were louder the next time.

PAISLEY ROBERTSON: I went to New York to work for Odetta after *The Last of the True Believers* came out. I was kick-starting Odetta's career and getting her home in order because she was such a pack rat. We went to the show and sat at a little round table. They both had been at Kerrville but had never met each other. Nanci starts singing her fabulous song "Mary and Omie" three songs in. I look over and Odetta's face was drenched in tears. She put her head down on the table because the song moved her so much.

DARIUS RUCKER: "Mary and Omie" is so great because she's telling this whole story of a post-Depression Black family who lives in the Deep South and moves to Texas. Nanci is something special. She's also one of the reasons I'm singing in country music today. I thought to myself when I heard that song, I'm missing something. I was listening to so much alternative music like Hüsker Dü and the Smithereens and not much else back then, but "Mary and Omie" made me realize I should be listening to a lot more country music. I put it on almost every playlist I have. I get that song, and I get Nanci.

[I first heard the song] when I was working in retail, playing in a band on weekends and selling records on Monday, Tuesday, and Wednesday, around 1988. I go into work one day, and one of my coworkers puts on this Nanci Griffith record. I had never heard her before. I'm walking to the back and am listening to the song. I get halfway to the back with my backpack and just stand in my tracks. I turn around, walk back up front, and go, "Let me see that record. How have I not been listening to this my whole life?"[20]

Country star Darius Rucker first gained national recognition as lead singer for the nineties pop band Hootie and the Blowfish. His "Don't Think I Don't Think about It" was the first number one country song for a Black artist since Charley Pride in 1963.

PAISLEY ROBERTSON: I wish I had known what Odetta's biography told me before I worked with her. I regretted not knowing what she had gone through. She was having a really rough time when I went to work for her and was not nice sometimes. We went to Washington, DC, one time to do a Democratic fundraiser. We had done brunch. I was sitting down from Ted Kennedy. Odetta wanted to see the desk where Lincoln had signed the emancipation proclamation. The door swings open, and Harry Belafonte starts singing, "Day-O." [Desmond] Tutu's nieces were there.

I was sitting next to Cesar Chavez downstairs and ran into Gloria Steinem. She was skinny as a rail with a dress that only had one shoulder. Odetta, who had a thing about her weight, was like, "Well, hi, you skinny little thing. How are you doing?" I saw Gloria Steinem blanch. Odetta thought anything skinny was good, but I said, "I know what you mean, Gloria. At least you're fatter than

I am." Odetta just tore me a new one as soon as we left. "You threw away my compliment," she said. "How dare you?" I worked for her for two months, and then I quit.

Odetta was so abused. Her father gave her to one of his work buddies to marry when she was just a little girl. Her mother was just a little girl. Odetta was treated differently because she was so Black. I remember someone from NPR was introducing her and said in a tasteful way, "Why do you think your career isn't doing anything?" She narrowed her eyes. "Honey," she said, "I would be on the top of the pile right now if I was white." All those people like Judy Collins and Joni Mitchell were all based on her, but she was a traditionally built Black woman. I mean, we all loved Harry Belafonte, but he's pretty white. They were all white versions [of Odetta].

Odetta was very bitter. She wasn't getting anywhere with her career. Look at those women I just said. They used her as a model and cannibalized her career. David Amram said, "She's so difficult to work with. Why don't you come up here and help me?" That's what I ended up doing. Odetta really wanted to meet [Civil Rights leader] Barbara Jordan. She and I really got along until I went to work with her. She was giving workshops. "You just have to do music," she would say. "Music is a blessing. It's not why or where or how you sound. You just do it." She thought she was gonna sing at Obama's inauguration even though there was nothing on the books for that. She died right before, but she was very happy about Obama.[21]

JOHN GORKA: People run from folk music, but Nanci knew it was a worthy genre. Two scenes come to mind when we recorded "Wimoweh." There was quite a commotion in the studio as people were gathering and chatting, but the room fell silent when Odetta walked in. Remarkable. Such was her presence. The room went silent without her saying a word. We were all in pretty high spirits that day. I remember John Prine saying, "I'm going to go home and vacuum for a couple hours and sing 'Wimoweh.'"

NANCI GRIFFITH: Odetta stopped the session at one point. She was like the teacher at the head of the class saying, "Everyone needs to remember what this song is about." Then she said, "It's about people's freedom. Let's get to the bottom of this. I know it's not your language, but pretend it is. This is 'We Shall Overcome.' That's where it should come from." I had already heard the history lesson because Pete Seeger had called me up and given me the scoop, [but] this song sums up the spirit of a time, a place, and a people.[22]

PETE KENNEDY: I played on twelve tracks on the *Other Voices* album. We did half the album—usually all playing and singing live in one or two takes—first in Nashville. I remember I was staying at Shoney's on Music Row and walked next door to Bob's Big Boy for breakfast. [Legendary Elvis Presley and Gram Parsons guitarist] James Burton walked in and took his place directly behind me. I turned and said quietly, "You play guitar, right?" "Yeah," he said. "C'mon, I'll buy you breakfast." We chatted over breakfast, and then he gave me a lift to Jack's Tracks in his Cadillac. Maybe that breakfast was part of the magic dust that sprinkled over that project from start to finish. The stars were aligned.

PAT MCINERNEY: I have a special memory of doing "Are You Tired of Me My Darling?" Jack's Tracks was laid out with the main room and then the drum room, which is isolated with no window. Chet Atkins came in to play on the song. You had to load out through the drum room because the door goes right out into the parking lot. Chet's got his guitars. I went up and said, "Can I help you, Mr. Atkins?" I picked up his guitar. "Mr. Atkins," I said, "it truly was an honor to play with you." "Son," he said, "what exactly did you do?" There was my brush with greatness squashed. "I played drums," I said. "Oh," he said. "You did a great job."

PETE KENNEDY: Then we camped out in Dublin and did most of the rest with a few latecomer cuts with Chet Atkins and Leo Kottke. I met Philip Donnelly during the *Other Voices* sessions at the Windmill Lane Studio in Dublin. I always thought of Philip as Nanci's real guitarist and loved his brilliant playing on her Rounder records, which are considered the classic Nanci sound. Philip had certain Stratocaster licks that sounded like pedal steel. They were such a part of Nanci's sound that I consciously imitated them sometimes to make the band laugh. Philip played on John Prine's original recording of "Speed of the Sound of Loneliness," so it was fitting that he played on Nanci's version as well.

"This Old Town" was a revelation. Perfectly constructed song with a great uplifting message. I laid back, and Béla Fleck played the basic instrumental hook. Then there was "Can't Help but Wonder Where I'm Bound" by our dear Tom Paxton. I played the little intro lick, a few fills, and the first half of the solo. Philip did lovely high filigree patters and came booming in with a really forthright statement for the second half of the solo. He was larger than life both musically and in person.

I've always played Stratocasters and Telecasters for my electric guitars, and volume swells are part of the Fender technique because of the placement of the volume knob near the strings. I did swells throughout "Comin' Down in the Rain" to suggest a sort of watercolor rain atmosphere. "Three Flights Up" begins with Nanci, Frank Christian, and me playing interlaced acoustic trio parts. I played the solo bits with the neck pickup of the Telecaster to get a deep rich tone that would sound like the timbre and cadence of Jerry Jeff

Walker's voice on "Morning Song for Sally," since he wrote the song. I thought that might suggest a sort of vocal duet even though Jerry Jeff wasn't actually singing on the song.

FRAN BREEN: The last album I did with Nanci was *Other Voices, Other Rooms*. I have to say that there were great days. Nanci was very benevolent and kind. She bought a house in Nashville and furnished it so we could live in it [while recording and touring]. She even bought a box of Major cigarettes and left them on the mantle because we both smoked those.

MAURA KENNEDY: The first time I played with Nanci was her *Other Voices* tour, which was the pinnacle for her. She had a nine-piece band with a drummer and a percussionist, stayed in the best hotels, and played the best theaters. She played two nights at Royal Albert Hall. I thought playing bars in Austin was the definition of success. [I joined the group because] Pete had sent me a set list of the songs Nanci intended to do on that tour. He also sent me a cassette of Nanci singing all the songs that would end up being on *Other Voices, Other Rooms* with just her acoustic guitar. I had a little four-track tape recorder and recorded every song on her set list. Then I recorded all the songs that would be on the *Other Voices* album. I remember what a big deal it was to scrape up the money to send it FedEx to where Pete was rehearsing with her for the sessions in Oregon.

Pete passed it along to Nanci. She asked a couple days later if I wanted to go out on the road with them. I couldn't believe it. No audition. Pete went into the rehearsal studio one day, and Nanci said, "I just listened to that tape that Maura sent. I wonder if she would want to come out on the road with us." [It was so trusting] for her to hire me without auditioning me or seeing me sing in a live setting. She didn't know how I sounded live or how I was onstage or if I would be a compatible person to share a bus with. She just liked it and trusted Pete or me to commit me to a two-month tour with them.

PETE KENNEDY: Our UK tour lasted three weeks from around Thanksgiving through around Christmas. I hadn't been in Nanci's band one week when we were playing at the Hammersmith Odeon [in London]. Mind boggling. Plus, everything was so fascinating since it was my first time in Europe. Nanci was a connoisseur of cool hotels, which was really different from the usual Nashville way to tour keeping costs down. You would stay in Holiday Inns or on the bus for those, but with Nanci we were staying at these hotels I could never have afforded on my own. That whole tour was cool just as a life experience, not to mention having a great gig. We toured behind *Other Voices* for two months when Maura joined the band.

MAURA KENNEDY: She had one day with a gig and one day off for the entire tour. We did thirty gigs with thirty days off in sixty days. The double joy of having a great gig with great material and a dedicated sold-out audience was being able to explore the next day. The *Other Voices* tour was a dream. The last adventure we had was toward the end in Northern Ireland. The theater was right next to the Unionist headquarters in Belfast. The headquarters had gotten bombed, but it hit the theater too. We didn't have a place to play. Our hotel, the Europa, was the most bombed place in Europe at the time. All the windows were blown out. We went to the hotel and saw all the windows boarded up except the few they replaced for us to stay in. We just wanted to get out of Belfast.

We weren't gonna be able to do the gigs. We had something like four or five there. Nanci was huge in Belfast and Ireland in general. We all chartered a bus and drove up to the Giant's Causeway, which is way up on the northern shore and the place where the cover for Led Zeppelin's *Houses of the Holy* was shot. There were all these cool, octagonal-shaped stones. We spent lots of time walking around London and Dublin on that tour plus York, England. There were narrow lanes and old villages there like walking around in a Harry Potter set.

Nanci had hits with "It's a Hard Life (Wherever You Go)" and "From a Distance" in Ireland. The Irish people had been through so much trouble and were so soulful. Nanci's songs were very personal about trials and persevering, which spoke to them as a people. They adored her and loved her voice and sense of humor. We still have friends that we met [on that tour] back in 1993. Nanci had only met them at the gig, but she acted toward them as if they were her own nieces and nephews. I asked her if she was related, but she said, "Oh, no, but they're such a lovely family." Nanci encouraged them. One boy is singing in the national choir now in Dublin.

I remember when Pete and I were a new couple and first on the road with Nanci. We were on the bus and snuggling. Nanci looked at us and said, "Some of us are alone." Nanci Griffith being lonely never occurred to me. She had this massive, dedicated audience that would show up wherever she went, but she had to give up that personal aspect of having a normal life and family to follow her dream of touring all over the world and playing the songs she wrote. I realized that what Pete and I had was really rare. Nanci clung to the comfort of the audience, but she was alone. I don't want to say she was lonely like she was sad because I think she liked her aloneness and didn't need a partner, but she was lonely at times.

MELANIE SMITH-HOWARD: Nanci was lonely. She was a female out on the road sometimes three, four, six months touring. You have to decompress and call people to say you're back when you get to town. It's harder on your love life for a female. You're constantly starting over and reconnecting with friends and family. I was aware of the sadness in her personal life from being on the road so much. I met several of her boyfriends. She liked intelligent men, but I don't believe she ever had true love. Maybe with her ex-husband, Eric, but I didn't know her then.

She was content being married to the job. I guess you have to give up something. Do you give up true love to be loved and adored by your fans? Those fans are from a distance when you get home. I would say her friendship with Harlan was one of the steadiest relationships she had. They adored each other. She's always adoringly looking at him in photographs. They're both smoking and drinking. They could have been father and daughter. They had a mutual respect club.

JAMES HOOKER: Townes, Guy, and Harlan lived rent-free in Nanci's head. We got them around us every chance we could get. Harlan Howard did a whole tour with us in Ireland. He didn't really perform. He and his new wife, Melanie, just came and hung out with us on tour. Harlan and Melanie stayed at all the same hotels as us. He would be sitting around the bar with us or go shopping around Dublin. He might have come onstage at a couple select places.

TOM PAXTON: Nanci had the towering power to make every song her own. Great artists can do that, which is why you hear a disc jockey talk about a Sinatra song when he didn't write it. Sinatra made those songs his. Jim Rooney deserves a lot of credit for his production on *Other Voices*. He worked with Nanci and stayed in the background, which I've [seen firsthand]. I've done albums with Jim, and he's a great producer. He guides you but lets you do your own thing. He has tremendous confidence to know when a song is done. I did an album with him called *Redemption Road*. Half the tracks on there are first or second takes. Jim can say after a first take, "You got it. Move on." Some producers will say, "Here's take forty-two." I like the way Jim works. He won't doggedly go over and over something in hopes of getting it perfect. "Let's get this done."

PETE KENNEDY: Jim Rooney's genius is that he works with really good people and songwriters. He gets really good people to play on the records. Then he just lets them do their thing. He might have a meeting with the artist to discuss what songs to do and little suggestions like putting Jerry Douglas on Dobro, but he's not hands-on with the arrangement or telling the singer how to sing. He just gets people who can come in and do it. Rooney was the easiest person to work with. We were barely aware of him once we went into the recording room. We were just the band playing together like we always did. We would be looking to Nanci [for direction], not over our shoulder at Rooney to see if he would change our part.

TOM PAXTON: Nanci always told a story with clarity. Look at "Love at the Five and Dime." Such a darling song. What she's talking about is so clear. Much like Townes Van Zandt's great song "Snowin' on Raton" that goes, "Snowin' on Raton / Come morning I'll be through the hills and gone." I love Townes's work. Guy was a songwriter's songwriter. Only a real confident songwriter writes "Homegrown Tomatoes," goddammit. I have a lot of time for that whole Texas group. I loved and treasured that when we were saying goodbye after the *Other Voices* taping in Austin, Guy said, "Tom, you're a sweet cat." I called him up one day and said, "Guy. This is Tom Damn Paxton," like how he introduced his guitarist Verlon Thompson.

Guy owned me. I thought anything he wrote was fabulous, like those lines in "Homegrown Tomatoes": "Only two things that money won't buy / That's true love and homegrown tomatoes." He was a sweet cat, a really lovely guy. I did a series of eight radio shows with BBC Scotland one time. We went to Guy's house. Picked up a bottle of Scotch on the way. We went down to his workshop and did the show. We played a couple songs, then spent the rest of the day getting drunk up in his house. Everybody came over. Guy was trying to get some smoke. Guy finally got some so he could be happy. I had to go to a dinner that night and barely made it out of there.

RILEY HICKERSON: I lived in Europe for eighteen years and was arrested for possession of fifty kilograms of hashish going into England from France in a car with Dutch license plates. Talk about asking for trouble. I was in a jail cell serving a six-year sentence in her majesty's prison when I got a package Nanci sent. The box was filled with her T-shirts and cassettes. The shirts said on the back, "Friends don't let friends vote Republican."

The prison guards were really impressed that I knew Nanci Griffith. They all knew who she was because Nanci was so popular over there. I told them we were next-door neighbors growing up. My brother Russell had given Nanci [the prison] address at a Holy Cross reunion, and this big box that she sent probably was one and a half feet by a foot wide and eight inches deep. She also included tapes by Joe Ely and others. I don't know if it helped how they treated me, but it certainly didn't hurt. Well, I did get furloughed after that, so maybe they were nicer. They just couldn't believe I knew Nanci Griffith.

My brother Russell later died from pancreatic cancer, and I was late getting to one of our Holy Cross reunions. Nanci waited and stayed such a long time because she wasn't gonna leave until she told me how sorry she was that my brother had died. We talked that evening. She was very sympathetic and went out of her way to express that she was sorry. It meant so much that she made it a point to stay. Nanci always treated me like I was her best friend. She never forgot the little people that she met on the way up. An amazing woman. Nanci had such a legion who loved her, but she never forgot my brother and me and always invited us backstage at her concerts when she came back to Austin.

I never met anybody like her in my whole life.

MICHAEL CORCORAN: I picked up my reviewer ticket at one Griffith show at the Majestic Theatre in Dallas in 1993 [and found out] it was front row center. That never happens with critics. I traded seats with someone in about the fifteenth row thinking I was being set up for an undressing in front of the whole crowd. I [later] realized maybe it was a peace offering by burying the hatchet with the best seat in the house.

• *Other Voices, Other Rooms* Tour, Carnegie Hall, March 25, 1993 •

CLIFF EBERHARDT: Nanci had Odetta, Gorka, Janis Ian, Julie Gold, Emmylou Harris, and me all sing with her at Carnegie Hall [on the *Other Voices, Other Rooms* tour]. Pretty amazing. This was great for all of us, and I ended up opening for Emmylou because of that show.

JAMES HOOKER: Bill Murray was with us at the Russian Tea Room. I was sitting beside Bill across the table from Emmylou Harris. She was talking about how she had burned the bread she was making and blamed it on the oven. Bill said something like, "Emmy, lots of men are pretty fond of warm ovens." She reached over and slapped the shit out of him. Then she continued talking to him. We went all over the city that night. A high point of my life was singing a duet on "Gulf Coast Highway" with Emmylou that night. Carnegie Hall was the first time I had played somewhere with a true upstage and downstage. The back of the stage is actually higher than the front and slopes down toward the audience.

JULIE GOLD: I got an expensive Tahari suit like a tuxedo with satin lapels because I didn't know what to wear at Carnegie Hall. Nanci was in a dressing room on the sixth floor when I arrived off the subway. A piano was in her room with a table with expensive food. We went down to the stage for sound check and found the place empty. Felt like walking into a dream. Nanci took a yellow rose, which I still have thirty years later, and pinned it to my lapel. I milled through the audience to find my whole family later. People kept coming up asking where their seats were.

All the usherettes were wearing exactly what I was except with a red rose in their lapel. My yellow rose made me look like the head usher. I eventually found my family. Beautiful show. That was my humbling experience that night, but I found my family and it was a beautiful show. I used to give Nanci a kiss after we would perform. She would have a little lip stain on her cheek at the end of every performance.

BRIAN WOOD: I remember Nanci pacing up and down, up and down in the green room at Carnegie Hall before we went on. She looked at me and said, "Aren't you nervous?" This is the beauty of being a sideman. "No," I said, "it's just another gig." We got up there and it was fine, but I could not believe that I was standing on the stage at Carnegie Hall. The curious thing about that gig was sound check. We were the last on the list to do ours. Guys were standing on the side of the stage with a stopwatch. "You have forty-five seconds to do your sound check."

We just made sure everything was plugged in and worked. I literally had to sprint off the stage watching this clown with his stopwatch. They ran a tight union shop. It would cost the producer of the concert if you didn't get off the stage in time. The whole thing was so ridiculous. The very next day I got my musician's union card, not because I wanted to but because I thought, I'm never gonna get thrown off the stage by these ghouls because I don't have this little card in my wallet.

Nanci always referred to me onstage as her right-hand man. She was great to me. She had [Carnegie Hall] in the back of her mind back in the *Poet in My Window* days. She never told me that directly, but I could see the trajectory of where it was going. Everything came to a head when she decided to move to Nashville. She really wanted me to move to Nashville, but I had this day job and couldn't make the finance work. Music means so much to me that I'm not sure I can do it for a living. I never wanted to feel like I was picking up my guitar case to go to work.

JOHN GORKA: I got a call one time when I was in Nashville and they were recording *Other Voices, Other Rooms*. They asked me if I wanted to come down when they were recording "Wimoweh." I happened to have the day off and got to sing on that record, which was one of my high points. I got to open a number of shows on that *Other Voices* tour in Minneapolis, Des Moines, and New York City at her Carnegie Hall show. The grand finale was at the Paramount Theatre in Austin.

Nanci was headlining the Carnegie Hall show. There was quite a cast of characters at that show: Emmylou Harris, Janis Ian, Odetta, Iris DeMent, Jim Rooney, Cliff Eberhardt, Frank Christian, and Harlan Howard. I played a song called "The Gypsy Life," which Nanci had sung with me on my record. The logistics were so tight that I couldn't use my own guitar, so the woman who sang backup for Nanci gave me her guitar. I played my only song at Carnegie Hall on a borrowed guitar. I was pretty starstruck and tend to embarrass myself when I'm around people like Emmylou.

MELANIE SMITH-HOWARD: Nanci invited us to go to Carnegie Hall when she played. Watching her at Carnegie Hall was awesome. Nanci played Harlan's song "Never Mind" that night. Harlan absolutely loved having his sweet friend play one of his songs at Carnegie Hall. That was on his bucket list. Buck Owens and others had done things when he wasn't in attendance, but he was there that night. Nanci called him out, and Harlan stood up and waved. Harlan loved the recognition.

Harlan was drawn to Nanci because she wasn't just so self-absorbed in her own work. She was involved in shining the light on lots of artists who opened for her and songwriters on albums like *Other Voices, Other Rooms*. She absolutely shined a light on your work if she loved it. Not many people did that. Nanci was a writer first. I think she would have been content being an author or songwriter if she hadn't had the gift of singing. Harlan and Nanci were both introverts, but they both loved words and playing with them like a crossword puzzle.

JOY LEWALLEN: I went to see her headline at Carnegie Hall. Phenomenal. The place was full and there she was: my friend. Onstage. Of course, I was proud of her. I loved how everybody was there to see her. She wasn't the opening act. She was headlining. We had a party afterwards at the Russian Tea Room, but she never came over to say hi to my friends and me. I realized that she was a star. She wasn't just Nanci. You have to be very well regarded and accomplish things to be asked to be on the stage at Carnegie Hall. I went to many sold-out concerts, but I wish she was here today to read all the accolades written about her after she died. Amazing.

Nanci's fellow songwriters appreciated her very much. She was such a champion of women musicians just starting out. There's a story about Kelly Willis being in the audience one time. Nanci said, "Come on up here and sing with me." My friend Denice Franke was a backup singer for her, and Nanci was a champion of her music. She appreciated good songwriting. John Prine was one hero of hers. She took his death really hard. John was a brilliant storyteller. You wanted to meet his characters like you did hers. She loved John. It was fun to watch them at concerts because you knew they were really friends. They would joke around and laugh backstage. You could tell by the way they interacted that they were close.

They were like old friends when I saw them interact. John had a killer sense of humor too. I don't think they had a starstruck thing between them. David Letterman did with her. You can tell when he's interviewing her. She charmed him for sure. I loved watching her on Letterman's show because I got to witness all of her hairstyles. She did some pretty cool things on his show and sung her heart out. You could tell she was shy the first time because it was her first television appearance, but she warmed up and fell into it. Nanci being so self-confident onstage came from her music. She was very confident about the songs she wrote and wanted people to hear them. She was proud of what she stood for.

PETE KENNEDY: Carnegie Hall was great. Carnegie Hall's opening night was Tchaikovsky conducting the *1812 Overture*. You can't get much bigger. Playing Carnegie Hall is the ultimate gig. You develop hopes and dreams for the artist as a sideman that put your own aside. So, as much as I thought it was cool for me to be onstage at Carnegie Hall, seeing Nanci really making it as a folksinger playing acoustic guitar at Carnegie and the ultimate English gig at the Royal Albert Hall made me so happy. She was so dedicated to her art. I got to see that her determination had really paid off.

It's a cliché to say someone gave it their all at every gig, but Nanci really did. I don't think she performed differently at Carnegie Hall because she would perform at the same level if we were in Aberdeen, Scotland. She was really on every night. She really enjoyed hosting Janis Ian, Emmylou, Julie Gold, Iris DeMent, and having them come out to sing with her at Carnegie Hall. She had an altruism that definitely extended to Maura and me. She had us as the opening act for her shows the next year. She knew that she was really getting up into the upper echelons and wanted to pull up others with her. Nanci's audience would give the stamp of approval to someone if Nanci had given hers, which was really helpful to Maura and me.

Nanci really enjoyed telling the audience who wrote the songs and helping others. Her whole life was about songwriters. She always acknowledged the writer when we did the *Other Voices* tour. Those were her people. "Please welcome Julie Gold, who used to be a secretary, but then she wrote this song. Now she's playing Carnegie Hall."

JULIE GOLD: Nanci included me every time she sang "From a Distance." I've had other songs performed on major stages, and people would say, "Julie, did you know so-and-so was singing such-and-such?" No. Would it hurt [for them] to call the songwriter who has lived for these moments? Would it hurt to say, "Thank you. I love your song. I'm singing it tonight?" Most people didn't. Nanci included me one hundred percent in the love, recognition, and popularity. What a gift.

PETE KENNEDY: Nanci loved doing that. Nanci and John Prine were like siblings when they were around each other. They had all this folklore between them. They would laugh all the time and nobody knew what they were talking about. They had so much chemistry. They were songwriting siblings. You knew they would last a lifetime.

CLIFF EBERHARDT: Nanci was headlining Carnegie Hall. Just walking onstage at Carnegie Hall was the greatest thing that had ever happened for Gorka and me. Some people just have empty holes in them that can't be filled. I have a lot of friends in this business like that. Nanci was always looking over her shoulder. "Well," she would say, "so-and-so never got a Grammy. I got a Grammy." "Okay." Nanci had a hard time being loved. I don't think love or even deep friendship felt comfortable for her. I would have loved to meet her parents.

Her family definitely was never talked about.

• • •

Nanci Griffith enlists powerhouse players (Counting Crows' Adam Duritz, the Indigo Girls, U2's Adam Clayton and Larry Mullen Jr.) and producers (R.E.M.'s Peter Buck and Elton John and Rush producer Peter Collins) for 1994's *Flyer* album. "[*Flyer*] is a departure for me in terms of writing technique," Griffith says. "It's all very personal. I don't want to pick out a specific [favorite] song because it's a new approach for me. I came up with a whole album of up close and personal Nanci Griffith songs instead of writing fiction. I wanted to use live vocals [on *Flyer*] [to] keep my music fresh and make me sound human."[23]

Critical acclaim follows quickly. "[Nanci Griffith is] a wide-eyed Texas waif," *Time* magazine writes, "who may just be one of America's best poets and for sure is one of its best songwriters." "Her songs show that inside the wistful farm girl," echoes the *New York Times*, "beats the heart of a steely moralist." The album's title track comes from real life. "The Flyer' is a very true story," Griffith says. "In fact, John Gorka, who is one of my good friends and one of the best songwriters I know, was there when the incident happened. We were flying together. 'The Flyer' is about that coincidence of allowing yourself to pass through people instead of bumping into [them]. John was really thrilled when it became a song. He said, 'I was there.'"[24]

"I was sitting on the other side of Nanci when we had the experience for her song 'The Flyer,'" Gorka says. "We were going from Houston to Austin. I was on the aisle and Nanci was in the middle. She got into a conversation with a pilot. I always seem to be present during these events. Nanci's songs had more depth than the average song lyrics. She had literary ambitions. She had written a book called *Two of a Kind Heart*. I got a chance to read it. The book was about a folksinger going into the Northeast to pursue her heroes."

Flyer reaches number forty-eight on the *Billboard* pop chart and peaks at twenty in the United Kingdom. The aforementioned guest stars boost the album. "The guys like Adam Duritz and Darius Rucker who came in to sing on *Flyer* were crazy about Nanci," Pat McInerney says. "Adam and Darius both put their heart and soul into it." "I love Adam," Griffith says. "He's a marvelous writer. There are two writers right now who all women are mad over because of the lyrics: Darius Rucker of Hootie and the Blowfish and Adam Duritz of Counting Crows. Their lyrics are incredibly sensitive to women's feelings." *People* magazine succinctly sums up Griffith's place in modern music: "She is our leading creator of folk-based pop songs."[25]

"Nanci's music evolved," Ken Levitan says. "Steve Ralbovsky was the A&R person who put *Flyer* together. We tried to expand Nanci's audience by having her contemporaries like Adam Duritz play with her. Big fan. Adam Clayton and Larry Mullen from U2 played bass and drums. Many contemporaries understood her talent." Standout tracks such as "Going Back to Georgia," "Talk to Me While I'm Listening," "On Grafton Street," and the buoyant closer "This Heart" give peers further proof. Additionally, Griffith notches her third Grammy nomination for *Flyer*.

However, Johnny Cash's iconic *American Recordings* wins the Best Contemporary Folk Album over Griffith, Shawn Colvin (*Cover Girl*), Iris DeMent (*My Life*), and the Indigo Girls (*Swamp Ophelia*) at the ceremony on March 1, 1995. "Getting the nomination was a thrill," says Indigo Girls singer-songwriter Emily Saliers. "There's the exotic [nature] of going out to Los Angeles and seeing all these music stars. Then we could go to the record company after-parties later. Maybe Michael Jackson or Bob Dylan would be in the room. You're like, 'Holy shit, is this really happening to us?' Those early days were quite heady."

PETER COLLINS: I started as an English pop producer and evolved into rock and more singer-songwriter music when I moved to Nashville. I was working project to project and didn't have time to listen to much of anything else back then, so I honestly wasn't too familiar with Nanci's music besides hits like "Love at the Five and Dime." Elektra's A&R guy Steve Ralbovsky asked if I was interested in working with Nanci. I was. I had just done an Indigo Girls album in Nashville and really loved Woodland Studio where we recorded, and Nanci was happy to record there. Nanci and I got on well when we initially met. Also, we had a really good budget.

One memorable moment was when I wanted to have a jug played on "The Flyer." I told Nanci that I thought that would work really well. She said, "Okay."

Nanci walked in in the middle of the song and said, "I'm not having flatulence on my record." I also remember trying to get a feel for a song—I think "These Days in an Open Book"—when we were doing preproduction. The band just wasn't getting the feel. We did it over and over. Nanci hurried out into the corridor and screamed. She came back in with the perfect temperament again.[26]

British-born producer Peter Collins has worked with Air Supply, Bon Jovi, Alice Cooper, Queensryche, Rush, Billy Squier, and dozens more. He lives in Nashville.

EMILY SALIERS: Peter Collins got us on *Flyer*. Nanci picked the songs ["These Days Are an Open Book" and "Time of Inconvenience"] for us. We had sung live together with Nanci by then, but it was an honor to be on her album. We recorded both tracks the same day. I remember we were trying to come up with harmony ideas and parts for "Time of Inconvenience." Nanci heard the harmony part we were doing and liked it, but that part was never intended to be the opening for that song [credited in the liner notes as "accidental a capella intro on 'Time'"]. They chose to use it as [the song's intro] in the end.

PETER COLLINS: I remember Adam Duritz being superprofessional during his sessions. "Going Back to Georgia" was fabulous.

ADAM DURITZ: Counting Crows were touring on our first album, *August and Everything After*, when Nanci and I worked on "Going Back to Georgia" for her *Flyer* album. [Steve Ralbovsky] tried signing us to Elektra Records the year before and knew I was a huge fan. He must have talked about me when they were planning out *Flyer*. He called and said, "Nanci Griffith would like you to sing on her record." I was totally floored. "Absolutely." They sent me a demo of an early version of "Going Back to Georgia" sung by Al Anderson. I was a huge NRBQ fan.

I got on a plane to Nashville at six in the morning, crashed for a little bit when I got there, and then Nanci picked me up. I had rewritten lyrics for my parts on the flight and was terrified that she wouldn't think they were okay. I mean, I loved Nanci's music, her songwriting, and her voice, especially on *Late Night Grande Hotel*. Her songs like "Late Night Grande Hotel," "Drive-In Movies and Dashboard Lights," "Trouble in the Fields," and "Ford Econoline" had deeply moved me and influenced me as a songwriter. Now I'm meeting my idol and asking if it was okay to change her lyrics? I very shyly brought it up and showed her the changes [in the studio]. She actually liked them and was very excited. We sang them in the control room.

The recording session was really great, easy, and quick. Nanci added harmonies when we came back to sing together in the last verse, which was really cool. Meeting your idol is always rough, but Nanci was wonderful. I had been so intimidated to do the duet on "Going Back to Georgia," but she immediately made me feel relaxed. "Going Back to Georgia" is the best guest vocal I've ever done because she brought out the best in me.[27]

Adam Duritz has served as lead singer and songwriter for Counting Crows since 1991. The chart-topping band's popular records—from the debut, August and Everything After *(1993), through the recent EP,* Butter Miracle, Suite One *(2021)—have sold more than twenty million copies.*

PETER COLLINS: I pride myself on being a vocal producer. I would say that [might be the best vocal performance of Adam's career]. I didn't have to do much work with him. The lyrics he rewrote for "Going Back to Georgia" were fabulous. He was very easy to record. Nothing but joyful memories working with him. I listened to the song today, and it still sounds great. The whole arrangement on that song is extremely good. Al Anderson came up with a wonderful motif on guitar. Getting a signature hook like that is hugely important for me in the production. You recognize that song as soon as it comes on.

ADAM DURITZ: The song is fucking spectacular. I'm sure Nanci would [have told me if she didn't like my rewritten lyrics]. You don't get to be Nanci Griffith by being mediocre. She recognized how nervous I was and just knew how to get that performance out of me. [Nanci set] a really good example for how to work with a young artist.

I was really lucky to be around people who did things the right way early on, like when Counting Crows were opening for the Rolling Stones that same summer. The Stones were really kind. We were not only welcome in their dressing room, but they would come get us if we weren't in there before the shows. [Rolling Stones guitarists] Ron [Wood] and Keith [Richards] wanted to play snooker with us. You know, they really didn't need to be that way. They're the Rolling Stones. They could have been assholes, but they are music lovers and were really great. Nanci was a music lover who was exactly the same as the Stones.

She told me Everly Brothers stories when we went out drinking after the session. So cool. Such a good memory for me. Fame and success change your level in life and how people see you. Fame does different things to different people. I don't understand why, but there are people out there who are fucking terrible to others. Nanci, the Stones, and Maria McKee were great to me and really became my best friends. I might have become the person I am anyway, but I know I had some really good examples at the beginning. They showed me how you can act with people.

Nanci and I kept in touch for a bit, and my parents and I went to see her play one time. She was so gracious and great toward them, but I have this bad and regrettable habit of being housebound and not staying in touch with people because of my dissociative [identity disorder] and insecurity. I don't think people want to hear from me so I don't bug them or stay in touch. Then time passes. I try to be better about keeping in touch with people now, but I was also so shy back then. That day in Nashville—the whole thing, getting there, working on the song, going out drinking after—was so incredible. Nanci was such a rocker.

The art is the real thing when you're an artist or musician. We immortalized "Going Back to Georgia." You make things that are timeless. That song is timeless and came back up when we were doing the Traveling Circus tour ten years ago. We had all three bands [Counting Crows, Michael Franti and Spearhead, and Augustana] on one tour playing the whole show together. [*Shameless* and *Phantom of the Opera* star] Emmy Rossum was my girlfriend at the time. Great singer. We decided to put "Going Back to Georgia" in the set. Emmy and I singing it was killer, amazing, the highlight of the set. We absolutely nailed "Going Back to Georgia." So cool to sing that song every night that Nanci and I wrote together.

PAT MCINERNEY: Adam was nervous [because he rewrote the lyrics to "Goin' Back to Georgia"]. You know, Nanci was always fine with that if she liked what someone wrote. She was up for collaborating. She knew how to work with people from [working in] the folk club scene in Houston. "You know," she said to me one time, "I have so many songs, I'm starting to forget lyrics. Hey, I know what I'll do. I'll just make them up. That's what I did in the first place."

ADAM DURITZ: Nanci had a way with words and melody and a way of singing that takes you in. You really get the person she's singing about in her songs. Maybe that's why "Going Back to Georgia" is such a joy for me. I feel Nanci and me when I'm singing it and when I hear it because that song really captured us both. Also, I wrote that Hank Williams quote into the song, "Long gone lonesome blue." I even sang it a little like that song. Singing that quote is such a joyful moment.

FRED KOLLER: Nanci was a writer who knew the characters she was portraying. Her songs told the story. You could tell she believed what she was singing. "The Last of the True Believers" really was Nanci. She believed in love and romance. We wrote "On Grafton Street" [on *Flyer*] at her house in Franklin. She started telling me the story, and we talked about Catholicism and the candles they burned. She told me about people she knew who had passed away. "I hear you live in Dallas now in a house out on the plains." She painted a clear picture.

Nanci wouldn't fight you over a certain word when you cowrote. I think we had some hesitancy thinking the line "far from the madding crowd" in "On Grafton Street" was too literary a reference, but we overcame that quickly. The line still works. She didn't care as long as the words were the right ones. Nanci cut "On Grafton Street" in Ireland because [bassist Adam Clayton and drummer Larry Mullen Jr.] from the band U2 were on the song. [Irish singer] Frances Black released her version of the song simultaneously, which didn't receive much play here but was very nicely done. I was always happy when Nanci recorded my songs or a song we wrote together.

NANCI GRIFFITH: Larry and I had talked for eight years about working together. We finally had time to get together. This was the first time that Larry or Adam had worked on anybody else's project but U2. I record very differently than they do. I record with everybody together in one room. Also, [R.E.M. guitarist] Peter Buck produced several songs for *Flyer*, and we ended up using two. Working with Peter was wonderful. [He was a] lovely producer not unlike Jim Rooney [in that] he was there to referee. He's more than happy to if you wanted him to play some guitar, but he's basically there to keep everybody from running amok.[28]

FRED KOLLER: I enjoyed talking with Nanci because there were more and more women in Nashville trying to just be vocalists at the time. Nanci wanted people to see that she was [a hard worker and] a reader who wasn't embarrassed to read books. Think about all the pictures of her holding books by people like Larry McMurtry. We had a couple conversations about Larry when we first met. She was finishing his early books. I asked what she thought happened to [the character] Danny Deck [from McMurtry's novel *All My Friends Are Going to Be Strangers*]. She knew his characters like she knew [those in her songs].

PETER COLLINS: Then we went to Electric Lady Studios in New York to put Larry Mullen Jr. and Adam Clayton from U2 on the record. I had heard terrible stories about problematic maintenance at Electric Lady so I called the manager and said, "Look, I have U2 coming in and we're flying up from Nashville. Can you please make sure the studio is one hundred percent checked over? Very important session." I walk in the studio and technicians have the desk [taken] apart an hour before we were supposed to start working. Not a good sign.

They got [the desk] all back together, but we had huge technical problems throughout. Just a nightmare. We didn't complete all that we wanted to, so I had to relinquish control to the drummer Larry Mullen Jr. The studio manager sent me a box of Cuban cigars as [an apology]. I thought, That's nice, but they were all flaking, counterfeit. Adam and Larry were very easy to work with. Larry is extremely creative as a drummer. The energy in the studio was incredible. He clearly wanted to produce but tolerated me. He mixed "On Grafton Street" and "This Heart."

• • •

Nanci Griffith employs a backing string section on 1997's *Blue Roses from the Moons* songs new (the opening Matthew Ryan cowrite "Everything's Comin' Up Roses") and old (the Darius Rucker duet "Gulf Coast Highway"), and the closing nod toward Guy Clark on his masterful "She Ain't Goin' Nowhere." Other key tracks include "Not My Way Home," "Saint Teresa of Avila" (cowritten years earlier with her sister Mikki and best friend Margaret Mary), and covers written by Sonny Curtis ("I Fought the Law") and Nick Lowe and Paul Carrack ("Battlefield"). Popular rock and roll producer Don Gehman (Hootie and the Blowfish, R.E.M.) steering the ship shows Griffith's heightened commercial appeal.

"Nanci was making what was supposed to be a big, successful record with Don Gehman," Jim Rooney says. "They were recording at Woodland Sound across the river with Jerry Allison, Sonny Curtis, and Joe B. Mauldin from the Crickets. I went over. I knew Don's reputation but didn't know him personally when I went [to the studio]. They had a bunch of people there—the Crickets plus James Hooker and Pat McInerney. I brought a Sony mike over with me. Don was lighting candles all over. He had his own drum set all set up, not one for Jerry. They were all sitting around, which isn't my style at all. I don't like musicians sitting around."

PAT MCINERNEY: The key to playing drums with Nanci was listening to her guitar and the cadence of the vocal. Listen to how she wants to sing. The vocal rhythm was even more important than the guitar. Nanci couldn't take playing with a click track. I had to listen to how she played the song, and everything came together. There wasn't a great deal of push and pull. I wasn't fighting her rhythm guitar. I locked into her vocal, and it would be there. Nanci didn't like to rehearse or do too many takes in the studio. She would sit there all afternoon on the early records and recut songs, but not toward the middle of her career. You really had to get her on the run-through or the first take. She drifted after that.

NANCI GRIFFITH: "Not My Way Home" took me four years to write. I would work on it at sound checks and the band wanted to get it finished. Finally, it took Sonny Curtis sitting down next to me on a sofa [during sessions] for *Blue Roses from the Moons* and saying, "I sure would like to sing harmony on that song you've been working on for four years." We sang the chorus, and he sang a beautiful harmony. Then our juvenile in the Blue Moon Orchestra,

Doug Lancio, sat down on the sofa and played the most gorgeous guitar solo. "Not My Way Home" took the longest and will always remain my favorite.[29]

MATTHEW RYAN: Nanci and I had close friends in common. She had taken an interest in me, which was a huge compliment because I was in awe of her work and also how she carried herself. She was strong and kind, smart and funny, and exactly who she appeared to be. She invited me to a party at her house one night, and then more nights and gatherings followed. A mentorship and maybe even a friendship developed, but it didn't feel like business. [We had] a true musical friendship, which was an education for me. Nanci was so generous. I still lean on her wisdom.

[Nanci and I] sat down late in the morning to write [*Blue Roses from the Moons*' opening track] "Everything's Comin' Up Roses" and were done by lunch. Took maybe an hour or two. I do think we were trying to tell each other something in some of those lyrics. She clearly understood the humor in praise, blame, skin, heartbreak, and deliverance. I was just starting out. Nanci had a kind of hazelwood stick when it came to songs, lyrics, and melodies. She knew what she liked and seemed to be able to sort what was useful and resonant in almost an autonomic way.

We were in a beautiful room at her place when we [wrote the song]. Outside was green, and the room smelled very nice and clean and had a ton of wood in it and even more books. We sat across a small table from each other. [Writing] felt easy. I was young enough at the time not to fully understand how uniquely graceful Nanci was. The tone and generosity Nanci had about her deepens and widens as time goes on. It really did inform so much of what she offered both privately and publicly and how I've tried to carry myself.

Nanci was one of the kindest rebels I've ever met. She was a true heart, a true believer. I felt like I was sitting next to a lake when I was around her. She was generous, sweet, funny, and smart as a whip and had insight into people and what we do. [She had] a sadness but not necessarily a darkness. She knew music inside and out and had one of the most beautiful smiles I've been in the presence of, which always [seemed] to say, "I know. It's ridiculous. We're ridiculous. The world is ridiculous, and it gets ugly, but the beauty available here in this experience far outweighs all the hurt and turmoil. Keep going. It'll be all right."

[Nanci's songwriting] had an effortlessness, an ease, clarity. She had—and still has—a unique ability to tell a listener hard things with a gentleness that honors the complexities of the human condition. Her songwriting is quietly provocative and compels a listener to be honest with themselves and what they did or do, what they have or have lost. Buddhists often call it "grandmotherly love." That's not a comment on Nanci as she aged, but that pure love of truth is what appealed to me in her work. Honesty in work and what we express acts like wisdom and passes something potentially essential forward.

Nanci always handled her vocation with humor and heart. Absolutely no one sounds like Nanci. Her uniqueness was present in her speaking voice and everyday spirit. She had a strong and direct kindness about her. She knew well the sorrows of living collectively and privately and yet exuded an unmoved compassion for what's always possible. She was a clear-eyed romantic because in romance there's hope and in hope there's music. Nanci carried everything gracefully whether it be social issues or the personal maps of love and friendship. She was deep water with a beautiful sense of humor.[30]

•   •   •

Nanci Griffith's slow personal and professional decline begins with the *Other Voices, Other Rooms* follow-up, *Other Voices, Too (A Trip Back to Bountiful)*, four years after her Grammy award win. "Nanci was really starting to slide into drinking and becoming a demanding diva by *Other Voices, Too*," says Jim Rooney, who again produces the folk collection. "She was obsessed with her success." "You can't talk about Nanci's life without acknowledging that she was a terrible alcoholic—especially during the second half of her life," echoes producer Thomm Jutz.

"Nanci had a horrific problem with alcohol."[31]

The expansive album—nineteen songs recorded mostly at Jack's Tracks in Nashville and Windmill Lane Studios in Dublin—receives mediocre reviews. "Nanci had given a serious boost to people like Odetta and Dave Van Ronk [with *Other Voices, Other Rooms*] when their careers weren't particularly buoyant," guitarist Brian Willoughby says. "Nanci was quite proud of the album and the book for *Other Voices, Too*, but unfortunately there's only so much critical acclaim you can get for that kind of thing where you're putting people together [to sing folk songs]. I suppose critics probably were already critiqued out after the first *Other Voices*. Then we toured the album."[32]

JIM ROONEY: Of course, then there was *Other Voices, Too (A Trip Back to Bountiful)*. "Let's do it again."

PAT MCINERNEY: Nanci won the Contemporary Folk Grammy for *Other Voices*. Rooney says in the liner notes to *Other Voices, Too (A Trip Back to Bountiful)* that we tried to hit lightning twice. We may not have quite made it. The record is good but not like the one we did before. We recorded that one all over the place. I loved Mickie Merkens's "Yarrington Town."

RON DE LA VEGA: The first album I played on was *Other Voices, Too (A Trip Back to Bountiful)*. We all helped with arrangements. The songs obviously were there, and Nanci had strong ideas about them. The bandleader James Hooker would put his twist to the songs, but we were all part of the process. We would add to the songs and take away, but we didn't necessarily rehearse. We didn't want to have a polished performance or recording because it was organic folk music. We wanted to leave it to the basic arrangements. The recordings really were a conversation musically. We tended to go full-on to get the conversation going.

Ron de la Vega served as bassist in Nanci Griffith's Blue Moon Orchestra.

PETE KENNEDY: We had become [the band] the Kennedys by *Other Voices, Too (A Trip Back to Bountiful)* and were no longer in Nanci's band. Maura and I had moved to the DC area but went down to Nashville to do a couple sessions for that record such as [the Tom Rush and Eric Von Schmidt arrangement of the traditional] "Wasn't That a Mighty Storm" and [Sylvia Fricker's] "You Were on My Mind." We were guest musicians by then.

BRIAN WILLOUGHBY: Nanci was there when I went to see Loudon Wainwright at 3rd and Lindsley in Nashville in the midnineties. I introduced myself as a friend of Pat McInerney's. Nanci was at her peak musically and was really friendly. She invited me to play on the *Other Voices, Too (A Trip Back to Bountiful)* sessions because I was in a band called the Strawbs. She wanted to do the song "Who Knows Where the Time Goes?" by Sandy Denny, and Sandy had been the lead singer of the Strawbs at one time. I had an absolutely fantastic time playing on that song and also playing on Richard Thompson's "Wall of Death."

I met people like Carolyn Hester, the fabulous Odetta, Tom Russell, Andrew Hardin, and the wonderful old character Dave Van Ronk. Three Irish girls were on it: Sharon Shannon on accordion, Mary Custy on violin, and Dolores Keane singing. We had a wonderful experience recording at Windmill Studios in Dublin, which was where I met Eric Taylor for the first time. The day we met was the day before the sessions would begin. We sat in the hotel bar drinking red wine longer than we should have. Nanci was not pleased, but you could tell they still loved each other as friends. He was a wonderful songwriter. I really enjoyed my time with him.

I remember playing with Nanci, James Hooker, and Pat McInerney on a show with the BBC Symphony Orchestra, one at the Jazz Cafe in Camden, and also John Dankworth's venue called the Stables. They were really enjoyable shows, but the most enjoyable one we did ourselves on the brilliant Gloria Hunniford television show. I found it really easy to embellish what Nanci was doing because she was a superb guitarist and the ultimate, consummate pro.

She was a great musician and songwriter, but she was even better with the audience. She had them in the palm of her hands.[33]

British guitarist Brian Willoughby has performed with the Strawbs, Dave Cousins, Mary Hopkin, and several others.

RON DE LA VEGA: Nanci had so many folk heroes on *Other Voices, Too*. I enjoyed the whole process working with everyone involved. The sessions definitely were upbeat. The difficulty in the studio sometimes would be communication because we're all human. Communication would fall or lapse, but we would step away. Nanci was great at that. We would step away and come back fresh. We rarely got mired down. Nanci pretty much coproduced whatever she did, and she knew [in that role] when to say, "Let's take a minute and breathe. Take the night. We'll come back." There were hiccups along the way, but nothing got bogged down.[34]

PAT MCINERNEY: [The atmosphere] in the studio for that album was different than the first. Nanci got really tired of the process in the middle of recording, and keeping up the momentum was difficult for Jim. We recorded in Dublin, New York, [and] Jack's Tracks in Nashville, which made it tiring as we did that at the same time as Nanci's live gigs. Rooney did a great job keeping it all together. I had the feeling that Nanci had overreached with *Other Voices, Too*. The performances became a little less personal than the first record. The tone was more like, "Let's just get it done." I talked to Jim, and he said, "We probably could have made one really good record instead of a double album." "Darcy Farrow" with just Nanci and me and "Canadian Whiskey" with Tom Russell were great.

• "Canadian Whiskey" (Tom Russell) •

TOM RUSSELL: Fast-forward about fifteen years. Boy, what a journey from that Kerrville campfire. I was now opening Nanci's sold-out show at the Royal Albert Hall in London, which is one of the most prestigious gigs in the world. The queen even has a private box there. Nanci Griffith had arrived. She was a folk hero in Ireland and the United Kingdom. I shared the stage with Nanci's guests on her *Other Voices, Other Rooms* tour: Donovan, Odetta, Dave Van Ronk, Carolyn Hester, Dolores Keane, and other legends. Nanci's journey was like Bob Dylan's in some sense. She learned from the masters and ascended with her dreams and songs.

NANCI GRIFFITH: We brought in Tom's mentor, Ian Tyson, to sing on ["Canadian Whiskey"]. I imagine [having] Ian Tyson there right in front of me with our microphones facing each other and to sing "Canadian Whiskey" was what it would be like for a lot of people if Bob Dylan was standing a foot away from them.[35]

TOM RUSSELL: Nanci loved the chorus on "Canadian Whiskey." She had an affinity for songs like "Tequila after Midnight" by Dee Moeller that made drinking sound alluring. I'm so honored that Nanci [said in] a live film of us singing "Canadian Whiskey" in 1988, "Of all the songwriters I've had the grace and privilege and honor to know, to me Tom Russell has been the most important. He was the first one to believe in me when I was sixteen years old." Her legacy is in the songs and in that unique Texas take on her life. She wrote her own book like Guy Clark, Townes Van Zandt, and a dozen others without playing up to cliché.

Nanci got into your heart. She was a star.

I recall the time we were late for the tour bus from Dublin to Galway in Ireland, over a hundred miles away. Nanci was given a private limo with a police escort all the way. I was riding with her. People had to pull off the road as we sailed by. Some waved. Hundreds of fans were waiting as we pulled into the parking lot. [People related to her because] she was so genuine in relating to audiences. You know, musicians have a special lingo and way of telling stories to each other when they're offstage. Sharing war tales from the road. Yarns spilled out in dressing rooms and after the gig. Guy Clark was a great all-night storyteller. Nanci was the same. She would stay up and swap stories with that old troubadour road humor.

• "Wasn't That a Mighty Storm" (Tom Rush and Eric Von Schmidt) •

CAROLYN HESTER: We did ["Wasn't That a Mighty Storm"] in Los Angeles. Jim Rooney directed the session, and Nanci wanted me to add my voice on the choruses. Emmylou was already doing the third [part harmony], so I had to do the fifth. I've always been the singer and have never done much harmony. I did harmonize on Tom Paxton's "Can't Help but Wonder Where I'm Bound" on the first *Other Voices, Other Rooms*, which was fun, but doing a fifth harmony? Jim played the song as it was with Nanci and Emmylou. Nanci questioned some note that I sang, so Jim listened to the song. "No, Nanci," he said. "What she did was right." I just wanted to make everybody happy. I didn't care if it was right or wrong. Also, Emmylou had baked a delicious cake before she left Nashville and brought it with her.

We knew how to have a good time.

• "Darcy Farrow" (Steve Gillette and Tom Campbell) •

STEVE GILLETTE: Nanci took part in a fundraising concert with Bonnie Raitt one time in Los Angeles. She met Tom Campbell there. Tom was my cowriter for "Darcy Farrow" and was producing the event. Nanci asked about our song, and Tom hastily wrote out the lyrics for her, awkwardly leaving off the second verse: "Her voice was sweet as the sugar candy / Her touch was as soft as a bed of goose down / Her eyes shone bright like the pretty lights / That shine in the night out of Yarrington town." Nanci recorded it [without that verse] with Jim Rooney at Jack's Tracks in 1996. She was very apologetic when the mistake was discovered after the album was released and wrote me a lovely letter. Of course, it wasn't her fault. Nanci deserves credit for Jimmie Dale Gilmore recording our song as well.

• "Yarrington Town" (Mickie Merkens) •

BOBBY NELSON: Brian Wood's wife, Mickie Merkens, wrote a song on the second *Other Voices* album called "Yarrington Town."

MICKIE MERKENS: Nanci had known about my song "Yarrington Town" since 1983. She called me one day [and said] that she would be recording that song for *Other Voices, Too*, and I swear she enjoyed telling me as much as I enjoyed hearing the news. Nanci loved connecting people and introducing musicians and players to her audience. She was so generous and giving. I was in shock when she called to tell me about recording "Yarrington Town." Nanci loved giving surprises, and that was a huge one. She went on to tell me in the same conversation that she would be singing my song with Emmylou Harris and Carolyn Hester.

NANCI GRIFFITH: I've always loved ["Yarrington Town"] because it's about a woman's coming of age, but it's also the essence of people finally [becoming] their own home, forming their own center. Emmy loves this song, Carolyn loves this song, and we all wanted to pass it on to the next generation.

MICKIE MERKENS: Legendary singers and writers singing with their daughters [on my song]. Nanci knew how excited I would be that she was doing that. I literally was in shock. I don't think I said more than a few words in that phone call. "Oh my god. Really?" Of course, her recording brought me to tears when I heard all those beautiful women singing together with the band arrangement. That was one of the most special gifts I've ever received. Carolyn Hester went on to record a version of the song on her *We Dream Forever* album in 2009. She's a folksinging legend. Carolyn would have never heard the song had Nanci not recorded it.

• "Desperados Waiting for a Train" (Guy Clark) •

PAT MCINERNEY: I remember "Desperados Waiting for a Train." Everyone was in the studio when we recorded on Halloween day, but Steve Earle was late. He came crashing through the door. He plunked his guitar on the ground and said, "Trick or treat, motherfuckers." Really funny.

JIM ROONEY: We were spending lots of money and had lots of guests on the tracks. That album was less successful and wasn't much fun. I did my best to ride with it, but the moment had gone by with *Other Voices, Other Rooms* as far as I'm concerned. There are good songs and performances on *Other Voices, Too*, but that album doesn't have the magic. There was stress with the people she was working with. Nanci didn't treat them well. Our wonderful tour manager Nineyear Woolridge almost committed suicide as a result of her behavior. Her behavior wasn't nice. Nanci was drinking a lot, throwing fits, and ordering people around. However, Nanci was still a worker and could deliver the goods, but I can hear the decline in her voice. The gang songs like "Desperados Waiting for a Train" didn't have any magic.

GUY CLARK: We used to go to the Gulf Days picnic in Odessa in [the subject of "Desperados Waiting for a Train" Jack Prigg's] 1938 Packard, and he would drink beer all day. I drove the car home. I was just a kid before I had a driver's license. [I would be] driving back to [Clark's hometown] Monahans [Texas] at thirty miles per hour. Jack was family. He had a room at the hotel, he didn't pay rent, but he paid the water bill and fixed things when they broke. He was there before I was born. "Red River Valley" was his favorite song. He was bald but would pass his hand over his head, and that's where [the song's line] "run his fingers through seventy years of living" came [from]."[36]

STEVE EARLE: "Desperados Waiting for a Train" was written when Guy was in his late twenties or early thirties about stuff that happened when he was eight. Guy was incredibly detailed—like details within details. I related to "Desperados" because I had a great-uncle named Gene Wall who worked for the railroad. He was a section boss in charge of maintenance for a section of the railroad. He got the section that went from Seguin, Texas, headed to Houston by Highway 90 for a while by complete serendipity. He would stay with us in Schertz, Texas. Naturally, he's like, "Where's the nearest beer joint?" He would buy me a Big Red and sit there and drink for three solid fucking hours until my dad got home."

TAMARA SAVIANO: Guy played a show at Las Manitas with Rodney Crowell and Nanci Griffith at South by Southwest [in 1998]. Griffith was gearing up to release her album *Other Voices, Too (A Trip Back to Bountiful)*, an album that included "Desperados Waiting for a Train." It thrilled Guy to be in the company of traditional and influential folk standard-bearers such as Stephen Foster, Pete Seeger, Woody Guthrie, Johnny Cash, and Ian Tyson.

It seemed like the beginning of a new era for Guy. He had influenced a small circle of artists and songwriters for many years, [but] now the ripple effect of Guy's influence on the greater world was undeniable in his late fifties with a profound body of work. Guy joined Griffith and friends to perform "Desperados Waiting for a Train" on the CBS *Late Show with David Letterman*.[37]

Tamara Saviano is the author of Without Getting Killed or Caught: The Life and Music of Guy Clark *(2016) and* The Most Beautiful Girl in the World: A True Story of a Dad, a Daughter, and the Healing Power of Music *(2013)*.

STEVE EARLE: Townes and I talked, but we didn't talk about songwriting. He just didn't want to talk about songwriting. Guy would talk about songwriting, especially if you asked him a technical question. Lyle, Keen, and Nanci came a little behind me, but I saw Nanci playing out long before I saw either of those guys. Guy and I were both huge fans of them. I was more contemporaries with those guys so we talked more. People liked Nanci. Letterman having a horrible crush on her didn't hurt.

DAVID LETTERMAN: Just listen to ["Desperados Waiting for a Train"], and everything will be fine. [Nanci Griffith] recruited the best names in the business for her masterful [*Other Voices, Too*], and I'm telling you something, this is just terrific. Performing with her [are] Guy Clark, Jerry Jeff Walker, Rodney Crowell, Steve Earle, Jimmie Dale Gilmore, Eric Taylor, and of course my hero, Nanci Griffith.[38]

David Letterman hosted Late Night with David Letterman *for more than a decade. He currently hosts* My Next Guest Needs No Introduction *on Netflix*.

RODNEY CROWELL: We did Guy Clark's "Desperados Waiting for a Train" on *Other Voices, Too* around the same time. Nanci basically called us up and said, "I'm working on this *Other Voices, Too* record. Can you come help out?" A phone call from Jim Rooney involved a ten-minute preamble before he would get to what we were talking about. I loved calls from Rooney. You would do anything for Jim because that first ten minutes could have been about anything. I think Burt Stein, who managed Nanci and managed me for a while, would have been very key to organizing the Letterman show. Burt knows everybody.

My memory from doing the Letterman show is just being in New York with Susanna and Guy Clark. We did New York up and managed to make it to the show in somewhat decent shape. I don't think I even watched the show after it aired. Letterman could be very standoffish. I've done his show several times. He didn't seem to engage musicians, but I remember David was more engaged about the song and the lineup and what it represented. "Wow. We got to Letterman with this one."

I remember walking from somewhere around 6th into the seventies and Columbus with Susanna. I was handing out dollar bills and fives to every street artist. Susanna had said she wanted to take a cab before we left. "No," I said, "let's walk." She said, "I told you it would be cheaper to take a cab." I just remember us all standing in line in that cold studio where they kept it fifty degrees so no one would sweat. There's that folky thing. Nanci had some Pete Seeger in her. She was an emissary for that. The rest of us would just go out and play. We weren't preserving it. We had Jerry Jeff, Steve Earle, Jimmie Dale, Eric Taylor onstage. We were the Great Credibility Scare right there on television. Way to go, Nanci.

We really did just one tour together around the same time in 1998. I was just starting to write my memoir, *Chinaberry Sidewalks*, and was walking through the airports with a notebook. I was always sitting and writing. Nanci would come over and say, "What are you doing?" She took an interest. "Well," I would say, "I'm trying to learn how to write prose." Our conversations centered around how to switch out of songwriting into the narrative on the page, which is an entirely different thing that took me years to understand. My only conversations [on that topic] were with Nanci. She never mentioned the book she was writing at the time. She was just curious. Figuring that out was a good way to spend the day on tour. It was something to do. Traveling can be boring. Nanci's curiosity was good food for me at the time. I didn't know what I was doing. I just wanted to do it.

JIMMIE DALE GILMORE: Nanci was really well loved by David Letterman. David once told me that he wanted Nanci and me to sing at his funeral. We were all together to record Guy Clark's "Desperados Waiting for a Train" on *Other Voices, Too (A Trip Back to Bountiful)*. We were all together having a really wonderful reunion. Those guys had all been heroes of mine for a really long time. That recording felt like a milestone. I felt like I was actually in the club now. That was totally thanks to Nanci. She orchestrated the whole thing, which really spoke to how much respect all of those people had for her.

ERIC TAYLOR: [We] were crowded into a tight circle in a sound booth in Nashville: Guy Clark with his guitar, Nanci to his left, then Rodney Crowell,

Steve Earle, me, and Jimmie Dale Gilmore to complete the circle. Jerry Jeff Walker sat off to the side because he also was with his guitar. Everybody in the circle was somehow Texas. [They] either [were] born there or had spent so much time there they wouldn't claim any other place. Nanci dealt out lines, made suggestions, and lit candles. We ran through the song, got our parts together, and nailed it next time around. Nobody from Texas would dare make that cut a difficulty. Griffith knew what she was doing. Maybe those nuts are right. Maybe Texas ought to be its own little nation.[39]

Peerless songwriter Eric Taylor's criminally underrated catalog includes the masterful albums Eric Taylor *(1995),* Scuffletown *(2001), and* The Great Divide *(2005). His ex-wife Nanci Griffith covered several of his songs.*

JIMMIE DALE GILMORE: I ended up doing the Letterman show three or four times—a couple times with the Flatlanders and that one time with Nanci. Everything is interesting and so different behind the scenes backstage. Everybody was imprinted with the way the set looked and the history of the Ed Sullivan Theater. The rumors of David Letterman keeping it cold in there were true. It was like a refrigerator, and we kidded around about that. I'm sure a couple of us went out after the show. We did a run-through of the thing earlier in the day. Rodney Crowell and I did a verse together and worked out the harmony. I did the harmony a little differently when we did the taping and Rodney gave me this funny look during the taping like, "Where did that come from?"

RODNEY CROWELL: Nanci liked to take a drink, smoke cigarettes, and shoot the shit until late in the evening. She was game and a good hang. I like that about her. She was a generous soul who was getting around in the world. That always seemed to be her least favorite thing. It took being on the road and traveling with Nanci before I caught on that she had that streak. I started to take her seriously after that. I understood then that she wasn't just a pretty girl coming in to sing some songs. She was the original article.

• "Streets of Baltimore" (Harlan Howard) •

JIM ROONEY: Nanci decided Hootie [and the Blowfish lead singer Darius Rucker] would do the harmony, John Prine would do the duet, and Harlan Howard would do the narration for his song "Streets of Baltimore." Harlan's recitation was the best part of the cut. Harlan is another person I met through Nanci. I was jealous because he had become her friend and thought she was great. I had been an admirer of his since Buck Owens started recording his songs in 1961 and eventually got to know him through Nanci. Harlan was just terrific.

He was being Harlan Howard at that point, and he loved being Harlan Howard. Everyone loved and respected him. He liked to hold court in a bar. I was more than happy to be admitted into his circle thanks to Nanci. We did become friends. We went to hockey games and played Scrabble together, which was one of the highlights of my whole Nashville career. I was ahead when we got down to the last words, but he got me on the last word.

MELANIE SMITH-HOWARD: Darius Rucker was supposed to be on Harlan's "Streets of Baltimore" when Nanci recorded it, but Jim Rooney ended up putting John Prine on that part. Darius was at the session, which is where I met him. I was a Hootie and the Blowfish fan. "Hey," he said, "you guys want to come to my concert at Starwood?" I wanted to go, but Harlan didn't do Starwood. They made him walk all around a chain last time when his seat was right there. "Here's my number," Darius said. "Call if you change your mind." I did. I talked Harlan [into going].

Darius said he would work it out. He sent a limo to our house. Harlan, Chet Atkins, Hootie and the Blowfish, Nanci, and John Hiatt, who opened the show, were in the green room passing the guitar around, which was even better than the concert. They set up a couple chairs onstage for Harlan, Nanci, and me to use. There was no walking anywhere. "Okay," Harlan said, "I've changed my mind on Starwood if you get me a backstage pass and a limo." Wonderful concert.

KATHI WHITLEY: Nanci's friendship with Harlan Howard and the way they nurtured each other's talent was one of the most wonderful things I ever got to witness. Of course, Harlan being the dean of Music Row gave Nanci lots of confidence. I mean, you're probably good when Harlan Howard says you're good. Harlan also was a friend of mine, and I got to pal around with those two. They took me to the Ryman for Emmylou Harris's famous shows when they were trying to tear it down. I was sitting between Harlan and Nanci going, "How did I get here? This is great." They just palled around. Harlan was great for having happy hour. Nanci would come over to his office, and they would play songs that they had written.

You know, Harlan didn't love everybody. They just had a kindred spirit. They shared a sensibility in story songs that they wrote about regular people. They both wrote very down-to-earth songs. Not lofty ones. Also, Harlan did love the ladies. He would always pick us girls when given the choice to hang out with ladies as opposed to a bunch of hairy-legged guys. I feel like it's true that Harlan gave Nanci his guitar once. I've heard several people have done something similar. Guy Clark gave Rodney Crowell his. I've been in a room when a songwriter will say, "Hey, I think I've gotten all the songs I'm gonna get out of this guitar. Yours are probably still in there."

JIM ROONEY: John Prine and I were doing his duets album *In Spite of Ourselves* at the same time. He considered putting that "Streets of Baltimore" cut on the album and had mentioned that to Nanci. She was excited, but John decided against it. "You're gonna tell her, aren't you?" I asked. I didn't want to be the one. Her fragility was getting quite serious by then. Nanci could be set off about anything, and she and John were gonna do a show together soon. "You're gonna have to tell her, John." He did. She wasn't happy but got over it.

CAROLYN HESTER: Nanci and Jim Rooney had fabulous taste. She had this genius, great art flowing as a musician, but she could also handle anything else business-wise. She was able to herd all these musicians in for her projects and take them on the road. I went on the road with her years later to promote *Other Voices, Too*. We went to Dublin for two nights plus days of rehearsal and an Irish television show. Odetta, Dave Van Ronk, Sharon Shannon, Philip Donnelly, Dolores Keane, and myself were there. Donovan showed up. Just wonderful. Then we took a plane to Glasgow and did two nights at the SEC Armadillo, which is a beautiful, huge concert hall. Nanci hired a chef to cook for us. Amazing.

BRIAN WILLOUGHBY: Europeans loved Nanci because she was an honest songwriter and very warm onstage. She would get the audience to sing along and knew how to entertain. She grew up through the folk clubs where you have to have an engagement with the audience and had been coming to England and Ireland for a long time by then. We also played a fantastic gig at the Olympia Theatre in Dublin on the *Other Voices, Too* tour. The folksinger Donovan joined us onstage. Nanci attracted people like him. Everybody wanted to play and be seen with her. People like the Crickets absolutely loved Nanci. She had it all.

Nanci was very friendly and good company socially and was a great musician, which helps enormously. She was quite an accomplished guitar player. I found it dead easy to play lead guitar with her. She was using metal finger picks and a bizarre thumb pick that was like a flat pick attached to a finger pick. Steel finger picks give you that extra poke when you need to be heard. I used to use finger picks years ago but abandoned them when I figured out that I have pretty good nails. I have tried to use them since, but it's a very cumbersome way of playing for me. I struggled. Very alien. Nails naturally bend around from the top whereas the finger picks bend around underneath so it's a totally different touch. She was always spot-on playing those harmonics between the chords on "Love at the Five and Dime."

The *Other Voices, Too* tour was like a huge family. Nanci obviously was the matriarch. You know, I'm not a singer. Nanci listed all the musicians in the tour book, and my entry said, "Brian Willoughby, lead guitar (definitely no vocals)." She was a very generous and kind soul. I don't think anyone on the tour would say she was being a diva. We all just played, sang, and got on with it. I don't remember anything disharmonious. Tom Russell was on that tour. His admiration for Nanci and their connection was obvious onstage. You can tell when people look at each other onstage. There's either admiration or hate. He had such admiration and loved Nanci. Same with Eric Taylor. Their interaction onstage was brilliant.

JIM ROONEY: I got to know this mountain climber who was part of the Irish expedition on Mount Everest in Ireland. We were just talking in a pub one time. He didn't know anything about me. He had given a talk about Everest, and he was a very likable guy who liked to sing and have a pint of Guinness. "What do you do?" he asked. "I produce records in Nashville." "Oh really," he said. "What kind of music?" "Folky people like John Prine and Nanci Griffith." "Nanci Griffith? I love Nanci. I take cassette tapes with me when I go to climb Everest and was listening to her." "What were you listening to?" "Tecumseh Valley."

I told him I would get him tickets to see Nanci in Dublin, but he already had some so I told him I would introduce them. I really believe it when I say music is a force for good in the world. Music gets people in their heart. Songs go into you. I've been a receiver in songs. Do you think Hank Williams thought a kid [like me] in Dedham, Massachusetts, would take in "I'm So Lonesome I Could Cry"? We don't know what happens to songs when we send them out there, but I do know that songs do mean something to people and change their lives, sometimes for the better. Never for the worse. I've never heard someone come up and say, "Your song ruined my life." I'm proud to be in the song business.

JOHN LOMAX III: I compared Nanci to the architect [Howard] Roark in Ayn Rand's *The Fountainhead* in my foreword to the book [*Nanci Griffith's Other Voices: A Personal History of Folk Music*] because they both had a vision and pursued that vision without worrying about what other people said or thought. They had a very clear idea of what they wanted and [knew they] would be best. They shucked off any criticism saying, "You should do this." There was this individuality in the character in Rand's book, and Nanci shared that in how she carried herself.

You had a few songwriters like Merle Haggard, Willie Nelson, and Johnny Cash who sang and wrote, but the whole Nashville ethos was that you had singers and you had writers. Not many newcomers were coming along as writers, so Nanci helped open those doors by doing the *Other Voices* albums. She also showed that a woman could get up there and sing and write and perform. You had Tammy Wynette, Dolly Parton, and Loretta Lynn, but you didn't really have many younger women making their way as singer-songwriters then.

Strange things went on because of that, like when she berated all the Texas writers for not championing her cause. She was calling out people. One [journalist] was like, "Why is she ragging on me? I didn't do a review but she's tearing me apart for one that didn't exist." Attacking what should be your biggest base of support seemed like an odd thing to do.[40]

VALERIE SCHUSTER: My husband and I met Nanci and Maura O'Connell for high tea at the Westbury Hotel in Dublin. Then we went to her show at the Olympia Theatre. She spent the first five minutes onstage talking about me, our friendship, and how I was living in County Mayo now. I saw her briefly before the performance. "You wouldn't believe who is here," she said. "Robert Plant from Led Zeppelin." I went backstage after the show and I wasn't able to see her, but I could see her crying. You know, Robert Plant recorded those albums with Alison Krauss. I wonder if he was looking at different women to record with and possibly she got word that he hadn't chosen her. She was in tears across the room.

JIM ROONEY: Nanci just couldn't stop thinking about herself and her career and judging other people and herself, which got in the way of having normal, healthy, fun relationships. That resulted in this totally lonely life.

• • •

Nanci Griffith produces one last seamless song cycle next. *The Dust Bowl Symphony* pairs her own Blue Moon Orchestra—bandleader James Hooker, percussionist Pat McInerney, bassist Ron de la Vega, guitarist Doug Lancio, guitarist Frank Christian, and guitarist and harmony vocalist Lee Satterfield—with the London Symphony Orchestra to record several classic songs ("Trouble in the Fields," "The Wing and the Wheel," "Love at the Five and Dime") and a few lesser known ("Nobody's Angel," "Waiting for Love"). They capture fourteen—including the new original "1937 Pre-War Kimball"—on *The Dust Bowl Symphony* during sessions at London's legendary Abbey Road Studios.

All involved find the former Beatles stomping ground inspiring as musicians. Additionally, they personally revel in soaking in the iconic band's most famous workspace. "Recording [*The Dust Bowl Symphony*] at Abbey Road Studios was an absolute treat," James Hooker says. "I couldn't wait to get out of the studio so I could wander around the other parts of the studio. I looked into the Beatles room in Studio Two. They still have [the space] just like it was back in the day. Hadn't changed a bit—at least back when we were there." *"The Dust*

Bowl Symphony was a joyous occasion," echoes producer Peter Collins. "'If my career is to end now,' I said at the time, 'this would be a glorious way to go.'"

PETER COLLINS: I guess *The Dust Bowl Symphony* was Nanci's idea. I had worked with the London Symphony Orchestra very recently producing the track "Written in the Stars" with Elton John and LeAnn Rimes. Nanci may have known that and said, "Why don't we do a record there?" Elektra funded it. I don't know what the budget was, but it must have been incredibly expensive.

EMILY SALIERS: Peter Collins likes to do orchestration with string sections and big budgets. He has very strong production ideas. Nanci was my first introduction to an artist having orchestration [backing them]. She [showed] me how that could work. I think orchestration is brilliant. Really keeps you on your toes. You get to hear your songs in ways you would have never imagined.

PETER COLLINS: We flew Nanci's whole band over and stayed at nice hotels. I had Darius Rucker fly to London for "Love at the Five and Dime." My old friend [and London Symphony Orchestra conductor] Andrew Pryce Jackman's arrangement on "Love at the Five and Dime" was fantastic.

TOM NORRIS: The arrangements on *The Dust Bowl Symphony* are breathtaking. I had joined the London Symphony Orchestra in 1998, so I hadn't been there long when we recorded the album with Nanci Griffith. Nanci's was actually one of the first commercial sessions I did with the orchestra. Many colleagues hadn't heard of her, but thankfully I had. I had that ex-girlfriend who got me into Nanci's music. There were a couple tracks on *Dust Bowl Symphony* I was really looking forward to because I knew them.

Listening now takes me right back to those sessions at Abbey Road. I remember Nanci in the [vocal] booth in the studio. We've done several similar albums, but the artists weren't there. We reworked their songs on those others, but they're not as reimagined as the ones on *The Dust Bowl Symphony*. Really exciting for me to be there. Those sessions were the best of both worlds. We had the possibility of what you could do with an orchestra and songs like hers. Pretty unforgettable being up close and personal to her voice as well [because] Nanci Griffith was the one who got me into Bob Dylan though her recording of "Boots of Spanish Leather." I loved the song and how Nanci did it. Then I heard Dylan's version and went, "Eh."

We were up close and personal with Nanci's voice in Abbey Road, but it wasn't just the voice [that moved me]. It was playing along with her live in the room. Magical. She was so lovely and sweet. I remember she had a bottle of bourbon on her stool in her booth. I thought, That's the way country stars like to do things.

PETER COLLINS: Nanci needed to sound like [Édith Piaf] for one song.

She wanted to get into character and had a bottle by the microphone to do so. Her vocals were live with the orchestra. [The session] had gone in the wrong direction by the fourth take. We had to overdub that one back in Nashville. Otherwise, what a fabulous record. Nanci's band handled themselves very well. Playing with the London Symphony Orchestra had to be very intimidating. I'm very fussy about musicians, and they didn't let me down. James Hooker was fabulous with the orchestra. Pat McInerney was terrific.

PAT MCINERNEY: We were in the big room where the Beatles recorded "All You Need Is Love" when we recorded *The Dust Bowl Symphony* with the London Symphony Orchestra. I was in a booth with a little metronome to remember the tempo. I would count off to the conductor and then he would conduct the orchestra while we played. Huge orchestra in that big room. I think the record is really good, but Nanci wasn't in top form during those sessions. We were in a nice hotel and everything, but she didn't seem to have the concentration necessary when playing with that caliber of musicians. They're standing around waiting to play and she shows up a little late again. Things were getting a bit difficult by that time.

TOM NORRIS: That very relaxed way of working really endeared her to the whole orchestra. She wasn't uptight. She was a little nervous to be in the room with the symphony orchestra, but more because of all this tech [we were working with]. Abbey Road is a massive space, but I remember there being this incredibly warm feeling in the room because she was so endearing. I also remember hearing her voice in my earphones, which is a disembodied thing to the rest of the track whether the singer is there or not. You don't even hear yourself in the headphones. You just hear the voice and maybe a little backing. Playing with this person feels very authentic and powerful as a musical experience.

RON DE LA VEGA: Recording *The Dust Bowl Symphony* album was like living a fantasy. We got to go spend a week with the London Symphony at Abbey Road Studios. Very surreal. Incredible. We were all upbeat and excited on the flight. We had dinner together the first night. Then we went into the studio the day before we started recording and got everything staged and set up. We got some sounds from the electronic instruments. The London Symphony Orchestra held a lot of value to me as a cellist. They were one of the best in the world.

I heard the symphony in the headphones and thought, "This sounds pretty good." Then I took the headphones off and thought, That's magic. We had something. I thought it was incredible to do that with them. We would play the song, and all the principal players would go in for the playback with the producer Peter Collins when we thought we had something. Hearing the discussions between the principals, the conductor, and Peter Collins was interesting. The recordings were fun.

JAMES HOOKER: I had never played with an orchestra until Nanci. Scary. I played with four or five guys all my life, and now there are seventy or eighty and one waving a stick. What a thrill. I have a photo somewhere with me sitting outside the studio with headphones on and the Abbey Road sign behind me. I went down to the crosswalk [the Beatles are walking across on the *Abbey Road* album cover].

RON DE LA VEGA: I have a personal note about my Beatles bass. I had an old Höfner, which was one of my first basses from the sixties. I just had to record with it at Abbey Road Studios. This bass has to soak up the vibe. I remember Peter Collins saying, "You know, Ron, the only person who can get a good sound out of that guitar is Paul McCartney, but if you must . . ." So, I switched it out with the bass I was supposed to play on this one track. I took the gamble. Could have come back to bite me and we would have had to spend an hour trying to replace it on the track. We went into the playback after playing the song, and I asked Peter how the bass sounded. He knew. "Damn you, Ron," he said. "It's good."

PETER COLLINS: I own a Beatles Höfner violin bass [like McCartney's] myself, and it usually sounds very thin. Paul obviously did something because his doesn't sound like mine. I'm sure I was reluctant [for Ron] to use it, but if it sounded good it sounded good. I don't care. I wasn't gonna be childish and say, "I said you couldn't play it. You can't play it."

RON DE LA VEGA: There was an ebb and flow like that working with everybody that was very nice. I figured I had to play the Paul bass. I gladly would have paid the session cost, but the Höfner had to be in there at least once. We actually ended up sneaking it in a couple times. Peter was great for that. We definitely had some things we had to do, but the creativity was still involved throughout the recording process. We didn't use the studio the Beatles used with the upstairs control room. That was actually our staging area because it was empty the days we were setting up. We were in the big room with the London Symphony and the strings and choirs.

The room sounded great and the vibe was very exciting. Really cool to be in the more famous room. We could see the stuff and walk through. I grew up with the Beatles, so it was a childhood dream. I remember when they were first on *The Ed Sullivan Show*. Truly a dream come true. This was a great thing for me because he had written some of the symphony bass parts for what I had played when we did the run-throughs for his arranging. We had to redo it when we recorded. They would say, "You're playing the wrong bass part." The songs would develop and mature as we played them and morph and take on a life of their own.

TOM NORRIS: You feel like you're entering the realm at Abbey Road. There are two studios, and the small one is the more iconic in terms of the recordings that happened in there like the Beatles. Sometimes we would put a smaller string orchestra in the small studio with the famous control booth upstairs. They're kind of in heaven up there with the band sitting down on the ground level, which is where Lennon and McCartney did *Abbey Road* and *Let It Be*. The big studio is the soundtrack studio. I associate the big studio more with John Williams and the *Star Wars* soundtracks. I'm fortunate that one of my other first sessions with the LSO was in the big studio with John Williams conducting the music for the *Star Wars* [prequels] one, two, and three, which were released after 2000. Four, five, and six were before my time.

The Phantom Menace was the first I was [involved with]. We had the screen as a drop-down at the back of the studio, which is the only studio I know where that happens. I'm sure there are loads in Los Angeles, but it's the only studio in London where you have an actual cinema screen there. John Williams is looking up there. He also doesn't work with a click track. We did for a few things just so the front and the back of the orchestra can be together, but John Williams is a consummate and singular musician. He's singular not only in the way that he can conduct his own music, but he does it in such a way that the ensemble isn't an issue. Also the ensemble to the picture [on the screen] isn't an issue. He's an absolute master. Those sessions—like Nanci's—were unforgettable.

Nanci's song "1937 Pre-War Kimball" on *The Dust Bowl Symphony* has a real groove, but I'm pretty sure we didn't have a click track on that. Frankly, you don't need a click when you have musicians like her band. You just use click to line things up. Pity that any music goes out the window just for the reason that you want to be together as a group. I remember "1937 Pre-War Kimball" had a chamber music vibe. The orchestra makes an appearance and then goes away. The song is beautifully charming. I love the fact that it's a goodbye song to a piano. The song is crystalline in personifying the relationship with her piano. Very sweet.

BETH NIELSEN CHAPMAN: So, I get this call from Nanci's manager Burt Stein one day asking me if I would come put some background vocals on a track. I had sung background on Suzy Bogguss's "Outbound Plane" and a bunch of other songs that Nanci wrote all in a little bouquet of time. I was fascinated by her and always looked up to her swagger. "Sure," I told Burt. "Are you kidding?" Nanci was there recording [overdubs for] "1937 Pre-War Kimball," which says, "I'd pretend I have the voice of Beth Nielsen Chapman." I had no idea when I came over that my name was in the song. Why would anybody do that? I was so blown away that she had this appreciation of me as an artist.

Nanci wanted me to harmonize the line with her. "Oh," I said, "you want me to sing, 'I'd pretend I have the voice of Beth Nielsen Chapman?' That might be a little weird." "Well," she said, "I think it would be funny." "Or," I said, "it could be really weird." I had to come up with some really good alternative to talk her out of the idea. "I have this great idea," I said. "How about I sing on the lines around that line?" "I don't know. I would have to hear that." "Just give me a track."

So, I built this step-up part on the track. You could hear this little wisp of my vocal going around Nanci on the track, which still was a little uncomfortable for me. "How about that?" She loved it and had me put it all over the song, which was great fun. I felt like I was entering into her world. She was such an amazing icon to me as a songwriter. I loved her wacky phrasing. Really cool.[41]

Beth Nielsen Chapman has written number one country songs for Willie Nelson ("Nothing I Can Do about It Now") and Tanya Tucker ("Strong Enough to Bend"). Sir Elton John performed her song "Sand and Water" during his 1997 tour.

TOM NORRIS: I remember "Late Night Grande Hotel" because that was my ex's favorite song. I got to know Nanci Griffith through that song and loved doing the orchestral version. I think it's actually a nicer representation of the song than the original. You don't always think that when there are outlandishly amped-up orchestral versions of songs, but it suits "Late Night Grande Hotel" very well. I think the arrangements for Nanci's album were super thought out. They sound like a very sensitive collaboration listening back now. The whole session had a very intimate vibe because she was there and interested in having a relationship with the whole band, including the orchestra. She seemed happy to be there.

Nanci's music is really sincere. So is her voice. She's not polished like Emmylou Harris, but she had a very distinct sound. Her voice was real and almost on the edge of being contrived even though it wasn't. Her voice has an amazing tenor, which she must have learned from Emmylou or Dolly Parton, very individual, direct, and smacks of sincerity. Sometimes we hear country music and go, "That's a bit clichéd." There's no reason her music should be any different, but it is. She went her own genuine road. Perhaps she was brave enough to stay with her own sound and articulation of what it means. Her songs are really touching.

Nanci was a very observant lyricist. She's talking about her feelings in the country tradition but found new ways to say those things. "Late Night Grande Hotel" is a good example. You wouldn't think you could make a song out of that, but she did. Also, her voice was incredibly childlike. She sounded very much like the young Alison Krauss. Alison was incredibly young, like sixteen, on her first albums. Supertalented on the violin. I got into Alison Krauss about the same time as Nanci. Their vocals were supersweet in the high-frequency clarity with a bell-like quality. She had that even more than Alison Krauss did. Nanci definitely was an influence for me.

I never really had a chance to shoot the breeze with Nanci when we were working together, but I would have been completely starstruck. I'm not very good at talking to very successful people, which is terrible because I'm sure we would have very interesting conversations. I did feel like there was a connection between her and us. Her investment in the whole project seemed very genuine. I remember there being a lot of chat from her, hearing her voice, and thinking we had the magic here in the studio. We all thought we [would have enjoyed a drink] when we saw her bring in the bottle of bourbon.

The vibe was in the glass.

• • •

Griffith joins legendary singer-songwriter Don McLean one night onstage in Austin between *The Dust Bowl Symphony* and *Clock without Hands* (2001). "Nanci was a very loving and open person," McLean says. "She was such a sweet person and excellent musician. I think she had grown up on my music because of her stepdad. The whole thing was quite touching and beautiful. She started telling me about Buddy Holly. I knew as a smart Texas girl that she was way into him." The moment—captured on the live concert film *Starry Starry Night: Live in Austin*—was a personal highlight for Griffith. "She screamed after we finished," McLean says, "'I got to sing with Don McLean.'"[42]

RALPH MCTELL: Don McLean says, "The world wasn't meant for one as beautiful as you." That applies to Nanci.

DON MCLEAN: Nanci sang on my live concert film *Starry Starry Night: Live in Austin* around 2000. I recorded there because I knew Terry Lickona from *Austin City Limits*. I was hired by the state of New York that year to sing in the Hudson Valley in 1969. They called me the Hudson Valley Troubadour. I sang in every river town on the Hudson. There was a radio station called WEOK in Poughkeepsie, New York, where I would do interviews. The owner employed a kid named Terry Lickona who used to interview me frequently, and we became friends.

So, I was going to do a PBS television special around 2000. Terry popped up and said, "I want to produce that out of Austin, Texas." I was happy because I knew the guy, but I wanted a female singer to be on the show. I had heard of Nanci Griffith but had never met her. Terry suggested her as an Austin, Texas, native. I said, "Sure." She had played at Caffe Lena in Saratoga Springs, New York, so we had that in common. I was a pop and rock guy, but I started out as a folkie like Nanci because I would sing anywhere I could get five cents.

I chose the songs we would do on that television special. They were "It's Raining in My Heart" and "And I Love You So." I had my arranger Tony Migliore make string parts for both songs. He basically took the string part from the Buddy Holly version of "Raining in My Heart." Garth Brooks was also on the show. I thought that Nanci was very, very good at singing her parts. I didn't tell her what to sing, but she did her harmony part extremely well. I'm telling you right now, produce those two songs with added strings and you could put them out as a record. They were that good. Nanci had brought her father along. Very nice guy.

Don McLean's "American Pie" and "Vincent" are undeniable folk music standards. His song "And I Love You So" has been recorded by Elvis Presley, Perry Como, Helen Reddy, Glen Campbell, and others.

L–R: Dave Alvin, Nanci Griffith, Vietnam, July 2001. Previously unpublished photo by Jim McGuire

L–R: Dave Alvin, Nanci Griffith, Vietnam, July 2001. Previously unpublished photo by Jim McGuire

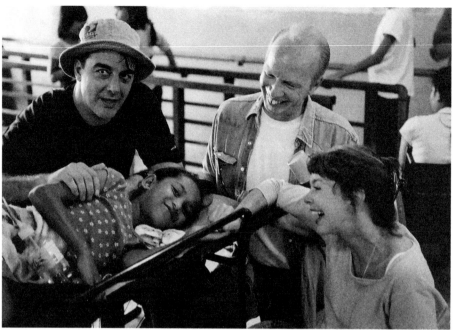

L–R: Chris Noth, Dave Alvin, and Nanci Griffith with the girl whose spine was severed by an axe, July 2001. Previously unpublished photo by Jim McGuire

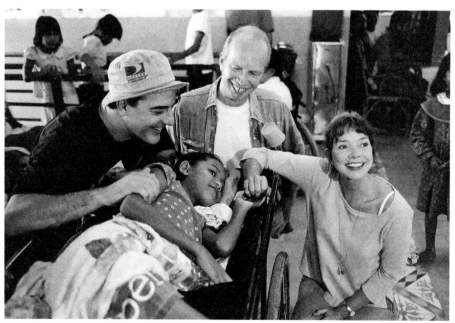

L–R: Chris Noth, Dave Alvin, and Nanci Griffith with the girl whose spine was severed by an axe, July 2001. Previously unpublished photo by Jim McGuire

L–R: Vietnamese girl and Dave Alvin, Vietnam and Cambodia trip, July 2001. Previously unpublished photo by Jim McGuire

Nanci Griffith, Vietnam and Cambodia trip, July 2001. Previously unpublished photo by Jim McGuire

Nanci Griffith, guitar shop, Vietnam and Cambodia trip, July 2001. Previously unpublished photo by Jim McGuire

Nanci Griffith, Vietnam and Cambodia trip, July 2001. Previously unpublished photo by Jim McGuire

Chris Noth with skulls, Vietnam and Cambodia trip, July 2001. Previously unpublished photo by Jim McGuire

L–R: Jim McGuire, Nanci Griffith, Soc Trang road sign, Vietnam and Cambodia trip, July 2001. Unknown photographer. Courtesy Jim McGuire

Nanci Griffith, Vietnam and Cambodia trip, July 2001. Previously unpublished photo by Jim McGuire

Nanci Griffith, rehearsal, Vietnam and Cambodia trip, July 2001. Previously unpublished photo by Jim McGuire

Nanci Griffith, rehearsal, Vietnam and Cambodia trip, July 2001. Previously unpublished photo by Jim McGuire

202

Nanci Griffith, Vietnam and Cambodia trip, July 2001. Previously unpublished photo by Jim McGuire

Nanci Griffith, Vietnam and Cambodia trip, July 2001. Previously unpublished photo by Jim McGuire

Nanci Griffith, Vietnam and Cambodia trip, July 2001. Previously unpublished photo by Jim McGuire

Nanci Griffith, Vietnam and Cambodia trip, July 2001. Previously unpublished photo by Jim McGuire

L–R: Nanci Griffith, Dave Alvin, Rockin' along the Mekong concert, Vietnam and Cambodia trip, July 2001. Previously unpublished photo by Jim McGuire

Nanci Griffith, Rockin' along the Mekong concert, Vietnam and Cambodia trip, July 2001. Previously unpublished photo by Jim McGuire

L–R: Nanci Griffith, Dave Alvin, Rockin' along the Mekong concert, Vietnam and Cambodia trip, July 2001. Previously unpublished photo by Jim McGuire

L–R: Nanci Griffith, Dave Alvin, Rockin' along the Mekong concert, Vietnam and Cambodia trip, July 2001. Previously unpublished photo by Jim McGuire

L–R: John Terzano, unknown, Nanci Griffith, Vietnam and Cambodia trip, July 2001. Previously unpublished photo by Jim McGuire

Nanci Griffith (center) with children, Vietnam and Cambodia trip, July 2001. Previously unpublished photo by Jim McGuire

Poster for Rockin' along the Mekong: A Concert for a Landmine Free World, with Nanci Griffith and Dave Alvin and *Sex and the City* actor Chris Noth as master of ceremonies, Hotel Le Royal Ballroom, Phnom Penh, Cambodia, July 2, 2001. Photo by Brian T. Atkinson. Courtesy Bobby Nelson

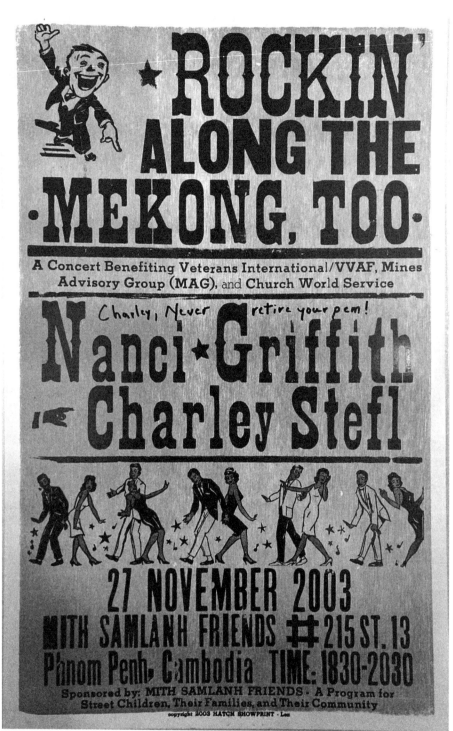

Poster for Rockin' along the Mekong, Too concert with Nanci Griffith and Charley Stefl, Phnom Penh, Cambodia, November 27, 2003. Courtesy Charley Stefl

L–R: Charley Stefl, Nanci Griffith, American Hotel, Hanoi, Vietnam, November 2003.
Courtesy Charley Stefl

Nanci Griffith with patient in Hanoi, Vietnam, November 2003. Courtesy Charley Stefl

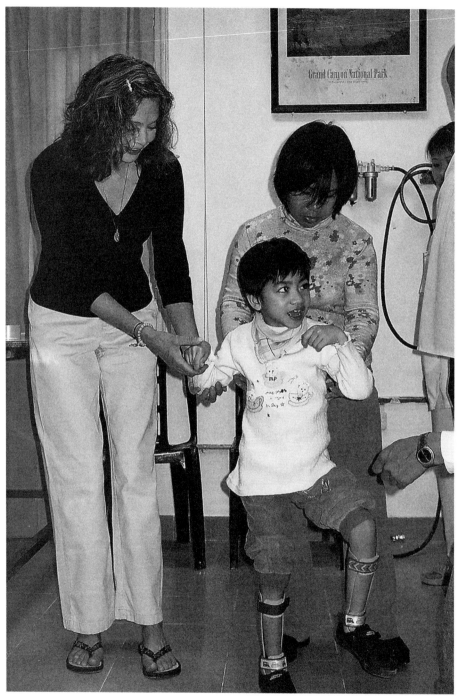

Nanci Griffith with patient in Hanoi, Vietnam, November 2003. Courtesy Charley Stefl

Bridge: Traveling through This Part of You

NANCI GRIFFITH TRAVELS through Cambodia and Vietnam several times while working closely with the Vietnam Veterans of America Foundation. They campaign for humanitarian causes such as landmine awareness. Griffith comes away with several songs inspired by these trips—most notably, one about ghosts Eric Taylor brought back from time served—for her forthcoming two albums. "Nanci and Eric's lifelong bond was [partly] due to him being a Vietnam vet and her association with the disabled veterans," Joy Lewallen says. "She said they gave a deeper understanding of Eric's demons and made her more sympathetic to the troubles that he had. She wrote a wonderful song about Eric called 'Traveling through This Part of You.'"

"Emmylou Harris connected me to Bobby Muller and the folks at the Vietnam Veterans of America Foundation for my trips to Cambodia and Vietnam," Griffith says. "My ex-husband was one of the reasons I wanted to go."[1] Blues blaster Dave Alvin, iconic Nashville photographer Jim McGuire, *Sex and the City* actor Chris Noth, and songwriter friend Charley Stefl accompany Griffith on various trips throughout the region. "I think there would be a greater outcry to ban landmine manufacturing if ranchers in West Texas experienced not being able to raise cattle or allow their children to play in fields," Griffith says. "These countries are dependent upon being able to farm [or] they will starve."[2] Griffith's *Clock without Hands* spotlights "Traveling through This Part of You."

JOHN TERZANO: Nanci wrote "Traveling through This Part of You" on her first trip back from Vietnam. She really captured the point of view. Most songs about Vietnam are about what veterans went through, but "Traveling through This Part of You" so poignantly captured what people who live with Vietnam vets—or are friends or married to them—go through. Such an extraordinary piece of insight and writing.

NANCI GRIFFITH: ["Traveling through This Part of You"] was inspired by landing [at] Tan Son Nhut [Air Base] and realizing that I was landing at ground zero of just about everything that went wrong with my marriage. Eric carried home a lot of losses in his person and a lot of problems from the war. I realized just how dear and sweet a friend he is to me in my life as I was landing at that airport. I've been through two of his divorces since we [were] divorced in 1982. Eric was very moved that I had written this sentiment to him, but he remarked that he would like to send all of his ex-wives to Vietnam. He's also a psychologist now, and I'm his best patient.[3]

SUSAN LINDFORS TAYLOR: Eric was really private about his experiences in the military. He was only in the military for a very short time. Walked in and almost quit immediately. He had a hard time with Nanci's song "Traveling through This Part of You" because he never went to Vietnam. He was only in Cambodia, but Nanci only talked about him being in Vietnam in the song. He really didn't like that because it wasn't true. Nanci's song also [brought up] all this stuff he never liked to talk about. Eric would never go there because it was so horrifying for him. "They flew us over there," he said. "We didn't know where we were going."

He said they landed in Vietnam, but then the plane took off again. The only reason they figured out where they were was because one guy in the unit saw a newspaper sitting on someone's desk one day. "Oh, we're in Cambodia." They were part of the secret war in Cambodia. Eric got up and quit. They said, "You're going to jail if you quit." "Okay," Eric said, "I'll go to jail." I think he was in jail for eighteen months. They flew him back to the States and he [did the time] over here.[4]

Singer-songwriter Susan Lindfors Taylor was married to Nanci Griffith's ex-husband, Eric Taylor, until he passed away in 2020.

JOHN TERZANO: I was familiar with Nanci Griffith's music when we met through the Vietnam Veterans of America Foundation in 1999. We had groups of artists who traveled around doing fundraising shows for a number of years. Emmylou Harris organized and brought along others like Nanci, Steve Earle, Mary Chapin Carpenter, Kris Kristofferson, Guy Clark, Terry Allen, and Patty Griffin. Nanci endorsed what we did wholeheartedly. She really got behind an issue. Nanci ended up doing three different trips with us to Cambodia and Vietnam and visited our project in Pristina, Kosovo, in 2004. We became good friends over the years, and the concerts and [2001's *Concerts for a Landmine Free World*] benefited our clinics.

BOBBY MULLER: We started Vietnam Veterans of America to address the needs and concerns of the Vietnam veterans and first led American veterans back to Vietnam [in 1981] to find out the consequences of oxi-herbicides.[5]

Bobby Muller is currently president of Vietnam Veterans of America, the organization formerly known as Vietnam Veterans of America Foundation.

JOHN TERZANO: I was part of the first veterans who went back to Vietnam in 1981. We were trying to get information for ourselves because we were being stonewalled by the veterans administration and the government on things like Agent Orange. Vietnam vets were ostracized back in the seventies, so trying to get any programs going through Congress was extraordinarily difficult.

BOBBY MULLER: We couldn't get answers from our government regarding our own population and were struck by the horrific situation in Vietnam. The war in many ways had not ended for Vietnam because the economic embargo and the political isolation were devastating. We felt a strong need to address what clearly was a legacy of our war on a human basis.

We realized that we had to get beyond our own needs and address the other victims of war. We were there to address the immediate needs of the Vietnam vets and also the broader aspects of war including humanitarian assistance and reconciliation. Our work with Vietnam brought us into neighboring Cambodia, which led us to understand [their] story better, and we recognized it was truly the greater tragedy of our war in Indochina overall. One reason we began the campaign to get rid of landmines was because of the recognition of how widespread and how profoundly affecting landmines are to a country. Their overall consequences are economically and socially devastating.

JOHN TERZANO: We were operating clinics in more than a half dozen war-torn countries around the world. Big ones were where we started the program in Cambodia and Vietnam, but we also went to Angola, El Salvador, and Nicaragua. Nanci was very generous, kind, and down to earth. You totally empathize as you're traveling to countries like Vietnam, which has so much meaning for our generation, and are seeing a child without a limb or with extraordinary birth defects. Nanci was one of the most empathetic persons I've ever known. She could feel someone's happiness and pain just by having a conversation with them. She absorbed your [emotions]. Her empathy comes through in her songwriting and the intimacy you see in her lyrics. She had this extraordinary gift to really listen to people, understand what they were going through, and turn that into something extraordinary.

Nanci also had an extraordinary thirst to learn about all the history. I [told her I] call Vietnam "the other side of the wall" because Vietnam is a living laboratory of where we dropped all these herbicides. We thought they might have some information when we arrived in Hanoi in December 1981. You go there and start taking a look at the suffering in the country you went to war with and realize your problems are minimal by comparison. Going back was a mind-fuck. That trip totally flipped our minds. "Okay, there are still things we've gotta do around Vietnam veterans, but there's a whole other side to this story to address."

Think about what our country went through after September 11, 2001, and all the hatred against the Muslims. The [Vietnamese people's] hearts and minds weren't still captured by a war over there, which is another thing that blew us away. America's hearts and minds were the ones captured. We were the ones who waged this war in Vietnam, but we were welcomed back in such an open way and really saw the beauty for the first time. That helps veterans get rid of those time-frozen images they had from the exploding tree lines and all the things you get from war. You go back in peace and aren't worried about gunfire coming from that tree line. You're not worried about, "Where is that smoke coming from?"

Their peacefulness with Americans is truly extraordinary. Mind boggling. "You know, our issues are not with you," the foreign minister told us. "You're just like anybody else. You did what your government asked you to do. Our issues are with your government: Nixon, Kissinger, Johnson, the people who ordered this stuff and made you do it. Yeah, you carried out the policy, but you didn't have a choice." They viewed us just as much a victim as themselves. They saw that we got caught up in the process. Another big part is the history of Vietnam. Vietnam has been around thousands of years. They have a long history and don't think in ways of immediacy [like] the Western world does. They're thinking in terms of those hundreds of years.

Vietnam was dominated by China for hundreds of years, but they managed to maintain their own culture, identity, and sense of independence throughout all that. You can see lots of Indian influence in Cambodia, Laos, and Thailand in terms of their architecture, culture, and gods. Vietnam is totally different. You don't see that influence because they maintained their identity. You had the French in there, then the Japanese came during World War II, then the French come back, then the Americans come in. The American War, as I've started calling it, was a speed bump to them. I think their own philosophies about that have a lot to do with how they think about [Americans]. Americans carry grudges much more.

DAVE ALVIN: Nanci Griffith and I were close for about a year. Nanci was a class act from another world who came into my life unexpectedly in an interesting time. We met at a wonderful New Year's Eve gig at the El Casino Ballroom in Tucson, Arizona, in 2000. I got a message that she would be at the show when I was on the way. We weren't just California and Texas different. She played singer-songwriter folk in the accepted definition, and I played folk music based on blues and rock and a more old-fashioned definition of folk. In other words, Nanci was acoustic guitars and slick production, and I was electric guitars and a sweaty band.

We thought both were folk music. We got close when she invited me to go to Phnom Penh, Cambodia. I had mixed feelings about going on the trip, but she convinced me. We had an amazing, life-changing time going to clinics and minefields. Her close friend John Terzano and a couple guys were dealing with landmine wreckage in places like Angola, Cambodia, and Vietnam where John's group was funding clinics. They were serving people who had lost arms and legs to landmines.

These very rural jungle regions had no medical help. Period. Clinics started being generalized, so you could go to one if you had the gout or flu. We spent time in clinics from the border of Cambodia and Vietnam to up near the Cambodia and Laos border. I remember one morning when John and I were in a hospital being run by this Christian aid group, which was one of the most heartbreaking, overwhelming moments of my life. People were looking at me for help, and I was like, "What the fuck? I'm just a fucking guitar player. I'm not even famous. What do you want me to do? I'll give you every cent that I have, but I don't have any." Heartbreaking.

We went to killing fields, which was a whole different experience. Nanci had been before and didn't go along to all the places. She was there for most, but some were too powerful and upsetting for her to visit twice. We spent two weeks over there and had some good drunks on a very emotional trip that ran the gamut. We did one gig swapping songs with acoustic guitars in Phnom Penh. Very few Americans were in Phnom Penh at that time, but almost all of them were at that gig with various Cambodian dignitaries and the American ambassador.

Sound check was funny. Picture Nanci and me onstage. We had two vocal mikes and two acoustic guitars. The sound system came from Singapore. The guy working the sound came from Thailand. The guys running the venue were from Cambodia. Guess what? No one spoke the same language. Hilarious. Just asking for something as simple as turning up or down the voice took gesturing for half an hour. Then the two guys would argue with each other in different languages. Somehow it managed to work.[6]

Southern California blues rocker Dave Alvin has performed with the Blasters, X, the Knitters, and Jimmie Dale Gilmore, but his solo work best represents his singular songwriting. He reached a pinnacle with the seamless King of California *(1994).*

NANCI GRIFFITH: The concert in Phnom Penh with Dave Alvin was really fantastic. I also enjoyed playing in Hanoi with the Vietnamese National [Symphony] Orchestra. I would say that was one of the defining moments of my career.[7]

DAVE ALVIN: I wish someone would have taped this great gig. I played my own songs but had just won a Grammy for my album of old folk songs called *Public Domain*. So I did several traditional folk songs from the record. Nanci would do her songs, but then, "This song was written by my friend . . ." We approached the same folk music differently. I would accompany her on lead guitar. Some people don't think I'm even a singer, but I'm certainly not a harmony singer. Nanci would say, "Sing harmony on this." "You're out of your fucking mind." She would sing beautiful harmony on my songs, though. She would figure out the chorus pretty quickly.

I knew "If I Had a Hammer" but had never done the song in my entire life. Nanci says to me, "Let's do 'If I Had a Hammer.'" "Well, I don't know that one." "You'll figure it out." I knew one verse of the Peter, Paul, and Mary versions and that the Weavers had done it originally, but the one I knew best was the Trini Lopez version. Of course, everyone in the audience knew that song. Nanci wanted to keep it going, so I started making up verses. "If I had a Ford, I'd drive it in the morning." Wonderful fun. That whole trip was a very intense, cherished memory. A couple things were [most memorable].

An absolutely gorgeous twelve-year-old girl was in one clinic. Her village in the jungle had been in warfare with another village. This girl had her spine severed with an axe. Nanci, John Terzano, Chris Noth from *Law and Order*, and I were around her bed. Words only go so far sometimes when something that bad happens with someone so innocent. This poor girl was in this clinic and they were hoping against hope. She was conscious and could speak. She even knew a little English. There's a photograph on the internet somewhere of us at her bedside. The injustice just ripped my heart out, man.

JOHN TERZANO: I remember that twelve-year-old girl. I have a very specific memory of Chris Noth, Dave, and Nanci standing around her. She's an example of one amazing thing with this work. You see these children who have gone through so much, and the joy [they maintain] is just extraordinary. My god, I would be so damn angry, bitter, and pissed off if I went through what these children did. Maybe that's the innocence of youth, but visiting these places and seeing kids who have had so many horrific things go wrong in their life both mentally and physically really puts things in perspective. We go back there and are like, "I have problems in my life, but look what this twelve-year-old girl has gone through already."

DAVE ALVIN: You're dealing with big ideas like political dogmas when you're talking about landmines. They think using landmines is right and, "We're gonna show you." This was just on the local, old-time, primitive level with one village attacking another. This little girl gets caught in it, and someone thought it was a good idea to put an axe into her spine. I'm getting pissed off now and have to calm down. The girl died about a year later. John kept in touch with the people at the clinic and kept Nanci and me informed. Life is a beautiful thing, but it's fucking brutal. I shared that experience with Nanci.

We also experienced one of the most gorgeous things when we were up at the Cambodia and Laos border and had almost died in a small, four-person Cessna plane. The pilot was a great Australian madman. He said, "Do you want to see the Grand Canyon of Cambodia?" "Sure." We were on our way up, and he flies us through this canyon that was stunningly beautiful. One positive side effect of a genocide is that the Cambodian landscape went back to being a jungle after Pol Pot had killed millions of his fellow countrymen. You're flying through this beautiful, remote canyon.

JOHN TERZANO: [The juxtaposition] of utter devastation and great beauty [throughout the countryside] is one of the fascinating things. What the hell did we go to war for? Look at this. These are beautiful, extraordinary people. They're survivors. We went to war against them. Then you see the beautiful countryside. We took our first trip over right before Christmas and we were commemorating the ninth anniversary of what was called the 1972 Christmas bombing. The United States dropped more bombs on Hanoi in a twelve-day span than Germany did on England throughout the whole World War II. We're walking around Hanoi, and people would come up to us asking, "Are you the American veterans?" "Yes." "Welcome to Vietnam." Now, think about that.

DAVE ALVIN: Then you come out of the canyon, and there's a flat jungle as far as you can see. These wind gusts hit us as soon as we came out and flipped the plane over two, three times like in a movie. I'm sitting next to Nanci looking out the window. "Now we're going all the way over. Oh boy. Oh boy." I realized what the headline was going to say: "Beloved International Folk Singer Nanci Griffith Dies in Plane Crash in Cambodia with Somebody Else on the Plane." Anyway, we landed on a dirt road because there wasn't an airport and spent the day at a silk farm. We got back into the plane in the late afternoon.

Then we had two days in Siem Reap and Angkor Wat. This was our treat after two weeks of killing fields and landmines. Imagine flat jungle as far as you can see. The sun started setting, which suddenly illuminated all the temples in the Angkor Wat complex that stretches for miles. There are stupas and temples sticking out of the jungle. They're all glowing orange, red, burgundy. Brilliant.

Nanci and I were sitting there, and it takes your breath and words away like the injured girl did. Beautiful.

I've never really spoken about this with anyone. The whole trip was very moving. "Moving" isn't even a good enough word. A moment at Angkor Wat was the first thing that came into my mind when Nanci died. We were at a famous main temple there during monsoon season. Nanci and I were sober and decided that it would be a really good idea to climb to the top of this temple in a fucking monsoon rainstorm. You can climb to the main temple's top on these narrow steps built into the side, but I'm not a big rock climber.

So, Nanci and I are climbing in the rain, wind, and the whole nine yards. I wear size twelve shoes, and these stairs are like size six. You have to do this on your hands and knees. I don't know what I was thinking. I guess the idea seemed good because we were so emotionally charged. Nanci was behind me and to my right. I made it to the top, but Nanci fell. I reached my hand out to grab her as she fell but couldn't reach her. She went down. She wasn't seriously injured, but her entire backside was incredibly bruised. I was battling against such feelings of utter helplessness and hopelessness during that moment. I thought about the little girl who was injured in the village warfare and didn't give up hope. She kept fighting until she died.

The people I met at these clinics were some of the bravest, most amazing people you could ever meet—particularly one doctor on the border of Vietnam. He had escaped from the killing fields twice. The one thing you don't want in your political paradise is fucking doctors. He managed to escape twice and eventually set up this clinic. You're battling against the evils humanity can do to each other. Then there's the helplessness of reaching for Nanci's hand to help her, but I wasn't able. That image is right where I went when she died. Like I said, we were close. Then we weren't. We lived in different worlds. I'm not a Nashville guy, and that was her world. Nanci was an A-lister. I'm a D-lister.

JIM "SEÑOR" MCGUIRE: Nanci took me back to where I served in Vietnam one time. I originally [served] very early on, from 1964 to 1965 when the Vietnam War was still being called the Vietnam Conflict. There were thirteen thousand Americans there when I arrived and two hundred thousand when I left. I was stationed at a place called Soc Trang, which was a little village about four hours south of Saigon. Soc Trang was right in the middle of the Mekong Delta [immediately west of Ho Chi Minh City]. My experience actually had been a good, life-changing year for me. I hadn't been interested in photography until I was in Vietnam and saw that part of the world.

I was there as a weatherman in the air force. We would give weather reports to any place with airstrips. They said they needed someone who could use a camera. I could and became the official camp photographer. They didn't have any good maps, which is why they needed a photographer. They needed to see the aerial landscape and hired an old Vietnamese guy who had a portrait studio in the village to come out and teach me how to develop film. We didn't have a darkroom so he would come out at night. We developed my first rolls of film in an army tent in the dark at night.

They would take me up in a light aircraft, and I would hang out to take aerial pictures so they could plan their missions. That's what I did the rest of the year once I learned how. They would see where the canals and roads were from my pictures. Vietnam was very primitive at the time. I would photograph these canals and villages from the air because there weren't roads. Transportation was by boat. They could see how canals connected all the rivers and villages in my pictures and would go on their mission to destroy these places. Then I would get to go in with them after the mission. These Vietnamese army officers would fly them in to do inspections. I would go so I would have the before and after photos of these places.

Nanci found out about this story and wanted to take me back to this village, but there wasn't any airport there. She went so far out of her way. We flew to Saigon, then took the four-hour drive to Soc Trang and looked up the family of the photographer guy, who had already passed away, but the photo studio was still there. His kids ran it in the same house. What an amazing experience. I was thrilled to go back. Everybody—Terzano, Dave Alvin, Chris Noth—went with us in a van. The thing I remember from that whole trip the most was that I couldn't wait to get out. Most places we went were prisons where there had been mass murders. Really horrible things happened there. Going to the prisons was eerie. You could feel death. There were places with hundreds of skulls of people who were killed in the mass murders. The whole country felt evil.

Terzano was the tour leader so he decided where we were gonna go. We went to one museum that was a death chamber back then. They sent prisoners there to torture and kill them. The museum had photographs on the walls. They showed people being mutilated and tortured and [after they were] dead. It was so god-awful depressing. I can't imagine why anyone would want to go through there, but I guess they're trying to preserve the history. I just thought it was disturbing, and I know Dave Alvin felt the same. We were sitting together on a bench when we came out of that prison. "God," he said, "get me out of here." So depressing and evil. That museum was one of the worst places I've ever been in my life.

CHRIS NOTH: I got involved with the Vietnam Veterans of America through my relationship with Nanci Griffith. She was a fan of my work on *Law and Order* and *Sex in the City*, and I'm a fan of her music. We [had] a friendship for years. She asked if I wanted to go to Vietnam and Cambodia and see what the VVAF was doing. The concert was fun, but it was the other things that I was shown along the way, like going to the VVAF school, the silk farm, and the clinics in Kien Khleang, Prey Veng, and Preah Vihear, that were a little more interesting for me. [We saw] people initially come out of the hills and jungles without limbs to be treated and then learn how to treat other people.

VVAF teaches victims to make prosthetic devices and wheelchairs for other landmine victims. I don't think there's a big consciousness in America. Look at me. I didn't know that much about it. Now, I have a fan base that writes letters with checks to VVAF for my birthday. I think there needs to be a better awareness of what VVAF is doing. Frankly, I feel they don't get the press they deserve, and I'm sure that's why people like Sheryl Crow and I have been asked to come along and witness it. It gave me hope to see an organization like the VVAF with all the corruption going on and the bad news in the papers. It's easy to be cynical, but VVAF is courageous and committed to making an enormous difference.

I walked into a dingy little museum in Vietnam called Requiem, which is the museum where they house all the photographs from the book *Requiem: [By the Photographers Who Died in Vietnam and Indochina]*. The museum tells the stories of all the photojournalists who died in Vietnam. Vietnam was unprecedented in terms of the access given to photographers and journalists. They recorded the war with pictures that brought the war home to Americans and showed us what was really going on. Many of the photos were shot a minute before the journalists themselves were killed. Really moving and intense.[8]

Chris Noth is best known as NYPD detective Mike Logan on the television show Law and Order, *Mr. Big on* Sex and the City, *and Peter Florrick on* The Good Wife.

CHARLEY STEFL: I was incredibly honored that Nanci asked me to go on a trip to Cambodia with her and John Terzano. Larrie Warren was head of the mines advisory group at the time and was working over in Cambodia. We flew into Hanoi and stayed at the Metropole about a block from the American Embassy, which was where our show was gonna be. We did some sight-seeing. Then we did sound check and got set up for the show. They had set up a really nice stage for us. The American Club at the embassy was presenting Nanci Griffith with Charley Stefl. We played for about an hour. Taylor donated two junior model guitars so we wouldn't have to carry our guitars. The travel was white-knuckle express.

We left the guitars for the kids to play with at a place called Mith Samlanh Friends in Cambodia. We did two shows: one at the embassy and another at this Friends place, which is for street children, their family, and the community. We were there to raise money for prosthetics for children and adults who had inadvertently picked up some type of unexploded ordnance. We went to the hospitals to visit patients who were undergoing fittings for these prosthetics. Nanci was so involved. She had been doing this for several years before. I was just tagging along. Nanci was beloved. Unbelievable how those kids took to her.

I went to this museum in Khmer Rouge where Pol Pot kept all his prisoners. He had turned this school into a prison. The educators and teachers were all arrested and tortured in this place. They were chained to steel bedsprings with no mattresses, and car batteries were hooked onto their extremities with alligator clips. They had all their photos on the wall. That's why Nanci and John Terzano couldn't go back. I was not a combat veteran, but it shook me to the core. Horrible. I couldn't sleep for the next two nights. Anyway, the main thrust of the trip was to raise money for the prosthetics. There are so many unexploded landmines there. We went to Laos too but didn't do a show there.

We got in a little sight-seeing when we were at Angkor Wat, which was absolutely gorgeous. I asked Nanci if they showed any resentments toward us Americans. She said that they called the Vietnam War the American War. I asked a native Vietnamese person about it. They said they weren't even alive during the war, and the older people don't talk about it. So many were killed in the war, but I didn't encounter any animosity at all, which I was fearing before we went. Nanci was fixated on things over there because of Eric's time there and [because] he had become an addict like so many during the war. She spent time in Ho Chi Minh City as well.

We wrote "Love Conquers All" for her *Hearts in Mind* album when we came back. Nanci was fun to cowrite with, but she already had so much of the song written when I went over to her house. Nanci sounds a little world weary and for good reason on that beautiful album. She had family issues as well, which she would talk about when she was in the right place. Her father, Griff, got very upset with her because of a procedure she had. Griff did not approve of the procedure and stopped talking to her. Nanci's stepdad, Pops, was the man she really looked up to. Nanci was devastated when he passed. She never reconciled with Griff.

Nanci told me about singing our song in Seattle later. "'Love Conquers All' got a standing ovation in a casino," she said. "The world stood up for us, Charley. It was an extraordinary experience that compared to the time I played

'Traveling through This Part of You' at a benefit for the Seattle Zoo in the rain where close to six thousand people showed up. I played the song without any introduction because I didn't know how [to introduce it]. One man with a cane struggled to gain his stance when I finished the song. He hollered, 'That is my song. Thank you. I [was in Vietnam] in 1967 and 1968.' Men were standing and giving their years in a wave across the audience.

"We could not move for at least two minutes as the wave continued. Everyone in the band was overwhelmed. I guess it's something you had to experience, like this incredible surge of love comes toward you. What we're about to do is so important. It might not seem so now, but when Cambodia isn't the lost, forgotten stepchild years from now our Thanksgiving concert will be remembered by every forgotten aid worker from every country working there as something they can take home in their pocket that we've done for them. They've worked so tirelessly for others."

JOHN TERZANO: Nanci wrote a song later on called "Not Innocent Enough" about Phillip Workman, who was convicted of murdering a police officer in Memphis, Tennessee. We started another group called the Justice Project, centered around criminal justice and reform and death penalty issues. Nanci became very interested in that and wanted to read and learn all about it. She wasn't just there to have a sixty-minute conversation about things. No, she wanted to learn, read, and talk to different people, which is the brilliance in her writing. She comes from a position of knowledge and having the empathy for whomever she's writing about.

Nanci's legacy will live on in her music and what she was able to give to this world. I often listen to her music. I love listening with headphones on so I can get totally immersed in the music. Take her songs apart and just look at the lyrics so you get the whole story and the simplicity in her words. She was truly, truly extraordinary, but not just in her own work. Ask her peers what the best version of Townes Van Zandt's "Tecumseh Valley" is. Nanci's name will come up. Her version is extraordinary. I remember her recording that with Maura and Pete in Washington, DC. She came into the office and said she was gonna do the song. Something was different when she came back after.

Verse: Clock without Hands

Nashville (The Later Years)

NANCI GRIFFITH RELEASES *Clock without Hands* around millennium's turn. "*Clock without Hands* is the title of Carson McCullers's last novel," Griffith writes in the liner notes. "As with her work, this piece of fictional art is based around the concept of complacency of emotion, allowing one's heart to go dormant, and the loss of innocent passion in life. Drawing inspiration from Jack London and John Terzano, once passion has been reduced to ashes the lights of life are flown and the soul has died in waking memory. This collection [is] my own awakening."[1]

High points such as "Traveling through This Part of You" and "Pearl's Eye View (The Life of Dickey Chapelle)" particularly resonate. "I remember one time right after she had some hand surgery," says Maura Kennedy, who co-wrote "Pearl's Eye View." "She called and said, 'Maura, I just discovered this woman Dickey Chapelle. She was a war correspondent. So cool. I really want to tell her story in a song, but I can't play guitar. I can send you some lyrics if you can work out the music.' She couldn't even wait for her hands to heal up [after surgery] before following this inspiration. She wrote like that. There were times on the road when she grabbed bar napkins and started writing because the inspiration came to her."

The Blue Moon Orchestra core—James Hooker, Pat McInerney, Ron de la Vega, LeAnn Etheridge, and Lee Satterfield—remains, with guitarist Chas Williams joining the fold. "The sessions for *Clock without Hands* were really cool," Williams says. "Nanci would play a song, then we would chart it and suss out the arrangement. I would decide if I was gonna play acoustic or electric guitar or Dobro. Then we would record a song two or three times and maybe throw in an overdub and be finished."[2]

The album's cover photo session was equally carefree. "There never was any wardrobe stylist for our shoots," Jim McGuire says. "Nanci always put thought into what she wanted to wear and how she wanted to present herself.

Clock without Hands was interesting. There was no concept. Those big, galvanized metal steel panels were left over from a shoot the week before. Nanci liked all the reflection off them. She just saw that and liked it with what she was already dressed in."

RON DE LA VEGA: We did some touring between *Dust Bowl Symphony* and [2001's] *Clock without Hands*, but Nanci would allow herself time to write at home, do interviews, and have meetings when we were off doing our stuff. We would get our bookings back in the studio. I took six months to tour with Engelbert Humperdinck. Then we would get back with Nanci.

CHAS WILLIAMS: I first played with Nanci when Pat McInerney suggested me to come play on the session for Nanci's song "Traveling through This Part of You." We had played several times before, and I guess Pat thought I would be a good fit for the session. The song came out really well.

Chas Williams has toured with Wynonna as well as Bread's lead singer David Gates. He is the author of The Nashville Number System.

RON DE LA VEGA: *Clock without Hands* was a fun album because it was so personal. We were very much involved with the arranging. Nanci would ask us all for input. We would take our chances. Sometimes something really wonderful would happen. Other times the hands would fall off the clock. We all put a lot into that album. Maura and Pete Kennedy were fun and very easy to work with in the studio.

Nanci crafted songs nicely. The stuff I had worked on before didn't have the care that Nanci put into her music, which really drew me to the songs. Also, her lyrics were beautiful. The funny thing was that Nanci would joke that she would write the same couple songs over and over. The structure of her chords and their movement were very interesting, which made it fun to play along with as a cellist and bass player. James Hooker and I would play around with different bass notes to put in the chords to make the song move differently. I would play the root notes sometimes, depending on the song structure.

Say the song was in C. We would naturally go to the five or G chord, but sometimes we would play the leading F-sharp into the G. Nanci's songs were deceptively simple. You would have to listen and look into the songs [to learn them]. They were complex. For example, "It's a Hard Life (Wherever You Go)" is a simple three-chord song, but at the same time that works for the song. That's one of my favorite songs, an anthem, which is the beauty. She knew when and when not to be complex. We could taper the arrangement from next to nothing musically into more of a huge thing with the same basic chords.

CHAS WILLIAMS: Sessions were quick. We would hang out in the lounge while people recorded their parts. The record sounded really great. Nanci didn't have much arranging to do, but [producer] Ray [Kennedy] helped out with that. We would do dynamics and band licks together, and Ray had some great ideas about how to craft the songs, like adding twelve strings or doubling up the slide parts.

"Shaking Out the Snow" was really cool. I was gonna play a slide part, and Ray said, "Try out this old Magnatone amp." The amp had this really cool tremolo sound that came out without using a pedal or anything. My slide part sounded so cool with that amp. "Hey," Ray said, "let's do that again." That was one of my favorite songs on the record. We recorded the album at the Room and Board studio that Ray co-owned with Steve Earle in Nashville. Steve showed up briefly a couple times, but I didn't really get a chance to talk with him. He would sit down and listen to the recording. James Hooker made final decisions on anything we had questions about.

We were gonna do this Paul Carrack tune ["Where Would I Be"], and they asked me to take it home and write a chart. The song had a half-diminished chord. Clive Gregson was on those sessions. "No," he said, "that's a diminished chord." "I don't know. What do you think, James?" He was the referee. We want to try something at rehearsal, but James would say, "Nah. Let's do this and that." He was a great guy and very diplomatic. He was so talented and always played the perfect B-3 or piano part. "How do you pull that off every night?" I asked one time. "Man," he said, "I'm scared to death."

I got a call six or eight months later to possibly join the band because Nanci's guitar player [Doug Lancio] was moving on. I said, "Heck yeah." The first gig I played with Nanci was in Birmingham, Alabama. I'm from Birmingham, so my whole family swarmed down there. I was flying by the seat of my pants. The gig was only two days after I got the call. They started handing me tour dates and gigs after that. I had been working with [front man for the popular seventies rock band Bread] David Gates, and gigs started to collide.

I realized I would have to pick one or the other. I chose the Blue Moon Orchestra and became a full-time member for the next three and a half years. Nanci was fantastic, supersweet, and nice. She really seemed to like what I was adding on guitars. The gigs were great because she had such reverent fans. They really paid attention. Man, you would think, people are really listening to what we're doing. They're not just here getting drunk at a concert. They were digging on every word.

I didn't realize she had such serious fans. You're right when you call them superfans. The Nanci web groups are very protective of her. They're almost protective to the point of fury, which is great. I remember playing in the UK once, and the applause died down after one song. Some superfan goes, "'Love at the Five and Dime,' Nanci." Then he goes, "Sorry." People wouldn't be apologetic over here for yelling stuff out. The depth of her fans' devotion was obvious.

Nanci and I both had trouble sleeping on a moving bus, so we would sleep at the hotel until eleven the next morning and roll out of our rooms at the same time. Nanci was supermindful of making everyone comfortable. You don't make much money doing most country music tours, and if you even get a hotel it's typically one room for everyone to shower in. We had our own rooms in excellent hotels with Nanci. She really cared for us well. Anyway, we would get up and wander into the hotel restaurant and usually see some other band guys in there. We would have breakfast together, then take a walk until sound check around three in the afternoon. Many artists don't do sound check, but Nanci was always there to practice.

We would get on the bus after the show, always had a good time, and would talk about the gig that night on the way to the next. We would sit up occasionally talking after everyone went to bed on the bus, but there wasn't too much one-on-one time. We mostly talked about music. I do remember playing with her early on in San Diego, and we found ourselves listening to Rodney Crowell after we played. "You ever do any drugs when you were younger?" she said. We were just getting to know each other. I remember having a Scotch with her at a supposedly haunted hotel in Ireland. She was telling me about the reported ghost sightings. We got along well.

One favorite gig with Nanci was outdoors in San Francisco on the Pier. The night was cold [while] we played with the San Francisco Symphony. We got about halfway through the show when the symphony players got up mid-song and started walking offstage. [That's how I found out] they won't play when the temperatures drop to a certain point. Nanci finished the show rocking after they left. We had to play so softly with the symphonies, I guess we were pent up. Nanci and the band really jammed hard. We had so much fun ending [the show] like that.

• • •

Nanci Griffith's *Winter Marquee* captures the songwriter in top form. The live album and concert film—recorded at the historic Tennessee Theatre in Knoxville on May 29, 2002, and released four months later—feature guest appearances by Emmylou Harris (on Julie Gold's "Good Night, New York") and Tom Russell (Phil Ochs's "What's That I Hear"). Both return for the Townes Van Zandt classic "White Freightliner Blues." "That night was exciting," Chas

Williams says. "Emmylou Harris was hanging around. I didn't get to talk with Emmylou that much, but a couple of us did get to ride back to the hotel in her car. She was supersweet."

CHAS WILLIAMS: I loved the sound of the finished product [2002's *Winter Marquee*]. There were a couple solos where I said, "Man, let me go back into the studio for that." One solo was on a fast country song, which sounded fine on the record, but the accompanying video sometimes showed my hands playing a different part than I was in the song. I laughed over that.

RON DE LA VEGA: There might have been some redos when we shot the live concert *Winter Marquee* at the Tennessee Theatre in Knoxville, but they only filmed the one show. They could edit like they did on *Austin City Limits* if a mistake or false start happened. We left most mistakes as part of the conversation unless one was huge and blatant. Say you stammer a little while talking, like I just did. You just [accept it] as part of the conversation, which is the beauty. Everything is good if it doesn't hurt your ears. Nanci could be very spontaneous when we played, which brings up a story about Fran Breen.

Fran was the drummer when I joined the band, but he had this method. He would read the charts to know what to play. He would ad-lib around that, but he was reading charts. I remember one time Nanci skipped a part of a verse, and Fran didn't let her in. She laughed. She was going with the flow of what was happening even though she was leading the band, but he's reading the chart. He joked about it later. "I'm gonna have to start following you at the gigs," she told Fran later. "You know the material better than I do."

Being onstage and watching Nanci perform every night was pretty incredible. I had the perfect stance behind her to see what she was seeing. I would find something different [in the performance] every night. Also, Nanci shared her humor and would have fun onstage. She and James Hooker especially connected well onstage. You know, there's that line in "Love at the Five and Dime" that goes, "So, Eddie ran off with the bass player's wife"? She arranged for the spotlight to come up on me for that line with the lighting guys once. I don't play on that part of the song. So, the spotlight shines on me, and she looks back at me. I thought I had missed my cue and look like a deer in the headlight.

Everybody was staring at me giggling. Hilarious.

• • •

Nanci Griffith follows *Clock without Hands* with *Hearts in Mind* three years later. Key tracks focus on the Vietnam War ("Heart of Indochine," "Old Hanoi," "Big Blue Ball of War"). The album also features cowrites with friends Elizabeth Cook ("Simple Life"), Charley Stefl ("Love Conquers All"), and the actor Keith Carradine (the United States–only bonus track "Our Very Own"). Additionally, Griffith covers former fiancé Tom Kimmel's "Angels." "I've had my songs recorded by everyone from Johnny Cash to Linda Ronstadt," Kimmel says, "but Nanci recording one meant as much to me as anything."

Pat McInerney and Griffith guide the journey together. "I coproduced *Hearts in Mind*, which was Vietnam heavy to me, but that's where Nanci was [in her songwriting]," McInerney says. "She wanted to get back to something more simple and centered on her songs with albums like *Clock without Hands* [and *Hearts in Mind*]. We had done the symphony dates, but she just didn't want to do them. She wouldn't come to sound check. Leeann Atherton would sing the songs during sound check. Nanci had grown tired of the symphony thing."

ELIZABETH COOK: Nanci had the idea for us to cowrite [the album's opening track] "The Simple Life." She knew that my mom had died, and hers died the day after we wrote it. She called me to come to her house and said she had a song we could write inspired by our mothers. She wanted to celebrate them in a song. Nanci had the skeleton of the song, and I think more than anything just wanted me there by her side to get the song out. I learned tidbits about her childhood from when we were touring, but I don't know much about her childhood or relationship with her parents. I know her stepfather was a positive male figure. She told me she took off by herself in a little car and toured. I can't imagine being brave enough to do that.[3]

Americana music favorite and Sirius XM's Apron Strings *host Elizabeth Cook has appeared on the* Grand Ole Opry *more than four hundred times. Her albums include* Balls *(2007),* Welder *(2010), and the postrehab collection* Aftermath *(2020).*

TOM KIMMEL: I didn't even really love the way she did my song "Angels" on *Hearts in Mind*, but it was just the fact that she did it. I wrote the song with my first wife, Jennifer Kimball. We met when we were students at the University of Alabama. I was fresh off the farm, so to speak. Small town. Jennifer had traveled to Europe and was really smart and well read. We hit it off in a big way and sang together and did everything together for five years.

"Angel" was first recorded by a contemporary Christian trio of Susan Ashton, Margaret Becker, and Christine Dente, who were three successful artists who got together and made a record. They did a lovely version. They even had the courtesy to ask if they could change a couple lines to make it more Christian. Artists often will change something without asking, so I really appreciated that. I've performed the song over the years myself. Nanci heard me do "Angels" with

Jennifer the night we met. She was at the Nashville Songwriters Association banquet because Julie Gold was getting an award for "From a Distance."

LEANN ETHERIDGE: The line and melody "back when Ted loved Sylvia" simultaneously popped into my head after reading an article about Ted Hughes in the *New Yorker* in 1998. I spent four years reading and learning about their life together, both professional and private, in order to finish writing the song ["Back When Ted Loved Sylvia."] My intention never was to take a side, just to tell their story. It was praise indeed when Karen Kukil, the curator of the Sylvia Plath archives at Smith College, remarked that I had found the middle ground after she heard the song.[4]

LeAnn Etheridge played acoustic and bass guitars and sang harmony vocals in the Blue Moon Orchestra. She is married to longtime Nanci Griffith drummer and producer Pat McInerney.

RON DE LA VEGA: The sessions for *Hearts in Mind* were the last I did with Nanci. That was a little more tense for me because I was leaving. Pat and I still were great friends, but we didn't play as well together. He knew I was leaving the band to pursue other genres and styles. I was looking at some classical and jazz [opportunities]. There was less communication between us because I was leaving. I remember Pat said a few times, "We're gonna have a blast going out to support this album." I had to remind him a few times that I wasn't. I was drawing it to a close for me. Pat was coproducing that record and the sessions all went great. Nothing bad.

JAMES HOOKER: Nanci's popularity in England and Ireland petered out about 2005. She was on top of the wave for years, but then it was time for someone else to ride it. The crowds still came, but the hullabaloo left. Her sense of humor usually was a little warped. She beat the shit out of thyroid and breast cancer. We had been off the road but went out again. We were backstage one night and Nanci said, 'James, do you want to see my new tits? They're not mine.'" 'No,' I said, 'that's all right. I'm sure they're wonderful.' She had this devilish grin, but then she started having trouble with her hands. Her illness was genetic and often in people with Nordic, Scandinavian, and Viking backgrounds and has been passed down hundreds of generations. Every few kids get it.

ELLIS PAUL: Nanci and I had Dupuytren's contracture in common. The illness makes your hand close in on itself. Your hands start to gather and tighten until your fingers close into a fist. I have a pretty bad case, which has affected how I play guitar. I heard that Nanci's case was painful. I heard she might have had surgery, which can lead to torn tendons that create lots of pain. I was always curious if that was one reason she stopped playing much. Dupuytren's contracture really affected her the last ten or fifteen years before she died. You can get treatment for it but have to adjust as a player. Surgery can cut a nerve and be pretty debilitating.

I've had to switch to a more flamenco-style strumming to use my remaining healthy fingers. Dupuytren's really affected my own music on piano the most. I don't have the reach anymore. Also, I have this zombie pinkie on my right hand that wants to play its own notes sometimes without invitation. I never met Nanci [for] more than a fleeting hello so I don't know the details of her condition, but it's very painful and makes being onstage very hard. You lose all the subtlety in your playing and can't engage the same nuances in your fingers. Miserable. I'm about to set up surgery for myself for next year, but I'm gonna record one more album before I take the big dive. The condition can be very debilitating even after the surgery.[5]

Maine-born songwriter Ellis Paul has released nearly twenty albums since his debut, Urban Folk Songs *(1989). He has won more than a dozen Boston Music Awards.*

JAMES HOOKER: Nanci could play guitar, but it was very painful. She couldn't do lots of signature things she had written anymore. We hired an extra acoustic guitar player to do those things. Nanci started cutting back on the band and did more intimate places with a trio. I could tell it was bothering her, but Nanci would change the subject real quick if I brought up her hands. "I don't wanna talk about it, James."

THOMM JUTZ: She had that weird thumb pick that Guy Clark had showed her that's a flat pick attached to a thumb pick. You can actually use it to play individual notes or as a flat pick. She used three finger picks, which might have contributed to the problems with her hands.

Thomm Jutz was named the International Bluegrass Music Association's songwriter of the year in 2021. The German-born Nashville resident's To Live in Two Worlds, Volume 1 *was nominated for a Grammy award the year before.*

TODD SNIDER: Nanci was a really great guitar player. She made that unique sound on her records, so it was a real [shame] that her hands got her in the end. She got that stuff I have so bad. She got the surgery but after a couple years had to stop playing guitar. I haven't had it bad in the last year or so, but I've had years where it just comes and goes. It's usually my neck and back, but my arthritis gets into my hands when it gets really bad. I think it's because I play guitar so much.[6]

Todd Snider has released nearly twenty records since his Tony Brown–produced MCA Records debut, Songs for the Daily Planet *(1994). The forthcoming* East Nashville Skyline: The Songwriting Legacy of Todd Snider *(Texas A&M University Press) tells his story.*

RON DE LA VEGA: I got a call a few years later to see if I would be willing to sub with the band, which I did, and it was like no time had passed. Thomm Jutz was playing guitar, but Nanci, Pat, and I felt like we hadn't missed a beat and were doing the same thing. We kept in touch some after that. Nanci always liked seeing my son, who is a special-needs adult now. Lives run in different directions, but I would hear every now and then that Nanci told someone to say hi to me. I feel bad because I didn't try to connect the last few years. I knew she wasn't doing well physically. I wanted to talk to her, but it was rough. That was my fault.

The Blue Moon Orchestra was more than a band to Nanci. They were her family. So, she felt like you were leaving a family anytime someone left. It was hard for her to take, and akin to a divorce in a way. I don't think her divorce with Eric Taylor was amicable at first, but then they maintained a great friendship beyond the relationship. Nanci gets bothered when you leave, but then time goes on and the personal mends itself.

NANCI GRIFFITH: [Eric and I] are a true example of people who can be friends after a marriage breakup. There doesn't have to be any ugliness. You have to remember that you once loved and respected each other. So much so that there is always that lingering feeling and tension. Eric sat in with us during an outdoor festival [one time], and his [ex-wife] Martha had gone to park the car. There was this huge storm, so everything got shut down. They're running to their car later, and Martha can't remember where she parked. It's hailing. Eric says, "Nanci, what the hell did you do with the damn car?" Martha stops and says, "I'm gonna tell you one more time. My name is Martha." "It's all right," Eric said. "That's the first name that comes into my head anytime anything irritates me."[7]

RON DE LA VEGA: Nanci was incredibly generous to a fault. She made sure her family was taken care of when we were touring. We had days off to sight-see. She even paid for some excursions she had been on before but didn't go with us. One guy complained one time, "I can't afford room service at this hotel." "We're being treated like royalty," we said. "You should be glad to be staying in a place where the suite is as big as your house. Walk around the corner to get McDonald's." You lose perspective sometimes. Nanci was a beautiful person.

Pat McInerney and I were so close for so long because we were the rhythm section. Pat was so easy to work with and would bring life to so much of what we were doing. Having Pat around was great for Nanci because they were such close friends. [Being in a band] is like working with a close relative, which isn't always easy to do, but they maintained a friendship throughout. Pat always had great ideas. "If you want a drummer that isn't a drummer," someone said, "Pat's the way to go." He played bluegrass. Drummers don't play bluegrass, but he was accepted into that, which was why Don Williams hired him. Pat was one of the core guys for the whole thing when I think of the Blue Moon Orchestra.

• • •

Nanci Griffith records songs old ("Late Night Grande Hotel") and new ("Brave Companion of the Road") for *Ruby's Torch*. She also records two Tom Waits songs ("Grapefruit Moon," "Please Call Me Baby"). The torch song album receives mixed reviews despite showstopping takes on Jimmy Webb's "If These Walls Could Speak" and Charles Goodrum's "Bluer Than Blue." "Nanci's writing definitely had dried up by *Ruby's Torch*," producer Peter Collins says. "She was nowhere near as prolific and hadn't made a record for a while. Also, Nanci had mellowed by *Ruby's Torch*. She wouldn't have gone out into the hallway and screamed like she did during the *Flyer* sessions. I was pleased with how *Ruby's Torch* [turned out], but it got some negative reviews."

PAT MCINERNEY: We recorded *Ruby's Torch* not far from Nashville. I listened to the album in the car this morning. Peter Collins was a very good producer who had worked some really big acts. Nanci wanted to do a torch song record, which we recorded live in the studio once again. Nanci didn't play guitar. She just sang. We had to be really set up when Thomm Jutz and I produced her. The mike would have to be in the right place, or she wouldn't have it. The band had to know the song when she came in. You had to get the song on the first take. I think some songs suffered from that, but others worked out great. She recorded like playing live. You go out and do it. That's the way she wanted it to be. Most results are great.

I think Peter was a little frustrated because we didn't have much time to record and Nanci really just wanted to record songs once. Don Gehman said to me when we recorded *Blue Roses from the Moons*, "She likes to cut lucky, doesn't she?" You get the first take and [find out if] you're lucky. The same applied to *Ruby's Torch*, which is a fine record that sounds really beautiful, but we maybe would have a little more variety in the material if she put herself more into it. The record sits in the same place too long, but the strings, rhythm section, and Nanci were all live.

PETER COLLINS: I would go to Kristin Wilkinson's house for arrangements. She would get her viola out, and we worked on arrangements note to note.

KRISTIN WILKINSON: Peter is a very knowledgeable and opinionated producer and would go over the direction he wanted for *Ruby's Torch*. Then he would give us time to work through it. I arranged in a way that was sensitive to the lyrics, the singer, and what sounded like it was serving the song, but Peter was driving the bus.[8]

Kristin Wilkinson is a Nashville-based composer, arranger, and orchestrator. The top-call viola player arranged and conducted the string sections on Ruby's Torch.

PETER COLLINS: I knew way up front what the record would sound like, which was very comforting as a producer. Sitting around and rewriting arrangements on the spot with an orchestra waiting around can be very stressful. So, *Ruby's Torch* worked out really well.

KRISTIN WILKINSON: Our system was really great because there are no surprises in the studio. Also, Nanci was not like some artists who are wrapped up in all these details, like "I don't like the B-flat in bar five." Nanci wanted the music to feel good. I thought she sang the Jimmy Webb song "If These Walls Could Speak" the best.

• • •

Griffith's penultimate album, *The Loving Kind* (2009), spotlights marriage equality (the title track) and capital punishment ("Not Innocent Enough") with hat tips toward songwriting heroes Townes Van Zandt ("Up against the Rain") and Dee Moeller ("Party Girl" and "Tequila after Midnight"). "Nanci said, 'Tell Dee to send me a couple songs,'" Moeller says. "'I'm getting ready to do a new album.' Of course, I did." Elizabeth Cook contributes harmony vocals on both Moeller tracks as well as Griffith's "Money Changes Everything" cover. Additionally, fellow Burt Stein management client Todd Snider guests on the updated *The Last of the True Believers* track "One of These Days."

Griffith writes (or cowrites) nine tracks on the album. "This was my first new writing in seven years," she says. "I had writer's block because I was very depressed about the direction our country was going in. I couldn't get anything out." She credits the shift in presidential administrations for inspiration. "The dam burst with the [Barack] Obama election [in 2008], and it all came out. [We] folk songwriters write about the people of your time to chronicle it for history, [but] the Bush administration was such a nightmare for me with the oppression of rights. The whole thing created this total wall for me."[9]

NANCI GRIFFITH: "The Loving Kind" is the story of Richard and Mildred

Loving. Reading Mildred's obituary touched my heart. I wondered, Why don't I know about this case, *Loving v. the State of Virginia*? She was Black and he was white. They had known each other since childhood and married each other in Virginia in 1958. They got thrown in jail because interracial marriage was illegal at that time. *Loving v. Virginia* is the reason there are no more laws banning interracial marriage. I sat and cried for four hours after reading her obituary. [Mildred] said in her last interview that she hoped that their case would be the cornerstone for marriage equality. What a blessing those two people were. The song wrote itself.[10]

JIM "SEÑOR" MCGUIRE: *The Loving Kind* photo shoot was [different]. Nanci had a hard time figuring out how to illustrate the title song. She decided on a portrait with her in a songwriter's mood with her guitar and notebook. She was sitting with my guitar on an old canvas backdrop in that photo. The journal and pen were hers. *The Loving Kind* was one of the more simple concepts. She was so easy to work with because she always came ready. We collaborated well and just worked out stuff as we went along.

THOMM JUTZ: Nanci was reluctant to go into the studio again when Pat McInerney and I coproduced *The Loving Kind*. We had the road band plus Barry Walsh on piano and Fats Kaplin on steel [guitar]. Really good vibe. We had four or five good days tracking, then Nanci didn't feel like being there anymore. We finished the vocals in my home studio, which is where Elizabeth Cook, John Prine, and Todd Snider came in to sing on tracks. Harmonious. Working with Nanci was at her own pace. You would never start before one o'clock in the afternoon and would want to have a bottle of wine ready, but she was easy to work with in the sense that she would do one or two vocal takes and say, "That's good enough. Do with it what you want."

She was very cool and a dream to work with in that way. She never micro-managed a note that I played. "You play what you play, and I'm not gonna tell you what to do." That's very, very rare. That gets you involved as a player because you feel like your work is valued. You play the music differently than if someone says, "Play this lick here, play this there, and don't play anything else." I really appreciated that leadership quality she had. Of course, she could walk onstage when she was on top of her game and hold the audience in the palm of her hand without doing anything other than singing and shaking her knee a little bit. She was magnetic.[11]

PAT MCINERNEY: Thomm and I went for a much more simple, acoustic-based approach when we produced *The Loving Kind*. Nanci was front and center on those records. Her rhythm and guitar playing were fabulous. She was back singing the songs she really, really believes in, which were the ones she wrote.

THOMM JUTZ: Nanci had reached out to me and her old friend Charley Stefl, a fellow Texan who did a Rockin' along the Mekong tour through Vietnam with Nanci one time [for help writing songs]. I don't think cowriting was something she was ever totally comfortable with, but she knew that Charley and I had written together and asked us. We went over to her house and wrote five songs together for *The Loving Kind* ("Up against the Rain," "Cotton's All We Got," "Not Innocent Enough," "Across America," and "Sing"). We had some ideas, and so did she. Then she found a few other songs other people had sent her.

We [originally started recording the album at] Signal Path in Berry Hill here in Nashville with David Ferguson engineering. Nanci loved him. He was a seemingly crude person on the surface by design, but he's also an incredibly warm soul and incredible engineer for acoustic music. Also, he could handle Nanci really well. He could critique her vocal performance, and she would totally accept it. Nanci was funny. Some people would say one wrong word to her, and she would snap like crazy. Others could be honest with her, and she would be just fine with their critique.

CHARLEY STEFL: I had written a couple verses of "Up against the Rain" and took the song over to Nanci the day we wrote five songs together with Thomm Jutz. "I wrote this song about Townes," I said. We finished it up. Then we did "Cotton's All We Got," which is about as autobiographically Nanci as you could get. Of course, she was born in Seguin, Texas, but her family is up around Stephenville. I remember being at a party one night where Nanci was talking with Lee Roy Parnell, who is from Stephenville. She said her grandparents were from around that area. So, that song was a true Texas experience of hers, but embellished, of course. Nanci had most ideas in place and knows where she wants to go with them as a cowriter.

I found that extremely helpful. You get together with people to write sometimes when nobody has ideas. Nanci was absolutely open to our ideas with lyrics [if they worked for the song]. "Not Innocent Enough" was Nanci's baby that we helped with. That song was used in schools around here. Nanci wasn't a practicing Catholic, but she wasn't shy about talking about it. She said in the fourth paragraph of a short story she wrote, "We were all of Catholic faith and attended the same school." I'm assuming she's talking about St. Edward's in Austin.

Thomm brought in the song "Across America." He had the first two verses and a chorus. Nanci loved the song. We finished that one, and I played it at the SESAC Awards with her in 2009. Nanci had the whole idea for "Not Innocent Enough." Our friend Richard Dobson was there. Of course, Thomm and Pat McInerney were there. Nanci got John Prine to sing at the very end, which was really cool. That was all Nanci all the way.

THOMM JUTZ: Prine came out to record his part with his manager Al Bunetta, who was a very colorful character. Nanci wanted to hang out with Prine. Al wanted to hang out with me and talk about our espresso maker in the kitchen. He was such a weird guy that you would hang out for an hour and talk coffee. Nanci was over on the other side talking to Prine, and I obviously would have rather been over there talking to Prine, but that's the way it was. We tried to promote the record, but Nanci was reluctant. She was tired. You don't feel like doing much when you're miserable being hungover half the day. That sounds flippant, but it's a reality. I had been fired by the time she recorded her last album, *Intersection*.

CHARLEY STEFL: We all came up with the song "Sing" together. You know, Nanci was having vocal issues along with the cancer and everything at the time. Nanci was most happy writing songs and singing, and she wanted people to know that's who she is. Her writer's block in the early 2000s [must have been depressing]. I said, "Let's write some stuff that you really want to write." That's how she came up with "Love Conquers All." She was so happy about that song and told me it was getting beautiful standing ovations.

DEE MOELLER: Nanci and I met here in Nashville at the radio station at the top of the Bridgestone Arena when Elizabeth Cook was doing an interview with her. Nanci gave me a copy of her new album *The Loving Kind*. I was amazed. My song "Party Girl" is about a girlfriend of mine who got married and her life changed. I don't remember where I got the idea for "Tequila after Midnight," but there was a year when I was hanging out with Willie Nelson and his group and got on a little tequila binge. Tequila wasn't a problem because I'm a real light drinker. Two drinks and I love everybody and am ready to go to bed. I wrote "Tequila after Midnight" in ten minutes when I got into drinking tequila then.

There was a club in Denton called the Office Club that I played [years earlier], and Nanci would drive up to those gigs when she was in college. I had no idea. It touched me a great deal when I found out. I was honored and thrilled that she did my songs and said those nice words about me on the back cover. We were [Texas women and] fans of each other, but [calling me her hero on the back cover] stunned me. We talked about that later. A problem she ran into when she moved to Nashville was her writing was so Texan. Many Texas artists could never quite connect with Nashville. You have to work within certain parameters here. Sometimes there hasn't been too much imagination in Nashville.

NANCI GRIFFITH: Dee Moeller was my hero when I was a teenager. She also wrote "Slow Movin' Outlaw" [recorded by legendary outlaw country singer

Waylon Jennings]. The honky-tonk she played in Denton was about two hundred fifty miles from my home in Austin. We would get together and borrow a parent's car [to drive there], and she was just mesmerizing. She was a great influence on me. I remembered these two songs of hers, "Party Girl" and "Tequila after Midnight." I said, "I'm going to start off by recording these two songs and surely that will break this writer's block. A cloud [had been] following me around."[12]

CHARLEY STEFL: Nanci asked me to help her onstage five minutes before we played at that SESAC Awards show, but I was so nervous I forgot. I'm sure that ticked her off. We played "Across America." Political times were highly [charged]. There were people in the audience who were not pleased, but it got a great reception overall. Of course, that wasn't the first time she stated things politically. She got flak for a show at the outdoor amphitheater at Arrington Vineyards here in Franklin. Williamson County is notoriously right politically.

My friend the musician Will Smith was at the show and said Nanci had made a snarky comment about Sarah Palin before one song. The people in front of him got up out of their lawn chairs, folded them, and left in a huff. "I've had enough of this." Will told me after, "We went to see Nanci's show on Sunday at Arrington Vineyards. She did a song you cowrote, but I missed one of the more entertaining portions of the festivities when apparently a political comment was made that got some Brentwood Republicans' knickers in a knot. [Nothing] bad. She just made a smart comment."

She told me the next day: "Hey, Charley. Those 'get over it' people can kiss my ass. Next thing you know they'll complain because I played 'Trouble in the Fields.' It's okay for [so and so] to stand onstage and spew his hate speech, but it's not okay to make a joke about Palin, however lame because she is her own best joke. There was never a poll in the paper calling overwhelmingly for me to leave the country. There was hateful letter writing. I was well aware of where I was [playing that concert]. One joke does not spouting politics make. Burt [Stein] is on this and will make sure that [they know] I did not say anything inappropriate. I've heard nothing but positive comments about the concert, and this stupid letter writing breaks my heart because my entire heart and soul go into every show I play."

THOMM JUTZ: Nanci's manager wanted me to tour Australia alone with Nanci one time. "You gotta be fucking kidding me," I said. "I'm not going anywhere without [former Gram Parsons road manager Phil] 'The Mangler' [Kaufman]." He wanted to save the money. "That's great," I said. "I'm not going." So, he put Mangler on the trip. The tour was grueling. We had just come off two or three weeks in England and Ireland. We were there for six weeks, and Nanci was not in good shape physically. She was miserable and didn't want to be there. We got along great, but six weeks together gets to be [too much]. We had done the Belfast Nashville Songwriters Festival and flew straight to Dubai and on to Australia.

BUDDY MONDLOCK: I saw Nanci at the Belfast Nashville Songwriters Festival. Nanci had a special love for the people in Ireland and especially Belfast and Northern Ireland. She was a huge hero over there. I had seen her a number of times in America, but seeing her there where the people really got her was something special. We ran into each other at the hotel in Belfast. This person who had just been onstage and the toast of the town the night before was now sitting alone and looking beat. I sat there to pass the time with her for a few minutes. You want the people you admire to be as happy with themselves as you are, but that's not always the way it works. Nanci was an amazing person, and I think she felt [how appreciated she was] onstage. Nothing beats when you're doing your thing well.

She needed to have moments like that onstage.

RALPH MCTELL: The last time I was in touch with Nanci was at a singer-songwriter festival in Belfast. Her minder said, "She doesn't leave her room very often, Ralph." So, I didn't actually get to see her. We spoke cheerfully on the phone and reminisced. My friend Brian Willoughby confirmed that Nanci was already having problems then. Nanci talked to me like she had known me for a long time when we first met. She told me she had a new sweetheart. She used those words. She talked about how much she loved going to Wales, where the Griffith family name comes from, and said she was looking for her grand-mother's face in the crowd. Sensitivity is a hard thing to maintain with the cyn-icism and rigors of the road when you have a mind that would notice things as gently and softly as Nanci would.

THOMM JUTZ: Playing Ireland with Nanci was crazy good. Playing in Ire-land is always different because music is part of their everyday life. They sing along. The Irish knew Nanci's music better there than people in the States. Everything was very warm playing there with Nanci. Ending our show every night with "Across the Great Divide" was always a highlight for me. So incred-ibly beautiful. The audience reacted to Nanci's interpretation so well, [but] she was drinking and smoking a lot on that tour and wasn't in a good place emo-tionally. She was frail, not eating right, and not exercising, but alcohol was the big thing no one really wants to talk about. Her output and the quality of her work reflected her problem.

MAURA KENNEDY: Almost twenty years had gone by when we did the last tour. Nanci didn't have a nine-piece band or two buses anymore. She wasn't doing whole tours. She was doing one-offs like one night in Seattle or two nights like Seattle and then Portland. Then we would fly to Belfast for one show and fly back home. I was talking with her one time and she said, "I want to be home with my dog." She had given more than thirty years to the road. She was retirement age. She had the right to retire if she wanted to, and she did. Nanci's hand problems had gotten worse. She might have even had a second surgery. She was petering out.

"I don't know if I can do the gigs," she said. "Well, we'll cover the guitar parts," we said. "You're a great guitar player, but people want to hear your songs and stories in your voice." She didn't play guitar at all on those last many gigs we did with her. I think that made her nervous because she was always behind a guitar and in total command of it. There's that line in "Love at the Five and Dime" that goes, "Eddie traveled with a barroom band until arthritis took his hands." She would hold up her own hands every time she sang that line in concert. That was the most personal to her at that point. Losing the ability to play guitar has to suck when you're so good. You could see that her hands would get cold. She would have to warm them up.

• • •

Nanci Griffith bookends her final album, *Intersection*, with the moving opener "Bethlehem Steel" and her idol Loretta Lynn's buoyant "High on a Mountain Top" at close. Several strong originals such as "Stranded in the High Ground," "Come On Up Mississippi," and the reworked and subtly retitled "Just Another Morning Here"—changed from *Late Night Grande Hotel*'s "It's Just Another Morning Here"—show her writing remains sharp despite poor health. The players accommodate by bringing the studio to her. "Nanci was deteriorating pretty quickly by the time we did her last album, *Intersection* [in 2012]," Pat McInerney says. "Maura and Pete Kennedy came down from New York with Pete's portable studio and set it up in the upstairs in her house. I brought a simple drum set."

The title track shapes the sanguine yet spirited set. Griffith delivers with a voice—much like Townes Van Zandt on his final album, *No Deeper Blue*, in 1994—housing weariness and wisdom enough for seven lifetimes. Their toll had been exacted. "Nanci [usually] was a pleasure, but the *Intersection* photo session was tense," Jim McGuire says. "She wasn't feeling well that day and wanted to do something quick. Mangler was there babysitting her. She wasn't up for anything extravagant or long. We shot at night on the street at a location I had already found. Nanci didn't want makeup or hair done and wasn't in a good mood. I'm sure drinking was part of it."

The album's cover songs—Mark Seliger's "Never Going Back," Ron Davies's

"Waiting on a Dark Eyed Gal," and Blaze Foley's "If I Could Only Fly" among them—double down with equal measures reach and regret. "Blaze and I were good friends, and I always wanted to do that song," Griffith says. "It took us three takes because we recorded this at my home. I [would go] downstairs and have a good boo-hoo to get what we got. You can still hear me crying on the track. I don't know that we'll be doing that song live because it's difficult to get through."[13] Remarkably, the album reaches number one on the United Kingdom's country chart.

JOHN LOMAX III: They were trying to get a record together because Pat McInerney wanted more ammunition to be out there touring. They tried to set up a session, but Nanci said, "I can't make it."

MAURA KENNEDY: Nanci used to love the process of going into a studio. We had been on the road with her, and she had been writing these songs. We told her she needed to do another record. "I don't want to go into the studio again." Pete packed up our studio and set it up on her top floor. We would do our weekend gigs and then drive or fly down.

PAT MCINERNEY: We recorded very simply. Pete played acoustic and electric guitars and bass, and Nanci played guitar. The idea was to do a very simple record, but it was hard to get Nanci's attention. Recording at her house seemed like a great idea at first. She can just come upstairs after we're set up. Then she can go downstairs, take a break, and watch television.

JOHN LOMAX III: They set up, but Nanci couldn't even deal with that.

PAT MCINERNEY: Maura Kennedy was a bigger presence than anyone on *Intersection*. She forced Nanci to sing better.

MAURA KENNEDY: We wrote four songs together. I would pull things out from what she would create. Nanci sent me lyrics to all the parts for two of them and said, "You put them in order. Tighten it up." Nanci didn't even try to rhyme "Pearl's Eye View (The Life of Dickey Chapelle)" when she sent me the idea. She just had a few lines and said put this and this in. She had all the ideas. I would sculpt it, but not for all songs.

PAT MCINERNEY: Nanci liked Maura. Maura has a lot of grit and pulled some performances out of Nanci we wouldn't have gotten otherwise. I did think some of the song choices were a little off, but you just couldn't tell Nanci, "That's just not a good song. Let's do something else." She had her head down at the time. She had been through some bad experiences a few months earlier that [showed up on] songs like "Hell No (I'm Not Alright)."

MAURA KENNEDY: Nanci was talking one time and just started singing "Hell No (I'm Not Alright)." That song is funny because she had said earlier that day, "I'm taking notes and naming names." She was writing it, and I said, "Nanci, you said this line earlier that would fit in really well there."

NANCI GRIFFITH: I have people come up to me in the grocery store and say, "Hell no, I'm not all right either." This record is up close and personal. Some people have said, "I didn't really want to know that. Too much information." Well, too bad. This is my twentieth album, and it's great if I want to get personal. I feel good about it. I'm fifty-eight years old, and it's about time.

MAURA KENNEDY: "Bad Seed" is one [that started] when we were in a hotel lobby. Nanci scratched out the words on a bar napkin and gave that to me. We had driven our studio down to Nashville [for the sessions]. She still had that set of lyrics when we did "Bad Seed." Reading the lyrics made me sad because she talks about her father. I knew Griff and thought he was a lovely guy. I don't have any idea of their personal feelings. I remember when she said she wanted me to set the lyrics to music I thought, Oh no. Oh no. I was trying to find a way to set the song to music so that the lyrics wouldn't stand out too much.

NANCI GRIFFITH: I was [my father's] good kid if I was nominated for a Grammy, but I was the bad seed who didn't turn out quite right if I didn't get one that year. I would have told [my father] the song is about him if we were speaking, but we're not. It really started fifteen years ago, and it went downhill from there. I finally said, "Enough is enough." There are occasional moments when I miss my dad because he has a great sense of humor, [but] I can't dig his politics.[14]

MAURA KENNEDY: I just didn't want to hurt Griff's feelings. How do you put such a dark song to music in a way that's gonna work? All I could think was using a [British eighties rock band] Rockpile melody. "We're gonna do 'Bad Seed,'" she said. "Did you write a melody?" I had been putting it off. I took Nanci's Taylor into the living room, put on my Rockpile hat, and came up with that pretty quickly. I took it up to her, and she sang it great. I never got into personal family stuff with her, which is why I was a little shocked when I read those lyrics. Griff was such a nice guy backstage at gigs.

PAT MCINERNEY: I would go home after we recorded. Maura would go back to their hotel room. Pete would be upstairs mixing on the fly and over-dubbing most of the night. Nanci didn't really record for long. You were really lucky if you got four hours out of her. She didn't want to put in too much time. Sometimes I would sit there with Pete and put more percussion on the songs. I thought that song "Bad Seed" was a bit paranoid. Nanci felt she was the bad seed of the family. She wanted the songs to sound angry like punk rock, so

Maura played electric guitar on "Hell No." Nanci wanted to express what she was going through at the time.

NANCI GRIFFITH: So many people are at an intersection of their life with the way the economy is with foreclosures and downsizing. *Intersection* is my musical crossroads. I came offstage [at Musikfest Café at SteelStacks in Bethlehem] and wrote "Bethlehem Steel" in about twenty minutes. It was devastating to the town when that mill closed, and we all lost a piece of America. ["Bethlehem Steel"] would have never been written, but they have a new arts center that's situated right in front. The stage of this huge arts center is one plate-glass window, and the backdrop is Bethlehem Steel. It was the first time in my career that I wanted to turn my back on my audience and just stare at this huge thing that looks like a movie set.

PAT MCINERNEY: We all wrote "Stranded in the High Ground." We were just upstairs messing around, and Nanci came up. This is how Nanci would work at that time. She came up, had a seat in front of the microphone, and didn't even say hello or anything. She just started playing "Standing on the High Ground" into the microphone. We knew that we wouldn't get it if we didn't get it right then. So, we all sat down and got this semireggae rhythm. "Hey, Nanci," Pete said. "Can we start again?" "Well," she said, "if we have to." Pete told her we hadn't been recording. We started again. One-take song. She had just been writing it downstairs and then disappeared.

ROBBIN BACH: I had met Nanci when my good friend Ken Beale told me about what they called "girls guitar night" at Brown's Diner. I had never been but knew where it was and asked who would be there. He went through the names: "Nanci Griffith . . ." I said, "Excuse me? *The* Nanci Griffith?" "Yeah." "You've got to be kidding. She's my favorite songwriter." He noticed I was going a little nuts. "Robbin, you have to calm down. This is their neighborhood. They don't like a big fuss." So, we go and I met her for the first time. I waited until Ken went to the restroom and went up to Nanci.

"Nanci," I said, "my name is Robbin. I just moved here from Jacksonville, Florida. I love your music and am a huge fan." Nanci asked about my family. I told her that my dad worked in the trucking business. She got up later to sing in this casual, tiny restaurant bar and goes, "I just wanna say hello to my new friend Robbin and dedicate this song to her." Then she sings [Townes Van Zandt's] "White Freightliner Blues." I felt like, Okay. Pinch me. So beautiful. Another thing Ken told me is that they would have a guitar pull where everyone shares a song if I wanted to stick around after. "You could play a song for them." I stayed. There were only about five performers. I played a song called "Davey's Last Picture" that night. Nanci ended up recording that on *Intersection*.[15]

Robbin Bach was Nanci Griffith's personal assistant. She cowrote "Davey's Last Picture," which Griffith recorded on her final album, with Bach's mother, Betty Reeves.

JOHN LOMAX III: The band realized that was pretty much the end of the line. Nanci wasn't gonna tour. Why should we hang around? They were waiting for her to get herself together. Never happened.

THOMM JUTZ: Everything got so bad that her manager decided there had to be an intervention. He hired a very top-dollar interventionist who set the whole thing up. He insisted that it be important for me, McInerney, and Mangler to be there. It was organized at a very, very unfortunate moment. I had warned him not to do it because she had been in a really good mood. "Look, man," I said. "She's doing great right now given the circumstances, and you're hitting her over the head with this? It's not gonna end well. Someone's head is gonna roll, and it probably will be mine. McInerney has been here for twenty-four years. He's her confidant. She can't fire you because no one else will manage her or take her on the road. I'm gonna get ass fucked here. You gonna resign too if she fires me?" "I would consider it."

Of course, he didn't. Of course, that's exactly what happened. She agreed to go to Eric Clapton's rehab for four weeks, and on the way home she got completely trashed and gave me a call in the next couple days, telling me, "You lied in front of all these people. You're fired." It was a relief at that point. It had been such a toxic atmosphere. Everyone was so anxious around her.

• • •

Nanci Griffith lives the decade following *Intersection* in relative seclusion by most accounts. Songwriting inspiration slows. Friends lose touch. "I used to go over to Nanci's house after [recording *Intersection*], but she started to see people less and less," Pat McInerney says. "We would talk on the phone and laugh, but she didn't want to be around people—even me popping in like I used to. She didn't seem enthusiastic about it." Griffith passes away on August 13, 2021. "Today I am just a sad man," Darius Rucker posts on Twitter that day. "I lost one of my idols [and] one reason I am in Nashville. Singing with [Nanci] was one of my favorite things to do." Griffith's family never discloses the cause of death.

JOHN LOMAX III: Pat McInerney told me that the last time they toured they were flying in and out of somewhere like Abu Dhabi. Nanci had gotten herself a first-class cabin while everyone else was in coach and was able to sequester herself for the entire flight. She was so soused when they landed that they practically had to carry her. She kept herself away from the band, and after a ten-hour flight you can do a lot of damage with unlimited alcohol. Booze just grabbed her. Vicious. Ate her alive.

THOMM JUTZ: You didn't know if she would make it through the gig or what shape she would be in when she showed up or have another meltdown. I was mad about it, but I was also like, "Yeah, fuck it. I'm good."

PAT MCINERNEY: I don't know why she got so isolated, but let's cut to the chase here. She had a terrible problem with alcohol. She really didn't look great anymore. She was painfully thin and lost interest. Food would sit on the table for a day. She had been in and out of rehab so much it might as well have had a revolving door for her. Phil Kaufman took her to Betty Ford on the West Coast once, and he said she got a plane ticket and was home before he was.

CHARLEY STEFL: We stopped communicating around 2008. We had an intervention for her, trying to get her off booze. She had been to rehab a number of times and once told me, "Why didn't you do an intervention for Townes? For Guy?" "That's not the point. We love you and you're killing yourself." She called me [around 2012] and was sounding a little loopy. That's when people started to notice her withdrawing and drinking more. Intervention was hard and didn't go over well. We all had to write letters. Then she really isolated herself. Very sad.

THOMM JUTZ: Alcohol was covering up deeper psychological issues that weren't addressed for many, many years.

PAT MCINERNEY: She was angry about quite a few things. She felt betrayed by the community that she grew up with and didn't think they appreciated her. That was never true. She didn't feel like she was part of that community anymore. I don't really know what the problem was with her family. I knew her family. Her dad was fantastic. Her sister was great. Nanci felt like she was the black sheep for some reason. She felt that Mikki was the glamorous one and she was the ugly duckling. She never really got over that. It went on and on and got worse to where she had all these provisions about where Mikki could be. She couldn't be within two hundred yards if we played in Austin. Absolutely ridiculous.

BETH NIELSEN CHAPMAN: People loved Nanci so voraciously. That's the thing about when someone has fallen into an addiction. They can't see how much love is waiting for them. The people who love them feel like they can't get in because the door has to open from both sides. Brutal.

PAT MCINERNEY: Maura and Pete Kennedy really were there in the last period, but things were getting difficult with Nanci. Nothing seemed to bring her pleasure. She was really tired. Nanci called me sometime later and said, "I would like to do more dates. Can you talk to Pete and Maura?" "Yeah, sure." I called them. They said they would love to do it and wanted to suggest a set list to Nanci with [songs that] longtime fans wanted to hear. The songs were primarily the earlier standards. Maura put together a set list and came down from New York.

"Let's not go to Nanci's house," I said. "Waste of time. She's too comfortable there and wouldn't work." So, we booked [Studio Instrument Rentals] in Nashville. Here's Nanci on day one ready and waiting before anybody got there. "Great, Nanci," I said. "Ready to do something?" "Yeah," she said. "Where are my guitars?" "Well, they're at your house." She was used to [a tour manager] handing her a guitar. I ran over and got them. We were a five-piece with Maura, Pete, and LeAnn on bass. We reworked "Late Night Grande Hotel" and "It's a Hard Life (Wherever You Go)" in a more acoustic style. We rehearsed for two days. Sounded fantastic. Then Nanci lost interest. Shame. The days we put in were absolutely incredible. Nanci looked good, sounded great, and played great. We all got on well.

Then she went back home.

THOMM JUTZ: Nanci wasn't aware what high esteem she was held in by people in Nashville, which made her a very sad person. Her hand had gotten really bad. I also think that some problems were because she was drinking and smoking so much that her body didn't heal properly after hand surgery. Her problems came back.

JOY LEWALLEN: The Dupuytren's was really deflating to her. She was an expert guitar player who wrote on the guitar. She had a rough patch to get through when she got that condition. I encouraged her to just get up there and sing with another guitar player. Many musicians do that, but playing and writing on the guitar was part of her heart and soul.

JOHN GORKA: Being able bodied is only a temporary condition. I tried writing emails to her, but Nanci said her hands would not let her [type]. Nanci had everything [before that]. I was congratulating her on all the accomplishments like winning a Grammy, and she said, "I don't think I've been that successful." My personal motto is "High standards, low overhead, and realistic expectations." I don't know. Some people have a grasp that's longer than their reach.

LLOYD GREEN: I don't know why she didn't [hit it big]. Labels? Timing? Nanci had great music. Whatever Tony Brown wanted was the way MCA cut records. For instance, they wouldn't let me bring an amp in through the studio door. They said, "Put it back in your car." We had to record direct on those sessions. Bizarre, but that's the way Jim Bowen wanted. Bowen changed Nashville forever when he came to town. Some good, some bad. Those other artists Tony signed around the same time were outrageously controversial. They had much more visibility. Nanci had to take a back seat. So unfortunate.

TONY BROWN: Maybe Nanci came along too early. I loved her voice, but it is an acquired taste. She had a little folk in it like Emmylou and was a great singer, songwriter, and presence. Me being involved in her career for a minute did as much for me as her. Nanci gave me credibility and made people think I actually had taste. I was so green with Nanci but learned a lot. I can't help but think the three albums I did with her helped her career.

She opened my eyes to how good people like Townes Van Zandt were. I never understood even though Steve Earle had held me on the ground and threatened to kill me until I listened to him. Townes was such an important figure, and Nanci was held in that same esteem. Nanci was the woman in that group who was stunning to look at in her own hippie way. She spoke her mind and wasn't afraid. I love that about her. I recorded a video interview for the Texas Heritage Songwriters Association last year because they inducted her into their hall of fame. I was thinking how timely it was. Maybe it would pull her out of her funk. Then, damn, she passed away, but I couldn't believe the press she got. She got as much as actors.

Nanci was considered a big star.

PAT ALGER: Nanci's is a big story in a certain way. She would have been surprised at the outpouring over her passing even though she was fairly confident that she was well respected. She didn't realize how she connected with a lot of people. Her songs have sentiment, but they're not overly sentimental. That's important. She put romance in [songs] that the guys sometimes left out, and I thought that was really impressive. She collected people like we all do. I mean, "Love Wore a Halo (Back before the War)." Interesting. She had "Nanci Griffith lines."

PAT MCINERNEY: This is what I would like to say: Nanci was a great friend. Difficult? Yes. What talented artist isn't? She was extremely talented. Generous to musicians? Absolutely. She never came in and told you what to play. "Oh, don't hit that cymbal." Never. She believed in the people she hired. She trusted us. I can't imagine a more generous person in that way.

THOMM JUTZ: I think Nanci will be remembered as one of the most important songwriters. She spearheaded a new movement of southern singer-songwriters and was a very strong-willed woman. She inspired other female songwriters to write truthful material and perform it really well. Nanci set a standard for sure. She understood the connection between her Texas singer-songwriter roots and what could be done in Nashville. She had an incredible artistic climax with *The Last of the True Believers*. I would argue that Nanci was one of the first women singer-songwriters who [blazed a trail]. She brought something that wasn't there before. She wasn't a product of Nashville or Texas alone. She made the two come together.

KATHY MATTEA: We had a lot of mutual respect and gratitude, but Nanci and I were never close friends. I wasn't in her inner circle, but I think she had a certain level of frustration over having so much respect by so many well-respected musicians and never becoming a big star on her own. I think that was hard for her. I can imagine her being so frustrated. "Everybody else is having hits on my records. Why am I not having hits on them? Why Kathy Mattea and not me? I wrote the freaking song. I cut my version in the same studio." That's part of the challenge and mystery of the music business. You roll the dice. You cannot control the outcome.

You ride the wave of whatever comes back to you. I got to take the big ride. Some people don't. Everybody's ride is different, and the system was very different back then. There were major labels, and she got on MCA with Tony Brown producing her. She made a run for it. She had a superloyal following, but it was very far beyond the bigger radar screen. We all have to make our peace with where we land. I think there were seasons where it was hard for her.

DEE MOELLER: Nashville never really understood Nanci. They never appreciated her like they don't appreciate many Texas artists. You gotta fit in here, but Nanci was never interested in [playing the game]. Joe Ely, Ray Wylie Hubbard, and people like that are so gifted, but Nashville never really got them either. I always felt bad for Nanci because she was the first who came here and did certain things that later worked for other people. For example, Mary Chapin Carpenter had more success than she did. She was different, but there was something easier to fit in than Nanci.

Same with Kathy Mattea. Also, I'm sure it was crushing to Nanci when she didn't have the big hit with "From a Distance." People might get Nanci in twenty, thirty years, like how much time it took Townes Van Zandt [to connect with a broader audience]. Nanci talked about Townes a lot. I always admired how Nanci worked so hard and never compromised. She was so true to what she did even if it cost her. She knew who she was, and she knew what she had to offer.

CHARLEY STEFL: Nashville can be a very cold place. People weren't paying attention to her the way they should have been in later years, which hurt her very deeply. "Nobody cares about me here anymore," she would say. "They go for the next big thing." Nashville just felt particularly cold to her.

Also, Townes had passed and Harlan Howard was gone. I think the lack of attention might have caused some of the problems she had later in life. She could cut you off. She cut off a lot of people, including family. She stopped communicating. That's a result of not feeling the love. She gave so much to people, yet I don't know what she would receive in return.

JULIE GOLD: Nanci left her mark forever. Not many artists have a cult following like she did. I don't know if she realized how beloved she was. I visit the Nanci Griffith fan page sometimes to see what people are saying. They remember what she wore, what she said, and the order of songs at gigs. "What do you think this song means? What do you think it means when she did this?" Really, really deep stuff. Nanci never discussed her writing with me. I have known her since 1986. Never once did she discuss her process. Never. "I'm in the middle of a new song," she would say. "You're gonna love it." Really. The most remarkable part of our relationship is that she was a songwriter [herself who] honored me throughout the course of her career by recording six or seven of my songs.

DARDEN SMITH: Any mentor situation always has a dark side. Nanci was fiercely competitive. Sometimes a door would close with her. I remember walking up to her once in Nashville, and I was like, "Hey, Nanci, what's going on?" "Oh, hi Darden." Nothing. "Oh, wow. I guess we're not friends anymore." I wasn't cool enough. Other people had told me that was coming. You were in until you weren't with her. That door shutting had nothing to do with me. I did nothing, but that took a while to realize.

Here's the deal. Nanci Griffith carved a path. She had an obituary in the *New York Times* for a reason. You can go back and reassess someone's personality for good and bad, but you only know the personality if you work with the person. My cousin loves Dwight Yoakam. Well, I did shows with Dwight Yoakam. There's a difference. You get a different perspective working with them in a club. The perspective you have from being in the club should not diminish from the music and the thing that someone like Nanci achieved.

DAVE ALVIN: I have heard stories about how she died but don't exactly know. I heard that her cancer had returned through the singer-songwriter hotline. Of course, Nanci enjoyed her beverages. We both did and enjoyed our cigarettes. Apparently, she really went for it with the bottle the last few years. I hadn't talked to her in maybe fourteen years. She was always inviting me to become a part of her world, but it ain't mine. I felt like so many of us had been holding out our hands to grab her. I just felt like, "Fuck it, my arm's not long enough." I think she was looking for something in life [that didn't exist]. I know there was a love she had.

She told me about the guy. He was her guy years and years and years ago, like a high school thing. The guy's dead. I know very little about Nanci and her life outside the time we were hanging around, but I feel like she was so smart and tough. She was successful in a way, but I know she wanted to be more successful. She should have been on one hand. On the other, fuck it. She sang with the Seattle Symphony Orchestra. That was happening before I knew her. You played with a symphony orchestra, you have a house, you can pay your bills.

What more do you want?

DENICE FRANKE: I know Joy stayed in touch until the very end. They were best friends. Joy was always there through thick and thin even if they had a falling out. Joy was always available. Joy knew Nanci better than any of us, but I know she and Bobby Nelson also were tight. Those two were her closest friends.

JOY LEWALLEN: Nanci and I talked almost every week for the past two years before she passed. She had been talking about doing a third *Other Voices* album and was telling me who she wanted to [include] on that album. I thought it was really great that she wanted to showcase the [folk] tradition. She always gave credit where it was due. Doing the first *Other Voices, Other Rooms* was purposeful. She chose songs that spoke to her and was very intentional with what she did. She had a huge arsenal of her own songs and didn't need anybody else. She had many years ahead of her, but she couldn't really play the guitar with the Dupuytren's contracture syndrome.

BOBBY NELSON: I like to remember [the good times] like having a hoot at parties with Rosalie Sorrels and Nanci. Rosalie could outdrink us all and keep playing the guitar until seven in the morning. Nanci really looked up to her. Rosalie was older and had pearls of wisdom about why she never really made it. Nanci knew that Rosalie was lousy with business. Nanci was determined to not only do her music and songwriting but do something that many male cohorts couldn't do, which was take care of the business. Nanci had such a wonderful persona onstage. She was very easy to be around. Nanci really influenced a lot of women with her songs.

PETE KENNEDY: Nanci had such a solid identity as a songwriter. I felt that way about guitar. You dedicate your life to something when you're a kid. That's why we were kindred spirits in a way. I always felt like Nanci was a sister to me. We would hang out on the road sometimes because she wouldn't want to walk around the streets by herself. I had so much respect for her as a songwriter. There was such a solidity to her, as creative as she was. You knew she would always be Nanci Griffith.

MAURA KENNEDY: No one knew the last show at The Ark would actually be her last show ever. I had been setting up a camcorder at some shows so I could see if I was screwing up at all. I remember setting up the camcorder at The Ark. "Aw, shit," I said halfway through. "I didn't turn the camera on." I realized that it was the best show by far from the last four years touring. You could feel that she was comfortable as soon as we walked in. Some places you could feel a little wall going up when she walked into the venue, but she felt completely safe there. Nanci was so charming and smart that night. Spontaneous. We walked off the stage, and she told Pete, "That was spectacular." She had never said that before. "That was spectacular."

PETE KENNEDY: Maura and I stayed friends with Nanci for years and years after we were in the band. Nanci kept friends for a long, long time, but they weren't usually also employees. She felt like we were real friends and kindred spirits, not someone looking to climb another rung up the career ladder. The last time we spoke with her was when Donald Trump was getting inaugurated in January 2017. We were in Nashville first on a southern tour. We went to her house one day, then went with Nanci to a rehearsal studio and spent two days practicing the songs.

We didn't pressure her to go back on the road or make another record. We just hung out. We would call her on the phone to see how she was doing. Nanci was about the same age as my younger sister, so I always thought of her as a sibling, never a boss or celebrity. I'm quite sure we would have been friends if we had met in a different life where neither of us played music. We just had a simple friendship, which is what really made all the difference over the years.

MAURA KENNEDY: Nanci was a really empathetic, strong woman. She didn't write about glamour. She wrote about hookers, farmers who were getting foreclosed on, the war correspondent who stepped on a landmine. The stories would get such a strong personal response from the crowd. She loved reading the *New York Times* obituaries and finding really interesting people who had lived quiet lives. Her songwriting legacy is giving voice to the voiceless and the interesting people who lived quiet lives. Where did that empathy come from? Maybe it had something to do with the pain of losing her boyfriend as a teenager. That always stayed with her.

DAVE ALVIN: Nanci was always searching for that guy from her youth again. Nobody could be that guy. I don't know what demons possessed her, and you never know with cancer, which goes away and comes back or goes away and never comes back. She was very proud of beating the cancers that she had. I was hearing on the songwriter hotline that Nanci had become reclusive when her cancer returned. She would reach out to me every now and again and want me to come to

Nashville. "That's okay," I would say. "I'm a Californian. I want to be in California."

Nanci was an incredibly generous person. I have never heard anyone say anything bad about her. She had a unique, literate, savvy voice that combined power and vulnerability to great effect. She was born with [those qualities], but you can evolve any character trait for effect when you're starting out. She was sensitive and vulnerable, yet inside Nanci was a pillar of steel even though she had to be very strong and resilient to strive and thrive in the music racket as a solo woman starting in the eighties. She knew how to play the game and took care of herself.

JOHN GORKA: I walked with a group after a show one time at the Bottom Line in New York City. Julie Gold and Bill Murray were there. Bill was a fan of Nanci's. "With Julie's songs and your outfits, Nanci," he said, "there's no stopping you."

DAVE ALVIN: The last time I saw Nanci was when I was headlining acoustic at the Bottom Line in New York. I was in a really angry, bad mood. I wasn't rude to her, but it wasn't a great way to say goodbye. The opening act was Tom Russell with his great guitar player Andrew Hardin. We were good friends and have written several songs together, but he pulled a show biz fast one and fucked me. [Late singer-songwriter Chris] Gaffney and I were driving in for sound check at three in the afternoon. That meant getting up hungover at seven in the morning in Boston and driving down I-95 to Manhattan.

Universal songwriter rules say that the headliner sound-checks first, then the opening act. We walk in and there's Tom Russell onstage. "What the fuck? I still have to go get a hotel room. I got shit to do. Goddammit, Tom." I notice he has Andrew Hardin on guitar, David Mansfield on mandolin, and Nanci fucking Griffith onstage. What the fuck? How am I supposed to follow Nanci Griffith? Man, I was pissed. I went to the sound guy at the Bottom Line and said, "What are they doing? They're not supposed to sound-check until five." "They got here early." Goddammit. Gaffney and I went to a diner to stew over everything.

We got our hotel and then came back to the Bottom Line around 5:30, which is two and a half hours after we were supposed to do it. "Yeah, the guitar works. The accordion works, great." Actually turned into a great show. Of course, Nanci didn't know why I was angry. Didn't have a clue. She thought she was being a good person by helping out Tom. She was. Then Tom turns around and does my song "Bus Station" with Nanci on Letterman.[16] How could I be mad? I wish I could have said goodbye or say, "Do you remember the temples and the sunset at Angkor Wat, Nanci?"

Never had a chance.

Tom and I discuss how Nanci's male fans pictured her as this helpless waif, this little girl with her cute socks. Nanci knew what she was doing. She knew her image, but her male fans wanted to protect her. "Poor little Nanci Griffith needs a big, strong man to take care of her." No. Never did. Nanci Griffith was more than capable of taking care of herself in any situation more than almost anyone. Nanci was very together. I didn't really fall into that trap except for that moment watching her fall down at the temple at Angkor Wat. That haunts me now. You go through those seven stages of grieving when your friends die. I really wish my arm was longer.

I wish that somebody had a strong arm to catch her.

RODNEY CROWELL: Susanna Clark was my really dear friend, and I've since come to realize that Nanci and Susanna were pretty similar souls. I saw Susanna regularly, but she retired [much like Griffith] the last fifteen years of her life [after Townes Van Zandt died]. I couldn't get her out of bed. There's something there. Nanci might be underappreciated in her passing, but I certainly hope not. I can say that when I learned that Nanci had passed, my thought was, Oh shit. I really should have reached out. I really rolled up my sleeves with other artists on their last legs, but I didn't with Nanci. I missed an opportunity to be a good friend, and shame on me. Townes was very palpable with the rambling and gambling image and "I'm never gonna get out of this world alive." I'm not sure Nanci's image translated.

Nanci's legacy might be too intricate and subtle for general consumption.

JOY LEWALLEN: Nanci needed a friend she could trust and who she could talk to without them wanting a piece of her. I can't say they're the reason she [cut herself off from everyone else the last years], but I think she was more tired of being on the road and wanted to stay home. Being on the road takes a lot out of you, especially when you're a single woman. She was a single woman in an all-guy band. I hate to sound this way, but sometimes you just need a girl-friend to talk to even though she was close with her band. She needed space. I can't tell you why she never went back, but I think it started with the hand and her needing time off.

I want people to know Nanci was a genuine, nice, caring, thoughtful person. I mean, she sent me birthday and Christmas gifts every year. She was a very thoughtful person who loved her dogs and was very politically involved. She wanted the best leader for the country. She was an advocate for doing the right thing. People should know that. She didn't make her talent about who she was. She didn't put that in the forefront. She was just about being a good, regular person. People miss Nanci as a performer, but I miss her as a friend. I miss coming home and having her message on my answering machine. Nanci was on the road for years. She was popular and drew sold-out crowds and never came home. Then she called me one time.

"Joy," she said, "I just wanna go home."

PAT MCINERNEY: I've never seen a better performer than Nanci. She completely understood her audience and how to make it work. Absolutely amazing. Nanci loved to be onstage. She just didn't love the other twenty-three hours of the day.

MAURA KENNEDY: Margaret Mary had just passed away when we met up with her before for the last tour after being away from her so long. Nanci and Margaret were closer than sisters. People would call out for "There's a Light beyond These Woods" during the shows, and Nanci would get really quiet. She always had a funny and spontaneous quip when people called out for something, but not for "There's a Light beyond These Woods." She would put her head down, get quiet, and say, "It's just too soon to do that. I don't know if I'll ever be able to do that song again." Everyone understood because she was being so honest.

The high point of the last tour for me as a fan was during our three nights at City Winery in New York. We were standing [side] stage after doing a regular encore at the end of the third sold-out show. The audience was still calling for her. "Well," Nanci said, "I've gotta do the song here if I'm ever gonna do it again." She didn't even tell me what song. She just said, "Come on." I think she gave it a little intro so I knew what song we were gonna do, but I couldn't believe it. I felt the blood rush through my feet when she started singing. I'm thinking, How am I gonna get through "There's a Light beyond These Woods"? How are we going to do this? I knew singing the song would be so hard for her.

You could see tears rolling down her face from the first line.

Real tears.

Tears from her heart.

Nanci opened herself up so wide to the audience and was able to sing the song, but her voice was trembling. I felt like she might have needed backup, so I very quietly sang harmony and kept focused on her so I could keep up with her phrasing. Then I realized there were tears coming down my face, too. I didn't notice [while we were performing] because I was so concentrated on getting Nanci through the song, but I looked out after we finished. You could literally see every pair of eyes in the audience glistening with tears.

That moment was the most stunning performance I have ever seen.

DAVE ALVIN: I admired the way Nanci survived an incredibly difficult business as a woman on her own terms. She never sold out. She was always about intelligent, literate songwriting. Thinking about her dying is overwhelmingly sad, but I know that Mary Gauthier had a beautiful experience with Nanci early on that really summarized her. Nanci had a passion for songs and song-writers.

Mary's story about Nanci is the real Nanci to me.

Generosity was Nanci Griffith—beginning, middle, and end.

Print that story. There's your book.

Nanci Griffith performing in the early 2000s. Photo courtesy Bobby Nelson

Poster for Nanci Griffith, Billy Joe Shaver, and the Cash Brothers, The Ark, Ann Arbor, Michigan, July 27, 2003. Courtesy Brian T. Atkinson archives

BIG BLUE BALL OF WAR (WORDS AND MUSIC BY NANCI GRIFFITH)

IN 1914 THIS BALL WAS AT WAR
IT WENT FROM BELGIUM ON THROUGH IRELAND
   THE CONGO, THEN BACK HOME
THIS BIG BLUE BALL OF WAR
   SPUN ON ITS OWN
SPINNING HISTORY IN LINES OF BLOOD
   WHEN NOT A SOUL FELL OFF

CHORUS: WE ALL RIDE ON (WE ALL RIDE)
      THIS BIG BLUE BALL OF WAR
      SOULS WITH TICKETS
         THROUGH THE VEIL, WE RIDE ON
      WE ALL RIDE ON (WE ALL RIDE)
      THIS BIG BLUE BALL OF WAR
      WE CHOOSE TO SPIN AROUND
         AND RIDE
            THIS BIG BLUE BALL OF WAR

ALMOST A CENTURY, THIS BLOOD HAS FLOWED
WE'VE KILLED OUR MEN OF PEACE
   AROUND THIS BALL
      AND REFUSED TO HEAR THEIR GHOSTS
WE SPEND OUR DESTINIES
   IN DEEDS OF HATE
HUMANITY UPON THIS BALL
   IS JUST A BLOODY FALL FROM GRACE

CHORUS

A REFORMATION MIGHT JUST SAVE US ALL
A VOICE OF HARMONY AND OPEN HEART
   WHERE THE WOMEN TEACH THE SONG
THESE MEN OF EVIL DEED CAN BE PROVEN WRONG

THIS BALL COULD SPIN IF WE JOIN HAND TO HAND
SO NOT A SOUL FALLS OFF...

CHORUS

Nanci Griffith's typewritten lyrics to "Big Blue Ball of War" from *Hearts in Mind*, December 22, 2003. Photo by Brian T. Atkinson. Courtesy Bobby Nelson

IN THE HEART OF INDOCHINE

I am on a Riverboat upon the Saigon River
Where the music's too loud while I try to have dinner
Stories I've been told of 1954
When the bodies floated ashore
   From that distant war
My friend Michael came here in '68
The bodies still floating
With the dinner boats sailing
   Beside the souls of the American war

CHORUS: Oh, deliver me to the river of souls
      In the heart of Indochine
      Oh, deliver me to a River of Peace
      In this twenty-first century
      All those souls that floated free
      In these dark war's waters
      All the souls now swim together
      The French the Viet Minh
         Those American boys
      The souls of the Saigon River
      In peace in Indochine

I am in a caffe' in Ho Chi Minh City
My friend Bobby Muller is sitting with me
This traffic is maddening
In his wheelchair he's napping
I wonder at times, does he walk in his dreams?
Later I walked all the way from Tu Do Street
To the banks of the river
With the dinner boats sailing
   Beside all of the souls of a River in Peace
(Chorus repeat)
Coda: Hoa binh...Hoa Binh in the Heart of Indochine

(words & music by Nanci Griffith/Nashville,TN 22 Dec, 03)

Nanci Griffith's typewritten lyrics to "In the Heart of Indochine" from *Hearts in Mind*, December 22, 2003. Photo by Brian T. Atkinson. Courtesy Bobby Nelson

Austin Chronicle cover, February 25, 2005. Photo by Brian T. Atkinson. Courtesy Bobby Nelson

Poster for "A Benefit for the Hall with Nanci Griffith and the Blue Moon Orchestra,"
Country Music Hall of Fame and Museum, Nashville, Tennessee, November 10–11,
2005. Photo by Erin Enderlin

L–R: Jim Rooney, Nanci Griffith, Jim McGuire, John Prine, Jim McGuire's photo
studio, Nashville, 2009. Photographer unknown. Courtesy Jim McGuire

260

Maura Kennedy,
Nanci Griffith, Pete
Kennedy, Belfast
school, February
2013. Courtesy
Maura and Pete
Kennedy

L–R: Maura
Kennedy and
Nanci Griffith,
Belfast school,
February 2013.
Courtesy Maura
and Pete Kennedy

Center: Nanci
Griffith with
children,
Strandtown
Primary School,
East Belfast. Photo
by Maura Kennedy

Left center: Nanci Griffith at The Ark, Ann Arbor, Michigan, spring 2022. Photo by BettySoo

262

Poster for Nanci Griffith tribute concert, Hole in the Wall, Austin, Texas, October 23, 2021. Photo by Brian T. Atkinson

Nanci Griffith photo, Texas Heritage Songwriters Association's hall of fame induction ceremony, February 12, 2022. Photo by Brian T. Atkinson

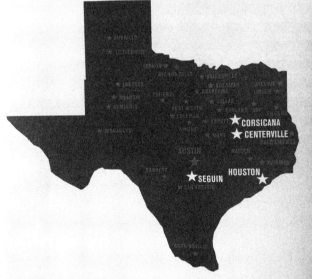

Program, Texas Heritage Songwriters Association's hall of fame induction ceremony, February 12, 2022. Photo by Brian T. Atkinson

NANCI GRIFFITH

Born in Seguin, Texas, on July 6, 1953, Nanci Griffith started playing in folk clubs at 12. Inspired by Townes Van Zandt, she made her way through the listening rooms and songwriter festivals, establishing her Currier & Ives pictures of small-town life that were the more innocent balance to Larry McMurtry's "Last Picture Show" version.

Releasing There's A Light Beyond These Woods, Mary Margaret in 1978 and Poet in My Window in 1982, she followed the trails blazed by Rosalie Sorrels, Jean Ritchie and Carolyn Hester as she made her way as a songwriter determined to show people their own lives in song. A 1985 performance on "Austin City Limits," to support her Philo Release Last of the True Believers launched the young woman in a handmade yellow dress with cabbage roses to national prominence.

Kathy Mattea would take "Love at the Five & Dime" from her second Philo release Last of the True Believers to #1 on the Country Charts; later Suzy Bogguss would also have a chart-topper with "Outbound Plane" (co-written with Tom Russell). That buzz would generate a deal with MCA Nashville.

Signed by Tony Brown as part of his progressive country quartet of Steve Earle, Patty Loveless, and Lyle Lovett, Griffith deemed her music "folkabilly" and set to building country music's most literate fan base. Lone Star State of Mind and Little Love Affairs merged Texas country, Kerrville folk, and a touch of her sweetness to create a singular sound. Lone Star also marked the debut of Julie Gold's "From A Distance," which made Griffith a massive star in Ireland, England, and much of Europe. Emmylou Harris regularly recorded her songs, including the seminal duet of "Gulf Coast Highway" with Willie Nelson, Griffith duetted with Harris, Jimmy Buffett, Counting Crow's Adam Duritz, Mac McAnally, Dolores Keane, the Chieftains, Darius Rucker, and John Prine, whose "Speed of the Sound of Loneliness" became a Wim Wenders' "Wings of Desire" inspired music video.

With 1989's Storms, Griffith's scholarly style moved towards the more alternative/progressive adult genre. Like 1988's One Fair Summer Evening, recorded live at Houston's Anderson Fair, and 1991's Late Night Grande Hotel, Griffith maintained the deep intimacy and warmth she'd always shared with her audience, but her emergence onto the world stage created broader canvases for delicate writing and both gutsy and whispered vocals.

Her MCA years set the stage for her most fruitful period. Always generous to other writers and artists, Griffith homaged her influences with Other Voices, Other Rooms. Her Elektra debut earned the 1994 Best Contemporary Folk Grammy.

Griffith traveled the world, most notably with the Blue Moon Orchestra, but she also toured with Buddy Holly's Crickets, and later with husband/wife duo The Kennedys, who co-produced with Griffith and McInerny Griffiths' final album Intersection.

A four-time Grammy nominee, she received the Kate Wolf Award from the World Folk Music Association and was inducted into the Austin Music Hall of Fame in 1995. In 2008, the Americana Music Association bestowed their Lifetime Achievement Trailblazer Award on the international songwriting sensation; BBC Radio-2's Folk Awards gave her their Lifetime Achievement Awards in 2012.

TEXAS HERITAGE SONGWRITERS ASSOCIATION

9

Program, Texas Heritage Songwriters Association's hall of fame induction ceremony, February 12, 2022. Photo by Brian T. Atkinson

Front row L–R: Nanci Griffith's black-and-gold embroidered hat, Cindy Walker's cowboy hat from the 1940s, Doug Sahm's black hat with brown leather headband, "Songwriters Est. in Texas" exhibit, Wittliff Collections, Texas State University, San Marcos, Texas, September 4, 2022. Photo by Brian T. Atkinson

Nanci Griffith's knit cap. Courtesy Brian T. Atkinson archives with special thanks to Tamara Saviano

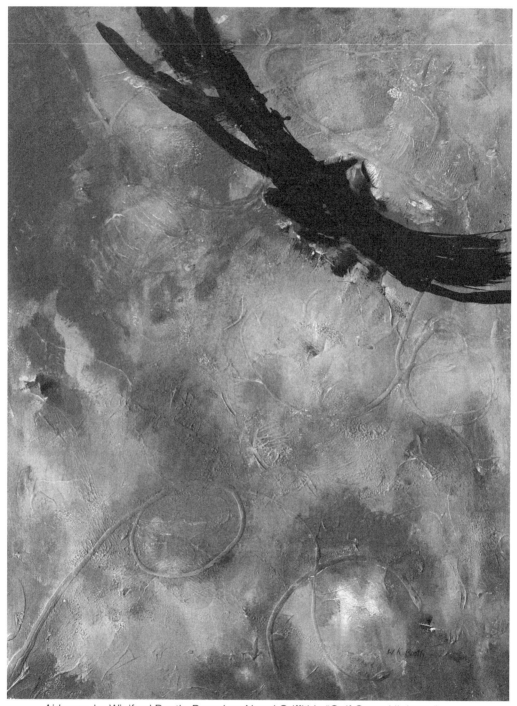

Airborne, by Winifred Booth. Based on Nanci Griffith's "Gulf Coast Highway"

Chorus: Love at the Five and Dime

The Songwriting Legacy

NANCI GRIFFITH'S SIGNIFICANT IMPACT on songwriters—particularly ambitious and independent-minded women—continues rippling in all directions. "There's that famous quote about how almost nobody bought Velvet Underground records, but everybody who did picked up a guitar and wrote a song," Adam Duritz says. "There would be no R.E.M. without the Replacements. No Counting Crows without Big Star. Nanci might not have been very successful—though she was bigger than those bands, for sure—but women heard her music and thought, I can write real songs about myself. I can talk about my life in a genre that's supposed to be about pickup trucks."

Griffith's approach and attitude equally energize songwriters today. "Women in Nashville revere Nanci," Suzy Bogguss says. "Nashville was the dude's community, but [male songwriters] had tremendous respect for her. Nanci could be a hard-ass if she needed to be. 'No,' she would say, 'that ain't right. I have something to say here.' That was the bolster we needed. Now there's a whole crop of songwriters in [Nashville and] Texas who are completely beholden to her. Nanci had balls. Anyone who has been a successful [woman] songwriter in Nashville would tell you Nanci knew how to maneuver without having to compromise herself. Having balls took courage. They could have totally shut her out. 'She's a bitch. Nobody hire her. Don't let her into the folk festival.'

"They didn't because they heard her songs."

GRETCHEN PETERS: Artists like Nanci Griffith who fell in between George Jones and the Rolling Stones were my bridge to country music. You can't separate Nanci from her songs. Nanci's songs belonged to her no matter how many times you hear other people cover them because her singing voice was such a part of her storytelling writer's voice. The storytelling is what always really intrigued me. I was always attracted to third-person story songs that were like little novellas set to music. Nanci's writing was more like that than a straight-ahead first-person love song, even though she could do that.

Those of us under the roots of the Americana umbrella all felt, "Where do we belong?" Nanci blazed a trail that way because she was making it work somehow. She was considered country but was a folkie for sure and made it all work for her. I think the idiosyncratic way Nanci sang influenced me too. She had that gorgeous, pure voice, but it was very much hers. She didn't sound like all the CMA female vocalists of the year. That was really important [for] those of us who never fit into the full-on, chest-voice holler, Nashville female singer mode. Nanci was a great beacon for us. "Hey, you can do this."

The entertainment and music worlds make it easy for you to disappear if you're not making the scene. People focus on what's right in front of them, and Nanci wasn't making the scene the last part of her life. She was reclusive, but there was huge, tremendous respect if you bring her up in conversation. You know that just from the outpouring that came out after she passed. Nashville has huge respect for her, but she wasn't someone who came out to gigs and was being seen. The last time I saw her was when she sat in with Tom Russell and me at 3rd and Lindsley in 2010. Steve Young also was there.

Nanci was superfun as a person, very sweet, funny, really quick witted, and not full of herself. She was really supportive. She was very egalitarian in the way she looked at herself and musicians. It didn't matter to her if you were a young singer-songwriter who hadn't done much of anything. She didn't look at songwriting as a competition. She was incredibly generous with people she felt had potential. She was incredibly supportive of Elizabeth Cook when no one knew who she was.

Nanci did very sweet things on her own accord. For instance, my husband, Barry, and I shared our story with her, and she ended up writing a song about us, which was incredibly touching. I mean, who does that? She was very, very open hearted. She just tossed off our song one day and sent it to us. Maybe she had been thinking about our story. Nanci thought of herself as a songwriter at the core, not so much as an artist, though she clearly was one. She was keenly aware that songwriters who aren't artists don't get recognized. Nanci was instantly familiar and intimate with me [when we were together], which made me feel like I could do the same. That's amazing considering she was a hero when I was living in Boulder wondering what the hell I was gonna do with this music thing.[1]

Gretchen Peters has been nominated for Grammy awards for writing Martina McBride's "Independence Day" and Patty Loveless's "You Don't Even Know Who I Am." She, Mary Gauthier, and Eliza Gilkyson tour as Three Women and the Truth.

MARY GAUTHIER: Nanci Griffith was a teacher to me. She showed me folk music, educated me on what came before, spoke my language, and sang her way into my being. I loved her music and saw her perform many, many times. I got to work with her when I was getting started and got to know her some after I came to Nashville. She was always kind to me, generous, a profound influence on me. Her spirit will always remain alive inside her music.

The first year I lived in Nashville I was invited to a party at Jim McGuire's house that became a song circle with Guy Clark, Lyle Lovett, John Hiatt, Joe Ely, Steve Earle, and Nanci Griffith. Wonderful night. I was on the edge of my seat, desperately wanting to go from being in the audience to swapping songs with that group of legends. I knew I was in deep waters, the new kid in town, but oh, how I longed to sit in that circle. I had deeply admired everyone in it for years. As the music was winding down, Nanci looked over and asked, "Mary, would you play us a song?" I knew her because I had opened a string of shows for her a month prior.

I was absolutely thrilled. I sat down in the chair she offered, took her guitar into my hands, and played my song "Our Lady of the Shooting Stars" [from 1999's *Drag Queens and Limousines*]. Other songwriters closed their eyes and nodded as I played. Some smiled. No wild applause, no pyrotechnics when the song ended, but the smiles and nods made me feel like I belonged. I still had a long way to go, but joining that circle was validation that moving to Nashville had been a good decision. Holding my own in that circle gave me confidence. Being around songwriters I deeply admired humanized them and made the star I was reaching for feel less distant.

I handed Nanci her guitar back when I was done. She shook her head and said, "Keep it." I froze, holding her engraved, signature sunburst Taylor 512 cutaway guitar in midair, question marks in both my eyes. "It's yours," she said. "When I moved to Nashville Harlan Howard gave me his guitar. I'm giving you mine." I was speechless but somehow found the courage to say, "Will you sign it?" She signed, "For Mary, because you will sing." I found out later that it's an old Nashville tradition to pass on a guitar, an attempt to stay on the good side of the muse and mystery. Some songwriters believe it is one way to keep songs flowing. Harlan gave Nanci one of his guitars because he felt there were no more songs left in it for him, but there might be some in there for her. Nanci had done the same for me.

"Welcome to Nashville, kid. Stay on the good side of mystery and paradox."[2]

Grammy-nominated singer-songwriter Mary Gauthier's songs such as "I Drink" and "Mercy Now" have been recorded by Bobby Bare, Kathy Mattea, and others.

She has released a dozen albums from Dixie Kitchen *(1997) to* Dark Enough to See the Stars *(2022) and the concert record* Live at Blue Rock *(2012).*

JAIMEE HARRIS: I finally got Nanci when Gauthier and I were jamming *The Last of the True Believers* on a trip a couple years ago. Her lyrics are incredible, but there's something about her sound that hits right at my sweet spot. She had incredible bands. I can listen to *The Last of the True Believers* over and over in my car. The way she uses harmonies is exactly in the spot I gravitate toward. The song that really hits me now that I've recently left Texas [for Nashville] is "One of These Days." That song soothes a homesickness in me.

I love being a Texan. My intention when I quit my job and moved to Nashville was to do the business, have a cheap home base, and then go back to Texas. Well, I met Gauthier, and now the story has changed. I have a deep homesickness and relate to Nanci's songs. They inspire me as a storyteller and being able to see narrators through different eyes. I'm not able to intellectualize it like I am with other writers. I have to listen and listen and let it enter my body. Something has to pass through me. Her combination of soaring melodies and the language [is inspiring].

I played with bands when I was younger, then started opening for Gauthier solo and realized, "Oh, my gosh. I've never done this before." Scared the shit out of me. Still scares me. All you have to work with are the songs, your voice, and an acoustic guitar. You have to do all three things really, really well like Nanci. Nanci saw Townes and Guy [going on solo tours] and thought, I can do it if they can. Her peers just [happened to be] men. Nanci's songs should be in the same pantheon as those guys. She was a first in lots of ways.

I've had an even longer relationship with Mindy Smith's music than Nanci's. I totally can hear Nanci's melodies in Mindy's. The range of their voices [is similar]. They both have this particular voice that they can use delicately but also bring power in the right moment. Also, they don't overuse it. They bring it with a deeper understanding of the song. I've noticed songwriters talking about songwriting at the highest form being literature lately. Nanci was a pioneer in that style of writing. She was intelligent and wrote literature.[3]

Jaimee Harris's debut, Red Rescue *(2018), caught attention throughout the folk world while earning her the title "the next queen of folk" from National Public Radio. The Texas native currently lives in Nashville and frequently tours with Mary Gauthier.*

MINDY SMITH: I had a really cool neighbor named Richard in Knoxville who would open my mind to different artists like Nanci Griffith. I really latched on to the timbre and warmth in her voice and how she wove together Ameri-

cana and folk sounds with Irish music qualities. Her lyrics sounded very familiar to me. Nanci really could paint a picture with her lyrics. You felt like you
were in a movie with "Love at the Five and Dime." She created this scene, and
you could feel where those people were. Nanci had such a visual way to write,
which isn't my strength as a songwriter. She lets you take that journey.

I always admire people who make you feel like you're living the story they
write. Nanci could move your heart. You feel the character she's singing. Also,
she made other people's songs her own. Not many people could take a song
and deliver it in the way that she did with the Bob Dylan song "Boots of Spanish Leather." She owned "Boots of Spanish Leather." She was so connected
with the music [on *Other Voices, Other Rooms*]. You could feel Nanci as a storyteller when she did John Prine's "Speed of the Sound of Loneliness." She
generated real emotion. Nanci owned songs so much that you wouldn't know
they weren't hers.

Nanci was so beloved among songwriters. The way she sang, picked guitar,
and presented herself onstage made her someone you wanted to know. Her
songs bring you back to where you were when you first heard them. She takes
me back to when my life was uncertain, and I had dreams and ambitions but
had no idea how to [make music my career]. Just knowing Nanci was there
doing it with other writers [was inspiring]. I should have reached out to her.

I met Nanci once. I had established a publishing deal early in my career
and was trying to find my way. Nanci invited me to lunch. I was so excited and
nervous that I didn't know how to behave. We ate at a steak house right by
Vanderbilt Children's Hospital. I didn't tell her I was a vegetarian and said,
"I'll meet you wherever you want to go." The steak house was such an understated place, which she picked because people approached her quite a bit. I
was wearing my black wool coat and didn't know if I should even take it off. I
didn't know what to say, but Nanci kept the vibe superchill and did her best to
put me at ease. People were just starstricken by her. Powerful experience.

Reliving when she took me to lunch has been weighing heavily on my
mind lately. She was so encouraging and went out of her way to do so, which
isn't a common thing. She sought me out, and I felt validated. I thought, Okay,
there is room for my voice here. Nanci opened the door to my heart and spirit
to keep me here. She encouraged me to keep on going. We have timelines in
life with moments that stand out, and having lunch with Nanci was one on my
timeline that marked my journey here. Nanci lifted me up so much.

I was going through papers the other day and came across her phone number from that day. I thought, What are the odds, right after we lost her? My
heart hurt because I could have reached out to her sooner and told her that I

loved her. I wonder because of what Nanci did for me if I should be [reaching out to younger songwriters] more often. Somebody might be the next songwriter of all time, and they might give up because they're not getting the interaction or support they need.

Nanci influenced a whole generation of men and women across the board, and those people now have gone on to influence people. Nanci was woven into our music's fabric by making the impact she did. Nanci and her songs influenced songs that are being written now. What an amazing accomplishment. We'll be writing a song and go, "That riff or melodic twist feels very Nanci Griffith." We forget to keep the people who influenced us in the forefront as we move forward. We have to take people with us. I've written so many songs that have such a Nanci Griffith vibe.

I wrote a song two weeks ago with a very strong influence from her. I wasn't thinking about writing a song like Nanci, but she came to mind during the writing process. I felt really connected to her as kindred spirits. Maybe I had a little angel on my shoulder named Nanci when I was writing that song. My songs are usually very sad, but this one wasn't. The song is called "I Only Have You to Thank," an odd little song about a piggy bank. The idea is that you know what's in this piggy bank, but you can't get it out unless you break it open. You like that piggy bank and want to keep it going, but you have to eat dinner at the same time. It's a comic relief song that got a really good response at a festival last weekend.

Nanci was tremendous. I'm so thankful for her music. She really did start the ball rolling for me. Many women my age had the same epiphany because of people like Nanci. "Wow, this is something you can do." She was one of the top five artists who really got me thinking I should give it a go. Nanci opened doors and took me down the rabbit hole to people like Gillian Welch. Nanci got me interested in people like Shawn Colvin and Patty Griffin when I was a Long Island girl who knew nothing.

I'm also thankful because I might not have known about Nashville if not for Nanci. She probably had to put up her dukes a lot when she was coming up in Nashville. This town isn't as kind to women as it is [to men]. I've had moments in my career when I had to speak up for certain things, which puts people off for some reason. I don't understand why. Being treated as if you know what you want can get ingrained in your spirit and weigh heavy on you. Dolly Parton and Nanci Griffith wouldn't have been as successful as they were if they didn't know what they wanted. Keeping that stamina up is a challenge.[4]

Mindy Smith turned heads throughout Nashville and beyond with her debut, One Moment More *(2004), and the follow-up* Long Island Shores *(2006). She won over legendary country singer Dolly Parton early on by covering her standard "Jolene."*

JAMIE LIN WILSON:Suzy Bogguss used to have [ladies' tea] nights for songwriters at her house. Erin Enderlin went one time and played a song in the circle. Nanci went up to Suzy and asked if that girl was okay. The song was about suicide. Nanci came up to Erin crying.[5]

Former Gougers and Trishas singer-songwriter Jamie Lin Wilson has made a name since with albums such as Jumping over Rocks *(2018). She contributed the track "Hi Fi Love" to Eight 30 Records'* Highway Prayer: A Tribute to Adam Carroll.

SUZY BOGGUSS: My first ladies' tea was at Nanci's house. Joyous. We were women celebrating being women songwriters. Nanci had artists and people who worked in publicity, but mostly we were female songwriters talking about how we were doing and getting along. The teas were a sharing experience. "How are you doing?" Nanci created such a great vibe. I knew that [communal] attitude about helping each other because I had come up through the folk clubs. Seeing females getting together to talk about that seemed remarkable. I thought we should carry that from one person's home to the next so it would keep going.

They fell by the wayside before too long. We only had four or five before everyone got too busy, which was a shame. They were the coolest thing. We had a beautiful group of people at my house one time with Beth Nielsen Chapman, Elizabeth Cook, Erin Enderlin, all these great young girls. We started with the English tea and cucumber sandwiches, but everybody broke out their instruments once the wine bottles came out. There were thirty-five or forty girls, and so many became so successful. We all brought someone young who was just getting started.

Erin Enderlin was still in college. Elizabeth was selling shoes. The music had started, but Erin had been sitting very quietly on the floor. She was being shy because Nanci was there. Nanci was her big hero. Then Erin got up to play. Her material is crazy emotional. She can go into a feeling like Merle Haggard and draw out all the beauty and tears. You can't always listen to her without crying. I feel like Nanci and Erin had similar backgrounds as young people. Erin's song hit Nanci because she related to it personally.

ERIN ENDERLIN: Suzy Bogguss was my mentor early on and invited me to ladies' tea at her house, which was a large gathering of insanely talented women. I met Beth Nielsen Chapman that day, and the best of the best in Nashville like Nanci and Elizabeth Cook were there. I was very socially awkward back then when I was nineteen and was hiding out in the kitchen. I'm sure some people thought I was with catering. Suzy came over and was like, "You have to come over here and play." So, I played my songs "Monday Morning Church," which Alan Jackson recorded later on, and "In My Blood," which is a cheery song about suicide.

Nanci walked across the room crying and bear-hugged me. "You wrote a song," she said, "that I could never write." I still have no idea what that really means. She gave me her phone number, and I would randomly call her like she was my aunt. "Hey, what's up? I'm working on this song." She would send messages like, "I'm in Europe and was listening to your music as we crossed the ocean." You know, I heard Nanci talking to Suzy after that tea. "That girl had a really hard life," she said. "Those songs are devastating." She gave me her therapist's number, which is how I got on antidepressants. Taking care of your mental health is important. I thought it was cool that Nanci could be so vulnerable to someone she barely knew.[6]

Nashville-based singer-songwriter Erin Enderlin's songs have been recorded by Alan Jackson ("Monday Morning Church"), Lee Ann Womack ("Last Call"), Luke Bryan ("You Don't Know Jack"), and others including Randy Travis and Terri Clark.

ELIZABETH COOK: Nanci came to town in Nashville's storied golden era in the seventies, which is the time when people compare Nashville to Paris in the twenties. Rodney Crowell and Steve Earle were the younger songwriters. John Prine, Townes Van Zandt, and Guy Clark were more established. They hung out all night with each other, wrote songs, and played them for each other. Nanci missed that sense of community and wanted to do something. She was the kind of person who wanted to do something about things.

Nanci started having these ladies' teas at her house and around town because she wanted female singer-songwriters to get together, play songs, and drink wine like they did [in the seventies]. She was an activist like with land-mine awareness and her political views, but she also was an activist for our community and women singer-songwriters. My mother was a big musical presence in my life and had just passed. Nanci stepped right in and became somebody I could look to [for advice]. I had never had a mentor like her.

She mentored me by proxy of example. I was nearby and watching her make those records, do tours, run her own band, and produce her music, which is the best mentoring there is. She never once told me what to do. She was always just there, reaching out, and including me so I got to watch her. Nanci knew what she wanted and how to get it. She cared about all the instruments on the records, how she wanted her music to sound, how she wanted those songs performed, and how she wanted to perform them onstage from an enter-tainment standpoint.

She wanted to put on a show.

I had known about Nanci because we would ride around in college listen-ing to her songs like "Lone Star State of Mind" and "There's a Light beyond

These Woods." I had not had exposure to an artist who was playing folk music with a country edge and the thoughtfulness of a woman in her lyrics. I defected from Music Row, but Nanci heard my song "Balls to Be a Woman" years later because I had a big record deal. Then Nanci heard me on the Opry and became a huge advocate. She was very revered by the singer-songwriters I was running around with.

Nanci had me go on tour with her. I couldn't believe it. The first shows we did together were three sold-out nights at the Birchmere in Alexandria, Virginia. Seeing someone succeeding at that level and in complete command of her music was mind blowing for someone like me who defected from mainstream country. Everyone was so excited she was playing, and they were there to listen to the show. I remember her audience buying so much of my merch. They were so loving and wonderful because of her being so passionate [about me].

Nanci liked to stay in nice hotels and have a night off, so we would have a travel day and a show day. She was able to afford to work at that pace and with the nice amenities. Nanci had put me in a bunk on her bus, so I stayed everywhere they stayed. I saw her years later in Norway when she had a night off. She insisted on coming to my show and introducing me to my audience. She was very passionate about what she thought they should think of me. She couldn't have been a bigger supporter. What she did was practically unheard of with women in the industry.

TODD SNIDER: I knew about Nanci and "Love at the Five and Dime" when I lived in Texas. Then Keith Sykes sent me a lawyer-slash-musician who was gonna teach me how to play to a click track. I drove up for a guitar lesson and Keith played me *One Fair Summer Evening* on cassette. He lent it to me, and I got the picture on the drive home. I went out and bought all her records. I studied Nanci because I knew she was the top female writer and troubadour of her time. I learned her songs, then met her at a Buddy Holly tribute we were both playing. She was really sweet to me and told me to take it easy. She was always really thoughtful to me.

We got closer when her manager Burt Stein started managing me. We would go to Brown's Diner. She and [legendary Rolling Stones and Joe Ely saxophonist] Bobby Keys would both go to Brown's, and you could hang with them. They mostly talked about songwriters. I never knew who the other people in the conversation with them were, but I assumed they were hit songwriters. Brown's is still a place where guys who have publishing jobs and have written three or four hits go. They throw out song titles and listen to their own songs on the jukebox. Nanci also told me that she really loved what Elizabeth Cook was doing.

She talked about Elizabeth all the time.

ELIZABETH COOK: I want to say she had a relationship with a guy who was a chef and worked at Brown's Diner. She was telling me about the same guy when I went to check in on her [in 2018], and we went to lunch at a little Mexican restaurant right off Music Row. She said she liked to have her own house and didn't want to live with anybody. Also, I remember these two girls sat down near us with a baby. They had to get a high chair. Nanci said in passing, "I'm glad I never did that."

I was her younger understudy so I didn't ask too many questions. I was just happy to be in her presence and soak up all I could. I do remember I had picked her up at her house for that lunch. She had someone who was there to help her, and they were fussing around in the kitchen over the cats and dogs. Nanci showed me her tomatoes. She seemed as happy as she could be. She loved being at home. She loved her animals and gardening. She had told her manager Burt that she wanted a year off. "Nanci," he said, "it's been a lot longer than that." She chuckled. The way she put it was, "I have traveled my whole life and just want time off." She just seemed happy.

Her health was better than I thought it would be. I was completely expecting to see a very depressing situation, but she seemed very clearheaded. I was checking in that day so I could lay eyes on her and understand what was going on with this person who so many people care about. No one had heard from her, but she was doing exactly what she wanted. Touring engulfed her for a very long time, and maybe she decided she wanted to live a different life. I don't know that it was an entirely dark thing, though it might have been on some levels.

Nanci had her holy grail when she was one of the many bright-eyed hopefuls who moved to Nashville: she wanted to be Loretta Lynn. She didn't see any reason why not with the way she could write, play, and perform, but country music radio changed a lot during that time. Nashville changed and became a huge gold rush with Garth Brooks and Shania Twain. What the record labels were interested in took a right turn toward money. I could see where Nanci could have felt that it could have gone better for her. [She] probably didn't understand why [she was] not doing better.

Maybe that's why she was so convicted and vocal about supporting singer-songwriters like me and the songwriting art form in general. [Griffith once called Cook this generation's Loretta Lynn.] I thanked her along the way, but I never told her how much that meant. She knew I loved her, but I didn't have the perspective at that young age to even know what I had stepped in and what would come to me in the business. I didn't know how much it meant for her to champion me and do it on so many levels in the music world. I had an example of someone who had completely carved out her own path and maintained total control with all the integrity that Grammys and Carnegie Hall bring. She was a great example of what you can have on your own terms.

I search for good new music and [musicians] to champion today like [Aaron Lee Tasjan]. I think you should find what you love and talk about that. I have that responsibility to help younger songwriters now because of how Nanci, Rodney Crowell, Guy Clark, the folks out at the Opry, and Loretta helped me out. I do everything for younger artists that I can. I try to get them on the Opry and introduce them to people who might help move the needle for them or just be a positive ear when their band van breaks down or the manager quits.

AARON LEE TASJAN: I was a little kid when I heard Nanci cover "From a Distance." Beautiful song. I moved to Nashville from New York City later on and was looking for some records related to this place. So, I went down to the record store and brought home *Little Love Affairs* on vinyl around 2013. Then I met Elizabeth Cook, and we worked up "Gulf Coast Highway" and "Late Night Grande Hotel" to sing together when I was subbing on guitar for her band. Getting inside those songs really deepened my appreciation for Nanci and her music.

I started listening more and watching her on *Austin City Limits*. Dawned on me that the rest would take care of itself if you're a really great songwriter. This was before I knew anything about Nanci's internal struggles within her own life. Dealing with depression, feeling isolated and lonely obviously drove the emotion and feeling behind her music. That certainly comes across when I hear songs like "Late Night Grande Hotel." She even references Greta Garbo. Hit the nail right on the head. Discovering her music helped me realize that you can be an artist who lets the music speak for itself.[7]

East Nashville favorite Aaron Lee Tasjan has performed with such diverse acts as Peter, Paul, and Mary's Peter Yarrow, the New York Dolls, Drivin N Cryin singer Kevn Kinney, and Todd Snider. His latest is Tasjan! Tasjan! Tasjan! *(2021).*

TODD SNIDER: I loved Nanci's lyrics and the attention to detail in her songs. She seemed like a female Ramblin' Jack Elliott, a Bob Dylan, and a Townes Van Zandt. She studied them for sure. She proved that she didn't just come up with herself whole cloth with that *Other Voices, Other Rooms* record. She knew her predecessors really well. The very first time we met was when I went with John Prine to a bank to see a benefit show she was playing. I remember the last thing she said to the crowd in this really high voice was, "Thank you for spending this fine summer evening with me."

Then she got offstage, her voice dropped an octave, and she said, "Where are my fucking cigarettes?" She immediately turned into Guy Clark or Townes Van Zandt offstage. Nanci was a rough-and-tumble woman who really lived and didn't have much fear. She was a rambling, scrambling woman. I found out later that her father was close friends with Townes. She said her father and Townes would do lots of acid together, and she had done acid too. I would have never guessed that, but lots of people who write good words take acid at some point. The end for Nanci was heartbreaking, but I'm not someone who wishes she was different so she lived longer. I'm just glad she was here for the time she was.

She fulfilled her destiny.

Burt said Nanci loved my record *The Devil You Know*. He said, "What if we had Nanci interview you for the press?" We had a really good conversation that day and then went over to Brown's after the interview. We were talking about Communism. I walked into this bar called the Chicken Shack another time when Nanci was alone and crying. I remembered noting to myself that she had the life I wanted, but she was crying in a bar at two in the afternoon. I didn't approach her or ask about it later. I don't even know if she knew I was there, but I took it as a warning. I totally related to why she was crying in that bar years later. Something hurt.

I still haven't put my finger on what broke her heart so bad. She reminded me of Jack Ingram. You want to see Jack really, really sad? Catch him the day after he wins an award. I don't understand it. This life feels like the mob in a way. I know that a bunch of our peers would say the same. You want this life? It's gonna take your boyfriend, your relationship to your mom, everything. There is a way to go about this that's a direct path to total loneliness. Almost everybody who does this goes through that trap at least once. Some don't get out.

AMY SPEACE: I discovered Nanci when I was in my first Kerrville Folk Festival songwriting contest. I'm from New York City and was playing music there during this post–Norah Jones time. Folk seemed like a bad word in New York City. We thought what we were doing was more indie acoustic, but then I got into Kerrville for that first time. Kerrville has a storied list who won the contest, and the famous one with those [like me] who didn't. I always say to people who didn't win, "I didn't win the contest, but I got the gig. Shawn Colvin didn't win. It's okay."

I was like, "Holy shit. This whole Kerrville world is doing the same thing I'm doing [coming down] from New York." I was so isolated in New York City music when I realized that these great songwriters were out there doing Kerrville. Also, folk wasn't what I thought it was. Folk wasn't Peter, Paul, and Mary. Folk is storytelling. I discovered Guy Clark, John Prine, and those names doing the Kerrville contest. I knew Lucinda Williams, but I hadn't followed the sled to the Texas writers. Then I went down the rabbit hole and discovered Nanci. I only knew "Love at the Five and Dime" as a Kathy Mattea song.

Nanci's voice is [interesting]. I heard Nanci and Iris DeMent for the first time and was like, "I don't know if I can wrap my head around this." Nanci's voice [was compelling] because it sounded like a little girl's. My first record was her cover record *Other Voices, Other Rooms*, and I loved her song choices. I had also just listened to Shawn Colvin's covers record *Cover Girl* and was very curious what songwriters the songwriters would pick to cover. *Other Voices* got me to listen to her other records. I thought it was interesting for such a great writer to do an album of cover songs like [*Other Voices, Other Rooms*]. Great songwriters do have great taste in songs, but [Guy and Townes] never would have done that.

Nanci's a folk icon.[8]

Former Shakespearean actress Amy Space has released ten albums, from her debut, Fable *(2002), to the standout* Me and the Ghost of Charlamagne *and her latest,* Tucson *(2022). She lives in Nashville.*

JAMIE LIN WILSON: *Other Voices, Other Rooms* was my real introduction to Nanci Griffith. Then we started playing Anderson Fair, which was a big deal because Nanci had made a record there. Anderson Fair is like a shrine to songwriters who were there in the seventies, so I feel like the room is sacred every time I step inside because Townes, Guy, Lyle, Robert Earl, and Nanci played there. Anderson Fair is my favorite room. I've been playing it since I was twenty-three. People still really care about songs there. Anderson Fair is recharging.

The venue feels like home, and it's the only place where I still get nervous. So intimidating. You walk into a pitch-black room. You can't even see the people in the front row. The room is so dark and quiet you might as well be in there by yourself. There's something about how intimate that stage is. I don't even need a microphone. I can step back to tune my guitar and mumble something to myself and hear somebody in the back laugh. "Wait, you heard me? Oops. Sorry."

Nanci's songs tell stories and have character development and a beginning, middle, and end, like "Gulf Coast Highway." They're short stories within three minutes. I loved Suzy Bogguss's "Outbound Plane" so much that I played it at my first talent show when I was nine. Nanci was so good at painting a picture and making you fall in love with her characters. I'm always amazed at how people do that. I can look at something and say, "This is what makes that thing so poetic," but it would be hard for me to write a song about two people who fall in love at Woolworth's and then the [man] joins this band and they have affairs and get back together and dance a little closer like "Love at the Five and Dime."

ANA EGGE: I was fourteen in a tiny town with just one store without a sign and one gas pump out front in North Dakota when my private hippie school had a guitar class. Our class quickly became a band with mandolin, guitar, and upright bass. We went to a bluegrass festival on my friend's farm called Pickamania, which had a couple homemade stages. This woman named Jean Horton sang "Love at the Five and Dime" in her set. I asked her how she wrote the song, and she said Nanci Griffith wrote it. "Love at the Five and Dime" was one of the first songs I learned to play. The bigger town Williston had a Woolworth's. Crosby was fifteen miles away with a Hallmark store and a co-op. They were dreamy. "Love at the Five and Dime" was such a beautiful song, so I learned more Nanci songs. She had so much tenderness and guts at the same time.[9]

Canadian-born singer-songwriter Ana Egge has toured with Jimmie Dale Gilmore, Iris DeMent, Shawn Colvin, and Ron Sexsmith. Her latest full-length collection, Between Us, *was released in 2021.*

JAMIE LIN WILSON: You saying that about her having those two sides says a lot about her songs. They're so sweet and so dark at the same time. All the anecdotes I've heard from people who knew her end up with her crying. Todd Snider told me the story the other day about seeing her when he first moved to Nashville. She was sobbing in a booth at the bar by herself with her head in her hands. "I didn't know what I was getting into," he said. We were having a conversation about whether or not to encourage people into the music business, and I said I wouldn't wish this on anybody. "Yeah," he said, "I know. I should have taken it as a sign when I saw Nanci Griffith. Here's the best of the best bawling her face off."

Nanci was a major influence on those of us who have gone into this storytelling folk world as young women songwriters who threw a guitar in a car and traveled around. Seeing her have the confidence to stand there with a band behind her and tell stories was an influence. I would think, Is it inconveniencing these guys to stand there and do nothing? I see her and I'm like, "No." She's charming and engaging. Her stories make people like the songs. Nanci makes us go, "Of course, I can do that."

ANA EGGE: Nanci had such attitude on "Ford Econoline," which was subversive for the time. "I don't need you or anybody. I've got my car and I'm good. I'm getting out of here. Everything bad is in my rearview mirror because I'm leaving." Very empowering. The song speaks of trauma and unrest without naming or blaming in any way, so it doesn't get sticky. "Ford Econoline" is about her making her own path and saying that freedom was in her own hands. There was no Goliath. She just needs to go, which is the hardest step.

"I Wish It Would Rain" has such a beautiful melody that speaks so perfectly to what the lyrics are [saying]. I love the lyrics: "I wish it would rain / Wash my face clean." Then, "The love and the memory sparkle like diamonds." That makes the diamonds line work so well. The feeling is so interior and perfect. The song is just magnificent and feels effortless because the melody goes with the lyrics. Nanci wrote unique melodies that make her songs so lasting and special. "I Wish It Would Rain" feels classic, like you already know the song.

ELLIS PAUL: Melodies have a staircase element like rhymes. You say the first phrase and know the potential rhymes. You know where it's gonna go. Nanci knew where to land the notes on the staircase in a way that was very interesting. She wrote hooks and great staircases like Paul McCartney. They're definable notes that follow this pattern that looks like a staircase that goes up and down, which is very hooky. That makes [listeners] not want to turn away.

LUCY KAPLANSKY: I think I'm gonna do "Ford Econoline" on my next album since I sang on the original recording [on *Lone Star State of Mind*]. "I Wish It Would Rain" feels and sounds right to sing. "Ford Econoline" is a really rousing song with a great hook about a woman's liberation. I always thought that the song was about Rosalie Sorrels, but I read recently she modeled the song after Kate Wolf. I admired Nanci. I covered "I Wish It Would Rain" on my album [*Everyday Street* in 2018].

MAURA KENNEDY: "I Wish It Would Rain" is a nice melodic Texas song. I remember when we were doing it on the road with Nanci doing an outdoor band show one day, and the audience was in front of us. There was a big black cloud coming our way from behind that we couldn't see. Everything was sunny where we could see. We launched into that song and the sky opened up right when we got to the second line. I think about that day every time I play that song.

ANA EGGE: The lyrics go, "Once I had a love in the Georgia Pines," which is all doot-do-doot-de-do. Then, "I wish it would rain and wash my face clean / I want to find some dark clouds and hide in here / Oh, love and the memory sparkle like diamonds / When the diamonds fall they burn like tears." The melody is descending right there. She plays a minor chord on "tears" and the lyrics feel ominous all of a sudden. The memory isn't so great even though there's something that's not all bad. It's tender and you can't let go of it even though you're not with that person.

Nanci's songs feel so available. They're an extension of the folk music that I grew up with and are much more in my experience compared to people like

Joni Mitchell. I love Joni, but the only song that I could relate with when I was a teenager was the one about the guy she dances with. All the others were like, "What? That's too out there." Same with the melodies. Nanci wrote simple beauty. You can't overstate simple beauty. Writing a lyric and melody line so you feel like you know the song is extremely difficult, a gift to the world she was tapping into these archetypes. John Prine had that ability too. They're not predictable, but you feel like you know what's happening.

DAR WILLIAMS: "Gulf Coast Highway" has one of the most beautiful melodies. Nanci really identified with the characters in the song. She had the gift of empathy. Her characters didn't have much, and I think people who struggle to keep what's important are important ones to write about. She presented these people as familiar to us rather than an alien phenomenon.[10]

Popular folksinger Dar Williams has toured with Shawn Colvin, Mary Chapin Carpenter, and Patty Griffin. She has released more than twenty studio and live albums since her proper debut, The Honesty Room, *in 1993.*

KATHY MATTEA: I started pulling out songs at the beginning of the COVID-19 lockdown, and "Gulf Coast Highway" just came to me. I spent days playing it. I sat in with Suzy Bogguss on a Facebook show and I was like, "We're doing this song. You better work up a harmony."

LAURIE MACALLISTER: My waiter friend Aubrey Hardwick gave me Emmylou Harris's *Duets* album with Emmylou and Willie Nelson singing "Gulf Coast Highway." I was stunned. So, so beautiful. I was busking in the subways then and worked up "Gulf Coast Highway." I would put out my guitar case and make fine tips. I could make a hundred bucks in a couple hours, but "Gulf Coast Highway" got more tips than any other song by far. You could break it down and say that was from the melody or lyrics, but it's just a spectacular song. People go crazy like, "What is this? I have to have it." People [almost always] would just walk by you busking even if they gave you money, but they actually stopped when I played "Gulf Coast Highway."

Fast-forward seven years. Red Molly were doing relatively well, making a living, and playing more than a hundred shows a year. We were at a gig in Pennsylvania one time, and [Red Molly singer-guitarist] Abbie Gardner shows up floored. I know exactly what she's gonna say. She had the same body language, expression, and excitement she always had when she found a song that would be incredible for Red Molly. Abbie had just come from a funeral where Fred Gillen sang. "I have just heard the most beautiful song," she said. "'Gulf Coast Highway.'" We worked it up and it became our [second] most requested song.

THE SONGWRITING LEGACY • 283

THE SONGWRITING LEGACY • 283

"Gulf Coast Highway" is one-in-a-million gold for singers. The song is inspiring, uplifting, and about dying. People fall in love with "Gulf Coast Highway" and come back for other shows because of the song. They tell their friends to come see us and buy our music. "Gulf Coast Highway" was so special for us. My ongoing love affair with Nanci was inspired by how important she's been in my own music career. I'm a fan of her music, and the Red Molly fans have been introduced to something they might not have by us sharing it. We had Fred Gillen sing the male part when we recorded "Gulf Coast Highway."

AARON LEE TASJAN: I imagine Nanci like a bird. She gets to these places where she's flying above all pain and loneliness she's singing about. She's literally saying on "Gulf Coast Highway," "We're gonna catch some blackbird's wing and fly away to heaven." That imagery matches up with the places she's coming from in those songs. I don't know if that was intentional, but I would have to assume so. She seemed to be capable of pulling back and recognizing these feelings that were hard for her to sit with. The heartbreaking part is there's really nothing that can be done to stop that. I walk away with this feeling that it's so hard to understand where that pain is coming from, but ultimately you don't know how to get past it in your life.

I remember talking to friends around Nashville who remembered talking to her when she was breaking down crying even though her career was on top of the world. She would feel isolated and didn't know if anyone around her loved her. "Am I loved?" I really hear that in "Late Night Grande Hotel." Then there's this beautiful simplicity in "Gulf Coast Highway." She talks about how these bluebonnet flowers only grow in this place at this one time. We only have the fragility of these moments, so we have to appreciate them in our hearts as best we can. Even the most beautiful things end up going away. Both songs hold a deep range of emotion within them.

MAURA KENNEDY: I remember thinking, "Gulf Coast Highway" is true. These are the bluebonnets she was singing about. So evocative to know that song wasn't just words. The song was based on something that Nanci knew and was ingrained in her experiences. My mother had passed away right before I met Nanci and Pete. I was so in love with that song the first time I went to Texas and saw all the bluebonnets that I ended up buying a packet of seeds and brought them back home. I waited until summer and tried to plant them at my mother's grave, but they didn't take because it wasn't Texas. I should have paid attention. That's the only place bluebonnets grow. There's not a misplaced word in that song.

AARON LEE TASJAN: Nanci's gift as a songwriter is Dylanesque in being able to hold these very relatable simple images in so many different ways.

Nanci definitely seemed willing to be honest and open in [her songs]. I some-times find it hard to listen to her songs if I'm in the wrong head space. I've felt that loneliness myself where it can be painful to listen to someone articulate it so honestly. Then there are other times when those songs make me feel way better. She's not a one-dimensional songwriter. Her songs have so much going on. I really end up treasuring songwriters like that. I listen to those songs over and over because there are different things I get out of them at different times.

MAURA KENNEDY: Listen to what she chooses not to say in the lyrics on "Gulf Coast Highway." Plus, the chorus starts with a melody on a minor chord, which gives the song a lonesome feel. The characters are already flashing for-ward to when they die and are already reckoning with the end of their lives. "Highway 90, the jobs are gone." Such a universal feeling about working-class folks who make it to retirement age and barely have enough to scrape by. The only thing they've ever owned is that little house right on the highway, which physically isn't prime real estate.

EMILY SCOTT ROBINSON: So much feels lonesome about "Gulf Coast Highway." They're talking about what they're gonna do, how they're gonna escape, and what their souls will do when they die. Plus, it's them against the world and the global economy that took labor to other countries. They're coming to the end of their lives but also the end to a way of life in the United States. "Gulf Coast Highway" is a photo negative of the American dream while being a beau-tiful love song at the same time. I love the line, "This is the only place on earth the bluebonnets grow." They're saying, "This is special. We couldn't go anywhere else. We wouldn't if we could. This is the only place bluebonnets grow."[11]

Emily Scott Robinson's Magnolia Queen *(2016) and* Traveling Mercies *(2019) led to a deal with John Prine's Oh Boy Records for* American Siren *(2021) and her latest,* Built on Bones *(2022).*

AARON LEE TASJAN: The "Gulf Coast Highway" story obviously isn't hers. She spent her life going all over the world singing the songs she wrote. Maybe there is something to the [theory that she could have written it as a wish for her own life]. The grass is always greener. Maybe the sadness in that song comes from when she comes back down from flying over it like a bird. She real-izes that's not what she's living. She doesn't have any stability, like having one person and one place for a stretch of time, watching the flowers come and go once a year in her own life. She's passing the time literally by constantly going from landscape to landscape rather than watching one change. I wish badly she was here to [explain].

EMILY SCOTT ROBINSON: "Gulf Coast Highway" feels channeled from a bigger place. I think when a writer truly knows a character in her bones and can sit down and have a conversation with them, the details are coming from a deeper place. Anne Lamott gives this writing advice about writing a lot of backstory for your characters, understanding how they would vote in the election, and [knowing] how many kids they would have. Then you select the details. The energy of the characters is in there. Nanci knew those people and their physicality. The details she gives hint at a deeper knowing. It's like [a method actor] writing about their character.

LAURIE MACALLISTER: So many things made Nanci successful. Her wholesome, homespun sound, and those melodies. The alchemy of all the factors did it, but the melodies are particularly captivating. The more rangy the melody is—how many octaves it covers—[the better]. Nanci seemed naturally melodic, but there's also making a song more melodic. You might do your first run-through of a song. Then you might write out the actual melodies and see melody isn't ranging very far. "How can I now edit the melody? Where can I substitute high notes for low notes?"

MAURA KENNEDY: I always think about that when I'm writing. I like the melody to go with the emotion. How would your voice modulate if you were telling this story? [Look at] the opening line in "Trouble in the Fields": "Baby, I know we've got trouble in the fields." Her melody goes with that emphasis. I don't think many songwriters do that so well. Her melodies were always connected to the lyrics. [Same with] "Gulf Coast Highway." I loved that song when I first heard it, which was before I moved to Texas. I went down for one early South by Southwest and rented a car. We were driving on the MoPac, and the median was filled with bluebonnets. I don't know if they still do that, but the whole median strip was so blue.

ELLIS PAUL: Nanci was talking about this really hard situation with farming on "Trouble in the Fields," but she wraps the lyrics in this really beautiful and melancholy melody. You're trapped by the beauty so the message is never too difficult to hear. So many folksingers can beat you over the head with their message [so] that they sacrifice melody and musicianship in delivering the message. Nanci didn't. She wrapped the message in beauty, which means you can hear the song a thousand times and the message really sticks. That's the thing about great songwriting. The song hooks you in, but then on the twentieth listen you go, "Holy shit. I didn't know what this song was about, but now I see it." That's like having a drink of whiskey and having the aftertaste happen. The aftertaste can be even better than the first sip.

LILY KEARNS: Nanci's song structures made me not afraid to throw something in my songs that might feel a little odd. Most songs today sound very, very similar. Nanci was shaping the tune around the lyrics. You either write the lyrics or write the music and fill in the lyrics. I always think the better songs for me are when I write the lyrics first. Nanci had a real gift for writing lyrics. The really cool part of "Trouble in the Fields" is where it climbs up to the chorus because you're not expecting it. You remember it for that reason.[12]

Glasgow, Scotland, native Lily Kearns sang Nanci Griffith's "Trouble in the Fields" with Teddy Ray in a YouTube video posted in 2021. She was twenty-two at the time.

EMILY SCOTT ROBINSON: I always come back to "Trouble in the Fields." I love the lyrics so much. Nanci knew those characters too. The older characters are seeing this way of life disappear, but they're also seeing that since it was hard for their ancestors it will be hard for them too. The children live in the city and don't understand. They never want the rain to fall or the weather to get colder, which shows this disconnect that the younger ones have with this way of life. The characters show their love for each other and the land they've worked for all those years. There's the commentary about the working class versus the banks and creditors and the changing way of life. "Trouble in the Fields" is a cross section of a geological time stamp like a carbon dating sample that feels so true. I love how she talks about her family being farmers and ranchers in West Texas on *One Fair Summer Evening*.

ELLIS PAUL: Nanci had a way with language. Her songwriting was really great, and she had a mission statement that said folk musicians were different than your standard pop songwriters who were trying to make a dollar out of writing about their own pain. Her songs weren't necessarily gonna go up the charts, but they were honest stories about the human condition. The singer-songwriter movement was about looking inward and your emotional state about what's around you. You start being a folksinger when you start writing about the collective rather than the self. She was writing "Trouble in the Fields" and social commentary like "It's a Hard Life (Wherever You Go)."

GLEN PHILLIPS: "It's a Hard Life (Wherever You Go)" takes you from Belfast to Chicago to her own idealism and how life can crush that. She brought that out with an effortless honesty and conversational quality. Nanci's songwriting simultaneously was so direct and universal. I might have known a little Tom Waits at the time, but seeing her lay out a story so specific that it could be about any person in any town really [influenced me]. She wrote songs that always felt applicable to your own life and not just the narration of something that happened to someone else. I was keyed into lyrics but only really knew the combination of words that were grand and vague like rock and roll. Nanci drew me in with straight-ahead narratives.

Glen Phillips serves as lead singer and songwriter for nineties hitmakers Toad the Wet Sprocket ("Walk on the Ocean," "All I Want"). He has released nearly a dozen solo albums, from Abulum *(2000) to* There Is So Much More *(2022).*

MICHAEL HALL: I liked the songs that poured out of Nanci like "It's a Hard Life (Wherever You Go)." What a great song and cool melody. She [wrote] that song like the way Dylan would borrow from old songs like [those in] Harry Smith's [*Anthology of American Folk Music*] and make something new. They're simple melodies over and over while singing something that gets at the heart of being a human being. Like, "Where did 'Blowin' in the Wind' come from?" It came from listening to all the songs in the Harry Smith compilations. I got the feeling Nanci did the same thing. "It's a Hard Life" really connected.[13]

Longtime Texas Monthly *writer Michael Hall launched a missile at Nanci Griffith in the feature "You Can't Go Home Again," a scathing character assessment published in the magazine in January 1999. Hall says he regrets the article today.*

GLEN PHILLIPS: I tend to write more about emotional ambivalence. The question is how you observe injustice in the world in a song that's honest but doesn't read like a pamphlet. The line "We poison our children with hatred" from "It's a Hard Life (Wherever You Go)" might have been less believable from another singer. Nanci could pull it off. Nanci took in Northern Ireland, racism in America, and her own disillusionment and distilled it down to simple facts: hate breeds hate, love breeds love, and you can't escape the fact that things are messed up. There's nowhere you can go and not face up to that. Also, she brought it back to that simple chorus while taking you on a trip around the world, then on back to her own experience and self.

I try to have those different levels in lyric writing. Take it from a relational point of view, then to a relationship to god or spirit, and then geopolitical and back to the original point of view. I learned a lot about how to zoom out while still keep[ing] it personal from Nanci and songs like "It's a Hard Life (Wherever You Go)." It's hard to talk about a large concept without being preachy. You want the lyrics to read like something you care about. I listened to "It's a Hard Life (Wherever You Go)" just this morning, and it still makes me tear up. She also could pull off a song like "From a Distance" that could be overblown. I love her version of the song. She makes it really intimate and personal. She was just sharing what was going on inside.[14]

ELLIS PAUL: Nanci was a folksinger. "Love at the Five and Dime" was a story song about these two people who fell in love really young and the troubles they came across and how their lives came full circle. Nanci had a good sense of the folksinger's role and how to go about it. I was never turned off by her stance in the songs. Nanci never preached. Many folksingers do, and you turn off the message. The fact that she was pretty and had a way around a melody with songs like "Five and Dime" made her an accidental country star, but she was a folksinger.

Nanci did the little repetitions that poets use like internal rhyme. "Hazel eyes and chestnut hair / She made the Woolworth counter shine / Eddie was a sweet romancer and a darn good dancer." You would never notice unless you were breaking the song apart like a songwriter would. Those things are internal hooks that pull you in. Also, she had such a presence onstage. She was confident but not in an off-putting way. She was casual, and the way she held herself was very inviting. She was tall, thin, and her posture was like the next evolution of man one more step from the gates. She seemed to be an inch taller than everyone else. Those things matter.

JENNY REYNOLDS: Nanci's introduction to "Love at the Five and Dime" during her *Austin City Limits* episode was both funny and poignant, familiar and new at the same time, which is hard to do. What makes Nanci familiar and new is the way she says things. She introduces the Woolworth's store in "Love at the Five and Dime" as "Woolworth" in that *Austin City Limits* taping, but in the song she refers to it as love at the "five and dime," which is so much more real, like you're chatting together. We had a Woolworth's in Dedham, Massachusetts, where I grew up. We always called it the five-and-dime.

Nanci talks to you like you talk to your friends and family. We're dancing in the freaking aisles at the five-and-dime? They didn't have to go anywhere else to dance. Martin Sexton has a song called "Diner" with the lyrics, "Diner, my shiny, shiny love." You don't know which diner. It's just the diner. Nanci calling the store the five-and-dime has a more direct connection with our hearts. Straightforward. "We were dancing in the aisles. We couldn't wait until we got home. We had to dance right there." There's such an immediacy in that song.[15]

Native New Englander but longtime Austin resident Jenny Reynolds enlisted several Central Texas musicians including Jaimee Harris, Scrappy Jud Newcomb, and BettySoo for her latest album, Any Kind of Angel *(2020).*

MAURA KENNEDY: The characters are not perfect in "Love at the Five and Dime." They screw up and then reconcile somehow. People relate to that. I remember Nanci asking, "Why do people always want to hear this song?" They love that the characters are flawed but they can still get together and share a happy, private moment at the end of the day. Then there's the energy, melody, and sass in "Ford Econoline." There isn't a weak spot in the woman's character. She was so strong and unstoppable. I love the energy she sings that song with. Plus, there's the way she hits those high notes. Her voice was so powerful in the higher range. That's still my favorite song.

EMILY SCOTT ROBINSON: "Ford Econoline" is another favorite because she's singing with a smile. The fact that she's chosen a Mormon woman to sing about is so great. "Ford Econoline" is a feminist anthem without being overt. Nanci writes stories of women eschewing their roles and going out in the world in a celebratory, powerful, free way. So amazing. I also love "Listen to the Radio" because it's also a really brilliant moment of songwriting with its feminist anthem. This woman is leaving these people who are depending on her to fulfill a role she no longer wants. She's not gonna cook dinner for the man waiting for supper. It's interesting that he's gonna call her mom to figure out where she's gone. "Hey, your daughter ran off again. Can you get her back here?" I love the production on that song because it's really fun and feels like classic country.

LAURIE MACALLISTER: Then there's "Lookin' for the Time (Workin' Girl)." Such a kooky song. We all brought in an avalanche of songs when we started Red Molly around 2004. Many were heavy, heartbreaking songs, which you'll find. All songwriters love sad songs, but we had this pile from us each bringing in twenty or thirty songs. One [former Red Molly member] Carolann [Solebello] brought in was "Lookin' for the Time (Workin' Girl)." The song has such a fun feel, superfun to play. You can be a really morose singer-songwriter and go sad song after sad song, but we knew we needed to be entertaining and break things up with different feels and subject matter.

"Lookin' for the Time" was an obvious song to include when we were coming up with our first set list. Carolann had a deep love of Nanci's catalog, and the song fulfilled that important role in the set with tongue-in-cheek humor. We already had that song worked up fully when it came to pick a song for the *Trouble in the Fields* tribute album. Our fans call themselves Redheads for Red Molly. The people who work our merch tables—both women and men— call themselves "working girls" because we sing "Lookin' for the Time."

Nanci left behind this massive legacy of love and talent. She has been a huge force in my folk music world. She would always be in people's top ten and has [earned] the same level of respect as John Prine. Nanci was so generous with so many people. Nanci was like the underdog. You root for her. You wanted her to win. Losing John Prine and Nanci were devastating blows. "No, no, she's too special. She is an angel. Don't take her." Nanci was a powerhouse. You know, I've been thinking about when you said you've been listening to Nanci twenty-four seven while doing this book. What an amazing way to spend one's time.

GLEN PHILLIPS: I grew up being into metal and disco and later got into punk rock and was very into the English postpunk and art rock scene. I remember Nanci being my first exposure to a singer-songwriter and storyteller. She was my gateway to a whole lot of other artists like Townes Van Zandt and Guy Clark, writing in a way I hadn't heard. I mean, *Storms* has "Drive-In Movies and Dashboard Lights." So good.

ADAM DURITZ: "Drive-In Movies and Dashboard Lights" reminds me of Springsteen songs and Bob Seger's "Night Moves." Such a great story song that paints a picture, which reminds me in a way of *The Last Picture Show*, a snapshot scene with the cinematic nature in the song. Springsteen songs conjure up the beachfront in New Jersey. "Night Moves" paints that late-night rock and roll thing. "Drive-In Movies" is [*Dazed and Confused* and *Boyhood* writer and director] Rick Linklater's Texas at night—the heat, the cars, the desert with great songwriting. That killer melody sweeps you up and transports you.

Nanci's songs can put you on the moon.

MATT HARLAN: I got into her collaborations on *Flyer* with contemporary folks I knew. I really like "Going Back to Georgia" that she wrote with Adam Duritz from Counting Crows. I said earlier the melodies aren't what sold me, but that one sticks in my head. I don't know if it's that contemporary assistance from Duritz, but I've loved that song since the first time I heard it. Makes sense. Counting Crows were a huge influence on me before I was into Americana music. I loved that Adam and Nanci both frequently use lots of words in their writing. They're shoehorned into the song in an unorthodox way. The melodies they use and where they chose to not sing and jump back in make that seem okay. Doing that only works with a strong framework.[16]

Houston-based singer-songwriter Matt Harlan appeared in For the Sake of the Song: The Story of Anderson Fair. *Austin-based label Eight 30 Records released his latest,* Best Beasts, *in 2019.*

ELIZA GILKYSON: We were just folksinger girls hanging out having a laugh and talking music and being supportive of each other, but the last time I saw her I noticed that she had built some defenses. I'm sure she had good reason. She really wasn't the kind of person who would change herself to fit in or adapt. She just wasn't gonna do that. She wouldn't have been able. The guys ruled the roost back in the day, but she absolutely was a good example for women songwriters. You have to be tough and stick to your guns. [Our folk world is] more friendly now than it was. You had to get into favor with the men who ruled the music business back then.

We always found that daunting because favors were expected in a way that wasn't gonna work for her or most of us. Nanci just toddled off with a smile on her face and a little clench to the jaw. "You're gonna get flattened if you roll over." We came up so much in the same period and were forming our sound at the same time but separately from each other. We were both pretty much set in our trajectories as writers when we came across each other, but she went a little nutty with our *Austin City Limits* taping. She had this song ["Clock without Hands"] that I thought was cute but not as refined, deep, and visceral as she had been in other incarnations.

I felt like fame didn't do her any favors. I didn't love "Clock without Hands" because she had lowered her bar a little bit. I've often thought if I had become a little more famous I wouldn't have kept growing my craft because I'm easily placated. Fame can be harmful. Everyone wants you to stay just how you are. Reinventing yourself becomes harder and harder, but I do love her song "Love at the Five and Dime." Beautiful. Also, Nanci was a folksinger at a time when being a folksinger wasn't cool.[17]

Cerebral singer-songwriter Eliza Gilkyson has released more than two dozen albums including the recent peaks Land of Milk and Honey *(2004),* The Nocturne Diaries *(2014), and* Songs from the River Wind *(2022). She lives in Taos, New Mexico.*

AMY RIGBY: I really loved doing the song "The Flyer" for Maura and Pete Kennedy's *Trouble in the Fields: An Artists' Tribute to Nanci Griffith* album. The song grabbed me because Nanci mentioned [my hometown] Pittsburgh. I also connected with the story and what it's like to be a single woman on the road. You're thinking you might have a connection with someone, but it's all so fleeting and random. Nanci made so much out of this one interaction on a flight. You have this little spark with someone that turns into something cosmic. She holds on to the idea of this guy, and they can track each other out in the world because of the work they do.

This was before social media, so we weren't all so interconnected through the internet. You had to actually track people down. Also, I love that the song takes flight melodically in the chorus, which would move me even if the melody didn't have words. Something in a songwriter's DNA shapes the melody. I like to think that she wrote them in that questing way like I write songs. I thought it took the mystery out of songwriting when I lived in Nashville and people wrote to a title. You set out knowing what you are trying to say. Nanci was more like a prose fiction writer.

I went to Pete and Maura's place after a gig in DC to record "The Flyer" for the tribute album. They had the track all laid down already. Maura was really producing the session, which I liked because I don't know that many female producers. They sent me the mix later, and Maura wrote, "Your track is magic." I hadn't heard it since we recorded, so I had forgotten what it sounded like. Wow, I thought, it was magic. I actually rerecorded it solo for my blog and loved singing it for people. That gave me a chance to say something about Nanci Griffith after she died. "Let's not forget this person." She seemed so literary even with her album covers. I felt like Nanci had more of a kinship with short story writers like Raymond Carver and Bobbie Ann Mason than any musical artist.[18]

Amy Rigby performed with Last Roundup and the Shams before launching her career as a solo singer-songwriter with Diary of a Mod Housewife *(1996). The Pittsburgh native's memoir,* Girl to City, *was released in 2019.*

ELIZA GILKYSON: Nanci was so sweet, funny, and intimate. We had mutual respect. Nanci was not just a songwriter. She was a very tenderhearted person who made every song her own and was a good player and musician. She constructed a song with so much musical knowledge. Her songs were visceral, but she was a quirky person with chops on her guitar, a great groove, and a sense of song construction. She wasn't gonna write a typical melody because her head didn't work that way. She strung chord progressions and melodies together in a way that wasn't predictable, but they had a familiarity when you heard them. [We knew she] would go someplace.

Nanci wasn't being different by putting together different chord progressions. She was wired that way. I [found that out myself] when I had some choices of songs to do for [the Red House Records children's lullaby collection *Down at the Sea Hotel*] and picked her song "Midnight in Missoula." Oh my goodness. "Are you sleeping now . . ." What a great chorus. The song showed her soft side and tenderness. She was a tough chick, but that soft side was apparent in the days when I knew her. Her tough side was never directed at me, but there was a defense that went up later to protect her. I don't know that it really helped her.

AARON LEE TASJAN: I did "Late Night Grande Hotel" for [Ken Levitan's] new Nanci tribute album, *More Than a Whisper*. I got with Doug Pettibone, who worked with Nanci. He had done some of my favorite music with Patty Griffin, so I came up with the idea to see what the song would be like as a conversation between two people. Doug brought in Patty to sing on the song. Singing a Nanci song with Patty Griffin was a dream come true for me. We did a very raw, open version. I was talking to [popular *Cocaine and Rhinestones* podcast host] Tyler Coe about the song and said, "You know, 'Late Night Grande Hotel' is such a lonely song. Do you think it's weird to do it as a duet?"

He said something that totally flipped me out: "There's no loneliness like the loneliness between two people." He told me it was the right thing to do.

CAROLINE HERRING: I discovered Nanci when I was in college in Mississippi. I listened to her much more when I moved to Texas. I heard her play once at an outdoor festival in Arkansas in my early twenties, which was one of my favorite concerts of my life. I was utterly and completely exhausted from working at a girl's camp but found joy in being outside in the mountains and sunset with Nanci and her iconic voice and songs. They made it a very joyful evening. Also, I loved that Anderson Fair record because she told stories between the songs. I could never quite figure out how to accompany myself with stories like she did.

I learned that storytelling [between songs] was allowed from her. People loved that. I listened to that whole record with "Love at the Five and Dime" and "Trouble in the Fields" probably ten thousand times. Great album. I was writing stories about other people [like Nanci was] and have always thought those are the best songs I've written. Nanci's songs were more fictional than mine, but I loved the way she described other people. She dignified them. Even the songs she covered like "Tecumseh Valley" and the way she and Townes Van Zandt dignified that life is interesting. She wrote about the joy and trials people had.

Nanci influenced how I wrote my song "Mistress" and a song on my first album called *Ringside Rodeo,* which talked about a girl growing up in the South. I wrote a song about three southern women on my *Lantana* album. I never would have known how to do that without Nanci's songs. I didn't know other women who did that like she did. I kept doing that even through my latest album, *Camilla*. I just got the idea that I could write about other people and dignify them from Nanci more than I've ever thought about. Those stories are important to me.

Nanci's song ["The Loving Kind"] is an interesting way to talk about race, but she wasn't the only one doing that. Tish Hinojosa is another. I wonder if they influenced each other in telling stories with historical significance. I would say that my songs like that are the most important that I've done as a songwriter. Obviously, listening to her album ten thousand times made me heavily influenced by Nanci Griffith and her storytelling. I still can hear the ping she played [to represent the elevator going up] when she sang about the Woolworth's store.

I wrote a road song about driving to Texas in a U-Haul for my first album, like Nanci did with "Ford Econoline." Peter Rowan talks about how Nanci would get in her car and drive up and down the coast. So few female musicians would do that. We're drawn to the empowerment in "Ford Econoline." Certainly you would be [empowered] if you've been married a while. She leaves, gets in her car, and she's alive and free. Life clamps down on you. Think about the roles of women in society and the South. Those roles are deeper and wider and stronger than I ever realized. "Ford Econoline" gives very basic empowerment. Being Mormon was an interesting twist.

TERRI HENDRIX: I was really drawn to songs like "The Wing and the Wheel" and "Love at the Five and Dime" when I heard Nanci's *One Fair Summer Evening*. She was really precise with her finger picking and strumming, and her guitar playing completely backed up her lyrics without interfering. Listen to those parts on "The Wing and the Wheel" and "Love at the Five and Dime" and compare them to contemporary music at the time. She was playing alternating bass lines with her thumb Guy Clark style. Nanci wrote song structures like they were short stories, which really had an impact on me. I liked the way she could write a universal narrative like "More Than a Whisper."[19]

Pioneering independent artist Terri Hendrix has released nineteen albums on her own record label and founded the Own Your Own Universe nonprofit arts center in Martindale, Texas.

DAR WILLIAMS: I love "Love at the Five and Dime" and her cover of "Once in a Very Blue Moon." Nanci picked great cover songs. *Other Voices, Other Rooms* was unparalleled. She was recording mostly songs written after the folk boom of the sixties on *Other Voices*. That album influenced my decision to record my covers album *Cry, Cry, Cry*. Many people have become successful by doing what they love. I could hear Nanci handpicking those songs and making them her own. She knew she could identify with them. I didn't hear them as her interpretation of the songs. She was singing with her heart. I have a song called "Traveling Again" where the melody basically was unintentionally stolen from the piano solo in "Listen to the Radio." I told her that at the Edmonton Folk Festival one year. She forgave me.

I think her really beautiful sense of melody set the bar higher for other songwriters. Nanci really held out for the right words and notes. She was part of a revival in the nineties we didn't know would happen. I thought as a teenager, Wouldn't it be amazing if we could get back to the time when songs and songwriters were so important to what we call American culture? They took that so seriously in the sixties. Nanci was saying we could harvest these amazing songs by writers like Townes Van Zandt, Frank Christian, and John Prine on *Other Voices, Other Rooms*. She gave us permission to sink into this song revival.

Other Voices, Other Rooms was so big and seminal. Nanci turned me and so many others on to these great writers and made their songs her own. I heard many of those songs for the first time on that record, which affects how I hear the originals still. I mostly prefer her versions because she embodied the songs so well. She had personal friendships with those writers, and some of the magic of the record was the storytelling she did inside the booklet. That added to the lore and romance of this songwriter life and how we feed and share with each other as we do our work. Sharing [allows] another writer to literally smell that flower, take in its beauty, reflect, and go back to their own desk and write.

Entering that world as a writer was exciting and called to me a thousand times more than it had before I heard *Other Voices*. Folk music had this goody-two-shoes image for a while, which it never was. Folk music was about people living their lives and doing what they needed to do like everybody. Sometimes it's messy. Sometimes it's scrappy because we don't make much money. [Not making money] is the truth, which can look romantic or tragic, but it's not Pat Boone. The struggle and truth is where the beauty comes from. You never know if you'll be writing in the depths of despair or feeling good in an attic somewhere.

I learned "Tecumseh Valley" immediately when I heard Nanci sing the song on *Other Voices*. I had never heard of Townes Van Zandt at that point, which was before I moved to Austin. I knew the song "Pancho and Lefty" because my parents had that Willie Nelson and Merle Haggard record, but I didn't know he wrote it. This woman [protagonist] Caroline lived such a hard life. Nanci was a woman who sung "Tecumseh Valley" with such care and tenderness. So powerful. So beautiful. Nanci's version is such a triumph.

EMILY SCOTT ROBINSON: I heard Townes Van Zandt's "Tecumseh Valley" covered at a summer camp once. Then I heard Nanci's version. Townes was so brilliant about writing characters, but I think "Tecumseh Valley" makes more sense and is sadder when a woman sings it. There's more implicit physical kinship and understanding with Caroline. There's something that feels a little sexualized hearing a man sing "Tecumseh Valley." There's a lot to unpack in there. A guy singing it is like, "Girl has tragic thing happen to her. She has to resort to sex work." Nanci made songs like "Tecumseh Valley" her own.

I always thought Kate Wolf's "Across the Great Divide" was a Nanci song. She connected with those covers so deeply. I felt like "Across the Great Divide," "Speed of the Sound of Loneliness," "Tecumseh Valley" are songs we as songwriters go, "God, I wish I had written that." Nanci embodied those songs. You could tell that she wasn't covering songs for popularity. They weren't songs that were a cool choice for the public. She was just doing songs that she loved. I know Nanci is famous for "From a Distance," but I don't care for that song so much. I understand that it's a big, broad anthem for world peace, but I don't think it's very well written.

DAR WILLIAMS: I lived in the middle of nowhere, so the idea of stage banter like she did on *One Fair Summer Evening* was like, "What? You introduce songs?" That record was all magical to me. I loved how she talked in between the songs and talked about things they shared. I felt so close to her even though I never saw her live or met her, but when I moved to Austin people played her songs. They were easy to start up a song circle. Everybody knew them. Sarah Elizabeth Campbell had her "bummer night" song swaps and would often do some Nanci songs. Rich Brotherton too.

Why aren't people covering Nanci's songs like they cover Lucinda Williams songs? I don't know, but again maybe it's because she disappeared. It takes so much to keep anyone's attention. How quickly generations turn as I get older is shocking. I just turned forty-five and it's like, wow. Townes's tragic life sadly really supported the endurance of his work because his death kept the story alive. Obviously, his work stands alone and always would, but people still need to find their way to it. The majority of people don't know Townes, but compared to what? The majority of Americans also don't know poets like Longfellow. Nanci deserves to be more well known and more injected into the canon more regularly.

TERRI HENDRIX: I didn't even think about Nanci as a "woman songwriter" until [Michael Hall's] article came out in *Texas Monthly*. I was so disappointed. Why would anyone write a piece like that? Why would anyone publish it? Why would you want to put your name on it and share a piece about her feelings about being an artist? I read that and went, "Oh, this is because she's a woman. She's not allowed to be like that." Todd Snider can throw a hissy fit and walk offstage, and everything is hunky-dory the next day. Jerry Jeff Walker can be irate in front of a crowd, but god forbid a woman does that.

MICHAEL HALL: I went back and looked at that [*Texas Monthly*] story I wrote about her when she died and was mortified. The story was really mean spirited. I wish I had written it in a different way because I was really dismissive. Man, I was an asshole to Nanci. I just piled it on with the easy [negative] stuff. She clearly was a needy person, and people love to pile onto a needy person in public—especially a successful needy person. Sally Field did that thing at the Oscars years ago when she said, "You like me. You really like me." People made fun of her because she was needy in front of millions of people.

Most people learn to cover that up, but Nanci didn't.

As Terri Hendrix points out, there was something there about attacking a woman. Men [in the press were] attacking this woman who was clearly having some emotional issues. There should have been much more prudence there. The worst part of the story I wrote was that I mocked her for not crying the way I thought she should during the [*Austin City Limits*] tribute to Townes Van Zandt, which is just horrible to read now. So fucking unfair. Townes said her "Tecumseh Valley" was the best cover of any of his songs. Maybe she was tapping into something. That song somehow got her on the emotional level to the point that she cried whether she was in front of people or not. Amazing. Getting an emotional Townes song right is really difficult. Somehow she did.

ANDREW DANSBY: I had a long week. I had to write a tribute for a colleague who died, which was a horrible task. I was like, "Finally, I am out of this miserable week." Then I heard that Nanci died and was like, "For fuck's sake." Then Michael Hall put out a tweet about how she tried so hard to be a Texas songwriter, but she was overemotional, which was such a textbook seventies, male rock critic dismissal with all these microdismissals, and I was just irritated on her behalf. Plus, I was hearing all these tangential things after she died. One person said Eric Taylor was the only person who could get her to shut up by punching her.

Someone else said the cover for *Other Voices, Other Rooms* made them want to choke her. I was wondering, Why is she creating this reaction? People I know who knew her very, very well have said she wasn't just a borderline alcoholic. She got deep into her cups and could be a complicated personality. I believe that, but on the flip side I can't imagine she doled out as much violent action as Eric Taylor. Eric was always really good to me, but he could be both physically and verbally pugnacious. Calling Nanci difficult was such a gendered thing.

Her behavior with the drinking, the volatility, and the outbursts that come with that wasn't any different than these songwriters who considered her a peer. She wasn't able to glad-hand. The language people were using seemed weirdly patriarchal. I'm looking at the cover of *Other Voices, Other Rooms* right now. Why would that make someone angry? It's just Nanci with her head back smiling and clutching a book. She did that on *The Last of the True Believers* with *Lonesome Dove* on the back. I forget which book Townes has jammed in his pocket on the front cover of *Delta Momma Blues*, but they both used books as props like little Easter eggs. Maybe she was more obvious than others, but Nanci saw songwriting as a specific writing art akin to some of the people who had work between two covers rather than the album.

TERRI HENDRIX: Nanci blazed a trail for me and other women. Songwriting has always been a boy's club in Texas, but Nanci cracked through and held her own. She became a hero to women in music. Also, she championed other women songwriters and their craft. Why write about an artist if you consistently don't like their music? Ignore them. Don't raise your hand just to be hurtful and say, "Ooh, ooh, ohh." There are so many great artists in the state of Texas to write about. Why pick on them? I felt sorry for Nanci having to deal with that piece in a national publication, especially because she also struggled through health crisis after health crisis.

Nanci had that baby-girl voice, but listen to someone else if you think that's put on. I always felt like that was part of her charm. Her voice was part of her inner child charm. We played a really fun show in New York once. We played, then she played, then Judy Collins closed. We all got onstage together at the end to sing "Send in the Clowns" and Buddy Holly's "Not Fade Away." Nanci held it down with a fantastic guitar part. I talked to her a little bit before the show, but not a lot because of the way backstage was structured. Judy Collins had pretty much sequestered the whole area so we couldn't get back there, but being onstage with Nanci was really wonderful.

ELIZA GILKYSON: Nanci going to Nashville was good because she was able to bend folk music toward country. She made it work for her career like Mary Chapin Carpenter did. They both were able to take their folk craft and sensibilities and turn right toward Nashville. The timing was good. She was carrying the folk mantle into enemy camp as far as I was concerned. Chapin and Lucinda Williams did the same when they all showed up in Nashville around the same time and took that folk fundamental and turned it into something very lucrative for themselves.

Songwriters like [Jackson Browne and James Taylor] were so on the outs in the midnineties when Nanci did the *Other Voices* records. She gave being a singer-songwriter validity with them. Honestly, I think that's one reason folk music stayed on the roster at the academy at the Grammys. Folk easily could have been homogenized into country or Americana later. I've been very vocally supportive of keeping folk separate from country or Americana. Folk has its own history and the connection to politics. Nanci carried the ball in a time when it could have been canceled completely.

Nanci will always be venerable among songwriters. She just had the classic insecurity that we artists all feel. We feel forgotten if we're not on top of things in the current time, which isn't the best side of our nature. We shouldn't indulge that bitterness and regret. We've been given so much and have it so good that we should be grateful and not go there. I say this to myself because I have lots of should'ves and could'ves. It brings me much more joy to [live with] the attitude of gratitude. She made choices that loosed her demons into her own mind.

I woke up with a sweet little memory in the middle of the night after we talked. Nanci and I were both booked at a little outdoor festival in the North-east. Nanci had an early day the following day and asked if she could go on even though she was the headliner. I agreed and watched her do her show as it started to get colder outside with a big unseasonable temperature drop. She ran over to me after her set and took off her beautiful scarf. I was getting ready to go onstage. She draped the scarf around my neck and gave me a big hug goodbye. I like to think that last contact was the real Nanci: generous, tender, and looking out for a fellow traveling songstress.

SARA HICKMAN: Nanci liked a scrappy underdog like me who stood up for herself. I remember we were being interviewed separately on tour in North Carolina when the journalist leaned in and said, "So, is there a lot of catfighting on tour?" I looked at him. "No. Just the opposite. Nanci asks me to come out every night during the encore and chats me up during the show. She has been really supportive. I don't feel we're competitive in the least. Can we get past that, please?" I put him in his place and Nanci did too.

We continued the tour. I was with my then-boyfriend Marty Lester, who is a recording engineer. We were driving in my car on the tour until we were in Kentucky where it was snowing very hard, and we got separated from the tour bus. We were approaching a river with a bridge overhead, and the car started spinning. I thought we were going to go into the deep, murky water. Fortu-nately, the car hit the rail barrier and stopped. We finally got to the theater, and I walked right into the building and straight onstage. I was still wet from mov-ing the car in the snow.

Marty went home. "That's it," Nanci said. "You're riding on the bus with me." I started riding on the bus with just Nanci, the driver, and her dog, Pops. What I witnessed was a very talented woman who was in some emotional tur-moil. She felt like she worked really hard and received a lot of accolades and awards, but she was struggling with her place. Her bus was really quiet. She didn't play music, and we didn't play guitars. Nanci was very blue. She had her head in my lap crying, and I was stroking her hair at one point. She essentially was heartbroken. I think it started with Bette Midler having the huge hit with Julie Gold's "From a Distance."

Nanci always felt overshadowed and couldn't understand why, which would lead to inconsistencies with how she would respond to different things. I even-tually got off her bus and started riding on the bus with the crew, which was completely opposite. We had loud music and were always dancing. The guys were hilarious and drinking and smoking. We had fun. "Hey," I would say to Nanci at sound check or the hotel. "Let's go to a museum or for a walk with Pops tomorrow." "Okay," she would say. "That sounds great."

She inevitably would disappear the next day and would be really sad when I would talk to her later. "I don't know why we didn't hang out," she would say. She was a conundrum. She wanted to be loved, but at the same time she didn't give people access to spending time with her. She was always so nice to me, but the tour was wrought with anxiety for everyone. She would get really angry and frustrated with members of the band. She sometimes would fire them in the middle of rehearsal, but then hire them back the next day because we were on tour. "I'm really concerned about Nanci," I said to my manager. "I want to talk to her." "Are you enjoying being on tour?" he asked. "Yeah." "Well," he said, "I would suggest not saying anything."

So, I didn't get to have a heart-to-heart conversation with her, but I did feel like she trusted me. She was lonely, which makes me want to cry right now. People would come to the shows, and her audience was amazing like mine is. I would get an encore every night from them, and Nanci was always really proud of me for that. I would go out and sell CDs after my set, and people would come up to me with flowers and teddy bears. It was really beautiful. "By the way," they would say, "can you give this to Nanci?" "Sure." Then I would go backstage and give her a plethora of gifts. She was so intimately loved. People felt they really knew her.

Why don't we celebrate musicians while they're here so they can feel adored and loved? Musicians would be lying if they said they didn't [need to be celebrated]. We express our feelings and develop a relationship onstage with the audience. So many people heard her songs on the radio and went to buy her music. Then they went to concerts. How beautiful would it have been if they were playing her music all over Ireland and the United States for her birthday or something so she could have felt that love? It makes me really sad for her. I think she would have been overwhelmed with gratitude—and relief that she had touched that many people.

I know a lot of singer-songwriters who say, "I wouldn't be a singer-song-writer if it weren't for Nanci Griffith." Rightly so. I feel for Nanci that she probably died feeling forgotten, but she was not. Jenny Reynolds and Eliza-beth Wills [have been influenced by her]. My friend Robin Macy, who was a founder of the Dixie Chicks, was a huge Nanci fan. I didn't listen to folk music growing up. I wanted to be a pop star, so I listened to music on the radio. Then Rod Kennedy invited me to play the Kerrville Folk Festival around 1989, and I was like, "Oh, wow. What is this?" I was exposed to this whole other world there outside Heart and the Rolling Stones. Kerrville was my awakening. Nanci was a big-time performer there.

Nanci's voice was her signature. Her voice was amazingly fragile and strong at the same time. Also, she loved, loved, loved being a songwriter and performing. I was so in awe that I had those opportunities for her to feel vulnerable. I wasn't obtrusive or demanding. I was just there and listened. She wanted someone to listen and make her feel valued even though she was incredibly valued. She had these tour buses. People were buying her music and bringing her gifts, but we don't always see outside ourselves. I've seen that happen with friends who have gone on to great success. They don't know what's happening and aren't sure who knows. Nanci knew she made a name for herself, but she had a deeper need to not be forgotten.

I met with Nanci once after we toured together. Art's wife at Artz Rib House in Austin called. "Hey," she said, "Nanci wants to meet you here at Artz." "Okay." The day was lovely and sunny, and I walked over to Artz. The whole place was closed, and Nanci was sitting at a table. They kept the place closed so she could feel safe. I didn't understand what the mystery was, but she could get mobbed. That was her way of saying, "I want to hang out with you, but I don't want anyone to know I'm here." Nanci loved their barbecue.

The love [between Nanci and the band] was so mindful and caring. People loved being a part of the band, which really was like a family. I'm still best friends with people in that band. The tour was so fun. Nanci was like a mother hen taking up all these different songwriters by taking us on tour or having us record or sing with her. Nanci didn't have a weak bone in her body and was determined, tenacious, and knew what she wanted. She taught me how I wanted to behave on tour with all the kindness she extended to me, which was an honor in the most sincere way.

I wish I could have gotten her off that tour bus.

Oh, I'm gonna start crying now.[20]

Sara Hickman has released more than twenty albums since her Elektra Records debut, Equal Scary People, *in 1989. She teamed up with the African Children's Choir for her latest,* Love Is a Journey *(2015). Hickman was the Texas State Musician in 2010.*

ANDREW DANSBY: I found it heartening that friends here in Houston were mourning her in a very sincere, public, emotional, earnest way. There was such an outpouring. It was nice to observe so many people mourning her because Nanci didn't get that late-career comeback like many do. Guy Clark and John Prine got their late-career recognition. Those guys got to enjoy being canonized and recognized for their entire body of work while they were still alive. I think it's a shame that Nanci never got to make that last record where everybody goes, "Oh, where has she been?"

I grew up on hypermasculine country music in a Waylon Jennings household with Emmylou Harris as a contrast. Emmylou was capable of some great writing, but I filed her more under "sensitive interpreter." So, I was excited to find Nanci Griffith and Lucinda Williams in short sequence when I was twenty years old. Nanci wrote really strong narrative songs. *The Last of the True Believers* had songs that stuck with me, like "Love at the Five and Dime" and "The Banks of the Pontchartrain." Then the album closed with "Fly by Night" and "The Wing and the Wheel." An album with two or three really strong last songs differentiates them from others for me.

The songwriting and execution on *The Last of the True Believers* felt really fully realized and never let up—especially with Béla Fleck, Roy Huskey, Lloyd Green, Philip Donnelly playing. The Anderson Fair people said Nanci had a weird push-and-pull with "Love at the Five and Dime." Kathy Mattea said Nanci expressed regret later that she bad-mouthed the song. She was probably just leery of being identified with one tune like anybody else.

No one stated it directly when I was writing the Nanci piece, but there was this constant sense of her wondering, Why are other people doing better than me? Some people doing the very same line of work don't care about having hits of their own. I feel like Nanci did. She thought of herself as a songwriter whose songs could be done by others, but she also definitely identified as a recording artist. Otherwise, she wouldn't have gone through so many sounds. We're not talking David Bowie, but there's an evolution that shows that she was interested in saying things in different ways. So, yeah, there was a sense of low-level disappointment with her.

WINIFRED BOOTH: Andrew Dansby wrote a really thoughtful article about Nanci in the *Houston Chronicle* after she passed, so I emailed him to tell him how much I liked his tribute. I also [told him about] this moment I had with a painting [inspired by "Gulf Coast Highway"]. I attached the painting to the email even though I didn't know what art he liked. Andrew responded with a really interesting email saying what he liked about the painting. So, I had a giclée print made and gave the canvas to him. He put the painting up in his music room, so Nanci's in good company.[21]

Contemporary Texas artist Winifred Booth lives in Houston. View her work at winifredbooth.com.

MATT HARLAN: I had friends who were like a second family [growing up] who played Nanci's music all the time. I definitely was not into her music back then, but I started getting into her songs in college. I checked out *Flyer* from the library and got *Other Voices, Other Rooms* from Columbia House for a penny. The songs she covered on *Other Voices* led me into her world. Nanci's songs have interesting instrumentation and melodies and great stories. She was alone among her contemporaries doing what people did before. You look at her and go, "Hey, this is how it should be." Other folks loved the way she sang and the melody, but that was never it for me. I was always into the songs themselves.

Break them down.

All her internal references were on point. She wasn't just throwing together words that rhyme well. The themes inside them worked. The details about the characters were thought through. Her characters were consistent and weren't disconnected. Nanci wasn't writing about truck drivers who also sold insurance. She fleshed out her characters. Look at her words: she just wrote, "Rita was sixteen years." She could have gone for a different rhyme or a nonrhyme. Most people go crazy about her vocal performance on "Ford Econoline," but the consistency of characters coming from Salt Lake City and understanding what that meant got me. A Mormon married a Jack Mormon, and she's got five kids.

All details are related and support the overall story. They're not just filling up space or false characteristics. They're small words here and there that add to the story, and you believe this is a real person. Nanci clearly knew the subject she was writing about. Also, I like her live at Anderson Fair record. She name-checks people I know. The folks at Anderson Fair were all intimately involved early on. They would lock the door and party all night when Nanci was there. I feel like that time starting out with Eric Taylor and Anderson Fair before they were successful was what really made Nanci.

I never met Nanci, but I've heard some hilarious stories like her asking for but not receiving her own bathroom at the Kerrville Folk Festival. "No, no, this woman's bathroom will be mine," she said. "You can't let anyone else in here." "No, this is the only one of these we have. We're not gonna shut this off so you can be a queen at this festival. You can go backstage, but you have to go to the bathroom like everybody else." I've also heard people say that she was so gracious and giving of herself and really nice to people who were up and coming. It's hard to know what to believe. She's a contradictory picture.

CAITLIN CANNON: Nanci had this childlike voice and that often can be translating childhood trauma. I had this boyfriend who every time I would talk in a baby voice would pop me out of it. "You're stuck at eight years old," he would say, "because that's when you had the trauma." Work becomes a catharsis for many of us. I identify with growing up and having parts of you that are childlike and a vessel for great pain. That can lead to being compelled to move around the puzzle pieces of words. Figuring out the perfect expression is a relief and great feeling. I'm drawn to Nanci because of that kindred spirit. Nanci gives us all permission to do that.

I go back to Nanci's songs because of the pain and power. I can feel both in her music. Our producer Doug Lancio told us lots of stories about playing with her. I know Nanci was reclusive and I think any good writer has that tendency. I think Nanci lived with an extreme loneliness and pain that she metabolized into her songs. She was extremely vulnerable, but that translates into extreme power. She had a very distinctive voice, but some people might not think that's good for popular music.[22]

Caitlin Cannon's The TrashCannon Album *made Saving Country Music's essential country records list for 2020. Cannon's and Alice Wallace's Side Pony collaboration released the debut* Lucky Break *in 2021.*

MATT HARLAN: You don't get an idea of who she was by the live show banter. You only get a hint in certain interviews. I watched this UK interview from the nineties and she sounds like a rough-and-tumble Texan, but then you see her onstage and hear the songs and she sounds so prim and proper. Her voice is this delicate thing you wouldn't associate with that side of life. She's like Alison Krauss. I've heard some hilarious stories about her not being the angel that she sounds like.

ALICE WALLACE: I spent a couple weeks really listening to Nanci's songs before I live streamed a tribute to her during the pandemic. Nanci was so masterful at writing a great lyric and melody, which makes singing her songs such a joy. I really learned about songwriting from Nanci in those weeks studying her songs. I was on the road with my duo Side Pony with Caitlin Cannon, and we listened to nothing but Nanci Griffith songs for a week straight. We did an acoustic "Love at the Five and Dime" the night we played in Austin, which became the closest thing I have ever had to a viral video, with thirty thousand views in the first week. We later spent two months on the road this summer and were traveling when we learned she died.[23]

Alice Wallace's fourth record, Into the Blue *(2019), made waves throughout Nashville and beyond. Wallace and Caitlin Cannon's Side Pony collaboration released the debut* Lucky Break *in 2021.*

CAITLIN CANNON: We had never done anything that did so well on YouTube as "Love at the Five and Dime." "Love at the Five and Dime" is one of the greatest love songs. Listen to the lyrics. The song tells the story of these characters that made horrible transgressions, but it's all love and all real. Nanci made it sound like becoming a songwriter was a choice. "You can do this, but just so you know, you're gonna be sad." Well, how bad will you feel if you don't do it? You have to make peace with the fact that there will be a certain amount of sadness.

Writing songs like Nanci did is the way out of the pain. I like the songs where people are vulnerable, show their pain, and rip themselves to shreds. I would rather hear honesty than an uplifting message. My favorite Nanci song, "Listen to the Radio," is upbeat but about being alone with no friends. "Ford Econoline" is an uplifting-sounding song, but it's also coming from a place of escape. Even Nanci's upbeat songs are about the person leaving or being alone.

JENNY REYNOLDS: [Nanci was] answering a calling that doesn't work nine-to-five as a writer. You ever think of a line at two in the morning and get yourself out of bed like a psycho to find a pen and a piece of paper? You want to date someone like us, right? I'm a slave to a Moleskine [notebook] and my cell phone. I've had a Moleskine in one form or another since high school. I have full shoeboxes. I left one on an airplane once, and I'm still sad about it. You gotta write stuff down. Even the experience of jotting it down will spur another line out of you. I put it in the reminders part of my iPhone when I'm really desperate and can't get to a pen and paper.

CAITLIN CANNON: We never know if we're gonna reach ten, ten thousand, or ten million people with our songs, but there's enough benefit in the connection and joy in the crafting of the songs for me to do it. Then you start working on the next. Writing anchors you to sanity. You don't feel as alone when you're crafting a song about a character. We all are actually alone. Tony Soprano's mother said, "You die in your own arms." That sounds a little cryptic now that Nanci is gone, but there have been periods of time when I'm happy [even though] I don't think life is about that. The pursuit of happiness is okay, but for me the question is more, is it meaningful?

We were just singing the other night with Emily Scott Robinson, who is a big Nanci Griffith fan. She knows her characters. I love to watch Emily's career unfold. She said onstage when she was about to play "Trouble in the Fields," "You have to care about people to be a songwriter." It's true. We listened to "Ford Econoline" after Nanci died. We [might] cover that, "Love at the Five and Dime," and her Kate Wolf cover "Across the Great Divide." I discovered that song through Nanci. I feel like it's our responsibility to sing those songs and keep the lineage going.

EMILY SCOTT ROBINSON: I grew up listening to Nanci Griffith from a really young age because she was my mom's favorite artist. Mom had *Flyer* and *The MCA Years* double album, which I listened to over and over. We only listened to Nanci and James Taylor's greatest hits in my house. My mom is a journalist and loves Nanci's storytelling and writing so much. I'm the same. I love the storytelling and her characters because she really understood people in their wholeness. Nanci was a romantic songwriter. You're generally rooting for her characters. I know I fell in love with them. I return to *One Fair Summer Evening* the most because I love hearing her tell the stories behind the songs stripped down, unpolished, and not produced. That album captures her essence. I love listening to her sing "Trouble in the Fields," "Gulf Coast Highway," and "Listen to the Radio."

BETTYSOO: I loved mix tapes my one older sister would make me from college. She would call and say, "You should find a CD by these people." The tapes had people like Shawn Mullins way before [his 1998 hit song] "Lullaby." I got into Nanci around the same time. Then I got *Other Voices, Other Rooms* and her Anderson Fair record, *One Fair Summer Evening*. They blew my mind. I was young enough to not be critical of accents and idiosyncratic singing like hers. Nanci had carte blanche with me. She was such an entrée for me into this whole Texas singer-songwriter world.

We all knew about Lyle Lovett because he was really close by [the Houston area], but I didn't know about Guy Clark and Eric Taylor until I got Nanci's records. I'm glad I got those two particular records, *One Fair Summer Evening* and *Other Voices*, because they immediately gave me context for this music. I still listen to so many songwriters today who I discovered on *Other Voices*, like Buddy Mondlock. The second *Other Voices [Too] (A Trip Back to Bountiful)* was great, but the first one really made the big impact on me. I learned to play songs like the John Prine and Jerry Jeff Walker songs off that album.

I also learned about Townes Van Zandt from Nanci because she did "Tecumseh Valley" on that first *Other Voices*. I already knew about Kate Wolf because I had seen her *Austin City Limits* show on my parents' tiny little black-and-white television. I was touring years later in the Netherlands and went to stay with my friend Fred for a few days. He was playing a DVD of that Kate Wolf *Austin City Limits* when I walked in. I freaked out. "Oh my god," I said. "That's the concert I saw as a little kid." I couldn't remember the songs or connect the dots. I think that's why I immediately connected with *Other Voices*. The first track had been part of the beauty and mystery of my early life.

Nanci didn't sound like a likely star, but she had so much to say. She had such a mousy and unique voice. I would hear stories about how people found her difficult, but listening to *One Fair Summer Evening* as a teenager she sounded so charming, thankful, and bowled over to be loved by the audience. I didn't know that Anderson Fair was this tiny little room. I was thinking this capital *R*, capital *A* "Recording Artist" was playing a live concert that must be at a big venue. Those were the only kind I knew about then. Here she is being so coquettish when I only had seen big stars who acted like they deserved to be there. Nanci was so different and had these songs like "Trouble in the Fields" and "More Than a Whisper."

Townes Van Zandt was lionized after he passed, but [he was an exception]. People are never gonna talk about most of us twenty years after our lifetime no matter how successful we get. Nanci Griffith is so famous in our world, but Joe Blow even here in Austin or Nashville probably would say "no" if you ask if he knows Nanci Griffith. That bugs some people, but I became comfortable early on knowing that I'll have no legacy. I just know Nanci's storytelling and earthy lyric play were revelations when I was young and only hearing really glossy, corporate music on the radio. She opened a whole different universe. I feel like it's my job now because of Nanci and *Other Voices* to open doors for others the way she did for me.[24]

BettySoo's albums such as Heat Sin Water Skin *(2009) and* When We're Gone *(2014) have established her as a standout singer-songwriter among Austin musicians.*

PHOEBE HUNT: Nanci's strength was finding really great songs that she could connect to as an interpreter. She went deep into understanding what the song means. I hope that's my strength as well. Doesn't matter who wrote the song. You're singing a message and translating that idea. Your goal is to convey that message. Also, I've listened to her music so much this past year that I'm sure—I hope—my songwriting has been impacted by her. Songwriting isn't something I can contrive.

My goal when I did "Goin' Gone" live was to be close to Nanci's version. I fell in love with that song. Beautiful. I did my best to sing the song with the same melody. My musical intuition can't help make it not exactly the same melody. We changed a couple arrangement things like starting a cappella with the chorus. I liked singing with [bandmates in the Gatherers] Makena [Hartlin] and Tabitha [Meeks], and the chorus felt strong. I thought we should start with that, but we kept it as true to the original cover that Nanci created as possible. Nanci's songs resonate and stand out because of the quality of the songwriting. There's no doubt that the quality in her songs is immeasurable. Her songs deserve the highest accolades.[25]

Austin native Phoebe Hunt cut her teeth with Belleville Outfit, performing blues and jazz hybrid roots music. Hunt's current Brooklyn-based Phoebe Hunt and the Gatherers shines on Shanti's Shadow *(2017) and* Neither One of Us Is Wrong *(2021).*

AOIFE O'DONOVAN: I went to see Nanci Griffith with Iris DeMent opening at Symphony Hall in Boston when I was nine years old. "Can you play 'Ford Econoline?'" I wrote in a note to her. "It's my favorite song." She said during the second half of the show, "This here is a request that a little nine-year-old sent backstage." Then she played the song. I remember sitting in the audience and being filled with so much joy that she had even read my note. I didn't know what that song was about when I was a kid, [but I probably liked it because] it's so upbeat. "She drove west to Salt Lake City . . ."[26]

Former Crooked Still lead singer Aoife O'Donovan has released the solo albums Fossils *(2013),* In the Magic Hour *(2016), and* Man in a Neon Coat: Live from Cambridge *(2016). She has performed with several others including Sarah Jarosz.*

SARAH JAROSZ:I discovered Nanci Griffith through my music-loving parents. They went to the University of Texas in Austin and would see Nanci, Shawn Colvin, and Lyle Lovett at the Cactus Cafe before anyone knew who they were, so I grew up listening to Nanci around the house. I remember really loving how her songs and voice sounded as a kid. I hadn't lived enough back then, but when I was an adult I appreciated the music on a deeper level. Her raw and straight-to-the-point voice stood out to me early on. Nanci had such a clarity of vulnerability. She was putting her heart on her sleeve, but her songs were never so personal that they were not relatable.

My parents took me to see Nanci at the University of Texas Union Ball-room when I was very young. So many early Nanci experiences were watching my mom cry or sing along to her songs in the car, and seeing my mom react like that was like, "Oh. Something is going on there with these songs. They're really touching her." "I Wish It Would Rain" was probably the first Nanci song I ever heard, so that's the one I gravitated to when I was looking into songs to work up for my set. I met Nanci backstage once at the Ann Arbor Folk Festival around 2011. She was very quiet and shy but also very sweet and gracious.[27]

Child prodigy instrumentalist Sarah Jarosz signed with Sugar Hill Records as a high school senior. Her debut, Song Up in Her Head *(2009), was nominated for a Grammy award. Her fourth,* Undercurrents *(2016), won two Grammys.*

LILY KEARNS: I heard Nanci's voice as a child on long car journeys because my dad is a big fan. We had four tapes in the car: Nanci Griffith, John Prine, Bob Dylan, and some Irish lady. I started rediscovering Nanci as I got older when I started performing in pubs and restaurants and was writing my own music. I went to this thrift store last year when I bought a record player, and I bought her record *One Fair Summer Evening* for seven pounds in a small record store on Glasgow's south side. I really fell in love with her music again.

Nanci's ability to reach the average person drew me to her songs like the same quality did for me with Bob Dylan and John Prine. She could relate things people understand on some level. Folk music really is storytelling and real-life experiences. Some are hers and some are people she met. I was really impressed by what we would call her stage chat on *One Fair Summer Evening*.

She could talk to hundreds of people as if it was just one person in front of her. She sang how she talked. I mean that as a huge compliment. Her talking voice is really singsongy, bright, and soft and has that charming southern drawl that draws everyone in along with the self-deprecating jokes. Then it's a continuation of her speaking as soon as she starts singing.

AOIFE O'DONOVAN: "Ford Econoline" isn't my favorite song now. "There's a Light beyond These Woods" kills me today because the song is about growing old, friendships, and the passage of time. Sarah Jarosz and I played "There's a Light beyond These Woods" a few times on the Cayamo cruise and bonded over our shared love of Nanci. Then Joe Henry and I sang "Gulf Coast Highway" at the Americana Music Association's awards [the month after Griffith passed away in 2021]. I used to do that one for Garrison Keillor, who is a huge Nanci fan. Doing that song with Joe was such a pleasure. I love the melody and words and how evocative the song is.

Nanci had such a clarity as a songwriter. She was such a consistently great singer and storyteller and is one of my all-time heroes. My parents were huge fans so I don't remember a time when I didn't know her music. *Once in a Very Blue Moon* was a huge record for my parents. They would play "Once in a Very Blue Moon" at parties where they would have what they called singsongs, which is like being at a pub in Ireland where people trade songs. My dad is from Ireland, and their music makes up the sonic fabric of my youth. My favorite album when I was a little girl was *Lone Star State of Mind*.

I knew the words to "Ford Econoline" even though I didn't know what it was about when I was younger: "She's salt of the earth / Straight from the bosom of the Mormon church." It was interesting to remain a Nanci Griffith fan into adulthood and go back into records like *The Last of the True Believers*, *Lone Star State of Mind*, and even *Other Voices, Other Rooms*, which came out when I was eleven years old in 1993. I had decided I wanted to be a singer by then and remember singing songs like all those covers like "Are You Tired of Me My Darling" at my cousin's. I was so impressed by Nanci's artistry and the way she put her own stamp on those songs.

Songwriters hold her in very high regard today.

SARAH JAROSZ: Nanci was the master who poured her soul out in genuine songs. The way she sings on "Ford Econoline" is incredible. The vocal on that song is the best example of a great, wailing vocal. Nanci was fearless with that performance. She inspired me to be true to my own voice. I have been listening to her almost every day since she died. She was so honest, which is really hard as a songwriter. I feel like the songs on my last record, called *World on the Ground*, were influenced by the Texas singer-songwriters I grew up listening to—and particularly Nanci. "There's a Light beyond These Woods" really influenced my song "Maggie." The way she describes the friendship is so beautiful and painful. I was nearly finished making *World on the Ground* when I was asked to contribute a song to an upcoming Nanci tribute record.

I had covered "I Wish It Would Rain" and several others in my live show, but I wanted to dig a little deeper. I picked "You Can't Go Back Home Again" because the song felt like an omen and so close lyrically to the songs I was writing for *World on the Ground*. I was looking back on my hometown and the complicated feelings of wanting to leave and come home. "You Can't Go Home Again" captured those feelings. Also, my parents brought the Thomas Wolfe book *You Can't Go Home Again* to a Cactus Cafe show one time. Nanci signed the book. The second page says, "To go home again. Nanci Griffith." My parents gifted me that book right around the time when I was having to choose a Nanci song to play for that tribute album. I encored with the song last time on *Austin City Limits*.

I felt like recording "You Can't Go Home Again" would be a cool way to honor my home. The song is about her complicated feelings about Austin, feeling alienated and not always welcome, but she shows her longing for it. They cut that *ACL* show down to thirty minutes so I don't think that song will be on the televised portion, but playing it felt really emotional and special on that stage regardless. I wouldn't have believed you if you told me as a kid that I would have played *Austin City Limits* several times by the age of thirty. I was fortunate to come up in a music community who are always simultaneously looking backward and forward.

LILY KEARNS: More people care about storytelling than we might perceive. I've shown Nanci's music to people who are into more popular music, and there are a few who are like, "Nah, that's not my jam." However, I've had other friends like that who say, "Wow. This is really beautiful music." You're right, we're moving away from this music, but it's always there under the surface. There's a really great folk festival Nanci played in Scotland called Celtic Connections that happens at the end of January. They get artists from all over the world to play folk music. People are hungry for folk music because there's so much crap out now. The musicians who play that festival are just ordinary people like Nanci Griffith.

I'm attracted to folk music because it's ordinary people telling ordinary stories, which is much more interesting than anything else. I heard "Trouble in the Fields" on *One Fair Summer Evening*, brought it home, and thought, I'll just chuck it on and see what's on there. I listened to the whole [album] through. "Love at the Five and Dime" stood out, but "Trouble in the Fields" particularly [caught my attention]. The song is about the Dust Bowl and the plight of ordinary people. Nanci sings that story about ordinary people who probably have been forgotten today as if it's happening to her. Amazing how fast we forget, but the stories live on through music.

I've been having fun getting back to more folky music. The best songs sometimes are just a lady and a guitar. Those songs have more impact most times than an eighties hit—although I do love an eighties hit. Nanci had an impact on lots of young musicians who just wanted to sing to big groups of people and nothing was gonna stop them. Nanci just said, "I'm gonna do this because it's what I have to give." She certainly had a big impact on me—especially by being so ordinary and also so extraordinary at the same time.

Folk music being an unpopular minority keeps it authentic. I'm gonna keep writing more songs and am trying to get my music out there, but I would like to do a covers album at some point of songs by great folk songwriters who have influenced me but might have been forgotten. People need to know them. Some of Nanci's best performances are covers. Obviously, her "From a Distance" is iconic, but I also heard her cover Bob Dylan's "Boots of Spanish Leather" somewhere. Oh, it's on what? *Other Voices, Other Rooms*? No, I don't have that one.

SARAH JAROSZ: Nanci had such a singular voice. I want to celebrate her songs moving forward. I think it [signifies] greatness when people don't necessarily click on all levels of popular culture. Nanci's music is so deep and real that her songs can always be appreciated later. They fit into the Texas music canon and the bigger singer-songwriter community in general. I fully expect that her songs will be sung years and years into the future because they weren't necessarily written for a certain time. She was writing from a real place, and that's when you get something lasting. I've read in a couple interviews [that] Nanci felt forgotten. So sad.

Nanci is beloved and revered all around the world.

I wish she knew.

Coda: Brave Companion of the Road

DAR WILLIAMS: Nanci always made things fun. I remember after a show in Pittsburgh when I was walking to my hotel. There was Nanci yelling out the tour bus to say goodbye. She was always insistent that we were all doing this big project to know ourselves through these songs—especially people trying to find out about different cultures and regions across the country. She went out of her way. We both had sets another time at Folks Fest in Lyons, Colorado. Nanci sent for me. I remember she was flossing her teeth when I got there. She came out of her dressing room just to say how much she valued my song "February." She was always trying to create this world of shared songs. She made sharing the spotlight her superpower. Nanci wanted us to understand what an important moment in time we were in together.

Essential Songs
as Ranked by Author

Written by Nanci Griffith

1. "Gulf Coast Highway," *Little Love Affairs* (written with James Hooker and Danny Flowers), 1988
2. "Trouble in the Fields," *Lone Star State of Mind* (written with Rick West), 1987
3. "Late Night Grande Hotel," *Late Night Grande Hotel*, 1991
4. "Love at the Five and Dime," *The Last of the True Believers*, 1986
5. "Going Back to Georgia," *Flyer* (written with Adam Duritz), 1994
6. "Drive-In Movies and Dashboard Lights," *Storms*, 1989
7. "The Wing and the Wheel," *The Dust Bowl Symphony*, 1999
8. "Ford Econoline." *Lone Star State of Mind*, 1987
9. "It's a Hard Life (Wherever You Go)," *The Dust Bowl Symphony*, 1999
10. "I Wish It Would Rain," *Little Love Affairs*, 1988
11. "Brave Companion of the Road," *The Complete MCA Studio Recordings*, 2003
12. "So Long Ago," *Little Love Affairs*, 1988
13. "Not My Way Home," *The Dust Bowl Symphony*, 1999
14. "Outbound Plane," *Little Love Affairs* (written with Tom Russell), 1988
15. "On Grafton Street," *Flyer* (written with Fred Koller), 1994
16. "Listen to the Radio," *Storms*, 1989
17. "There's a Light beyond These Woods," *There's a Light beyond These Woods*, 1978
18. "Cold Heart/Closed Minds," *Lone Star State of Mind*, 1987
19. "I Don't Want to Talk about Love," *Storms*, 1989
20. "If Wishes Were Changes," *Storms*, 1989
21. "More Than a Whisper," *One Fair Summer Evening* (written with Bobby Nelson), 1988
22. "One of These Days," *The Loving Kind*, 2009
23. "Anyone Can Be Somebody's Fool," *Little Love Affairs*, 1988

24. "You Made This Love a Teardrop," *Storms*, 1988
25. "Down 'N' Outer," *The Complete MCA Studio Recordings*, 2003
26. "Bethlehem Steel," *Intersection*, 2012
27. "This Heart," *Flyer*, 1994
28. "The Last of the True Believers," *The Last of the True Believers*, 1986
29. "Intersection," *Intersection*, 2012
30. "Working in Corners," *Poet in My Window*, 1982

• *All songs written by Nanci Griffith unless otherwise noted, and ranked in hierarchical order*

Covered by Nanci Griffith

1. "Across the Great Divide," *Other Voices, Other Rooms* (Kate Wolf), 1993
2. "Tecumseh Valley," *Other Voices, Other Rooms* (Townes Van Zandt), 1993
3. "The Sun, Moon, and Stars," *Late Night Grande Hotel* (Vince Bell), 1991
4. "Speed of the Sound of Loneliness," *Other Voices, Other Rooms* (John Prine), 1993
5. "Storms," *Storms* (Eric Taylor), 1989
6. "Boots of Spanish Leather," *Other Voices, Other Rooms* (Bob Dylan), 1993
7. "From Clare to Here," *Other Voices, Other Rooms* (Ralph McTell), 1993
8. "Once in a Very Blue Moon," *One Fair Summer Evening* (Pat Alger, Eugene Levine), 1988
9. "From a Distance," *Lone Star State of Mind* (Julie Gold), 1987
10. "Morning Song for Sally," *Other Voices, Other Rooms* (Jerry Jeff Walker), 1993
11. "Goin' Gone," *The Last of the True Believers* (Pat Alger, Bill Dale, Fred Koller), 1986
12. "Deadwood, South Dakota," *One Fair Summer Evening* (Eric Taylor), 1988
13. "Do Re Mi," *Other Voices, Other Rooms* (Woody Guthrie), 1993
14. "Can't Help but Wonder Where I'm Bound," *Other Voices, Other Rooms* (Tom Paxton), 1993
15. "Lone Star State of Mind," *Lone Star State of Mind* (Fred Koller, Pat Alger, Eugene Levine), 1987
16. "Tower Song," *Poet: A Tribute to Townes Van Zandt* (Townes Van Zandt), 2009.
17. "This Old Town," *Other Voices, Other Rooms* (Janis Ian, Jon Vezner), 1993
18. "Are You Tired of Me My Darling," *Other Voices, Other Rooms* (G. P. Cook, Ralph Roland), 1993

19. "Three Flights Up," *Other Voices, Other Rooms* (Frank Christian), 1993
20. "Desperados Waiting for a Train," *Other Voices, Too (A Trip Back to Bountiful)* (Guy Clark), 1998
21. "Davey's Last Picture," *Intersection* (Robbin Bach, Betty Reeves), 2012
22. "Southbound Train," *Little Love Affairs* (Julie Gold), 1994
23. "Never Mind," *Other Voices, Other Rooms* (Harlan Howard), 1993
24. "San Diego Serenade," *Late Night Grande Hotel* (Tom Waits), 1991
25. "I Would Change My Life," *Little Love Affairs* (Robert Earl Keen Jr.), 1988
26. "Bluer Than Blue," *Ruby's Torch* (Charles Randolph Goodrum), 2006
27. "Yarrington Town," *Other Voices, Too (A Trip Back to Bountiful)* (Mickie Merkens), 1998
28. "Heaven," *Late Night Grande Hotel* (Julie Gold), 1991
29. "If These Walls Could Speak," *Ruby's Torch* (Jimmy Webb), 2006
30. "Tonight I Think I'm Gonna Go Downtown," *Poet in My Window* (Jimmie Dale Gilmore), 1982

• *Ranked in hierarchical order*

Set List for Carnegie Hall Concert, March 25, 1993

1. "Trouble in the Fields"
2. "Listen to the Radio"
3. "Three Flights Up"
4. "I Wish It Would Rain"
5. "Across the Great Divide"
6. "Gulf Coast Highway"
7. "Are You Tired of Me My Darling"
8. "One Blade Shy of a Sharp Edge"
9. "Ford Econoline"
10. "Speed of the Sound of Loneliness"
11. "Tecumseh Valley"
12. "Outbound Plane"
13. "Can't Help but Wonder Where I'm Bound"
14. "Boots of Spanish Leather"
15. "So Long Ago"
16. "This Old Town"
17. "The Sun, Moon, and Stars"
18. "Don't Forget about Me"
19. "Gypsy Life"
20. "Wimoweh"
21. "It's a Hard Life (Wherever You Go)"

ENCORE
22. "This Heart"
23. "The Wing and the Wheel"

Notes

Foreword

1. Emily Saliers, interview with Brian T. Atkinson, May 6, 2022.
2. Amy Ray, interview with Brian T. Atkinson, May 6, 2022.
3. Lyle Lovett, interview with Brian T. Atkinson, January 18, 2022.
4. Kathy Mattea, interview with Brian T. Atkinson, September 14, 2021.

Prelude

1. John T. Davis archives, Elektra Records press release, accessed June 2, 2022, inspiringquotes.us/author/33343-nanci-griffith; Arloki272, "Nanci Griffith - Telluride, CO - 6/20/1998," YouTube video, 23:45, August 14, 2021, https://www.youtube.com/watch?v=iMYg
WceQCfo

Introduction

1. Nanci Griffith, "Love at the Five and Dime," *The Last of the True Believers*, Philo/Rounder Records, 1986.
2. Kathy Mattea, interview with Brian T. Atkinson, September 14, 2021.
3. Adam Duritz, interview with Brian T. Atkinson, October 13, 2021.
4. John Jobling, "Nanci Griffith - New Country Gettin' Tough 1987," YouTube video, 9:14, July 15, 2020, https://www.youtube.com/watch?v=Iw9CthS283Y
5. John T. Davis, interview with Brian T. Atkinson, December 3, 2021. "I think people like Townes Van Zandt and Guy Clark [get more attention] than Nanci because of the personas they created for themselves," Davis says. "They were the hardcore troubadours who were hard-living and hard-drinking outlaw characters. They assumed a larger-than-life quality. I don't think Nanci was interested in crafting a larger-than-life persona. Their work obviously speaks for itself, but I feel they lived their public lives in a much more flamboyant way than she chose. She was more private. They lived that life in public offstage and on.

"I certainly saw Nanci's badass, hard-drinking side, but she didn't want to be an outlaw chick singer like Miranda Lambert. We [got along because we] both liked to take a drink every now and then. We would sit, bitch, moan, and swap lies. Sitting down with Nanci was like sitting down with a friend without any facade or [need] to keep up any conversation. Nanci had a wry and even bawdy sense of humor that didn't always manifest itself onstage.

"We enjoyed each other's company."
6. Dar Williams, interview with Brian T. Atkinson, November 19, 2021. "Nanci wasn't overly wholesome, but her songs feel like a clear step from the Carter Family," Williams

says. "I'm sure Nanci influenced me as a songwriter. I've sung her songs over and over again. I loved the storytelling aspect of 'Five and Dime,' which was like a *Romeo and Juliet* in small-town America that I could relate to. Nanci isn't talked about as much as some songwriters, which probably is at least a little sexism, but she also disappeared. I moved to Austin from 1995 to 2000, and Nanci was nowhere to be found. She had already moved to Nashville. She was doing what she needed to do. She wasn't playing the festivals or the circuit. I mean, I even got to hang out and play with Willis Alan Ramsey."

7. Tony Brown, interview with Brian T. Atkinson, December 23, 2021. "I knew you had to cut hit records to keep your job," Brown says. "The whole idea was to make the company money, but then I played [guitar in the band] on the road with Rosanne Cash and Rodney Crowell and was stung with this elitist thing they had. You had to be elite to hang out with Guy Clark, Rodney, and Rosanne. You know, I inherited George Strait and Reba McEntire when Jimmy Bowen left MCA to go to Capitol Records. How lucky was I? I remember an interviewer interviewing me said, 'I hear you're doing Reba McEntire's new album.' I was almost embarrassed for a moment. I look back on that and think, How snooty was I? I got so full of myself."

8. Amy Speace, interview with Brian T. Atkinson, October 31, 2021. "I'm so fascinated by the craft in Nanci's writing and the love that she put into the characters she wrote. I saw her at the decline, and I know enough about Nanci through others that she was not a happy woman at the end. I think about people I admire being like that and am like, 'How did they not know?' Maybe the covers album was her way of getting more widely known. Nanci was out of it the night I saw her at the Bluebird Cafe with Peter Cooper and Eric Taylor, who I had seen play before and became buddies with. Eric and I talked a lot. 'Holy crap, this is gonna be interesting.' Her hands were shaking and she didn't seem like she was wide awake, but she stepped up whenever she played.

"Eric and Nanci were a train wreck together."

"Having my husband on the road with me makes a huge difference," Suzy Bogguss adds about staying healthy. "You leave a show with such a high because you've just experienced this tremendous energy that's passed between you and the audience. Then you go back to your room and it's so frickin' quiet, which sometimes can spawn beautiful songs, but I think about huge stars like Tanya [Tucker] going back to their hotels after being in front of thousands of people. No wonder people drink themselves to sleep or find another mode of chemical relief to wind down. You have such a serious high followed by a serious low. You have to catch yourself early enough to keep track of that.

"I got a meeting with Dolly Parton one time when I was working at Dollywood because I had opened shows for her when I was the female headliner at the park. That was one of the very first things she said to me. First she said, 'Jim Foglesong is a real gentleman. You will love him. He will never do you wrong.' Then she said, 'Don't do drugs. Don't get caught up in that stuff. It's really easy. They'll be there. They make things easier. Don't do that.' You don't forget Dolly Parton giving you advice in her fancy negligee."

Amy Speace: "I'm an alcoholic in recovery. Many songwriters watched Nanci go downhill. I was miserable on the inside before I quit drinking, but it looked real shiny on the outside. My career looked like it was going well, but I was suicidal. I didn't think I was enough. I thought I was a mistake. I didn't just have shame. I was shame. I was in a horrible, dark place. I thought my songs came from the thin line I was crossing between living and dying. I was really scared to get sober. I wondered who I would be without the darkness. The people who brought me into recovery are great, Grammy award–winning songwriters. They literally brought me into the room and then guided and shepherded me.

"I would say I started writing my best songs within four years [after getting sober]. There was a give-a-shit that went away. I was really concerned with what everybody thought of me before and climbing the ladder in the business. I became less interested in that the longer I stayed sober. I now just want to write a great song as honestly as possible. I had to shake the demons out of my system. I can see the writer's pain in what I wrote before. I wasn't able to talk about other people's pain to let the audience see that. I was more like, 'Let me just bleed on the paper.'

"Nobody needs that.

"I was three bottles of wine in and had a bottle of Ambien in my hand the night before I went to Alcoholics Anonymous. I was screaming at a god I didn't believe in, 'Can I take all this and solve everything?' I called a person I knew was in AA. They picked up at two in the morning. I'll never forget that. I've had other times where I've been on my knees since then wrestling with things, but I don't have my hands on that bottle of Ambien anymore. You never really beat the disease, but getting up is quicker now. The disease is so hard, which is why I have such compassion for Nanci. We watched her go downhill. People rarely stay sober. Alcoholism is a horrible disease."

Suzy Bogguss: "There have been many times when I catch myself and say, 'I have to take a break from drinking for a few months'" (Suzy Bogguss, interview with Brian T. Atkinson, March 3, 2022).

Amy Speace: "Stopping drinking changed my writing for the better and made me less of an asshole. The fear about what other people think about you is still there, but when you drink you're just drunk and numbing the same feelings. You have no way of getting past it. You walk through it when you stop drinking and then learn and evolve into the next place on the other side. I noticed how much drinking Nanci was doing when I started doing shows together, which was really disconcerting because she was really small. However, I will say that she stood backstage and listened to my entire opening set. Shocked me. Nobody had done that for me."

9. Beth Nielsen Chapman, interview with Brian T. Atkinson, November 19, 2021.

10. Jobling, "Nanci Griffith - New Country Gettin' Tough 1987."

11. Nanci Griffith and Joe Jackson, *Nanci Griffith's Other Voices: A Personal History of Folk Music* (New York: Three Rivers Press, 1998), 23–24.

12. Peter Cooper, interview with Brian T. Atkinson, February 14, 2022.

13. Thomm Jutz, interview with Brian T. Atkinson, January 13, 2021.

14. Julie Gold, interview with Brian T. Atkinson, September 10, 2021.

15. Darden Smith, interview with Brian T. Atkinson, October 30, 2021.

16. Peter Blackstock, "Remembering Nanci Griffith, the Greatest Austin-Raised Singer-Songwriter Ever," *Austin American-Statesman*, August 27, 2021, https://www.statesman.com/story/entertainment/music/2021/08/27/nanci-griffith-obituary-austin-singer-songwriter-dead/8188421002/

17. Amy Grant, interview with Brian T. Atkinson, January 24, 2022.

Verse: There's a Light beyond These Woods

1. Nanci Griffith Rarities, "Nanci Griffith - Other Voices, Other Rooms (Part 1) [1993]," video, 30:09, July 12, 2020, https://www.youtube.com/watch?v=r9oXw2fH2i8

2. Bobby Nelson, interview with Brian T. Atkinson, October 5, 2021.

3. Stephen Doster, interview with Brian T. Atkinson, October 17, 2021. "Nanci called me years later when she was recording in Nashville and asked if I knew a guitar player who played like I did," Doster says. "'Yeah,' I said. 'I know one.' I had been doing various things like working with James Honeyman-Scott from the Pretenders, but then he died. The engineer stole the tapes [we were working on]. Nightmare. I was ready to get back to where I got started when Nanci called me. I went back to playing my acoustic guitar. *Once in a Very Blue Moon* was the same with live recording. We probably overdubbed Béla Fleck when he came in, but we sat in the same room.

"Lyle Lovett was on that record and had come into the fold by opening shows for us. The first was at Emmajoe's in Austin. Lyle had just gotten out of school. His friend Robert Earl Keen came along and got up at the Cactus one time to do a silly song called 'Swervin' in My Lane.' Lyle had it all together. He had a strong vocal presence and was strongly influenced by Willis Alan Ramsey. He would say he was just trying to do him. Lyle would find out what kind of tennis shoes Willis wore so he could go buy some. Anyway, Lyle was a standout, opening our shows with the songs on his first record. Nanci recognized that and invited him onto the record to help get him to the next level."

4. Blackstock, "Remembering Nanci Griffith."

5. Charley Stefl, interview with Brian T. Atkinson, January 28, 2022. "Nanci came walking into the West End Amoco in Nashville one night after I had moved there," Stefl says. "I was floored. I didn't even know she was in town. She had run her car off [the road] around Centennial Park. She either had a flat tire or some problem with the engine and needed a wrecker to tow her car home, but all our wrecker drivers had gone home. She called Pat Alger, who was one of her initial contacts when she moved to Nashville. He came to get her. Her career was just starting to take off. She wrote me one time, 'Charley, never retire your pen.' She was always encouraging other people."

6. Mike Williams, interview with Brian T. Atkinson, December 5, 2021.

7. Lyle Lovett, interview with Brian T. Atkinson, January 18, 2022.

8. Mickie Merkens, interview with Brian T. Atkinson, February 18, 2022.

9. Griffith and Jackson, *Nanci Griffith's Other Voices*, 109.

10. Nanci Griffith Rarities, "Nanci Griffith - Other Voices, Other Rooms (Part 2) [1993]," YouTube video, 30:09, November 3, 2021, https://www.youtube.com/watch?v=oPmSOO3PXTU

11. Griffith and Jackson, *Nanci Griffith's Other Voices*, 23, 26.

12. Pete Kennedy, interview with Brian T. Atkinson, December 30, 2021; for more on Pete Kennedy, see Pete Kennedy, *Tone, Twang, and Taste: A Guitar Memoir* (self-pub., Highpoint Life, 2018).

13. Raised on Radio, "Nanci Griffith - A Tribute with Archive Interviews and Session Music - Radio Broadcast 19/08/2021," August 23, 2021, accessed June 3, 2022 (site discontinued).

14. Valerie Schuster, interview with Brian T. Atkinson, November 9, 2021.

15. Raised on Radio, "Nanci Griffith - A Tribute."

16. Paul Johnston, "There's a Light beyond These Woods (Mary Margaret)," Austin

News Story, May 23, 1998, austinnewsstory.com/Interviews/Maggie/maggie.htm

17. Riley Hickerson, interview with Brian T. Atkinson, December 30, 2021. Riley Hickerson passed away on May 1, 2022. His obituary was in the *Austin American-Statesman*, https://www.statesman.com/obituaries/paco0208601?fbclid=IwAR1rufErKpyjVs BPJzD7imxIL_SdFTdb_THj4eR7KPIRgwymHBSpBBh4Avs

18. Darden Smith, interview with Brian T. Atkinson, October 30, 2021. "I loved what Nanci did, loved her music, and loved what she taught me, but at a certain point you go, 'That was then. This is now.' People are like that, and this business feeds it. There's a massive amount of bullshit and ego feeding in the music business. People want their ego fed. People think they need to feed egos. Then people on both sides believe it, which creates weirdness. Then you meet people like Joan Baez and Emmylou Harris, who are totally aware of who they are. They're nice, sweet. Yeah, they're the center of attention, but there's no bullshit when you're working together. There are enough of those people. Doing this takes a certain amount of self-focus where you can put yourself up there to stand in the light and pour your heart out.

"Turning off that self-focus when the light isn't shining on you can be hard. That focus is really a burden to yourself and people around you especially if the accolades don't add up to what you think you deserve or what they used to be. Those are two flavors of the same sword.

"Nanci was a massive mentor to Lyle until it went weird. So, she did help guys, but she mostly opened up doors for females behind her like Shawn Colvin, Brandi Carlile, my friend Amy Speace, and so many female singer-songwriters. Guy and Townes opened the door for me, but that was from listening to their records and not by meeting them. Nanci opened a massive number of doors with her music and her tremendous attention to detail in her music. Her records are pretty meticulous whether you like them or not. Her singing and choice of language were incredible. She understood what she could gain from moving to Nashville. She knew exactly what she was doing and knew that wouldn't happen in Austin, Texas.

"Also, Nanci had dark pain inside. People really respond to pain when someone steps up to the microphone. They're not responding to the lyrics. The lyric is the vehicle for the pain and the beauty that comes through. People dig that. They don't say, 'I'm coming for the pain,' but they say, 'Oh my god, I'm so moved.' I know people who are pretty famous who sing flat. They don't hit the note, but what they're singing is true. That's what people dig. Nanci did that for so many people—both musicians and nonmusicians. She was totally a pioneer and had a massive career.

"I did a couple shows around Portland in 1995. My agent called me up: 'I have two shows with Nanci Griffith in Portland. You wanna do them?' 'Yes.' Those were my last times opening for her. The band was all there. I walked into the dressing room and everyone was reading. No one was talking besides the drummer Pat McInerney. 'Hey, Darden, how you doing?' He's funny as shit, but everyone else was just reading novels. Very serious. I'm walking by thinking, This is heavy as shit. Nanci didn't say a word to me at the gigs. I was like, 'What the fuck? Really?' Then she spoke very sweetly onstage. There you go. That's the mirage. You have to shake your head and go, 'Whatever.'

"This is a business at the end of the day. Musicians and songwriters are way more open around songwriters than most people would be. We live with our heart totally exposed, but it's not uncommon for people to have a wall up like what I experienced at that show in Nashville. Bam. I slammed up against the wall. 'You're not really in my club anymore.' Very competitive nature and a control thing probably. Doug Hudson and Denice Franke got fired from a tour in Ireland because they went to a pub. Nanci had told them not to go there. 'Fuck that, we're going to the pub. It's right next to the hotel.' Nanci fired them because it was known as a pub that catered to one side of the Irish argument, and Nanci was very pro the other side. Who fires someone for that? She's not U2.

"Hey, everybody has a monkey. Nanci drank a lot of booze. She drank a six-pack of beer while she was singing 'Two Dollar Novels' on my second record. [Asleep at the Wheel leader] Ray Benson was producing. Ray looks at me when she left and goes, 'That woman can drink.' Ray fucking Benson is saying that. Ray knows. At the same time, all of this negative stuff—all of this—doesn't take away from the beauty. You don't know anything about this if you didn't know Nanci. You have to remember that. What she did was so profoundly beautiful and influential. Millions of people got massive amounts of beauty, joy, and light from Nanci's records and performances, which is important to realize."

19. Bobby Nelson, interview with Brian T. Atkinson, October 5, 2021. "Nanci cut off all her Austin contacts about ten years ago," Nelson says. "I don't understand what happened. She had real trouble with her father and sister, but she got along with her brother. Things were up and down with her sister. Her sister married a very wealthy person who is real famous for raising cranberries somewhere in the north. Most times Nanci wouldn't talk with her. I think a lot came down on her when she was unable to play the guitar anymore. 'What have I done with my life? I never really made it and now I can't play guitar or lead a band.' She cut herself off from us in Austin including Brian Wood. We so adored her, and she knew it. She just had such bad, bad feelings about Austin."

20. Denice Franke, interview with Brian T. Atkinson, December 5, 2021.

21. Kevin O'Hare, "Nanci Griffith Talks about Music, Politics," MassLive, October 18, 2009, https://www.masslive.com/entertainment/2009/10/nanci_griffith_talks_about_mus.html

22. Jimmie Dale Gilmore, interview with Brian T. Atkinson, September 17, 2021. "Nanci took me out opening a couple tours after she had become a pretty big star," Gilmore says. "We stayed in touch with an occasional phone call at other times. We would at least go out and have dinner together when I was passing through Nashville. We might go to a show. We were all busy by that time. Musicians don't get to spend much time with their old friends unless you happen to be in the same band because you're all on the road. That's how it was with Nanci and I. We were very close but didn't see each other much because of the circumstances."

23. Janet Gilmore, Facebook post, August 16, 2021.

24. Brian Wood, interview with Brian T. Atkinson, November 17, 2021.

25. John Hill, interview with Brian T. Atkinson, February 17, 2022.

Verse: Once in a Very Blue Moon

1. *For the Sake of the Song: The Story of Anderson Fair*, directed by Bruce Bryant, 2009.

2. *Townes Van Zandt: Be Here to Love Me*, directed by Margaret Brown (Palm Pictures, 2005).

3. Bryant, *For the Sake of the Song*.

4. Joy Lewallen, interview with Brian T. Atkinson, November 5, 2021. "My neighbor across the street was older and had been going to the Old Quarter so I went with her," Lewallen says about starting work at Anderson Fair. "There were nights when whoever was running the bar had to leave. I was always sober so they said, 'Joy, you have to run the bar.'

I ran the bar at the Old Quarter until 1973. Then a couple of my friends opened a new club called the Sweetheart of Texas. I was the manager there for a year. I lived right down the street and had been going to Anderson Fair for the music. The same thing as [happened at] the Old Quarter happened at Anderson Fair in 1974. Someone would go for a cigarette break, and I started tending bar by default. Anderson Fair was the laid-back beer and wine neighborhood bar.

"Nanci and I were just regular friends. She was never a star to me even when she became one. I've had this conversation with lots of people and especially Lyle Lovett. He thanks Anderson Fair every time he plays here. He thanks those of us in the audience by name if we're there, which is phenomenal. Nanci and I were sidekicks until she died. Vince Bell also was right in that we all supported each other. You still got spaghetti even if you didn't have any money. I bought Mickey White's guitar for him because he needed an upgrade.

"Nanci was working on a novel and some songs the last few years. We talked about what her novel would be about. I jokingly asked her if she would put me in it because I'm such a character. We laughed about that. They weren't lengthy conversations. She was just checking in. I would come home from school and find a message, then call her back. I wasn't interested in jump-starting her career or wondering what she regretted."

5. Dalis Allen, interview with Brian T. Atkinson, December 4, 2021. "Nanci last played Kerrville during our twenty-fifth anniversary in 1996," Allen says. "We had huge crowds. People were parked up and down the highway to see her. The sheriff's department didn't like that, but we had a very successful festival. The festival went for twenty-five days. Of course, we never did that again. My god. We were a bunch of zombies. We had Nanci, Carolyn Hester, Guy Clark, Michael Martin Murphey, Dar Williams, Lucinda Williams, Jerry Jeff Walker, Ray Wylie Hubbard, and Odetta on the lineup. Nanci was in her heyday. I wasn't backstage much at that point because I was running the office and being one of the photographers, but I remember there were cars parked on all the roads.

"We couldn't fit another person in the campgrounds but people were still coming. I'm guessing some people had to turn around and go home. Our theater wall-to-wall holds about five thousand people, and our typical crowd would be fifteen hundred to three thousand, which is where you're getting tight. It was a free-for-all. I'm not sure all those cars moved. I just remember everyone going outside and saying, "Oh my god, what are we gonna do?" How the heck we got Nanci out with that many people in the way [baffles me].

"I saw Nanci in person for the last time when Eric Taylor called when they were recording his album *Live at the Rock Room* and said, 'You have to come. You have to be here.' This was during the festival. Me driving to Houston from Kerrville and back while running eighteen days of the festival was [crazy]. I asked my friend Kim to drive. We drove to Rock's studio, and Nanci and Lyle were there with a [French] guitar player. Susan Lindfors Taylor, Denice Franke, and the Anderson Fair crowd were there. Fun. That show was like the old days. Nanci and Eric were sparring together onstage. 'Oh, that's not the way that goes.' We had lots of laughter. They remained close until he passed."

6. Steve Earle, interview with Brian T. Atkinson, December 7, 2021.

7. Wayne Miller, interview with Brian T. Atkinson, January 3, 2022. "Nanci started writing a book while we were together called *Two of a Kind Heart* in the early eighties," Miller says. "She was pecking away on a typewriter. I read parts of *Two of a Kind Heart*, but I don't remember how far along she had gotten."

8. Dee Moeller, interview with Brian T. Atkinson, September 20, 2021.

9. Vince Bell, interview with Brian T. Atkinson, October 11, 2021.

10. Bryant, *For the Sake of the Song*, 2009.

11. Lucinda Williams, *Don't Tell Anybody the Secrets I Told You: A Memoir* (New York: Crown Publishing, 2023).

12. Rod Kennedy, *Music from the Heart: The Fifty-Year Chronicle of His Life in Music (with a Few Sidetrips!)* (Austin: Eakin Press, 1998), 205.

13. Carolyn Hester, interview with Brian T. Atkinson, October 15, 2021.

14. Tom Russell, email interview with Brian T. Atkinson, September 20, 2021.

15. Robert Earl Keen, interview with Brian T. Atkinson, October 12, 2013.

16. Nanci Griffith Rarities, "Nanci Griffith - Other Voices, Other Rooms (Part 2) [1993]."

17. John Gorka, interview with Brian T. Atkinson, October 24, 2021. "Nanci would later sing on my record *Writing in the Margins* when I did the Townes song 'Snow Don't Fall,'" Gorka says. "I had seen her do a show at The Ark in Ann Arbor, Michigan, with Chris Smither and maybe Maura O'Connell. 'John,' Nanci said, 'sing Townes's songs.' So I recorded 'Snow Don't Fall.' I came down to Nashville for her to sing on that and a couple others. Nanci had just gotten back from a landmine removal tour with Emmylou and Steve Earle that morning but came in prepared with multiple parts for my songs."

18. Tom Paxton, interview with Brian T. Atkinson, November 16, 2021.

19. Steve Gillette, email interview with Brian T. Atkinson, April 17, 2022.

20. Tish Hinojosa, interview with Brian T. Atkinson, November 28, 2021.

21. James McMurtry, interview with Brian T. Atkinson, November 13, 2021. "The second gig on our second tour was way up the Upper Peninsula in Ishpeming, Michigan," McMurtry says. "That was the first time I had ever come off that big hill by Duluth, Minnesota, and looked down at Lake Superior like you're looking down at the end of the world. We had to race from the first gig in Minneapolis along the Superior shore and up the peninsula to get to the venue, which was a high school auditorium. We roll up and Nanci's road manager said, 'Nanci rejected the sound system. Don't load in just yet.' Their sound man was bitching that they only had forty-two inputs. Only forty-two inputs? They were trying to get the exact sound from the record.

"We went next door to Hickey's Bar and proceeded to drink all afternoon while waiting for someone to drag a sound system four hours up from Green Bay. Then we had time for a five-minute line check before we had to play. Ninety degrees outside. We would look out the bar and see people waiting in the street. They were getting madder and madder and were mad at us when we hit the stage just because we were the ones there. Everybody calmed down when we dedicated the first set to the patrons at Hickey's Bar."

22. Fred Koller, interview with Brian T. Atkinson, November 19, 2021.

23. Peter Rowan, interview with Brian T. Atkinson, December 1, 2021.

24. Jim Rooney, interview with Brian T. Atkinson, January 6, 2022. For more on Jim Rooney, see Jim Rooney, *In It for the Long Run: A Musical Odyssey* (Chicago: University of Illinois Press, 2014). "Pat McInerney was a true friend to Nanci," Rooney says. "He continually tried to help Nanci the last eight or ten years of her life. The Kennedys did too. I liked her manager Burt Stein, but he refused to understand her mental state in the last years and kept thinking she was gonna get out there and play. I said, 'Have you seen her? Have you been to her house? You would be shocked. There's no way she could get onstage.' The Kennedys would go to her house to rehearse, but she was totally unprepared and couldn't do

it. She had health problems, but mental health was her main problem. Nanci drove people away. She was a recluse in total isolation besides having her employee Robbin to go to the liquor store.

"I've done three tracks for Ken Levitan's Nanci tribute album. Kathi Whitley and I had talked about the album [before I committed]. I couldn't see working with Nanci at that point, but I couldn't see working on it without her. I called her. She was drunk when she answered so I didn't even bring up the subject. I called Kathi and said, 'I don't see how I can do this.' They went ahead with the project so I said, 'I can do some tracks.' We did 'Love at the Five and Dime' with John Prine and Kelsey Waldon at Jack Clement's in the same wonderful room where it all started for me with John, Iris DeMent, and Nanci, so it made sense.

"The last time I saw John was when I brought him a mix of 'Love at the Five and Dime' coming up on Christmas. Well, Christians were supposed to visit the sick, so I visited Nanci one time about eleven on Sunday morning. 'I'm in town,' I said. 'I would like to drop by.' 'Okay.' I went over and went in the door. She was in her pajamas. She had a can of beer in her hand but wasn't drunk. She didn't invite me to sit down, which was a little strange. I eventually said, 'Can I sit down? Are you aware that they're doing an album of your songs?' She was."

25. Lloyd Green, interview with Brian T. Atkinson, February 15, 2022.

26. Pat Alger, interview with Brian T. Atkinson, September 14, 2021. "I hadn't seen Nanci in a long time when she passed," Alger says. "I really regretted that. I thought she was a lot younger. I was really sad when she died. I remember going down to Anderson Fair and really getting a sense of what Nanci Griffith meant to Texas. I stayed at her dad Griff's place. We went to an Astros game and had a really ordinary adventure. I had my first migas there. I made migas for myself this morning as a matter of fact. Nanci's sister Mikki might have been singing with her at Anderson Fair. Her dad was a singer, too. He was a barbershop quartet singer. Quite good. Nashville is the headquarters of the barbershop quartet organization, and he came here a couple times for that. He was a graphic designer and did the artwork for *Once in a Very Blue Moon*. I think I met her mother in passing."

27. Michael Corcoran, email interview with Brian T. Atkinson, January 5, 2022.

28. Buddy Mondlock, interview with Brian T. Atkinson, November 10, 2021. "Guy Clark had taken an interest in me on my first trip to Kerrville in 1986," Mondlock says. "I wandered up the hill where Nanci was talking with Guy when she was playing the festival a few years later, and Guy said some nice things about me. I was a little in awe of meeting Nanci.

"Nashville songwriters were always rooting for Nanci. She had a major label deal, lots of fans, and deserved it all. She was a hero to guys like me and helped me in a couple significant ways over the years, but Nanci could be standoffish and not the warmest person if she was in a bad mood. For example, I ran into Nanci one time at the post office, and she was looking pretty ragged. I said, 'Hello.' She blew me off. I'm not sure she even recognized me, but she certainly didn't go out of her way to be friendly. Otherwise, she generally was very sweet, like the time she let my bass player and me stay at her apartment my first time in Dublin."

29. John T. Davis, interview with Brian T. Atkinson, December 3, 2021.

30. Marcus K. Dowling, "In Memoriam: Five Must-Listen Nanci Griffith Songs," cmt.com, August 16, 2021, https://www.cmt.com/news/uamj03/in-memoriam-five-must-listen-nanci-griffith-songs

31. Ken Levitan, interview with Brian T. Atkinson, December 18, 2021.

32. Andrew Dansby, interview with Brian T. Atkinson, October 15, 2021.

Chorus: Gulf Coast Highway

1. Paisley Robertson, interview with Brian T. Atkinson, February 15, 2022; Richard Skanse, "The 25 Greatest Album Covers in Texas Music History," *Texas Music*, Fall 2021, https://txmusic.com/the-25-greatest-album-covers-in-texas-music-history/. "The Last of the True Believers" ranks twelfth among the twenty-five greatest covers. "[The cover] finds Griffith (clutching a biography of Tennessee Williams)," Skanse writes, "standing outside of a Woolworth's flanked by four friends: music writer John T. Davis and Paisley Robertson playing the couple on her left and Dianne Warren slow dancing on her right with some long, tall gent named Lyle Lovett."

2. Kathy Mattea, interview with Brian T. Atkinson, September 14, 2021.

3. Raised on Radio, "Nanci Griffith - A Tribute."

4. Peter Cooper, interview with Brian T. Atkinson, February 14, 2022. "I'll never forget seeing Nanci on an award show singing Loretta Lynn's song 'The Pill,'" Cooper says. "She was immediately recognized as a real-deal talent. I believe her first calls when she got to town were from Chet Atkins and Harlan Howard. Harlan told Nanci she reminded him of Loretta Lynn, which is high praise from on high. Those MCA albums didn't set the woods on fire commercially, but they were a signal artistically that something new and great was going on. Some songs like 'Outbound Plane' and 'Love at the Five and Dime' should have been radio hits for Nanci, which is saying nothing about Suzy Bogguss's and Kathy Mattea's incredible voices. Rodney Crowell had years like that. Other people were recording his songs, but he couldn't get on the radio. Finally, he was able to break through in the late eighties, but that music wasn't necessarily fully representative of his artistry.

"I called Nanci when I was making my first record, *Mission Door*, and said, 'I was wondering if you would sing on a song.' 'What song?' 'Well,' I said, 'Mission Door.' '*Eric's* song?' she said. 'Yeah,' I said. 'I thought it might be a touchy subject.' They were long divorced by then. 'I love that song,' she said. 'Tell me when to be in the studio and I'll be there.' I think there are lots of opinions about what makes a great songwriter, but you're probably a pretty great songwriter when your ex-wife wants to record your songs—especially when she has the song sense of Nanci Griffith."

5. Terry Myers, interview with Brian T. Atkinson, February 5, 2022.

6. "Nashville Skyline: Nanci Griffith, a View from the Rooftop," *Wood and Steel* magazine, Taylor Guitars, year and issue undetermined.

7. Melanie Smith-Howard, interview with Brian T. Atkinson, February 21, 2022.

8. Suzy Bogguss, interview with Brian T. Atkinson, March 3, 2022.

9. "Nashville Skyline: Nanci Griffith."

10. "Nashville Skyline: Nanci Griffith."

11. Jim "Señor" McGuire, interview with Brian T. Atkinson, March 6, 2022.

12. Tony Brown, interview with Brian T. Atkinson, December 23, 2021.

13. Rodney Crowell, interview with Brian T. Atkinson, November 21, 2021.

14. Julie Gold, interview with Brian T. Atkinson, September 10, 2021.

15. Lucy Kaplansky, interview with Brian T. Atkinson, September 22, 2021.

16. Maura Kennedy, interview with Brian T. Atkinson, December 21, 2021.

17. Nanci Griffith, introduction to "Trouble in the Fields," *One Fair Summer Evening*,

MCA Records, 1988.

18. Laurie McAllister, interview with Brian T. Atkinson, January 6, 2022; James Hooker, interview with Brian T. Atkinson, April 19, 2022. "I had spent one-third of my life with Nanci [when I left the band]," Hooker says. "One-third is longer than any woman I've been married to. I loved Nanci to death. I would do anything for the woman. She would have done anything for me. She was loyal. We might fuss and fight on the bus, but don't come on our bus and fuss and fight with us. You'll get a whole load of people down your neck. 'We can talk about family, but don't you talk about our family.'

"We had talked on the telephone, but I hadn't seen Nanci since 2007. [My wife] Jessica and I tried to hook up with Nanci after we bought a house in Nashville in 2018. She was slurring the couple times I called. Then one time I got her bright and chirpy. She was gonna meet us at Brown's Diner. We went to Brown's at the appointed time and waited and waited. I called an hour later, and her assistant answered the phone. She said, 'Nanci's not gonna be able to make it.' I talked to her on the phone about a year later. She was chirpy again and wanted to write songs. I started writing some instrumentals I was gonna send to her. We never hooked up."

19. "Nanci Griffith - Gulf Coast Highway, First Performance: 25/06/1988," video, accessed June 4, 2022, https://www.coveredbybrucespringsteen.com/viewcover.aspx?recordID=522. "[Nanci and] I later recorded her song 'Gulf Coast Highway' for my album *Modern Art* in 2003," Tom Russell says. "I was always drawn to the song after touring for a few years with Nanci. She sang this classic duet every night with her piano player James Hooker. 'Gulf Coast Highway' reminded me of early Ian and Sylvia songs like 'Lonely Girls.' Nanci and I were very much influenced by Ian and Sylvia in both our songwriting and vocal arrangements. 'Gulf Coast Highway' also has the Guy Clark touch that truly resonates with Texas geography as well as a Woody Guthrie touch with its working-class point of view and great melody."

20. Amy Grant, interview with Brian T. Atkinson, January 24, 2022.

21. Pennstatefan1, "Nanci Griffith & James Hooker - Gulf Coast Highway - Live," YouTube video, 3:41, December 3, 2010, https://www.youtube.com/watch?v=DUqLleoZxtM

22. James Hooker, interview with Brian T. Atkinson, February 7, 2022.

23. Blackstock, "Remembering Nanci Griffith."

24. Pat McInerney, interview with Brian T. Atkinson, January 12, 2022.

25. Mark Costigan, "Fran Breen on Nanci Griffith," YouTube video, 11:10, August 25, 2021, https://www.youtube.com/watch?v=Ou7SqblYudQ

26. Kathi Whitley, interview with Brian T. Atkinson, January 12, 2021.

27. Tom Kimmel, interview with Brian T. Atkinson, November 26, 2021.

28. Amy Ray and Emily Saliers, interviews with Brian T. Atkinson, May 6, 2022.

29. Cliff Eberhardt, interview with Brian T. Atkinson, October 14, 2021. "Nanci came up to New York and sang on my second album, *Now You Are My Home*. She called me one day. 'I'm gonna come sing on your album,' she said. 'I don't want you to pay me. I'll buy the airfare.' That was typical Nanci. I sent her demos of every song on the album, and she said, 'Okay. I want to do the song 'Now You Are My Home.' The only thing she asked was that it just be the engineer and me in the studio, which I was fine with. The session was at ten in the morning. She came in and had worked out three different harmony parts. 'Okay,' I said, 'let's do them all.' She came up with a pretty complex part.

"Nanci was singing sharp when she was first rehearsing the song. I turned to the engineer. 'You're the producer,' he said. 'You have to tell her she's singing sharp.' I hit the talk button and said, 'Nanci, I think you're a little sharp.' She said, 'I would put somebody's eye out if I was any sharper.' She was a total pro. Julie Gold was my best friend in New York, so we had that connection. Nanci used to stay at Julie's apartment. We would all get together, drink, and hang out when Nanci was in town. I also got together with her when I went to Nashville.

"Nanci was unreachable in ways. You're talking to her and having a great time, but you go, 'I'm never gonna be able to get in there.' We were never gonna completely connect. She always kept something on the back burner, but she was [generous]. I did a showcase at this eight-hundred-seat theater in New York one time playing for labels because Wyndham Hills had gone out of business. Nanci flew up from Nashville just for that show to support me. You don't see that in many other songwriters. I think the reason she [would go out of her way to be nice] is that she didn't perceive me as a threat. We played very, very different music. I think it was like Nanci giving her guitar to Mary Gauthier. Mary was no threat to Nanci. She had a competitive side, so she treated people who weren't in her genre the best.

Verse: Across the Great Divide

1. Mary Wood Littleton, "An Interview with Nanci Griffith," August 30, 1994, http://brisbin.net/Nanci/nancimwlart.html
2. Littleton, "Interview with Nanci Griffith."
3. Nanci Griffith Rarities, "Nanci Griffith – Other Voices, Other Rooms (Part 2)."
4. Nanci Griffith Rarities, "Nanci Griffith – Other Voices Other Rooms (Part 2)."
5. Elektra Records press materials for *Other Voices, Other Rooms*, John T. Davis personal archives.
6. Joe Jackson, email conversation with Brian T. Atkinson, April 9, 2022; Griffith and Jackson, *Nanci Griffith's Other Voices*, 54.
7. Caroline Herring, interview with Brian T. Atkinson, November 23, 2021.
8. Raised on Radio, "Nanci Griffith - A Tribute."
9. Time Capsules by Tim Van Schmidt, "'Love Letter: An Hour with Kate Wolf' 1985 Interview by Tim Van Schmidt (2021 Version)," YouTube video, 1:06:50, April 13, 2021, https://www.youtube.com/watch?v=64GqR3Beihs
10. Nina Gerber, interview with Brian T. Atkinson, December 7, 2021.
11. John Terzano, interview with Brian T. Atkinson, February 3, 2022.
12. Griffith and Jackson, *Nanci Griffith's Other Voices*, 67–68.
13. Harold Eggers, interview with Brian T. Atkinson, December 4, 2021. "Townes and I were at Richard Dobson's girlfriend's place when I saw a girl over to the side at the party," Eggers says. 'Townes, who is that?' I asked. 'She looks like she's twelve years old.' She was dressed in those little-girl white socks. 'Harold,' he said, 'that's Nanci Griffith.' 'I'm not going to that side of the room, man. I'm sure I'll be accused of something I shouldn't be doing. Look at her. The way she looks is so innocent and shy.' 'Oh, no, no,' Townes said. 'She will eat you alive if you rile her up.' 'Wow. Okay.' Nanci was married to Eric Taylor, who was out there and full-blown darkness back then."
14. Janis Ian, email interview with Brian T. Atkinson, April 6, 2022.
15. Tom Norris, interview with Brian T. Atkinson, November 12, 2021.
16. Jonathan Bernstein, Jon Dolan, Patrick Doyle, Christian Hoard, and Joseph Hudak,

"John Prine: 25 Essential Songs," April 7, 2020, Rolling Stone, https://www.rollingstone.com/music/music-lists/john-prine-25-essential-songs-974926/

17. Griffith and Jackson, *Nanci Griffith's Other Voices*, 102–3.

18. Fiona Whelan Prine, Facebook post, August 13, 2021.

19. Ralph McTell, interview with Brian T. Atkinson, January 7, 2022.

20. Andy Greene, "Darius Rucker: Five Songs That Changed the Way I Heard Music," April 4, 2018, Rolling Stone, https://www.rollingstone.com/music/music-lists/darius-rucker-five-songs-that-changed-the-way-i-heard-music-630045/

21. For more on Odetta, see Ian Zack, *Odetta: A Life in Music and Protest* (Boston: Beacon Press, 2020); the book mentions Griffith only once but points out that Odetta also drank excessively. An excerpt: "It was during this chapter of her life, as her career and personal life [floundered], that friends began to realize that Odetta's drinking had become a serious problem. The singer Nancy [*sic*] Griffith recalled Odetta once telling her, 'All god's children needs vodka,' but now Odetta had trouble stopping" (204).

22. Griffith and Jackson, *Nanci Griffith's Other Voices*, 102–14.

23. Nanci Griffith, Elektra Records press release, "For Nanci Griffith, It All Begins with a Song," September 1994, John T. Davis personal archives.

24. Littleton, "Interview"; Michael Walsh, "MUSIC: Little Gifts That Just Happen," *Time* magazine, October 3, 1994, accessed June 15, 2022, https://content.time.com/time/subscriber/article/0,33009,981519,00.html; Stephen Holden, "POP REVIEW: Dreaminess Just behind the Twang," *New York Times*, November 5, 1994, accessed June 15, 2022, https://www.nytimes.com/1994/11/05/arts/pop-review-dreaminess-just-behind-the-twang.html

25. hadji828, "Nanci Griffith Interview on WRLT 1995," YouTube video, 9:23, February 12, 2022, https://www.youtube.com/watch?v=dLIpkCbWMDQ

26. Peter Collins, interview with Brian T. Atkinson, April 25, 2022.

27. Adam Duritz, interview with Brian T. Atkinson, October 13, 2021. "Country music is so divided between roots country and modern Nashville country," Duritz says. "Popular country is very different and very produced. Think about the most popular music ever made like Shania Twain. Mutt Lange produced so it's not a surprise, but listen to a Shania Twain record and it sounds exactly like a Def Leppard record except the guitars are quieter and there's a mandolin or pedal steel over the top. Then there's the other side with Waylon Jennings and Willie Nelson, Steve Earle, and Nanci Griffith. I think of that as Austin country, which [carries on] the legacy of Hank Williams. Nanci was a big part of that for me."

28. hadji828, "Nanci Griffith Interview."

29. Arloki272, "Nanci Griffith - Telluride, CO - 6/20/1998."

30. Matthew Ryan, email interview with Brian T. Atkinson, May 7, 2022.

31. Thomm Jutz, interview with Brian T. Atkinson, January 13, 2021. "I knew Nanci had recorded my friend Richard Dobson's song 'The Ballad of Robin Winter-Smith' on *Once in a Very Blue Moon*," Jutz says. "Then Richard told me about Nanci when I moved to Nashville from Germany in 2003. Someone in Knoxville who Dobson worked with wanted me to produce a record for him, but I literally had only been in town a week or two. I called Richard. 'Hey,' I said. 'Do you have contact information for Pat McInerney and Ron de la Vega?' Ron wasn't available, but Pat was. We became really good friends. I was playing with Mary Gauthier, and Mary would be invited to parties where Nanci was. So, I was invited.

"I had idolized people who would come and go at the parties like Guy Clark. Some parties were at the photographer Jim McGuire's house. I remember one great Christmas party with Nanci, Guy, Joe Ely, Lyle Lovett, Shawn Camp, and John Prine. The party was right at the end of that incredibly rich era with Guy and Nanci. I felt there was a lot of jealousy and weirdness going on between the people at times, but that scene was still going on. They all were still hanging out and would [pass the guitar around]. One party was the time when Nanci gave Mary Gauthier her signature Taylor guitar. Nanci was very giving and gracious like that.

"James Hooker was on the way out then, so the band's sound was changing. Nanci knew he was irreplaceable, but she wanted to downsize the band. I was the natural choice as Nanci looked for a new guitarist because McInerney and I knew each other really well already. Also, Nanci liked my playing and that I was from somewhere else. We started writing together as well. Nanci was not someone who wanted to rehearse, and I was cool with that. I did my homework and showed up.

"The songs on *The Last of the True Believers* are special. Nanci was on top of her game. Some of the greatest players in Nashville like Pat Alger, Jerry Douglas, Béla Fleck, and Kenny Malone were playing live on that record. Nanci had the best of the best for playing acoustic singer-songwriter music. The record was a new benchmark in presenting an intersection of distinctly Texas songwriting with the cleanliness and quality of Nashville playing. The songs were incredibly inspired. The material is so good, and the songs sound like everyone was just glad to be there. I think *The Last of the True Believers* set a standard. What's so unique is everything is amazing, so I don't have any favorite songs.

"I've always loved when Nanci interpreted Pat Alger songs. His sense of melody and advanced chord progressions provide a really nice counterpoint to her vocal, which is more raw, folky, singer-songwriter. Pat comes from a more harmonically advanced James Taylor influence. Pat's song 'Once in a Very Blue Moon' that she did on the album before *Last of the True Believers* has such an incredible melody. Nanci gave that song such a great vocal performance. That song could be a little sweet if someone else sang it, but not with Nanci. She made that song amazing.

"I produced her track 'The Giving Tree' for the [*Twistable, Turnable Man*] Shel Silverstein tribute. I think she loved that story because she used to read that story to kids when she was a kindergarten teacher. She said, 'You guys book the studio and the band. I'll show up and sing. When it's done it's done.' It was a one-off. I think her vocal on that was really nice. I really appreciated her vocals in the later years. Ironically, it got a lot lower from all the smoking, but her voice had an interesting tone and especially on that song.

"I would like to say that Nanci was a really, really good guitar player. There are clips on the internet of her playing the 'Love at the Five and Dime' solo right after it had come out. Her sense of timing was so good. She was easy to play with. You just played to her vocal. There was no push and pull. She was a great leader that way. Also, I'm not ashamed to talk about the more dicey stuff we talked about. It was true to what I experienced. I do not want to come across as bitter. My life became a lot better after I worked with her. I could concentrate on producing and writing more.

"The danger of the Nanci gig was that you would stick with it forever and a day. Great touring and money. Other people who stayed and didn't get fired didn't have a pleasant experience. 'Hey, man,' [road manager Phil] Mangler [Kaufman] always told me. 'Her firing you was the best thing that ever happened to you.' I have to say in hindsight that's true. I have no hard feelings. I still consider Nanci a friend. She was funny. Conflict was scorched earth with her. 'It's over. We can never reconcile this in any way.'"

32. Brian Willoughby, interview with Brian T. Atkinson, January 14, 2022.

33. Brian Willoughby, interview. "Nanci lived very close to us in Nashville," Willoughby says. "We had one absolutely fabulous New Year's Eve at our local watering hole Brown's Diner. They shut the pub down, and Nanci, Pat McInerney and his wife, Lee Ann; my wife, Cathryn, and myself sang old folk songs like 'Stewball' after a few beers. Nanci was in her element that night. The last time I saw her was also at Brown's. She was with Don Everly's wife. 'You have to meet Brian Willoughby,' Nanci said. 'Tell the boys that Brian's the man if they ever need a guitar player.' She was unnecessarily generous to Cathryn and me. We have a statue of Saint Francis in our garden here in Ireland that Nanci gave her. She gave the statue to us because we were on tour in England when Cathryn's dogs died. Nanci made sure that the dogs were buried.

"Nanci was a really nice human being even outside the music world."

34. Ron de la Vega, interview with Brian T. Atkinson, January 26, 2022.

35. Griffith and Jackson, *Nanci Griffith's Other Voices*, 151.

36. Tamara Saviano, *Without Getting Killed or Caught: The Life and Music of Guy Clark* (College Station: Texas A&M University Press, 2016), 149.

37. Saviano, *Without Getting Killed or Caught*, 284–85.

38. Saviano, 285.

39. Griffith and Jackson, *Nanci Griffith's Other Voices*, 161.

40. John Lomax III, interview with Brian T. Atkinson, December 10, 2021.

41. Beth Nielsen Chapman, interview with Brian T. Atkinson, November 19, 2021. "Nanci had this really weird accent when she sang. I always wondered what that affectation was about, but she was Nanci Griffith. She got to do whatever she wanted. Then I would be invited to her fantastic teas for women, and women singer-songwriters in particular. Emmylou and all these women from unknown writers to established legends were at her house. She would have wine on one end of the table and coffee and tea on the other. I went in thinking she would be someone I couldn't access, but she was so friendly. We weren't super-close friends after that, but I felt that we established a mutual respect that made me feel really good."

Chapman on Griffith's influence on her as an artist: "I was trying to get a record deal as a country artist at the time, and it seemed during the five years between 1985 and 1990 the Tony Brown signings had a moment in time. I didn't [feel like] a country artist, and I know Nanci felt the same about herself, but she was doing the country thing and having hits with more established country artists. I studied her. Then I started having hits years later through country artists and was approached by labels to be a country artist myself. I was talking with Jim Ed Norman about all these concerns one day. 'Beth,' he said, 'Nanci Griffith is a great artist and songwriter. You're a great artist and songwriter. You guys can jump in and out of any genres.'

"Easier said than done, but I saw that Warner Bros. let me be more flexible. Nanci and her outlandishness really paved the way for me getting my record deal. Nanci did what she wanted to do. That's what makes someone the ilk of an artist like Nanci Griffith or Joni Mitchell. They do what they're gonna do whether the world goes along or not. That influenced me a great deal as an artist. I've put out sixteen different albums. One is in Latin, another is in sixteen languages. One is a children's book on astronomy. I never wanted to be put into something I had to stay in.

"Nanci influenced me as a songwriter to the extent that great songwriting is what I feed on. I appreciated and learned from her brilliant masterpieces. Some people are great songwriters who go in the direction of quirky two clicks too far and the song becomes more of a novelty. Nanci had that edge, but she stopped way short of going too far so the songs became classic. 'Love at the Five and Dime' is a classic song. Maia Sharp, the Accidentals, Kim Richey, and I were learning 'Outbound Plane' for our upcoming tour. Amazing song. I went back and listened to Nanci's and was fascinated by how different it was from [Suzy Bogguss's version]. I guess you could listen to the two versions and go, 'Well, Suzy Bogguss's is more commercial.' Nanci had a growl. 'That's who I am. Take it or leave it.' That's richer to me in some ways."

Chapman on quitting drinking: "You know, Nanci was partly the reason I quit drinking. Well, to be clear, it wasn't just like, 'Oh, Nanci's a mess, so I should quit and not be like her.' I just found myself noticing that I really wanted to have a drink at the end of every day. I was using it as a way to relax.

"My son had his first child right around then. I talked to him a couple months later when he was up by himself drinking a couple shots of whiskey. I thought, That sounds like fun. 'Do you do that often?' He indicated that it might be a regular thing. This red flag went up in me. 'Listen,' I said, 'there's alcoholism going through both sides of your family. So enjoy it, but realize it's a loaded weapon when you pick up a drink. It can be a problem or not depending on which way the weapon is pointed. Be really aware.' I was also a breast cancer survivor. A new study had just come out and said people who have had breast cancer should only drink a teeny bit, and I was way past that. I felt like I wanted to make a change. 'I really need to stop,' I told my son. 'Mom,' he said, 'I think you really need to quit.'

"'Yeah,' I said, 'but I can't do it on my own.' I said that to trick him. It worked. He volunteered to quit with me. 'Oh, what a good idea.' We both stopped at the same time. That was when I was talking to Burt Stein a lot, and Julie Gold had come into town to teach a workshop. 'Have you talked with Nanci?' I asked. 'I haven't been able to get through.' She hadn't. Nanci was isolated to the point where people who loved her dearly didn't want to bother her. Meanwhile, I was looking at myself and how alcohol can really [take over]. You think you can get it under control, but you don't. I remember Nanci being one of the people I was looking at during that time and saying, 'There might be a better choice for me.' I'm so grateful. Neither my son nor I have had another drink eight years later."

42. Don McLean, interview with Brian T. Atkinson, November 17, 2021.

Bridge: Traveling through This Part of You

1. "Interview with Actor Chris Noth, Singer/Songwriter Nanci Griffith, and Founder and President of VVAF, Bobby Muller," *Washington Life* magazine, undated, accessed April 16, 2022, https://washingtonlife.com/backissues/archives/03apr/vvaf.php
2. "Interview with Actor Chris Noth."
3. Steve Wilkison, "Nanci Griffith - Traveling through This Part of You - Her Song for Eric Taylor," YouTube video, 7:11, March 10, 2020, https://www.youtube.com/watch?v=pmPQZPum1LM
4. Susan Lindfors Taylor, interview with Brian T. Atkinson, December 28, 2021.
5. "Interview with Actor Chris Noth."
6. Dave Alvin, interview with Brian T. Atkinson, October 7, 2021.
7. "Interview with Actor Chris Noth."
8. "Interview with Actor Chris Noth."

Verse: Clock without Hands

1. Nanci Griffith, liner notes for *Clock without Hands*, Elektra Records, 2001.

2. Chas Williams, interview with Brian T. Atkinson, December 20, 2021.

3. Elizabeth Cook, interview with Brian T. Atkinson, November 10, 2021.

4. LeAnn Etheridge, liner notes for *Hearts in Mind*, New Door Records, 2004.

5. Ellis Paul, interview with Brian T. Atkinson, November 3, 2021. "I was coming up in the Boston folk scene in the late eighties and saw Nanci a couple times when she was a mainstay favorite who would play several times over a weekend at Club Passim," Paul says. "She eventually outgrew the room but would come back to do fundraisers after she had become somewhat famous. Also, her voice stopped me in my tracks when I would hear her on the radio on WERS 88.9 FM. Nanci doesn't sound like anybody else. Her voice was like being photogenic. You don't notice until you see a photograph when someone is photogenic. Voices are like that. She had an audiogenic voice that was captivating.

"I'm all for her and people like Mary Chapin Carpenter having a foot in country and folk and being a star because they championed songwriters. Seeing someone succeed like that was really beautiful. Nanci was fulfilling a way to become successful without being in the confines of a folk club. Also, she chose well-written songs by people I knew like Julie Gold and Buddy Mondlock when she wasn't doing her own songs. She tapped into the gold mine of unknown songwriters and knew where to dig. They were perfect songs for her voice and mythology. Nanci had a beautiful vocal range. She knew how to lift out of the verse coming into the chorus.

"Knowing how to do that is a function of not only her songwriting but also the voice she had, which could be really warm and then biting later. Her voice gave her a dynamic that not everybody else would have. I always go back to 'Love at the Five and Dime' because I've had it on rewind for so long. I wonder, What is it about that song that kills me? She has a couple songs like that. She goes up into the chorus, which is just so vulnerable and lifts beautifully. She had such a good sense of melody and phrasing. She was a poet who sang well. There was no way she wasn't gonna be a star. She was like a decathlete who did everything well.

"I go back to the Buddy Mondlock song she covered on *Other Voices* called 'Comin' Down in the Rain,' but 'Trouble in the Fields' and 'It's a Hard Life (Wherever You Go)' are in my DNA. I've heard those songs enough over the years that pieces fall into my own music. I can only hope that some of that is happening in my own music. Nanci's impact on songwriters and listeners is enormous. Her lyrics influenced me because they seem like simple storytelling in that John Prine way. Simple language sucks you into the songs. She never seems like she's overwriting. Nanci's writing was so conversational."

6. Todd Snider, interview with Brian T. Atkinson, January 5, 2022. "I opened for Nanci a bunch of times. I went to a foreign country with her for a tour once. The 'road mangler' Phil Kaufman, who set Gram Parsons on fire after he died, was her tour manager. He was epic. We roared. We all drank lots. Nanci had a big audience here, but the same around the world. I always play a smaller venue when I go to London. I remember she had a brand-new song called 'Hell No, I'm Not All Right' that we were all excited about. She was playing that a lot. I remember noticing that she was very, very popular wherever we went, but it's an easy hole to fall into, thinking you're not.

"Fiona [Prine] told me that John felt that way sometimes. I've always been the opposite. I'm so easily talked into the notion that things are going well. I've never wondered why I wasn't a bigger star. I've always just wondered how I'm still standing. I haven't ever thought,

Damn, I'm not Bruce Springsteen because of the industry. No, I think I really got lucky. I made up a song about a group from Seattle that didn't exist [Snider's early hit 'Talking Seattle Grunge Rock Blues'], and thirty years later I still have a job. I see it like I beat the casino, but some people like [Nanci, John], and Jack Ingram are like that."

Snider on being an MCA recording artist like Griffith: "I told Tony Brown I didn't want to be a big star when I signed with him. I wanted to be like Nanci. She was writing songs for MCA that were art. Tony's such a good cat. Nashville was his town when I got here. There was a joke going around. 'How does Tony Brown change a light bulb? He doesn't. He just declares darkness an industry standard and everyone goes with it.' Tony was really good to me. Go back to where all these young songwriters come from and it traces back to Tony Brown and Susan Levy. Those two started with Guy, Nanci, Lyle, then Chris Knight and me. Tony was so into underground singers.

"He was a master of getting people together and making things positive. He told me when I made my first record, 'I'm just gonna guard the door for you.' He just let me do what I wanted and sat there to make sure nobody came around to fuck with it. I don't think they gave a shit about what I did once they had the Seattle song. I had artistic freedom because of one funny little song. 'Do what you want because this one's gonna fly.' It did. I never even wrote that song down. I knew the words and how talking blues songs went. I can't believe I played a song I wrote that morning at a label showcase."

Tony Brown: "Jimmy Buffett was moved from ABC Records to MCA Records in Los Angeles and became a platinum-selling artist when Irving [Azoff] managed him. [MCA president] Jimmy Bowen told Buffett, 'You know, your first two records were cut here in Nashville with Don Gant. Nashville's opening up to acknowledging that people like Kenny Rogers could be country and pop. Your music fits right in.' He moved Jimmy to our division for *Riddles in the Sand* and *Last Mango in Paris*. 'I've got a guy in Memphis working with Keith Sykes,' Buffett said. 'You need to cut a record on him and coproduce with Mike Utley.'

Todd Snider: "I was offered two record deals with MCA, and I took the smaller one. They offer you tons of money to succeed on a linear level. Then they have other people like Lyle, Nanci, and Steve who they call 'integrity artists' but don't spend as much money on. The artists didn't mind. Tony said it was always good to have people like them on your label. It's still good to have Steve Earle on your record label even if you're trying to make hits for Reba McEntire. He said it gave credibility to their commercial artists to have Nancis and Steves. They also might write a genuine hit song for one of the commercial artists. That used to happen all the time. You know, Willie made a small one and Patsy Cline would have the big hit."

Snider on songwriters and songwriting: "I heard Susanna Clark say one time that songwriters were so boring because all they ever talked about was songwriting, but Nanci knew all the lore about how Kristofferson found Prine and how Guy met Jerry Jeff. She was really well [educated]. There are so many young people coming up behind us now who see that you can have a job as a singer [because of those like Nanci] and you don't have to be in a Pepsi commercial. You can become a singer and tour around in a bus and play shows every night without your aunts and uncles ever knowing about it.

"You live this life like a stripper, and Thanksgivings with strippers are different. They're seedy and lonely. I'm not knocking strippers either. I've just seen lots of people including myself get trapped into the whirlwind of only living for the next song and consistently letting everybody else down in every way. The last couple years have been so hard. John Prine had really great insight into being happy. I don't know how he pulled it off, but he was a really happy man by the time he was fifty-five. He stayed that way, but Nanci was like Townes. Jerry Jeff could be too. They could break out the sadness at the happiest occasion on earth.

"I agree when you say you think Nanci felt left out. I think she was. I'm in that spot myself, but I don't mind. I'm fifty-five. I grew up with guys in sports who are like, 'Remember how far I threw the ball when I was thirty-eight? Don't you want to cheer for me again now that I'm fifty-five? I can't throw the ball that far anymore, but does anyone want my shirt?' Nanci didn't write anymore at the end. I've always liked women troubadours. I like having women who aren't funny open for me so it's a juxtaposed show.

"Most girls like Rorey Carroll and Sierra Ferrell who have opened for me idolize Nanci.

"Our world with traveling troubadours really took a ton of hits the past few years with people like Nanci, Billy Joe Shaver, Prine, Jerry Jeff, and feels rudderless right now, but someone will come along and be the new Johnny Cash. I opened for a kid named Tyler Childers who played waltzes at an arena in Kentucky. I thought I was on the moon. I had met him and knew he liked me, but then someone called and said, 'Do you want to open for him?' Open for him? Wow. That happened fast. I saw the show and it was like watching a Townes Van Zandt concert while this guy played his lyric-driven waltzes except there were twelve thousand people there. It really feels like the Great Credibility Scare might be coming back around with Margo Price, Kacey Musgraves, Sturgill Simpson, and Jason Isbell.

"Those would be some good ones if you put posters of musicians on your wall."

7. Griffith and Jackson, *Nanci Griffith's Other Voices*, 168–70.

8. Kristin Wilkinson, interview with Brian T. Atkinson, April 28, 2022.

9. Nanci Griffith Rarities, "Nanci Griffith Interview at Tavis Smiley (2009)," YouTube video, 12:17, September 25, 2021, https://www.youtube.com/watch?v=L8XJQLW0_HQ

10. Nanci Griffith Rarities, "Nanci Griffith Interview at Tavis Smiley (2009)."

11. Thomm Jutz, interview with Brian T. Atkinson, January 13, 2021.

12. Kevin O'Hare, "Nanci Griffith Talks about Music, Politics," MassLive, October 18, 2009, https://www.masslive.com/entertainment/2009/10/nanci_griffith_talks_about_mus.html

13. Raised on Radio, "Nanci Griffith - Talks about Intersection LP & Autobiographical Lyrics - Radio Broadcast 91/03/2012," September 7, 2021, accessed June 16, 2022 (site discontinued).

14. Raised on Radio, "Nanci Griffith - Talks about Intersection LP & Autobiographical Lyrics."

15. Robbin Bach, interview with Brian T. Atkinson, February 10, 2022. "I was Nanci's personal assistant for ten years from 2004 to 2014," Bach says. "I saw Pat Alger at the post office when I was first asked to work with Nanci. I love his music. I had seen him at Merle-Fest. 'Pat,' I said, 'I just got a job with Nanci Griffith.' 'What are you gonna be doing?' 'Well, I'm gonna be her personal assistant.' He got quiet and looked at me. 'I think I'll do okay,' I said. 'I've been around and have been a lot of stuff: nurse, chauffeur, mental health supporter.' He looked at me and said, 'That might work fine, Robbin.' Like he was saying, 'We all need a good mother.'

"I was totally starstruck when I started working for her, but I got smart really fast. I went out with Nanci to Ray Kennedy's farm. They were recording a show Steve Earle was doing. Peter Collins was standing under a tree. Peter saw my face and said, 'It looks like you're pretty excited to be working with Nanci.' 'Oh yes. I can't believe it.' He looked at me and goes, 'Keep it professional, if I could give you a little advice.' I realized that was important. I listened. Nanci and I were able to have a professional relationship with those boundaries."

16. Dave Alvin, interview with Brian T. Atkinson, October 7, 2021. "Tom Russell could have done eight million of his great songs on *David Letterman*, but he and Nanci were so incredibly nice to do my song 'Bus Station,' which they recorded on his album *Modern Art*," Dave Alvin says. "What an honor to hear my words coming out of their voices on the show. They finally did 'Bus Station' the way it was supposed to be, which I didn't even have the guts to do when I recorded the song on *King of California*. I had written 'Bus Station' as a duet in the Loretta Lynn and Conway Twitty vein, so it meant a lot to me for them to sing the song together. Tom let me know that he and Nanci were recording the song. Blew my mind. I wanted the song to be a bittersweet, melancholy, sad ballad. I think that version is what Tom and Nanci knew. Hearing Nanci sing the words to the song that first made me feel like a songwriter. She made me feel like I was in heaven.

"I wrote the song about a bus station in Northern California and a hungover morning in Saint Louis after I was in those situations. Usually takes me about ten years after experiencing something to write about [it in] a song. 'Oh, there's a song there.' 'Bus Station' means a lot to me because I wrote it when I was a fry cook and my brother [Phil Alvin] and I were starting the Blasters. I was suddenly in a rock and roll band playing blues covers like Junior Parker and Howlin' Wolf and rockabilly like Carl Perkins. We were doing whatever we wanted to do, but we realized we had to write songs to get a record deal. Being a songwriter where I grew up? Yeah, that's not what happens. You go get a job at the steel plant in Kaiser, California, or become a fry cook or longshoreman in Long Beach.

"I had to come up with more songs for the Blasters album when I remembered the overwhelming sadness in the situation I was in at the bus station. That tied into the alienation people were feeling in the early eighties economically. I knew I was a songwriter when I was getting near the end of writing 'Bus Station.' Everything else was like, 'I wrote that? How did I do that?' I slaved over 'Bus Station.' I liked the way the Blasters did it, but it wasn't the way I wanted it to sound, so I recorded it on *King of California*.

Chorus: Love at the Five and Dime

1. Gretchen Peters, interview with Brian T. Atkinson, September 15, 2021.
2. Mary Gauthier, Facebook post, August 13, 2021.
3. Jaimee Harris, interview with Brian T. Atkinson, April 12, 2022.
4. Mindy Smith, interview with Brian T. Atkinson, October 21, 2021.
5. Jamie Lin Wilson, interview with Brian T. Atkinson, November 22, 2021.
6. Erin Enderlin, interview with Brian T. Atkinson, March 22, 2022.
7. Aaron Lee Tasjan, interview with Brian T. Atkinson, January 25, 2022.
8. Amy Speace, interview with Brian T. Atkinson, October 31, 2021.
9. Ana Egge, interview with Brian T. Atkinson, November 22, 2021.
10. Dar Williams, interview with Brian T. Atkinson, November 19, 2021.
11. Emily Scott Robinson, interview with Brian T. Atkinson, November 10, 2021.
12. Lily Kearns, interview with Brian T. Atkinson, December 3, 2021.
13. Michael Hall, interview with Brian T. Atkinson, June 9, 2022.
14. Glen Phillips, interview with Brian T. Atkinson, January 21, 2022. "I threw Uri Geller into the song 'Nanci' that I wrote [for Toad the Wet Sprocket's 1994 album, *Dul-*

cinea], like the Beatles threw Sweet Loretta Johnson into 'Get Back,'" Phillips says. "'Nanci' was a bit of a nonsense lyric, but it was definitely a nod to Nanci Griffith in the way that it was spelled. I thought Nanci was wonderful. I talked about Loretta Lynn in the song, too, but I didn't know anything about her back then. I now know Loretta Lynn is a badass. So, it was a tip of the hat to Nanci but not about anything really, which was half of what I wrote in those days.

"Nanci has albums that are more timeless than *Storms* with the eighties elements, but the songs are just so good. Nanci crossed lots of musical boundaries. Frankly, the more pop production on that album might be what let me really hear the songs at the time. Then there was *One Fair Summer Evening*. I had never heard a singer-songwriter tell stories like she did before. I only had heard rock and roll banter. The way she talks about the twelfth-fret harmonic on 'Love at the Five and Dime' being the up button in the elevating was a beautiful detail. She sets you up for success to have a deeper listening experience. That's an art. It's easy to say, 'This is a song about a guy who meets a girl,' but proper banter is like a good trailer that leaves you curious without spoiling the best moments."

15. Jenny Reynolds, interview with Brian T. Atkinson, September 27, 2021. "Nanci Griffith got my ears up through her standout ['Tower Song' cover on] the Townes Van Zandt tribute record *Poet*," Reynolds says. "Everybody around me was like, 'Duh. You should have known about her.' I'm a huge believer that simple is not easy, and Nanci's guitar-picking style is really simple and great. Martha Stewart wouldn't make so much money if simple was easy. Nanci's style was a very straightforward picking pattern that supports her melodies beautifully. Also, I liked the way she interacted with her audiences.

"Guy Clark and Townes were simple and straightforward lyricists like Nanci. Townes's song 'Pancho and Lefty' is pretty straightforward. John Prine's 'Hello in There' has some double entendre, but you know what's going on in there. I think recognizing what you should say and what you leave out is important. What you leave between the lines is where the story's completion exists. The songwriter's job is to say what needs to be said and have a very good understanding of what the audience could fill in between the lines. Judy Collins was more complex and figurative.

"You could tell that Nanci Griffith read. She supported her art with books like an athlete supports his sport with nutrition. Her nutrition for songwriting was not always sung. I like her songs 'Listen to the Radio' and 'Late Night Grande Hotel.' Look at her face in You-Tube videos. She just looks happy onstage and has this unadorned look on her face. Just a smile. Look at Sting's promotional photos. He looks like he has a migraine. G. K. Chesterton was a big Christian guy but also was a Shakespeare critic. He has this quote: 'The world is a comedy to those who think and a tragedy to those who feel.' I feel. Nanci was someone who feels. Lucinda Williams too. Life is a tragedy to us. Everything is a bittersweet symphony to a thinker.

"Everything is mired in one thing or another you go through if you feel."

16. Matt Harlan, interview with Brian T. Atkinson, October 30, 2021.

17. Eliza Gilkyson, interview with Brian T. Atkinson, December 8, 2021.

18. Amy Rigby, interview with Brian T. Atkinson, January 16, 2022.

19. Terri Hendrix, interview with Brian T. Atkinson, October 14, 2021.

20. Sara Hickman, interview with Brian T. Atkinson, September 22, 2021.

21. Winifred Booth, interview with Brian T. Atkinson, October 20, 2021. "I had known about Nanci Griffith since the late eighties when I moved from Northern Ireland to Texas,"

Booth says. "I saw her on *Austin City Limits* and had been very aware that she was very popular in Ireland around then. Her popularity in Ireland may have something to do with the fact that not only was folk music popular in Ireland but so was mainstream country. [The Irish] like authentic storytelling. Nanci was so authentic and captivating and had a Woody Guthrie thing about her music. I agree that mainstream [is not very authentic], but there are two different audiences in Ireland with mainstream country and folk who like music with personal ideas.

"I liked Nanci's Texas twang, crystalline voice, and cadence. She had a clear voice and a passion that came through which made her relatable like the girl next door. She was very endearing. In addition, she had a fierceness as well that I really admired in a time when women weren't so popular in the folk music genre. I really felt like she believed in her songs. She was a great musician and songwriter who just got after it. I really love her version of the Sandy Denny song 'Who Knows Where the Time Goes?' and her own songs 'Listen to the Radio' and 'Trouble in the Fields.'

"I watched a video of her doing 'Who Knows Where the Time Goes?' from the *Transatlantic Sessions* with Maura O'Connell and other Irish musicians. Nanci seemed quite emotional. I think people who do a cover song well almost take over the song and believe in it. Doesn't matter that they didn't write it. Nanci doing 'Who Knows Where the Times Goes?' is like hearing it for the first time. She had a great ability to wear her heart on her sleeve with other people's work."

22. Caitlin Cannon, interview with Brian T. Atkinson, November 17, 2021.

23. Alice Wallace, interview with Brian T. Atkinson, November 5, 2021.

24. BettySoo, interview with Brian T. Atkinson, October 8, 2021.

25. Phoebe Hunt, interview with Brian T. Atkinson, November 16, 2021.

26. Aoife O'Donovan, interview with Brian T. Atkinson, October 27, 2021.

27. Sarah Jarosz, interview with Brian T. Atkinson, October 10, 2021.

Discography

1. Rachel Syme, "Nanci Griffith's Lone Star State of Mind," October 16, 2023, accessed November 25, 2023, https://www.newyorker.com/culture/listening-booth/nanci-griffiths-lone-star-state-of-mind

SELECTED DISCOGRAPHY

Nanci Griffith Studio Albums

1. *There's a Light beyond These Woods*, B.F. Deal Records, 1978
2. *Poet in My Window*, Featherbed Records, 1982
3. *Once in a Very Blue Moon*, Philo Records, 1984
4. *The Last of the True Believers*, Philo Records, 1986
5. *Lone Star State of Mind*, MCA Records, 1987
6. *Little Love Affairs*, MCA Records, 1988
7. *Storms*, MCA Records, 1989
8. *Late Night Grande Hotel*, MCA Records, 1991
9. *Other Voices, Other Rooms*, Elektra Records, 1993
10. *Flyer*, Elektra Records, 1994
11. *Blue Roses from the Moons*, Elektra Records, 1997
12. *Other Voices, Too (A Trip Back to Bountiful)*, Elektra Records, 1998
13. *The Dust Bowl Symphony*, Elektra Records, 1999
14. *Clock without Hands*, Elektra Records, 2001
15. *Hearts in Mind*, New Door Records, 2004
16. *Ruby's Torch*, Rounder Records, 2006
17. *The Loving Kind*, Rounder Records, 2009
18. *Intersection*, Hell No Records, 2012

Nanci Griffith Live Albums

1. *One Fair Summer Evening*, MCA Records, 1988
2. *Winter Marquee*, Rounder Records, 2002

Nanci Griffith Compilations

1. *The MCA Years: A Retrospective*, MCA Records, 1993
2. *The Best of Nanci Griffith*, MCA Records, 1993
3. *Country Gold*, MCA Records, 1997

4. *Wings to Fly and a Place to Be: An Introduction to Nanci Griffith*, MCA Records, 2000
5. *20th Century Masters: The Millennium Collection; The Best of Nanci Griffith*, MCA Records, 2001
6. *From a Distance: The Very Best of Nanci Griffith*, MCA Records, 2002
7. *The Complete Studio Recordings*, MCA Records, 2003
8. *Ghost in the Music*, Rox Vox Records, 2015
9. *Nanci Griffith: Working in Corners*, Craft Recordings, 2023

Nanci Griffith Tribute Albums

1. *Trouble in the Fields: An Artists' Tribute to Nanci Griffith*, Paradiddle Records, 2012
2. *Dance a Little Closer: The Kennedys Sing the Songs of Nanci Griffith*, independent release, 2014
3. *More Than a Whisper: Celebrating the Music of Nanci Griffith*, Rounder Records, 2023[1]

Nanci Griffith Books

1. *Two of a Kind Heart: A Novel*, JRP Books, 2023

INDEX